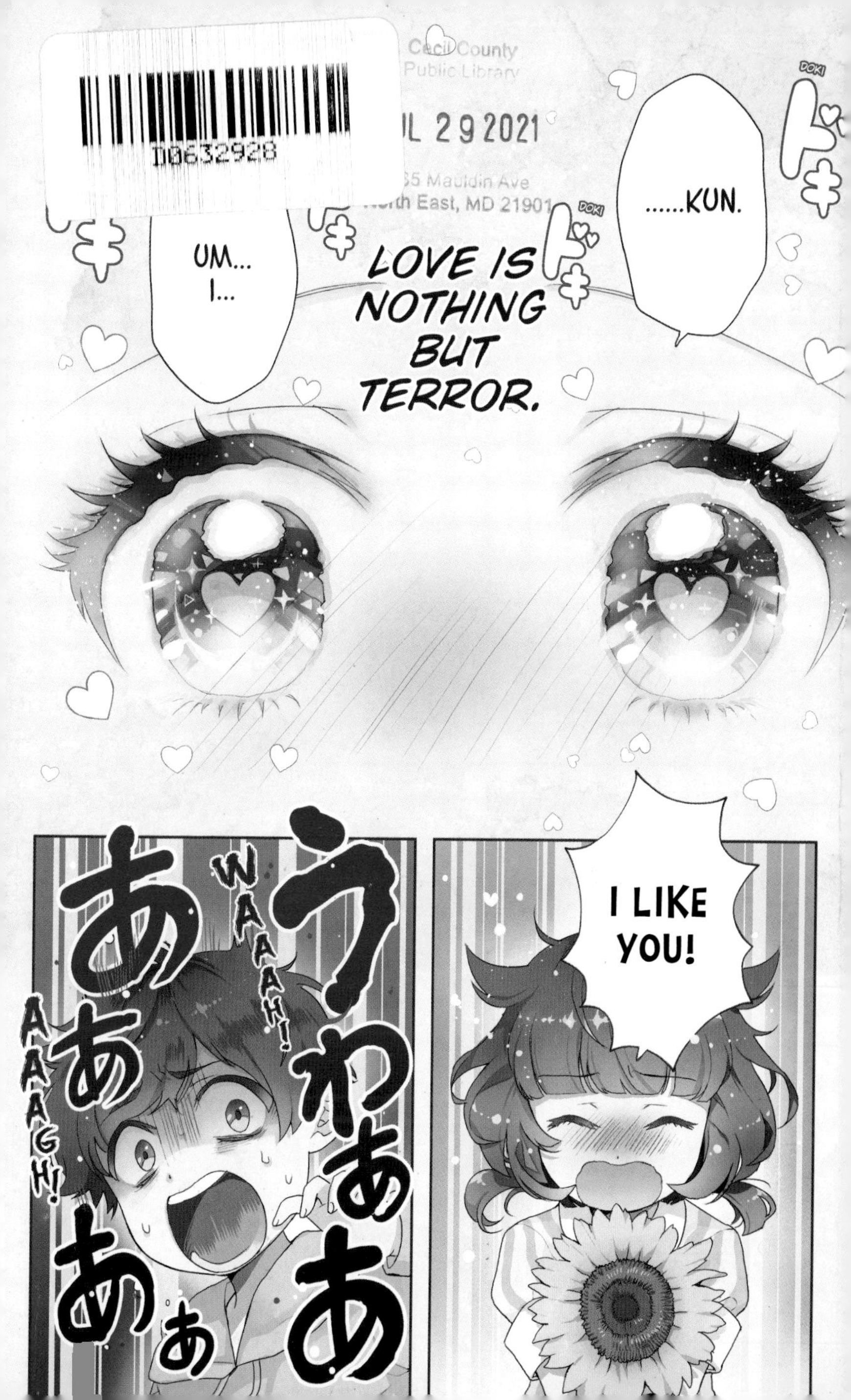
DOKI DOKI
......KUN.
DOKI DOKI
UM...
I...
LOVE IS NOTHING BUT TERROR.
I LIKE YOU!
うわあああぁ
WAAAAH!
AAAAGH!

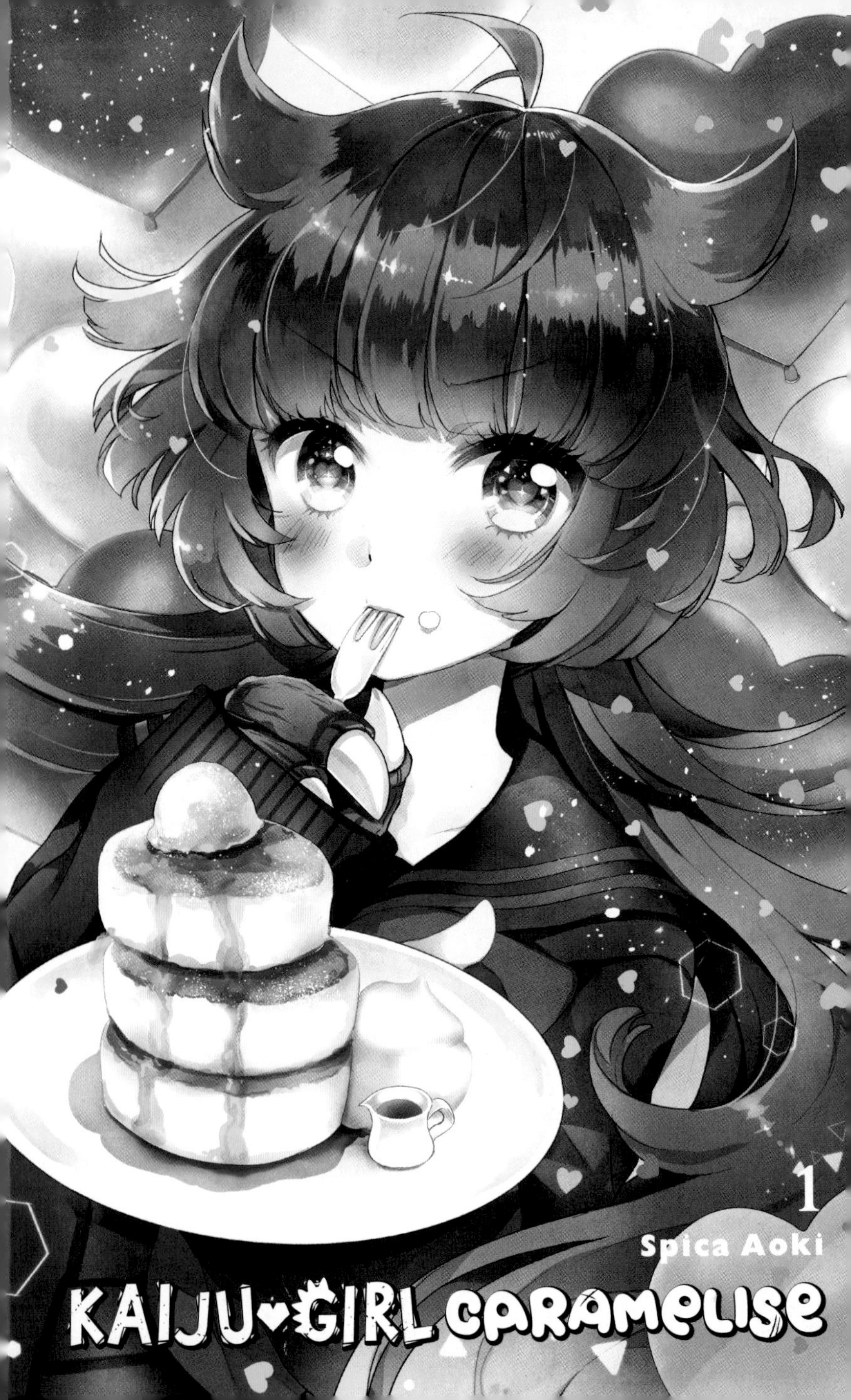
1
Spica Aoki
KAIJU♥GIRL CARAMELISE

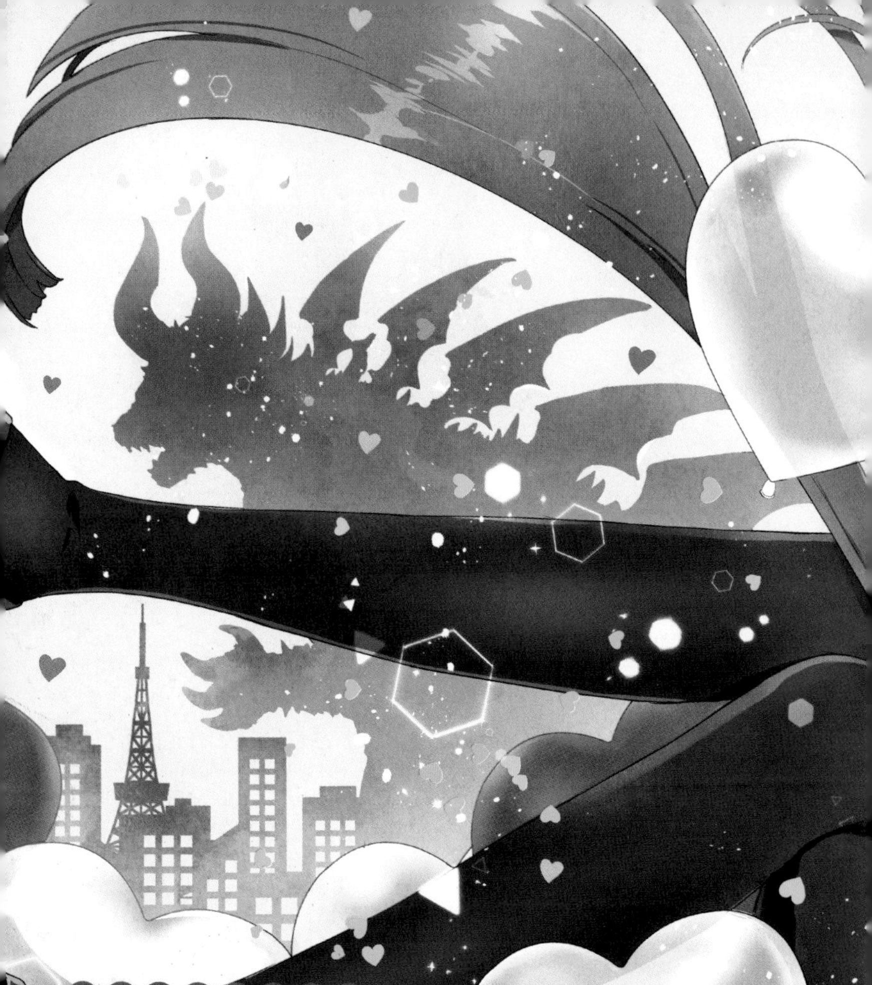

contents

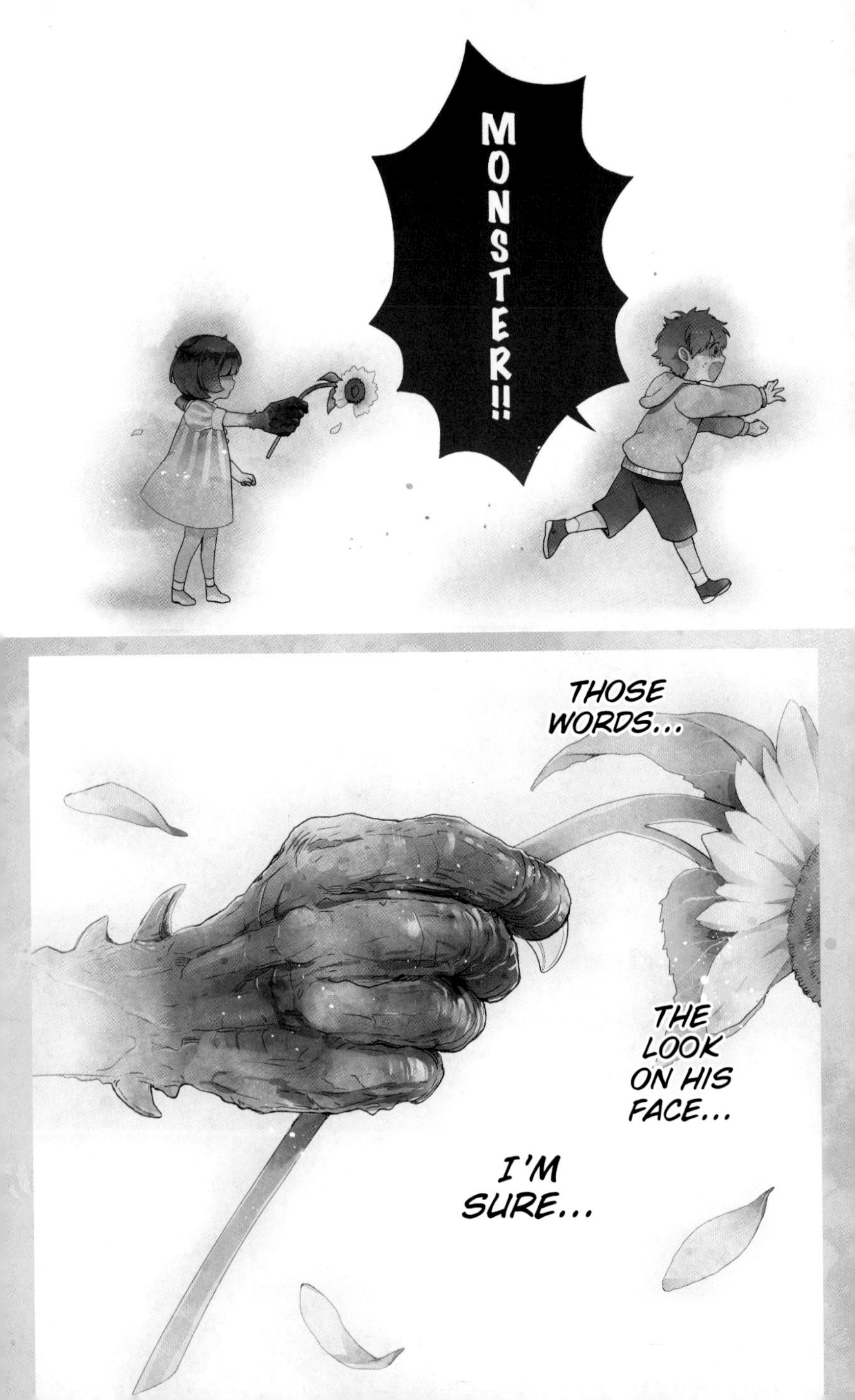
MONSTER!!
THOSE WORDS...
THE LOOK ON HIS FACE...
I'M SURE...

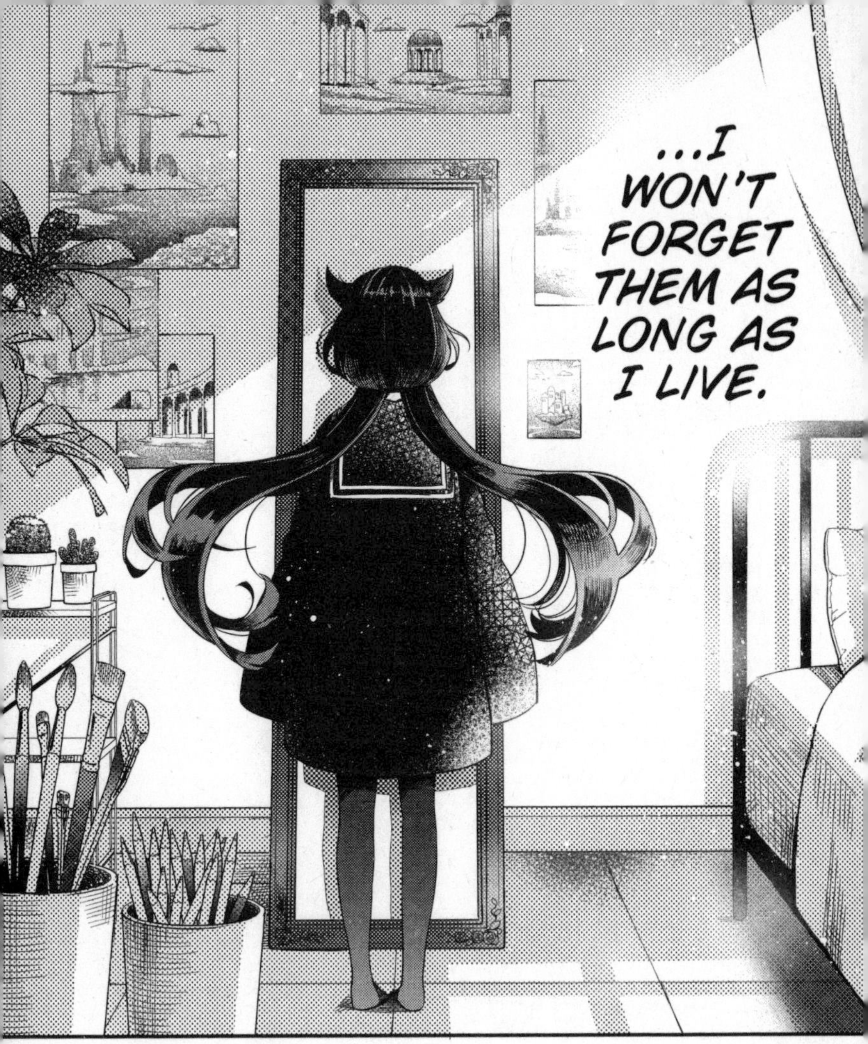
...I WON'T FORGET THEM AS LONG AS I LIVE.
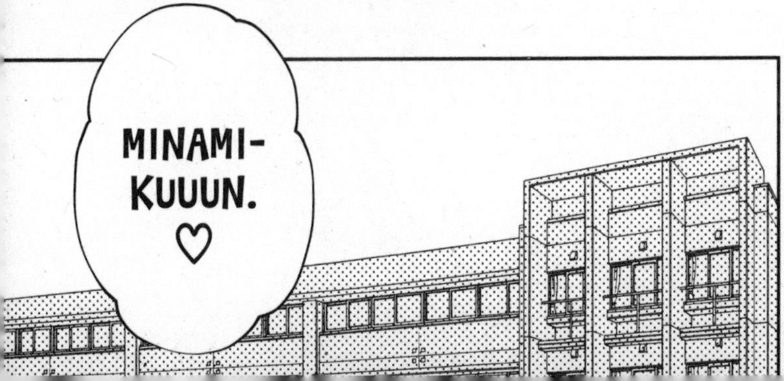
MINAMI-KUUUN. ♡

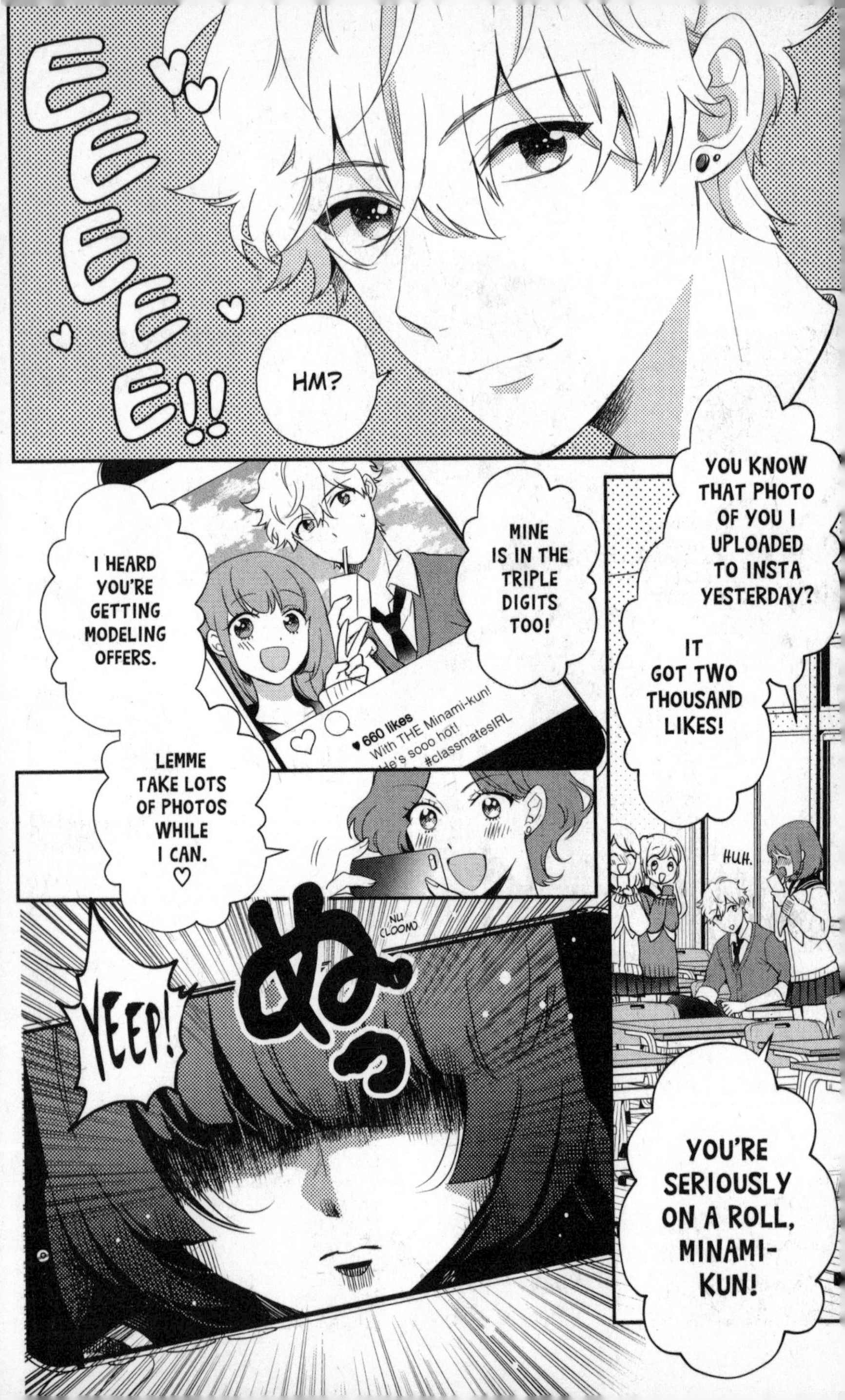
EEEEE!!
HM?
YOU KNOW THAT PHOTO OF YOU I UPLOADED TO INSTA YESTERDAY?
IT GOT TWO THOUSAND LIKES!
HUH.
YOU'RE SERIOUSLY ON A ROLL, MINAMI-KUN!
MINE IS IN THE TRIPLE DIGITS TOO!
I HEARD YOU'RE GETTING MODELING OFFERS.
♥ 660 likes
With THE Minami-kun!
He's sooo hot!
#classmatesIRL
LEMME TAKE LOTS OF PHOTOS WHILE I CAN. ♡
ぬっ
NU (LOOM)
YEEP!

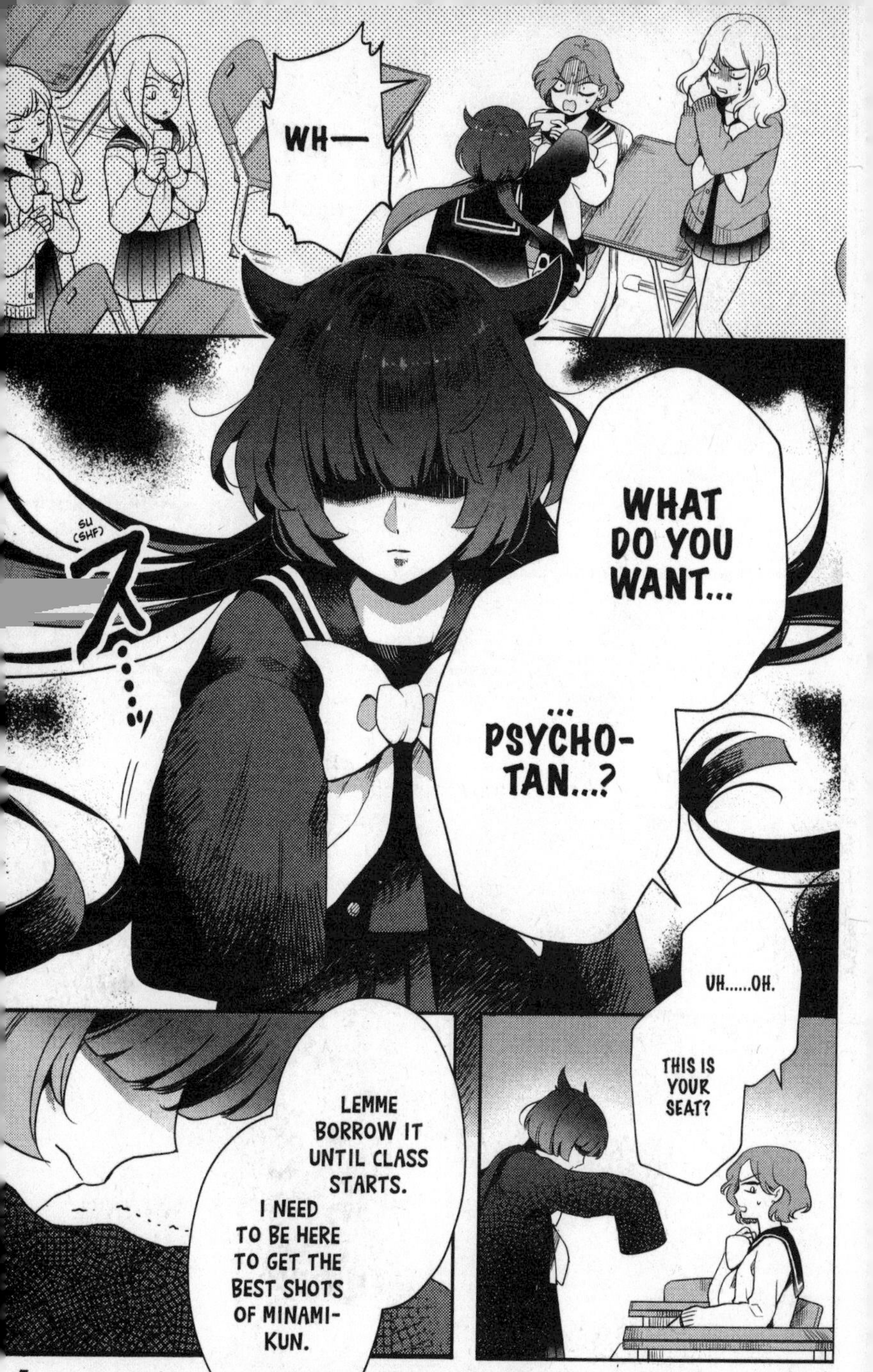
WH—
WHAT DO YOU WANT...
...PSYCHO-TAN...?
SU (SHF)
UH......OH.
THIS IS YOUR SEAT?
LEMME BORROW IT UNTIL CLASS STARTS.
I NEED TO BE HERE TO GET THE BEST SHOTS OF MINAMI-KUN.

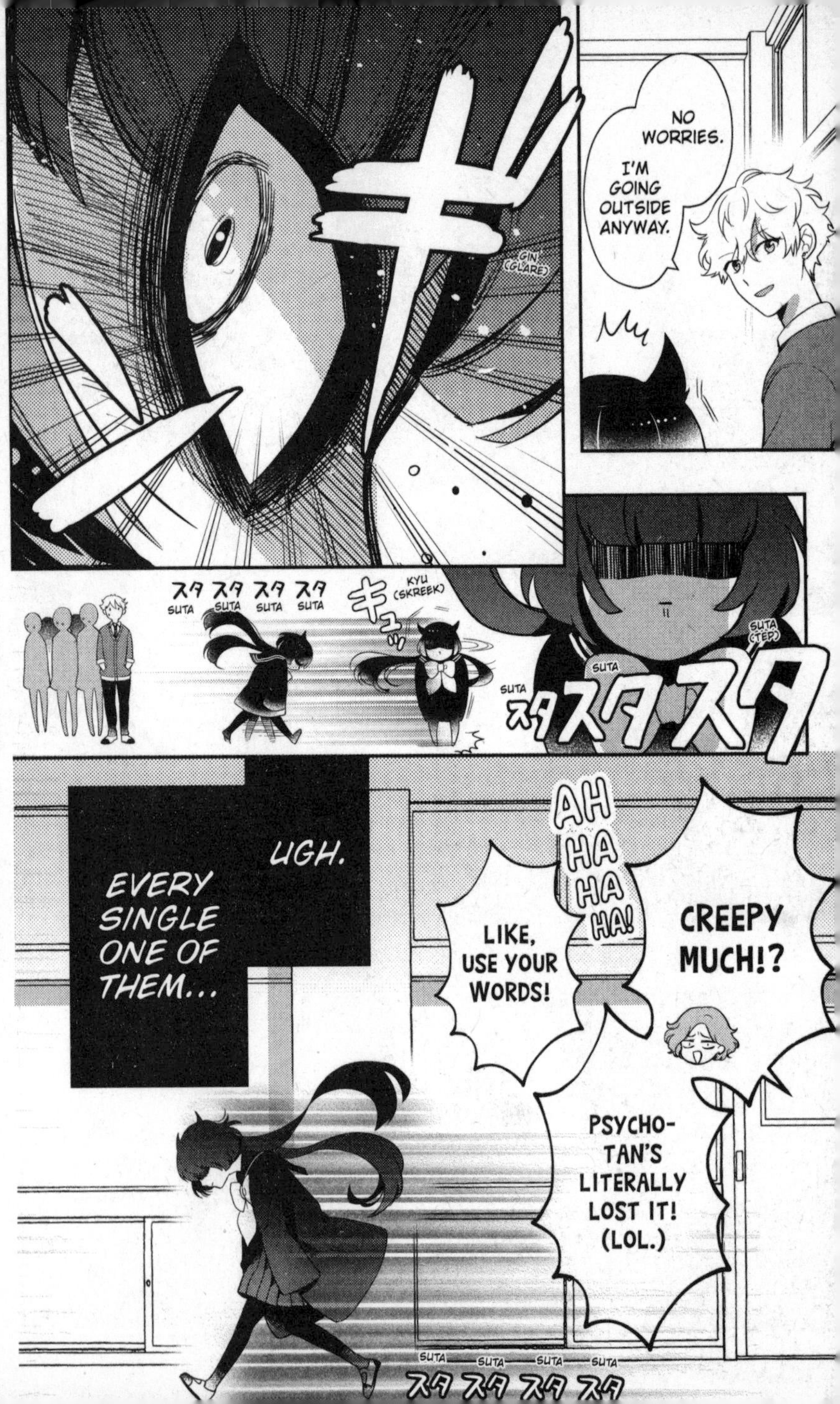
NO WORRIES. I'M GOING OUTSIDE ANYWAY.
GIN (GLARE)
SUTA (TEP)
スタ SUTA
スタ スタ SUTA
キュッ KYU (SKREEK)
スタ SUTA スタ SUTA スタ SUTA スタ SUTA
AH HA HA HA!
CREEPY MUCH!?
LIKE, USE YOUR WORDS!
PSYCHO-TAN'S LITERALLY LOST IT! (LOL.)
UGH.
EVERY SINGLE ONE OF THEM...
スタ SUTA スタ SUTA スタ SUTA スタ SUTA

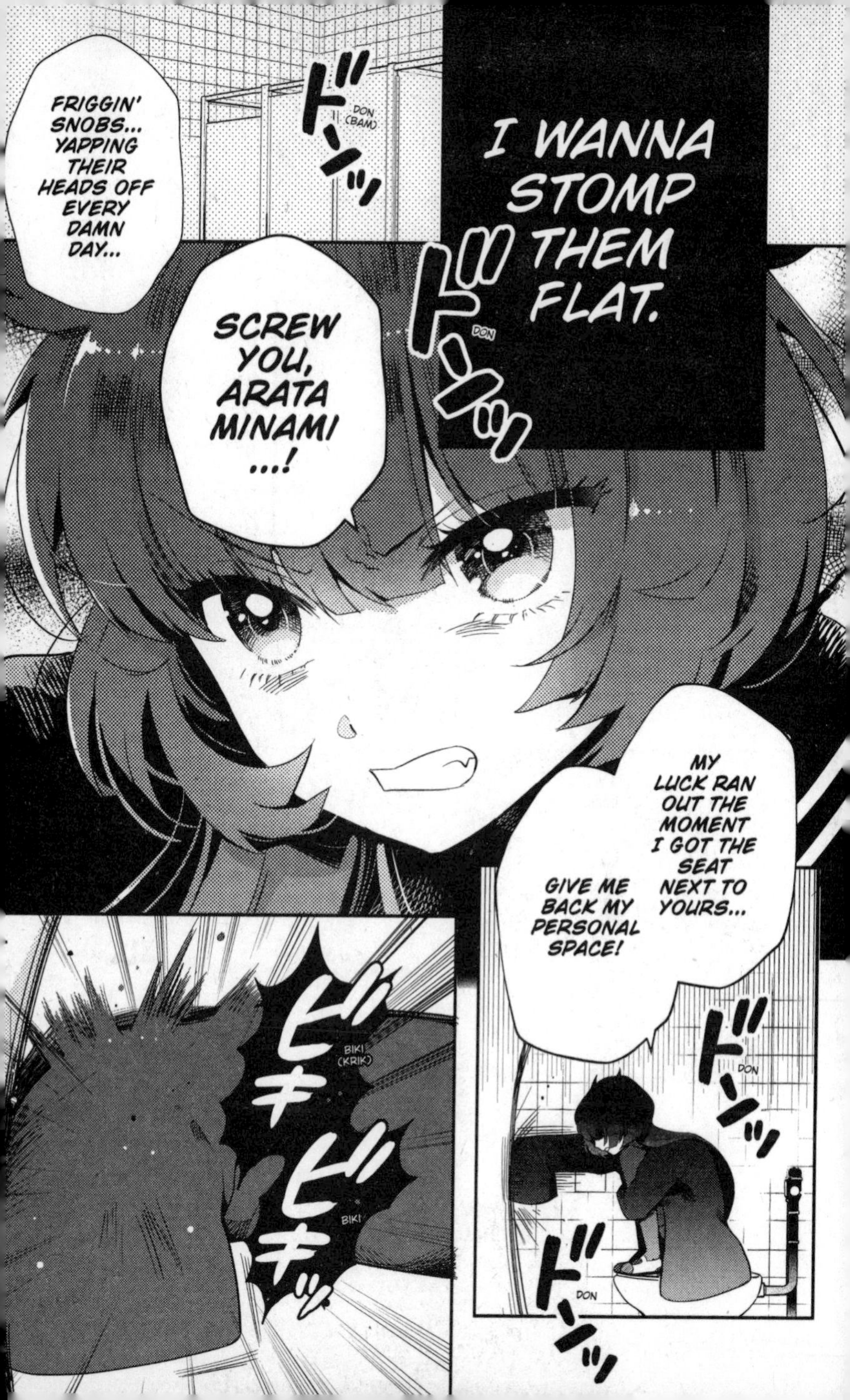
I WANNA STOMP THEM FLAT.
DON
DON (BAM)
FRIGGIN' SNOBS... YAPPING THEIR HEADS OFF EVERY DAMN DAY...
SCREW YOU, ARATA MINAMI...!
MY LUCK RAN OUT THE MOMENT I GOT THE SEAT NEXT TO YOURS...
GIVE ME BACK MY PERSONAL SPACE!
DON
DON
BIKI (KRIK)
BIKI

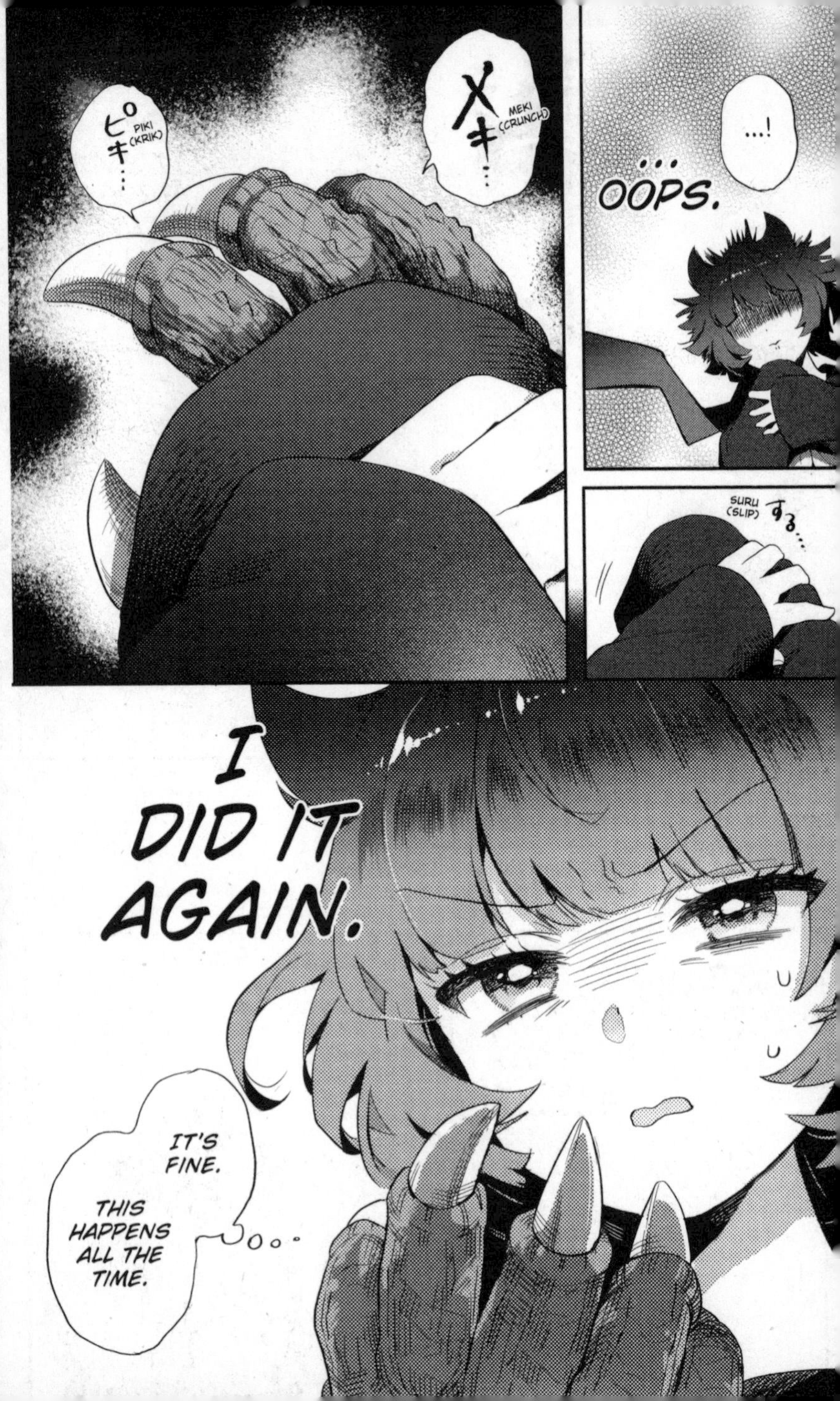
...!
... OOPS.
SURU (SLIP) する...
メキ...
MEKI (CRUNCH)
ピキ...
PIKI (KRIK)
I DID IT AGAIN.
IT'S FINE. THIS HAPPENS ALL THE TIME.

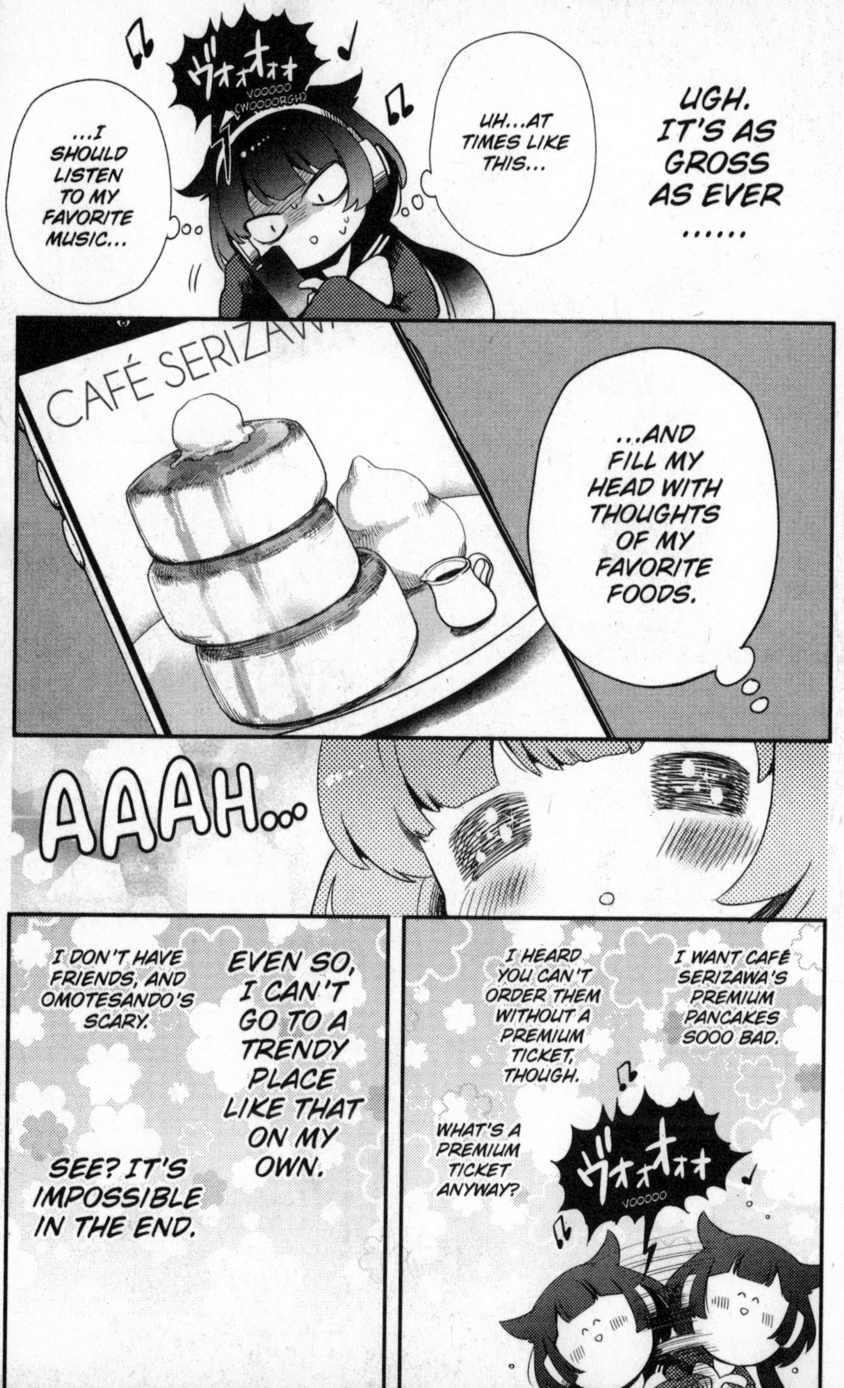
UGH. IT'S AS GROSS AS EVER ......
UH...AT TIMES LIKE THIS...
ヴォォオォォ
VOOOOO (WOOOORGH)
...I SHOULD LISTEN TO MY FAVORITE MUSIC...
CAFÉ SERIZA
...AND FILL MY HEAD WITH THOUGHTS OF MY FAVORITE FOODS.
AAAH...
I WANT CAFÉ SERIZAWA'S PREMIUM PANCAKES SOOO BAD.
I HEARD YOU CAN'T ORDER THEM WITHOUT A PREMIUM TICKET, THOUGH.
WHAT'S A PREMIUM TICKET ANYWAY?
ヴォォオォォ
VOOOOO
EVEN SO, I CAN'T GO TO A TRENDY PLACE LIKE THAT ON MY OWN.
I DON'T HAVE FRIENDS, AND OMOTESANDO'S SCARY.
SEE? IT'S IMPOSSIBLE IN THE END.

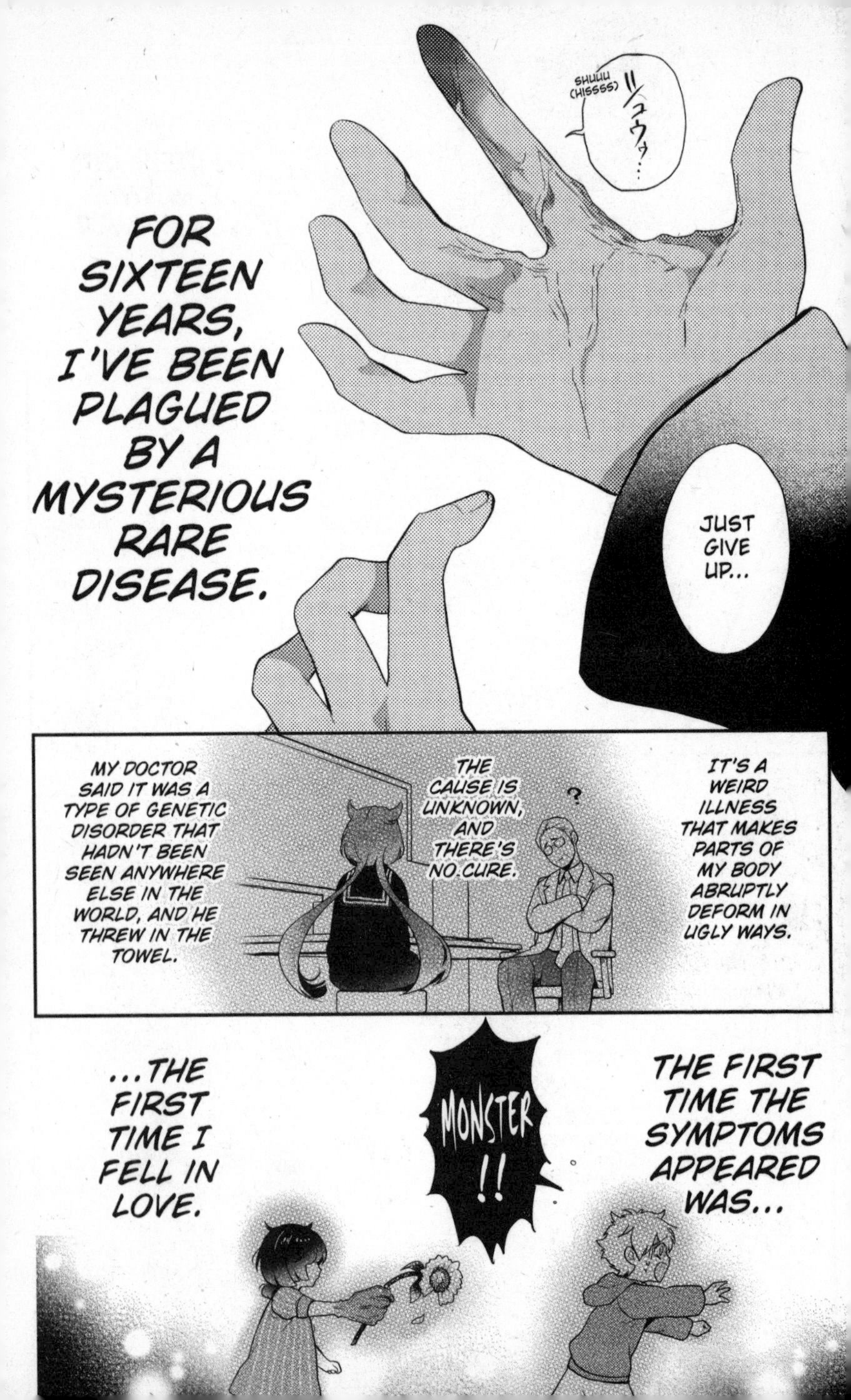
SHUUU (HISSSS)
JUST GIVE UP...
FOR SIXTEEN YEARS, I'VE BEEN PLAGUED BY A MYSTERIOUS RARE DISEASE.
IT'S A WEIRD ILLNESS THAT MAKES PARTS OF MY BODY ABRUPTLY DEFORM IN UGLY WAYS.
THE CAUSE IS UNKNOWN, AND THERE'S NO CURE.
MY DOCTOR SAID IT WAS A TYPE OF GENETIC DISORDER THAT HADN'T BEEN SEEN ANYWHERE ELSE IN THE WORLD, AND HE THREW IN THE TOWEL.
?
THE FIRST TIME THE SYMPTOMS APPEARED WAS...
MONSTER !!
...THE FIRST TIME I FELL IN LOVE.

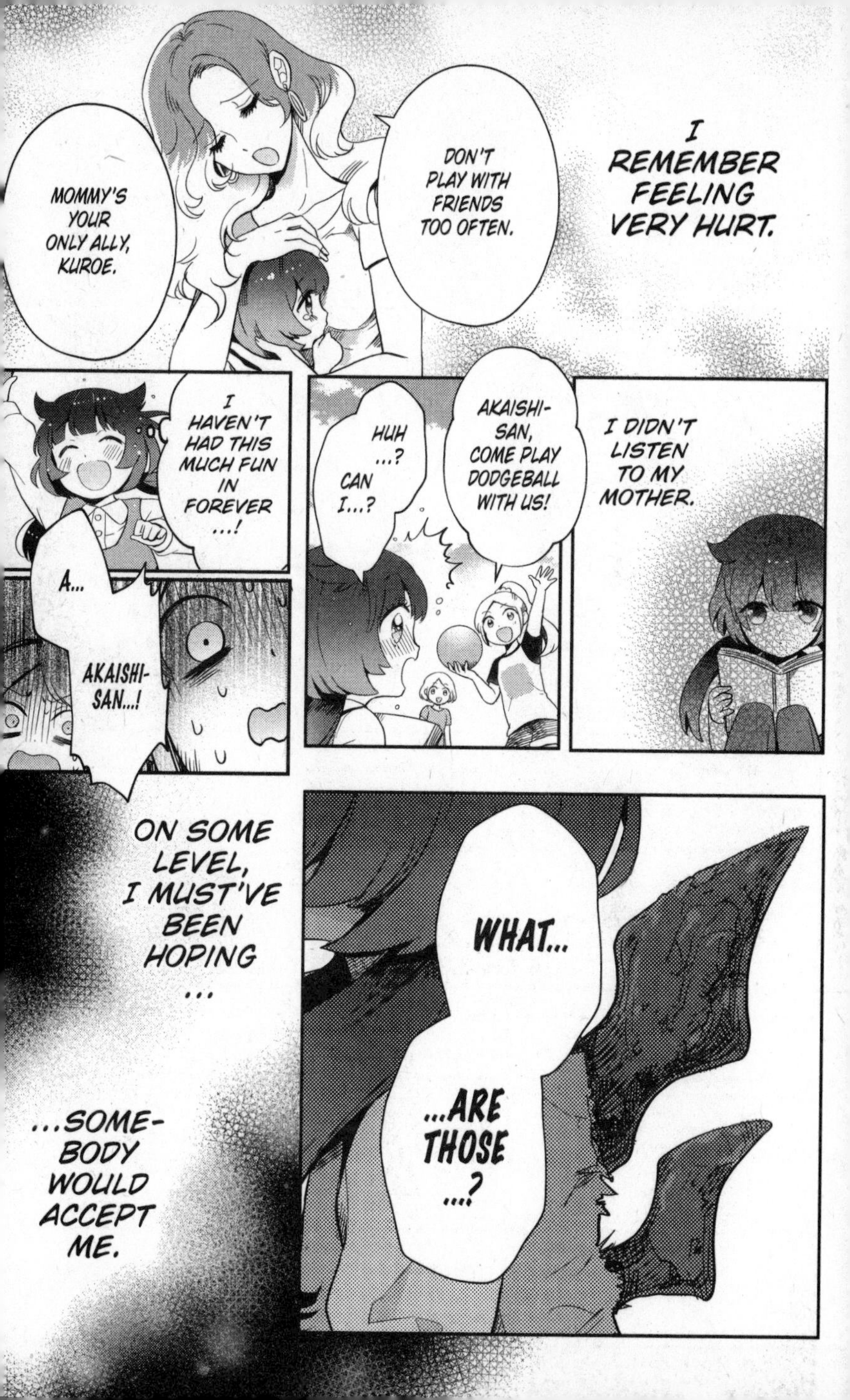
I REMEMBER FEELING VERY HURT.
DON'T PLAY WITH FRIENDS TOO OFTEN.
MOMMY'S YOUR ONLY ALLY, KUROE.
I DIDN'T LISTEN TO MY MOTHER.
AKAISHI-SAN, COME PLAY DODGEBALL WITH US!
HUH...? CAN I...?
I HAVEN'T HAD THIS MUCH FUN IN FOREVER...!
A... AKAISHI-SAN...!
WHAT... ...ARE THOSE...?
ON SOME LEVEL, I MUST'VE BEEN HOPING...
...SOMEBODY WOULD ACCEPT ME.

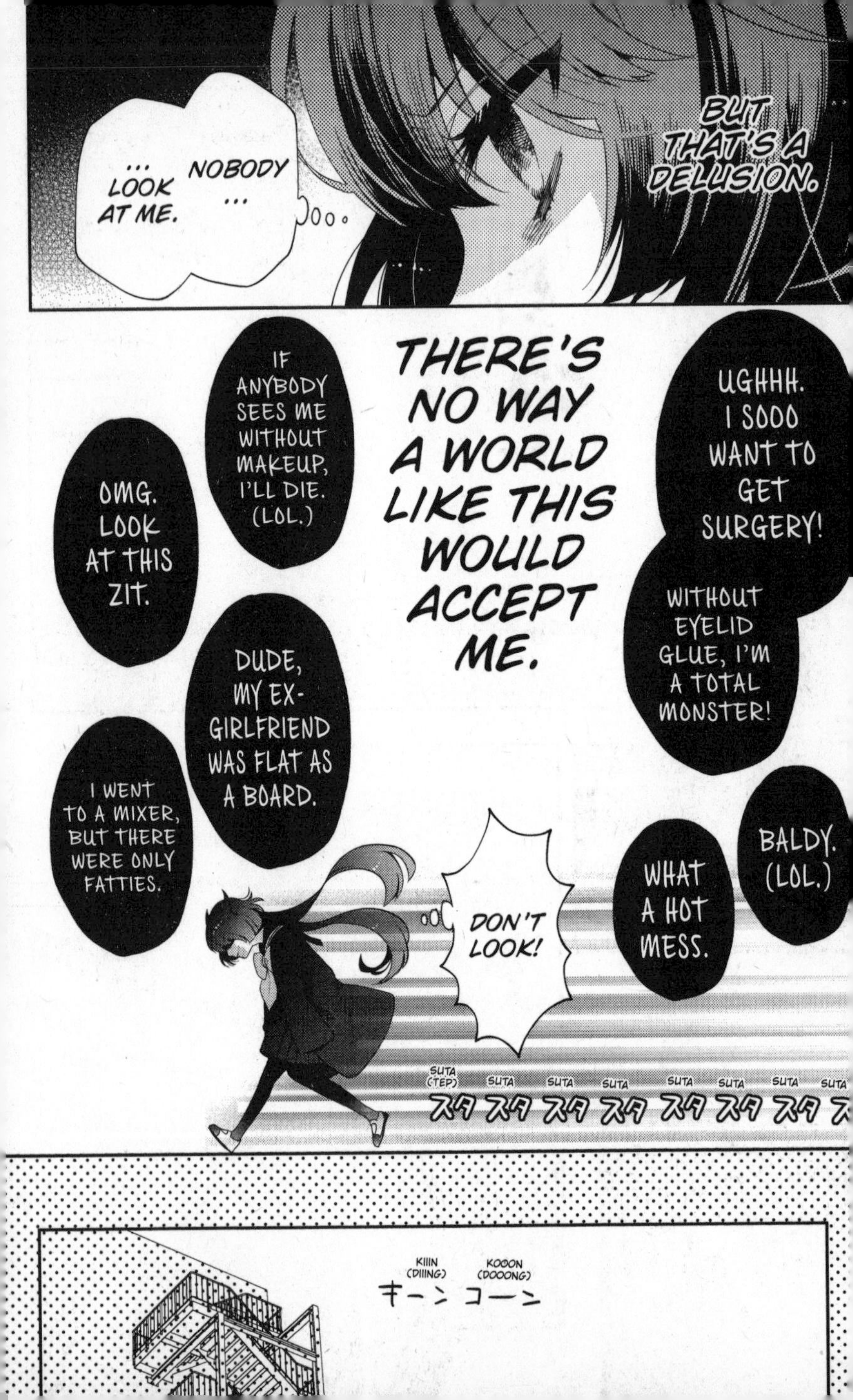
...NOBODY... LOOK AT ME.
BUT THAT'S A DELUSION.
UGHHH. I SOOO WANT TO GET SURGERY!
THERE'S NO WAY A WORLD LIKE THIS WOULD ACCEPT ME.
IF ANYBODY SEES ME WITHOUT MAKEUP, I'LL DIE. (LOL.)
OMG. LOOK AT THIS ZIT.
WITHOUT EYELID GLUE, I'M A TOTAL MONSTER!
DUDE, MY EX-GIRLFRIEND WAS FLAT AS A BOARD.
BALDY. (LOL.)
WHAT A HOT MESS.
DON'T LOOK!
I WENT TO A MIXER, BUT THERE WERE ONLY FATTIES.
SUTA (TEP) SUTA SUTA SUTA SUTA SUTA SUTA SUTA
スタ スタ スタ スタ スタ スタ スタ
KIIIN (DIIING) KOOON (DOOONG)
キーン コーン

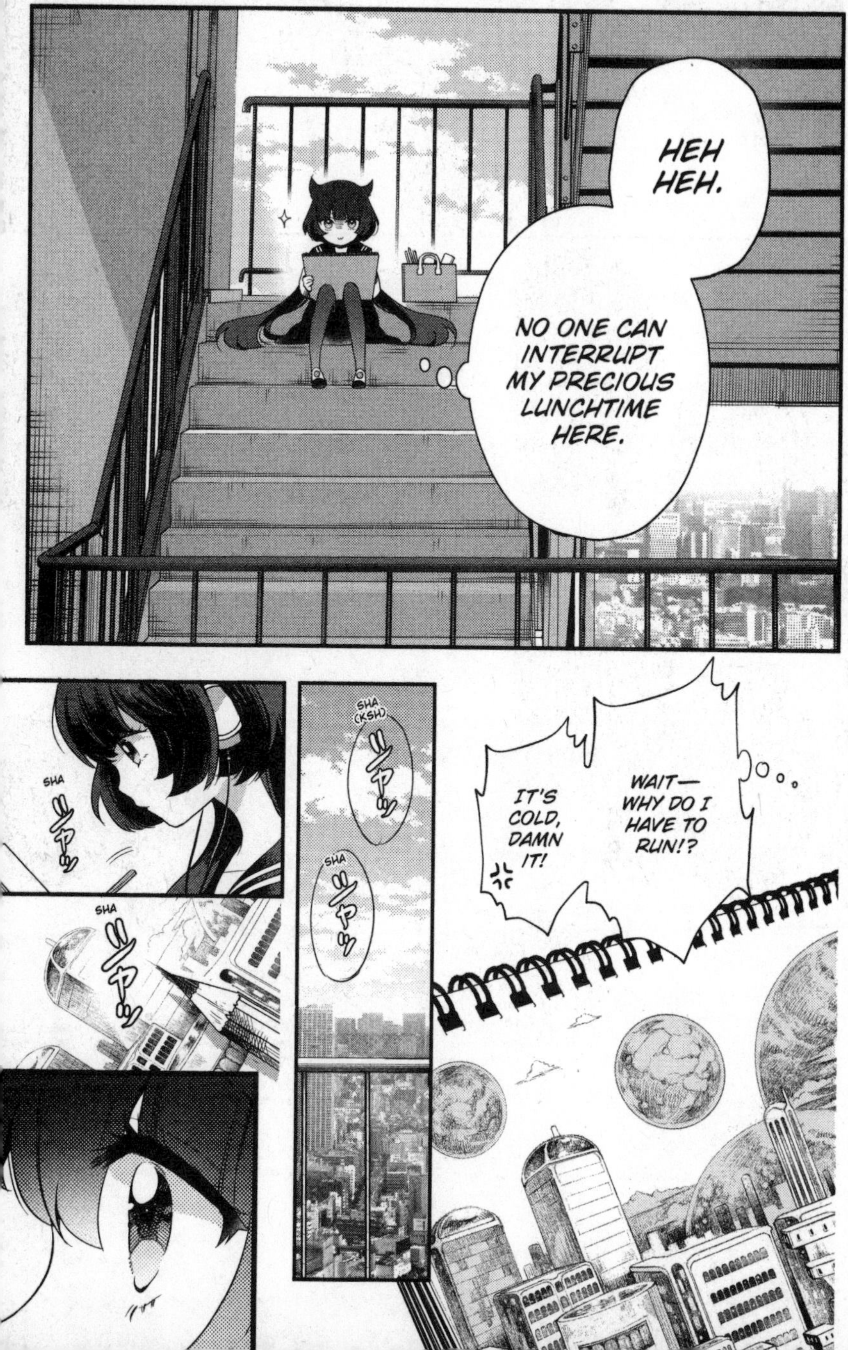
HEH HEH.
NO ONE CAN INTERRUPT MY PRECIOUS LUNCHTIME HERE.
WAIT— WHY DO I HAVE TO RUN!?
IT'S COLD, DAMN IT!
SHA (KSH)
シャッ
SHA
シャッ
SHA
シャッ
SHA
シャッ

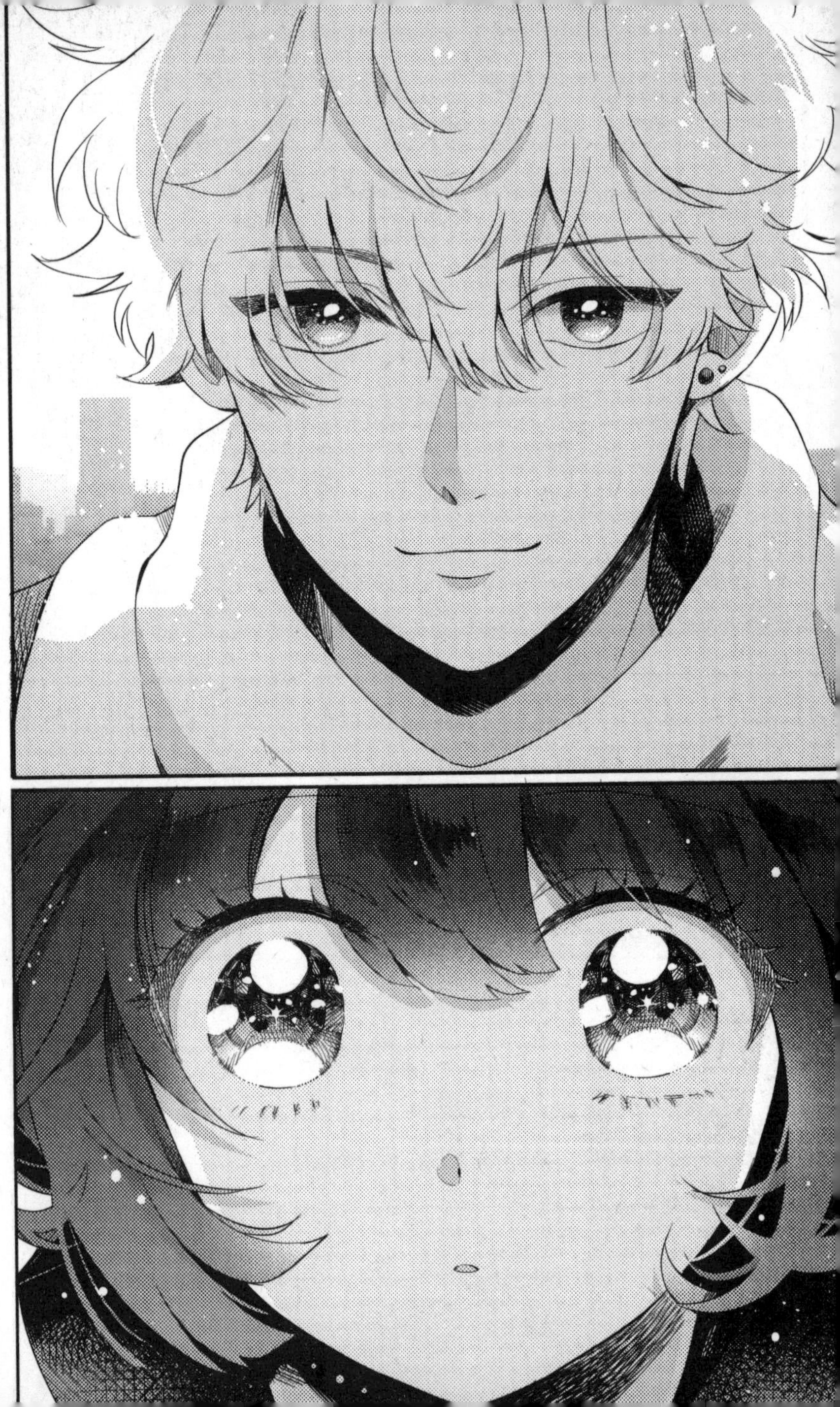

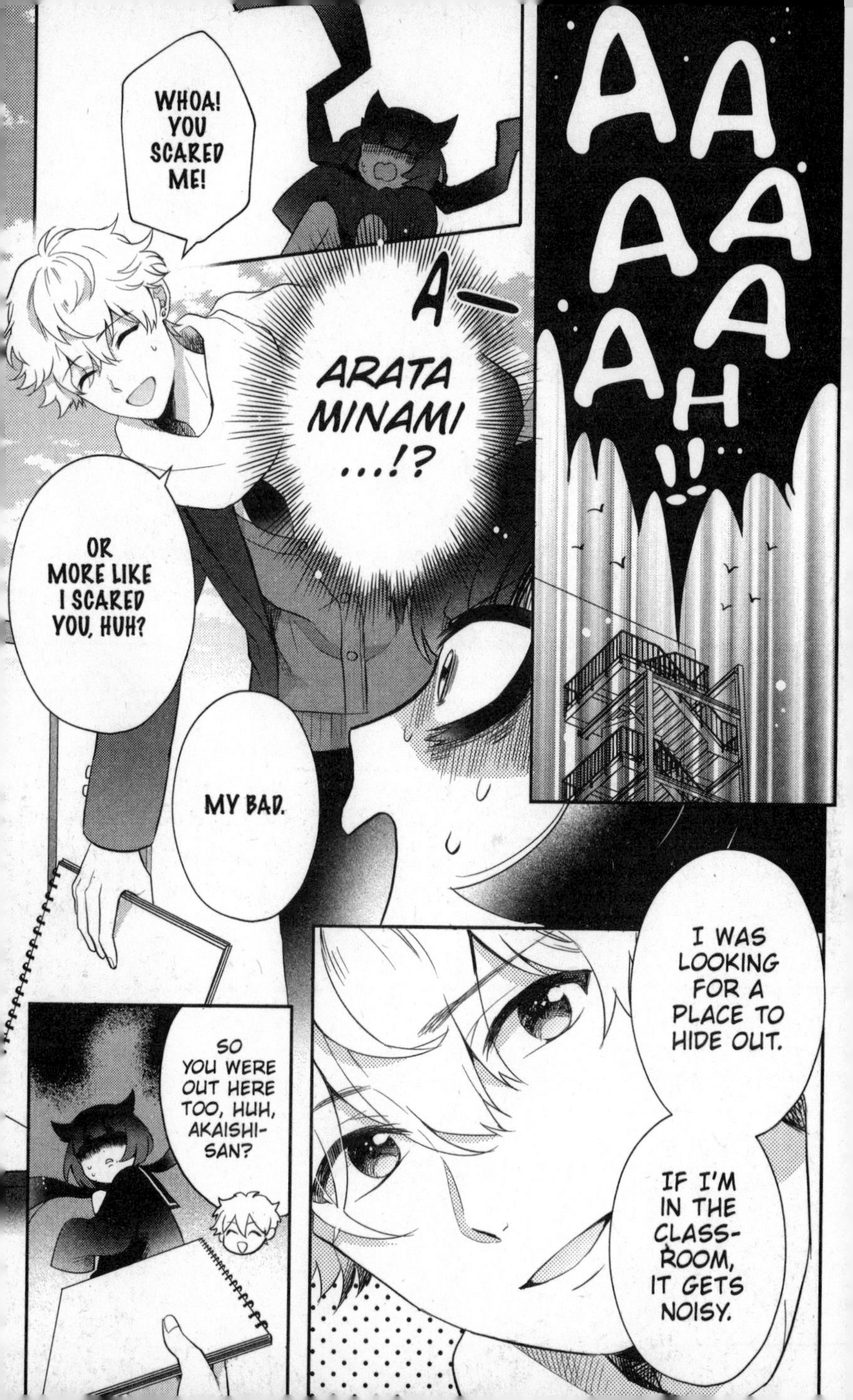
AAAAAAAH!!
WHOA! YOU SCARED ME!
A—
ARATA MINAMI ...!?
OR MORE LIKE I SCARED YOU, HUH?
MY BAD.
I WAS LOOKING FOR A PLACE TO HIDE OUT.
IF I'M IN THE CLASS-ROOM, IT GETS NOISY.
SO YOU WERE OUT HERE TOO, HUH, AKAISHI-SAN?

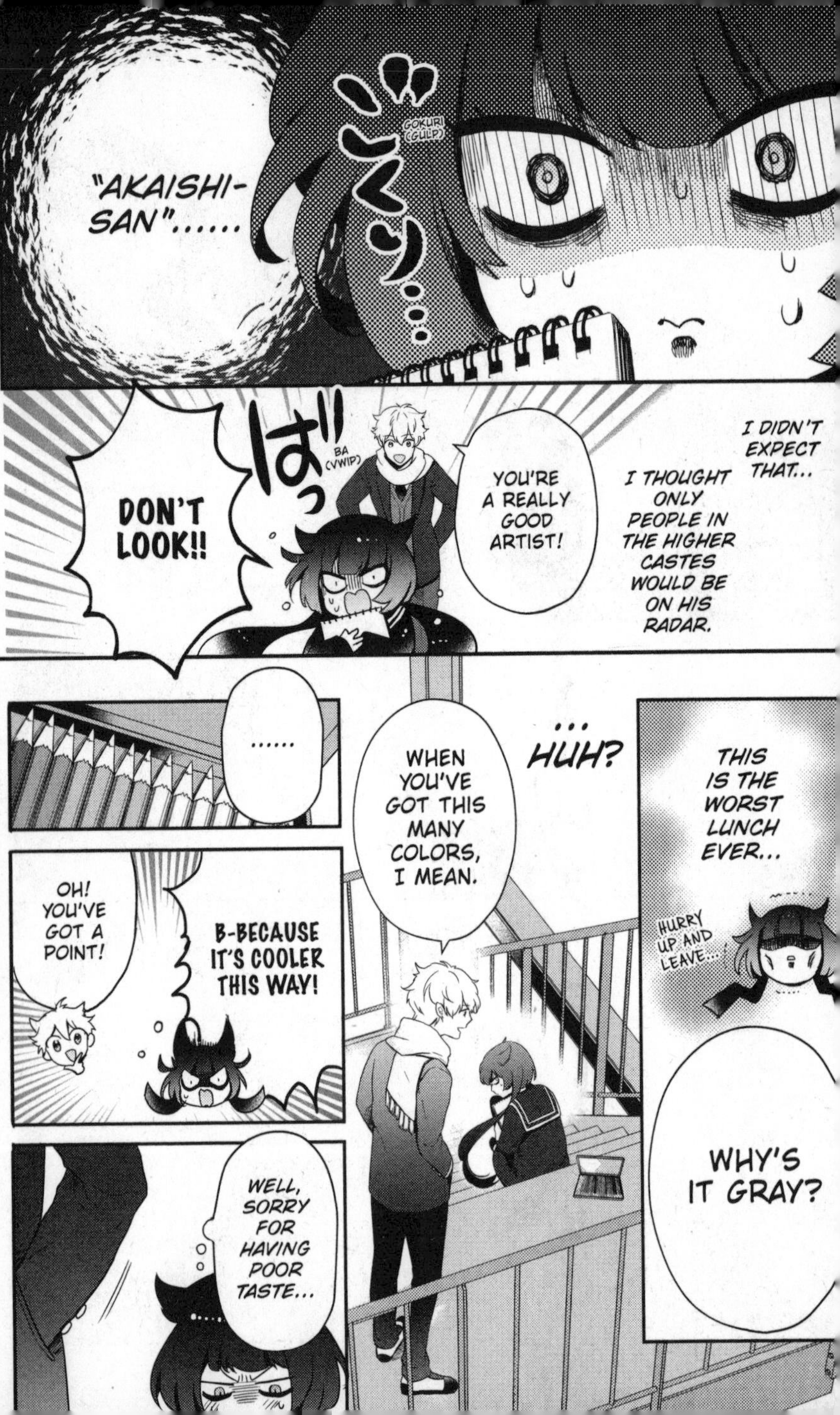

ごくり…
GOKURI (GULP)
"AKAISHI-SAN"......
I DIDN'T EXPECT THAT...
I THOUGHT ONLY PEOPLE IN THE HIGHER CASTES WOULD BE ON HIS RADAR.
YOU'RE A REALLY GOOD ARTIST!
ばっ
BA (VWIP)
DON'T LOOK!!
THIS IS THE WORST LUNCH EVER...
HURRY UP AND LEAVE...
WHY'S IT GRAY?
...HUH?
WHEN YOU'VE GOT THIS MANY COLORS, I MEAN.
......
B-BECAUSE IT'S COOLER THIS WAY!
OH! YOU'VE GOT A POINT!
WELL, SORRY FOR HAVING POOR TASTE...

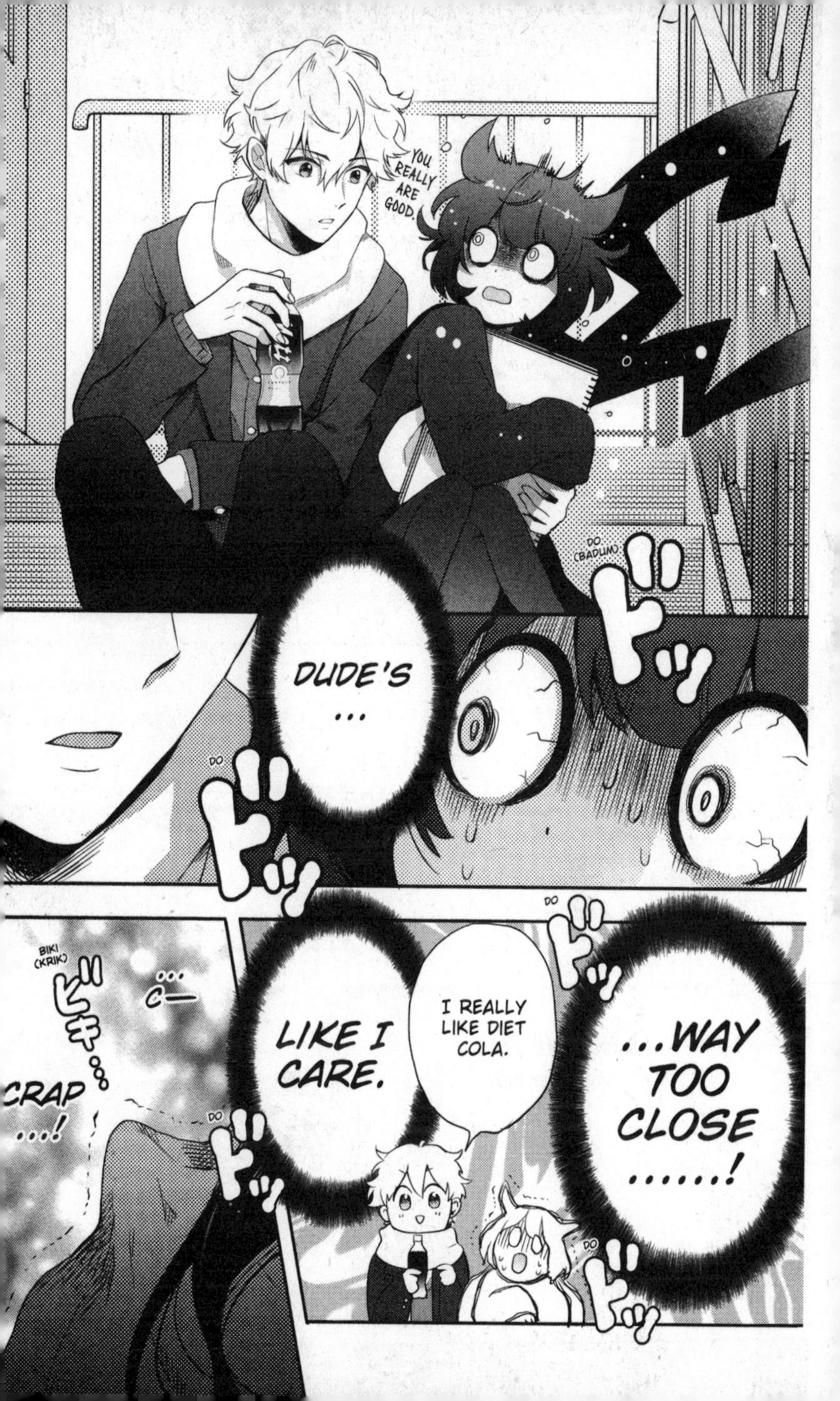
YOU REALLY ARE GOOD.
DO (BADUM)
ドッ
DUDE'S ...
DO
ドッ
DO
ドッ
...WAY TOO CLOSE ......!
I REALLY LIKE DIET COLA.
LIKE I CARE.
DO
ドッ
DO
ドッ
... C—
BIKI (KRIK)
ビキ...
CRAP ...!

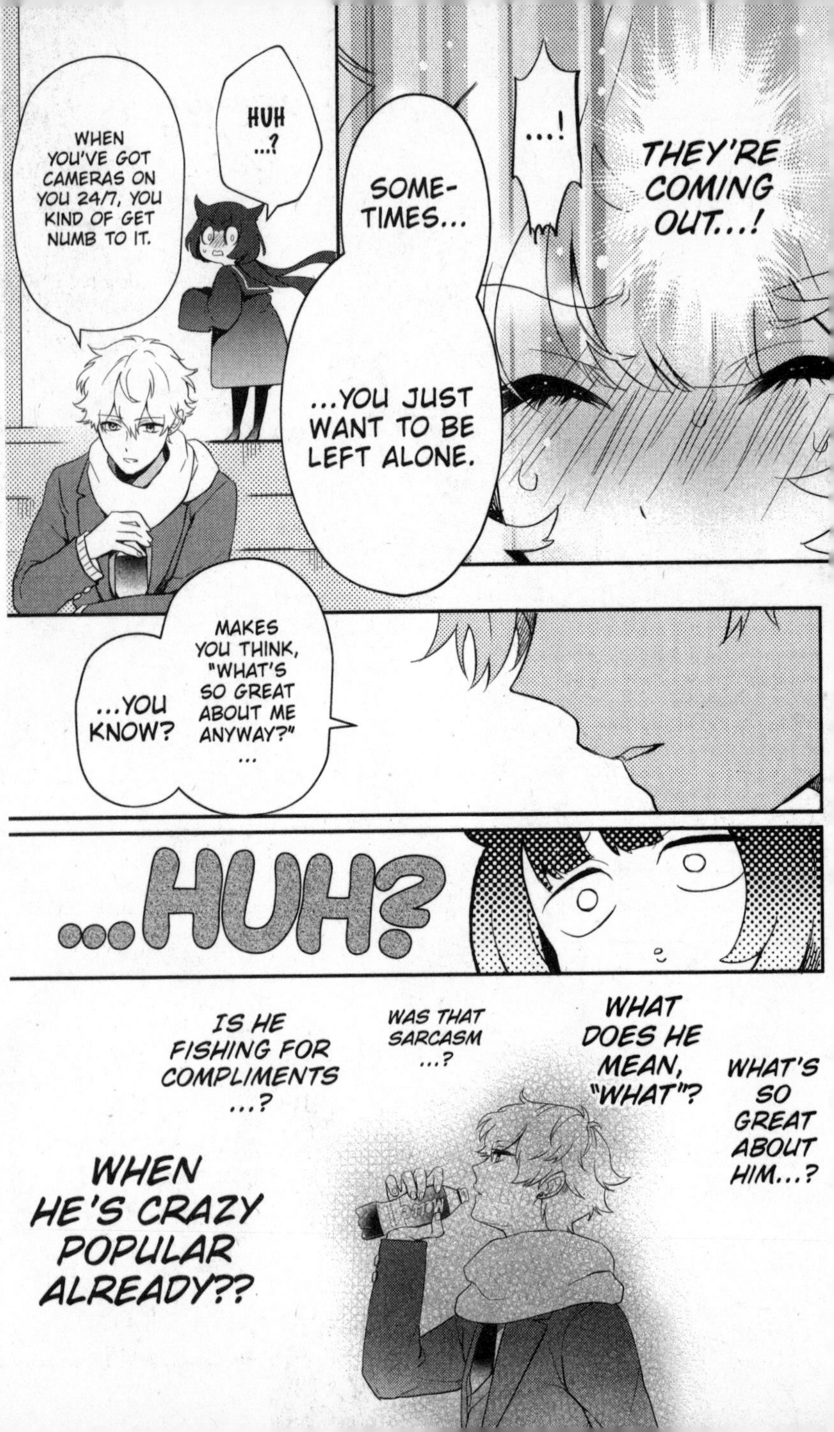
...!
THEY'RE COMING OUT...!
SOME-TIMES...
...YOU JUST WANT TO BE LEFT ALONE.
HUH ...?
WHEN YOU'VE GOT CAMERAS ON YOU 24/7, YOU KIND OF GET NUMB TO IT.
MAKES YOU THINK, "WHAT'S SO GREAT ABOUT ME ANYWAY?" ...
...YOU KNOW?
...HUH?
WHAT'S SO GREAT ABOUT HIM...?
WHAT DOES HE MEAN, "WHAT"?
WAS THAT SARCASM ...?
IS HE FISHING FOR COMPLIMENTS ...?
WHEN HE'S CRAZY POPULAR ALREADY??

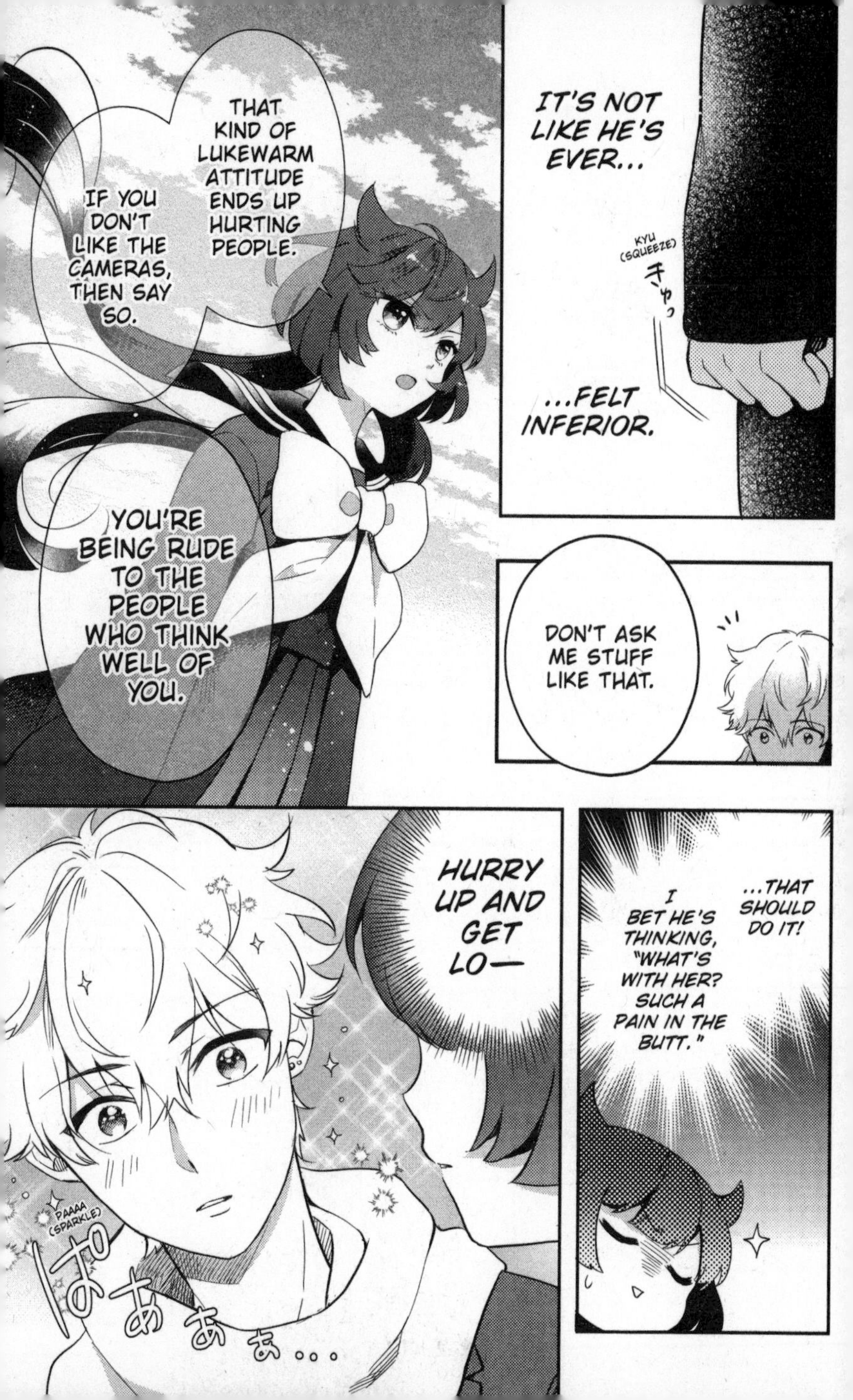
IT'S NOT LIKE HE'S EVER...
KYU (SQUEEZE)
キュッ
...FELT INFERIOR.
DON'T ASK ME STUFF LIKE THAT.
THAT KIND OF LUKEWARM ATTITUDE ENDS UP HURTING PEOPLE.
IF YOU DON'T LIKE THE CAMERAS, THEN SAY SO.
YOU'RE BEING RUDE TO THE PEOPLE WHO THINK WELL OF YOU.
...THAT SHOULD DO IT!
I BET HE'S THINKING, "WHAT'S WITH HER? SUCH A PAIN IN THE BUTT."
HURRY UP AND GET LO—
PAAAA (SPARKLE)
ぱあああ...

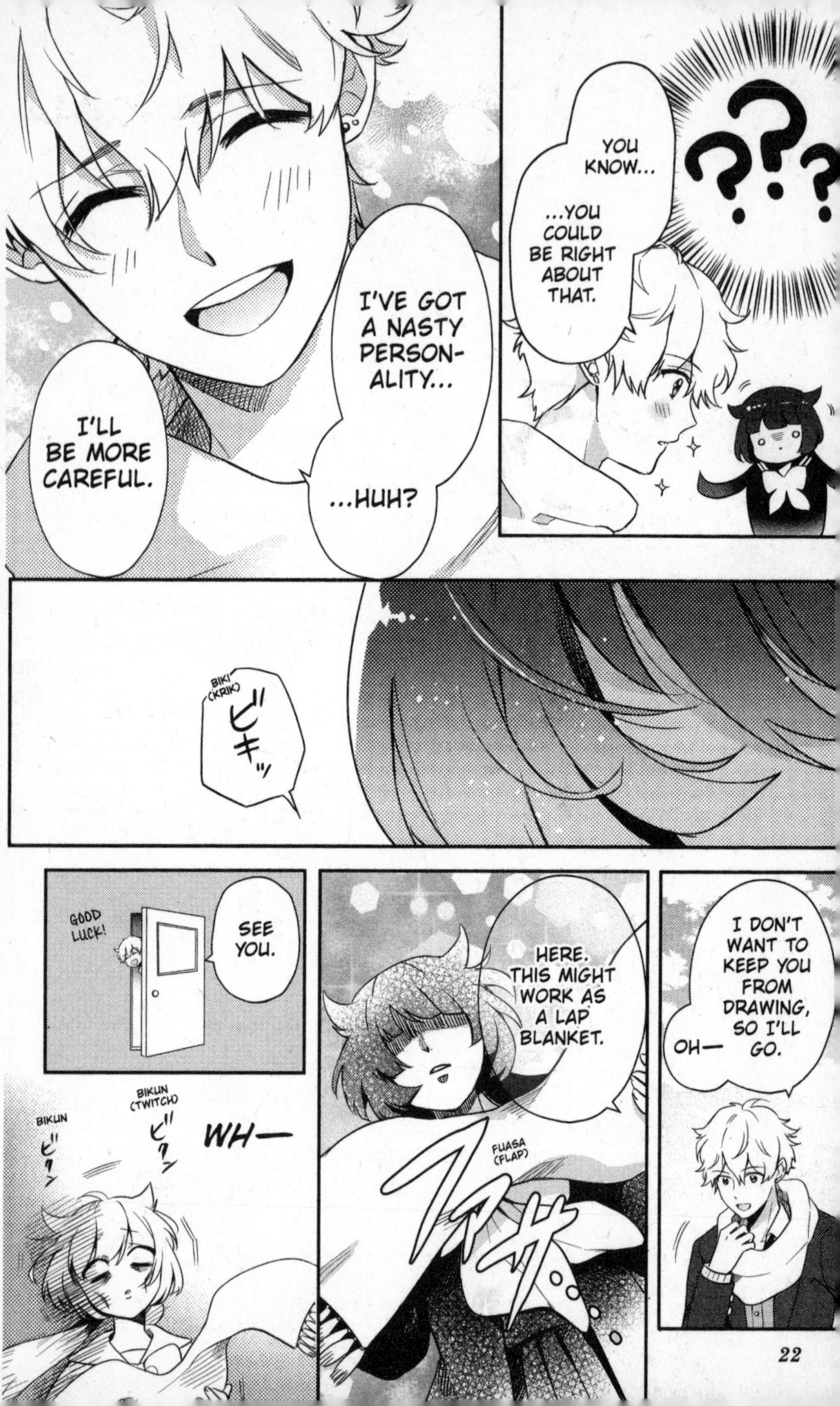
YOU KNOW...
...YOU COULD BE RIGHT ABOUT THAT.
I'VE GOT A NASTY PERSON-ALITY...
...HUH?
I'LL BE MORE CAREFUL.
BIKI (KRIK) ビキッ
I DON'T WANT TO KEEP YOU FROM DRAWING, SO I'LL GO.
OH—
HERE. THIS MIGHT WORK AS A LAP BLANKET.
FUASA (FLAP) ファサ
SEE YOU.
GOOD LUCK!
WH—
BIKUN (TWITCH) ビクン
BIKUN ビクン

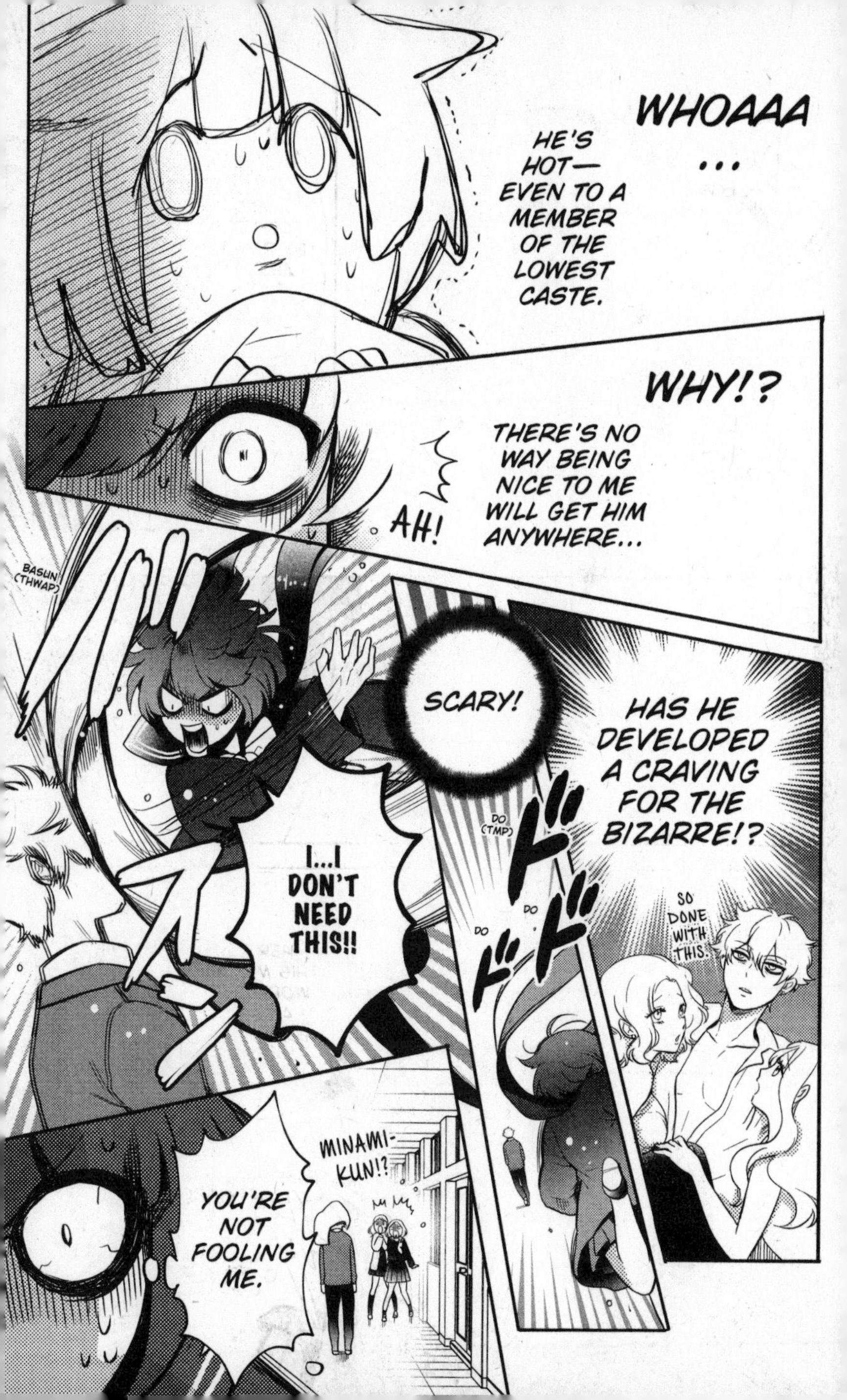
WHOAAA ...
HE'S HOT— EVEN TO A MEMBER OF THE LOWEST CASTE.
WHY!?
THERE'S NO WAY BEING NICE TO ME WILL GET HIM ANYWHERE...
AH!
SCARY!
HAS HE DEVELOPED A CRAVING FOR THE BIZARRE!?
DO (TMP)
DO
DO
SO DONE WITH THIS.
BASUN (THWAP)
I...I DON'T NEED THIS!!
MINAMI-KUN!?
YOU'RE NOT FOOLING ME.

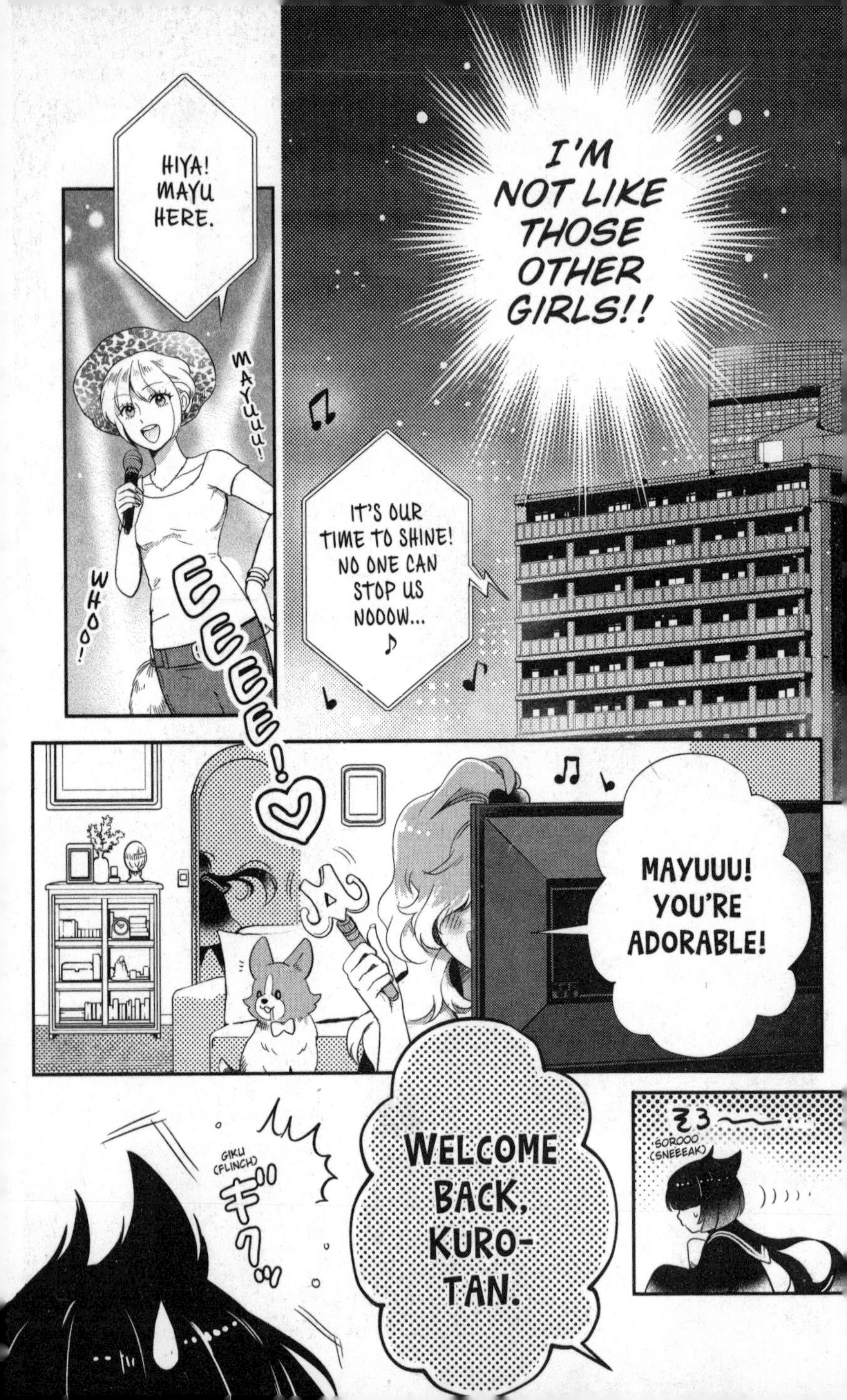
I'M NOT LIKE THOSE OTHER GIRLS!!
IT'S OUR TIME TO SHINE! NO ONE CAN STOP US NOOOW... ♪
HIYA! MAYU HERE.
MAYUUU!
WHOO!
EEEEE! ♥
MAYUUU! YOU'RE ADORABLE!
SOROOO (SNEEEAK)
WELCOME BACK, KURO-TAN.
GIKU (FLINCH)

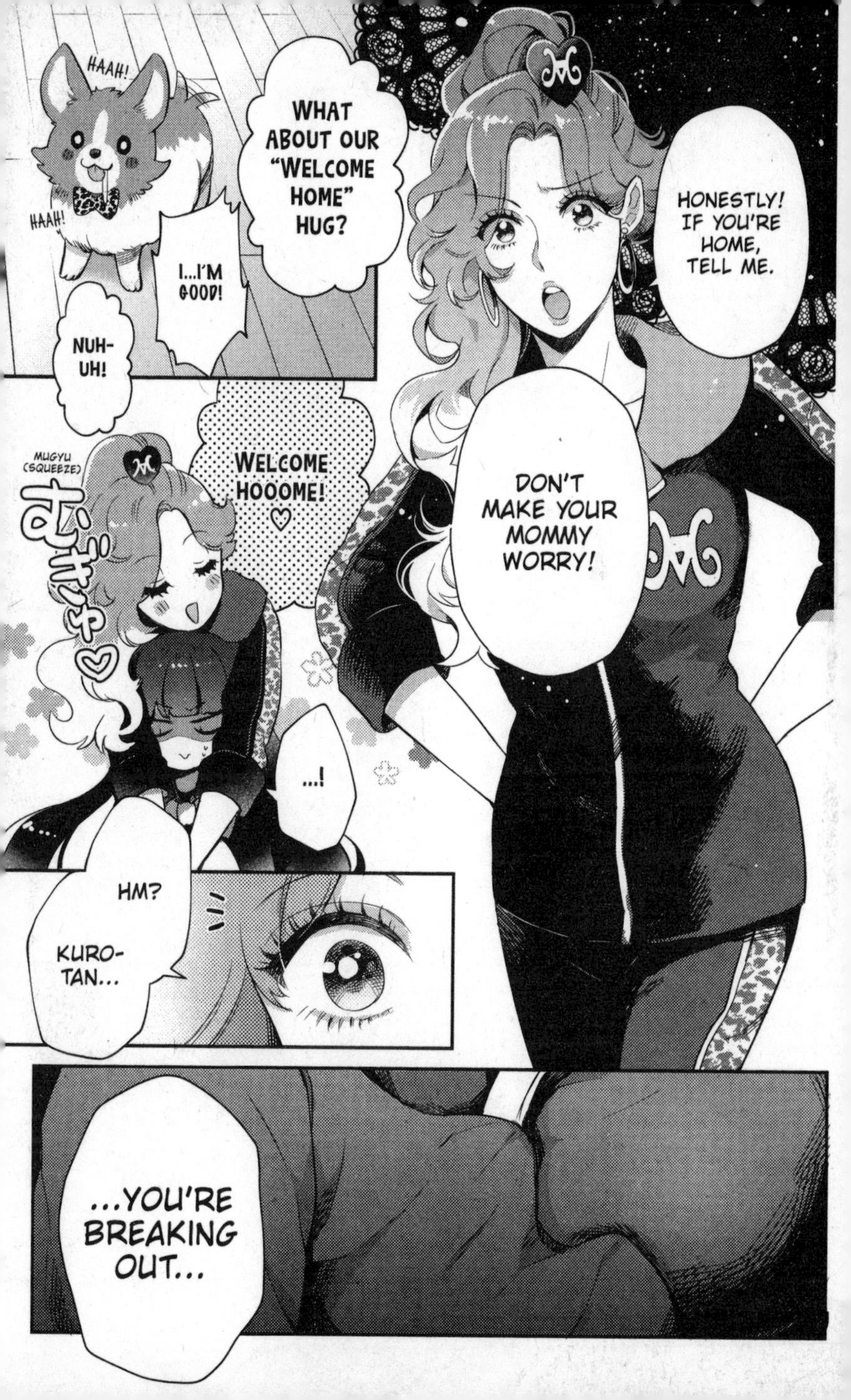
HONESTLY! IF YOU'RE HOME, TELL ME.
DON'T MAKE YOUR MOMMY WORRY!
WHAT ABOUT OUR "WELCOME HOME" HUG?
HAAH!
HAAH!
I...I'M GOOD!
NUH-UH!
WELCOME HOOOME! ♡
MUGYU (SQUEEZE)
むぎゅ♡
...!
HM?
KURO-TAN...
...YOU'RE BREAKING OUT...

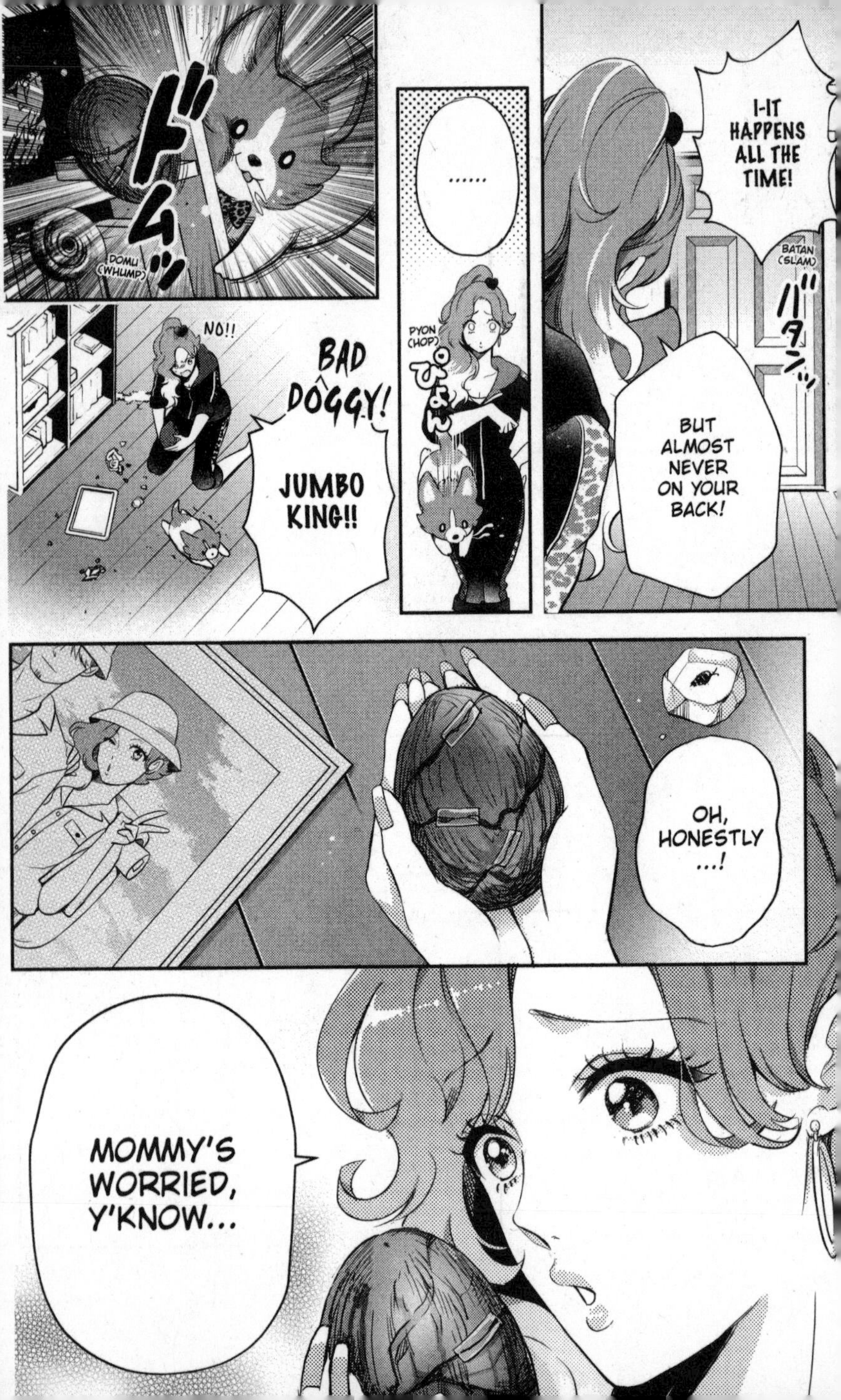
I-IT HAPPENS ALL THE TIME!
BATAN (SLAM)
BUT ALMOST NEVER ON YOUR BACK!
......
PYON (HOP)
DOMU (WHUMP)
NO!!
BAD DOGGY!
JUMBO KING!!
OH, HONESTLY ...!
MOMMY'S WORRIED, Y'KNOW...

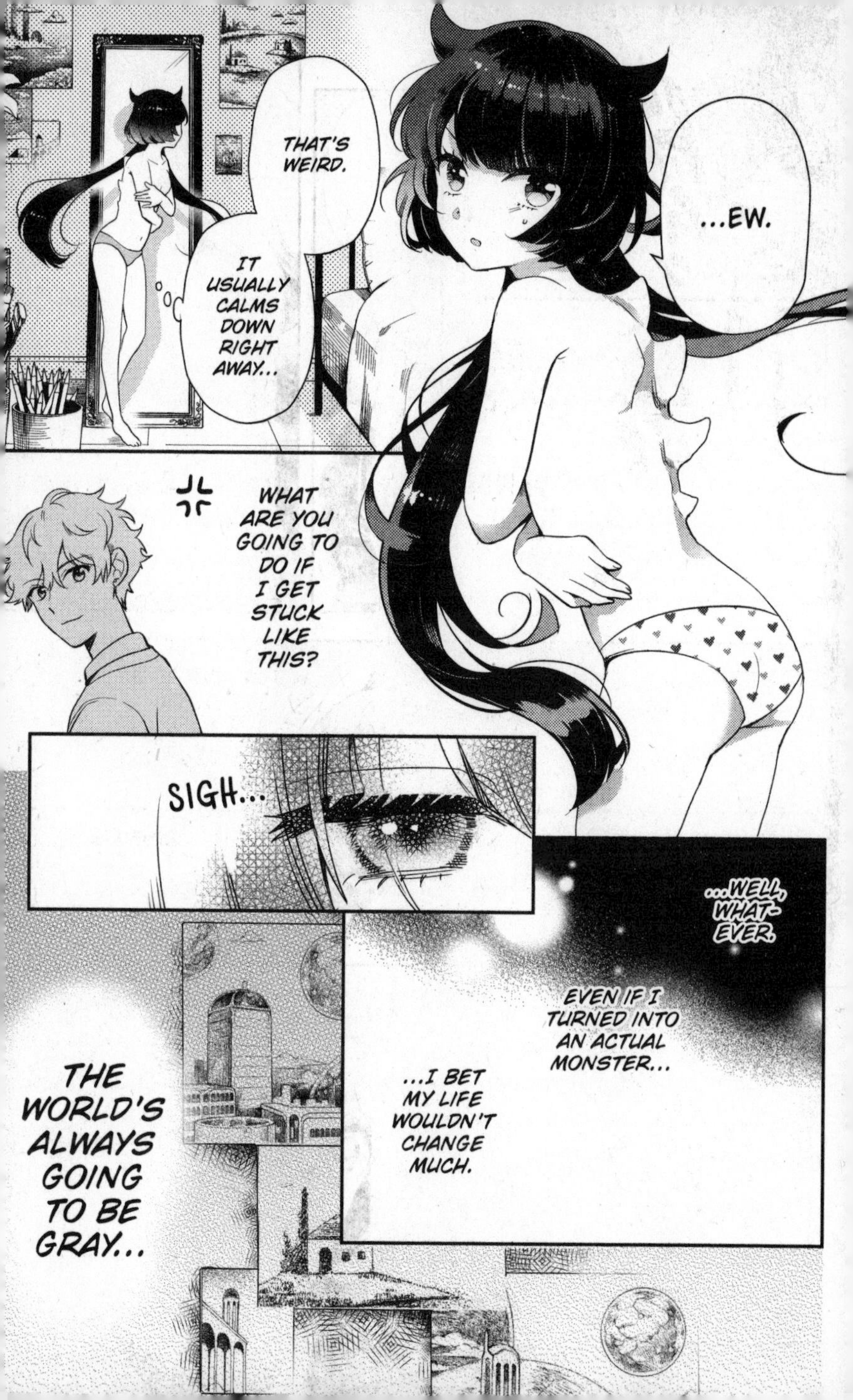
THAT'S WEIRD.
IT USUALLY CALMS DOWN RIGHT AWAY...
...EW.
WHAT ARE YOU GOING TO DO IF I GET STUCK LIKE THIS?
SIGH...
...WELL, WHATEVER.
EVEN IF I TURNED INTO AN ACTUAL MONSTER...
...I BET MY LIFE WOULDN'T CHANGE MUCH.
THE WORLD'S ALWAYS GOING TO BE GRAY...

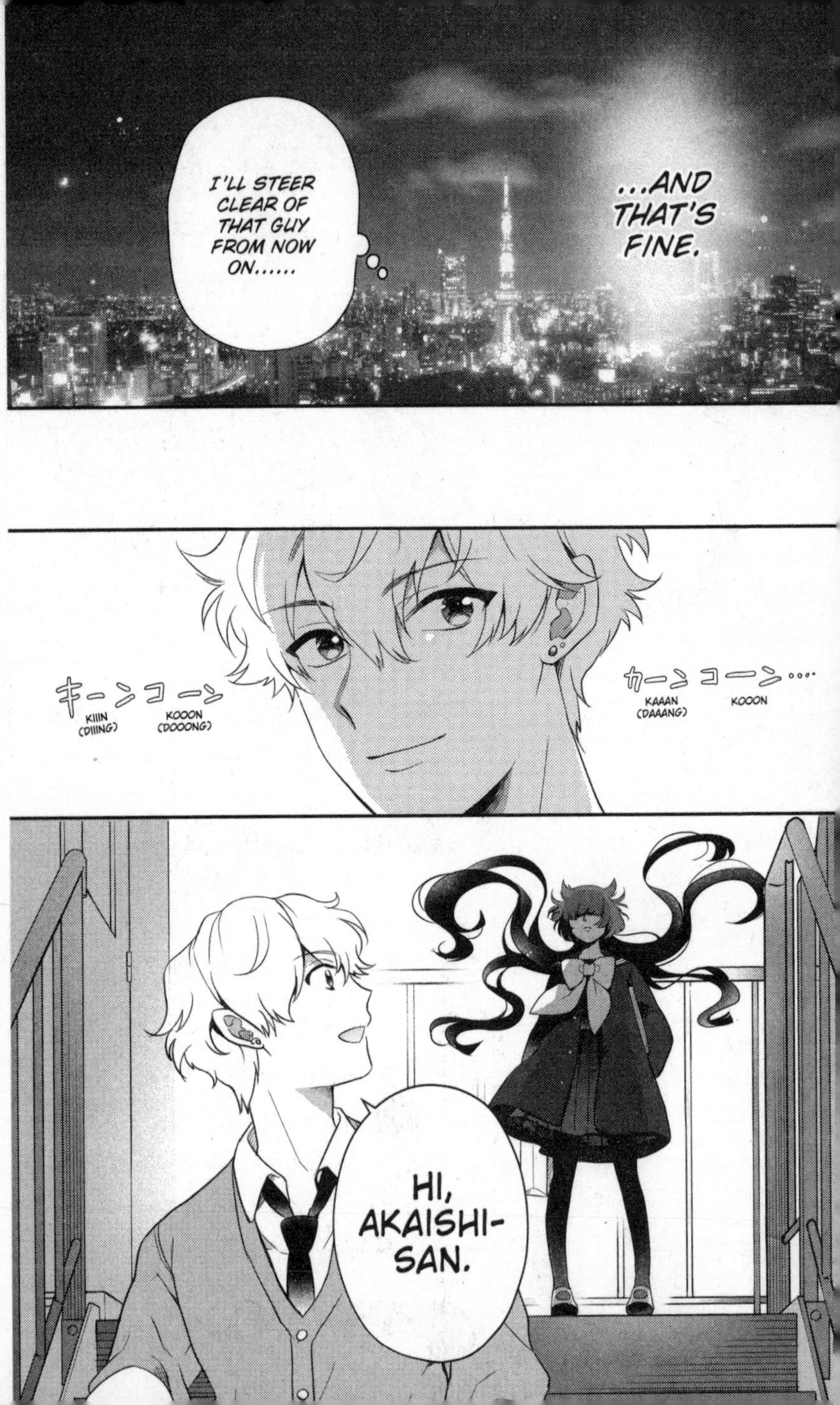
...AND THAT'S FINE.
I'LL STEER CLEAR OF THAT GUY FROM NOW ON......
カーンコーン...
KAAAN (DAAANG) KOOON
キーンコーン
KIIIN (DIIING) KOOON (DOOONG)
HI, AKAISHI-SAN.

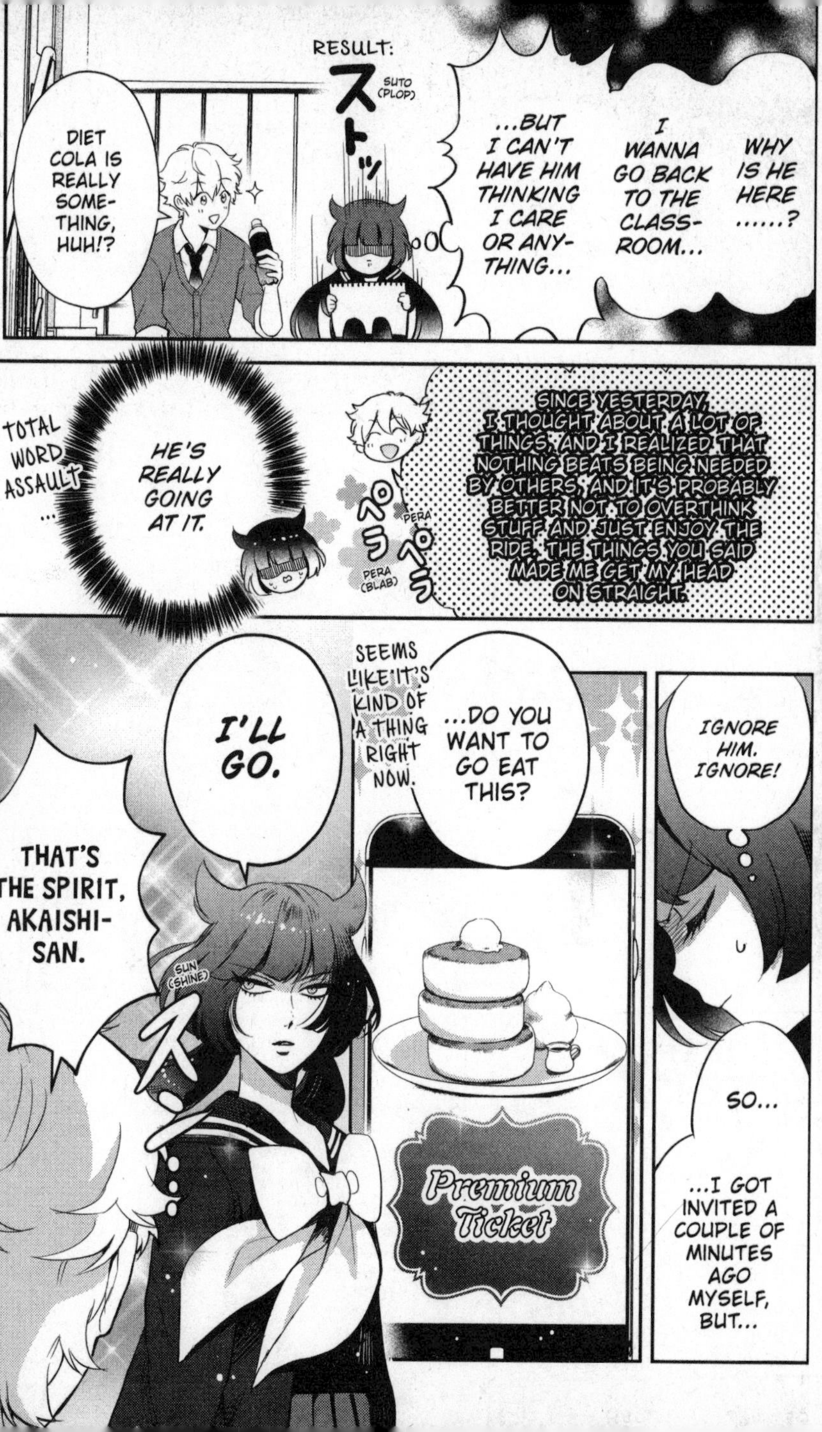

WHY IS HE HERE......?
I WANNA GO BACK TO THE CLASSROOM...
...BUT I CAN'T HAVE HIM THINKING I CARE OR ANYTHING...
RESULT:
ストッ
SUTO (PLOP)
DIET COLA IS REALLY SOMETHING, HUH!?
SINCE YESTERDAY, I THOUGHT ABOUT A LOT OF THINGS, AND I REALIZED THAT NOTHING BEATS BEING NEEDED BY OTHERS, AND IT'S PROBABLY BETTER NOT TO OVERTHINK STUFF AND JUST ENJOY THE RIDE. THE THINGS YOU SAID MADE ME GET MY HEAD ON STRAIGHT.
ペラペラ
PERA PERA (BLAB)
HE'S REALLY GOING AT IT.
TOTAL WORD ASSAULT...
IGNORE HIM. IGNORE!
SO...
...I GOT INVITED A COUPLE OF MINUTES AGO MYSELF, BUT...
...DO YOU WANT TO GO EAT THIS?
SEEMS LIKE IT'S KIND OF A THING RIGHT NOW.
Premium Ticket
I'LL GO.
ス
SUN (SHINE)
THAT'S THE SPIRIT, AKAISHI-SAN.

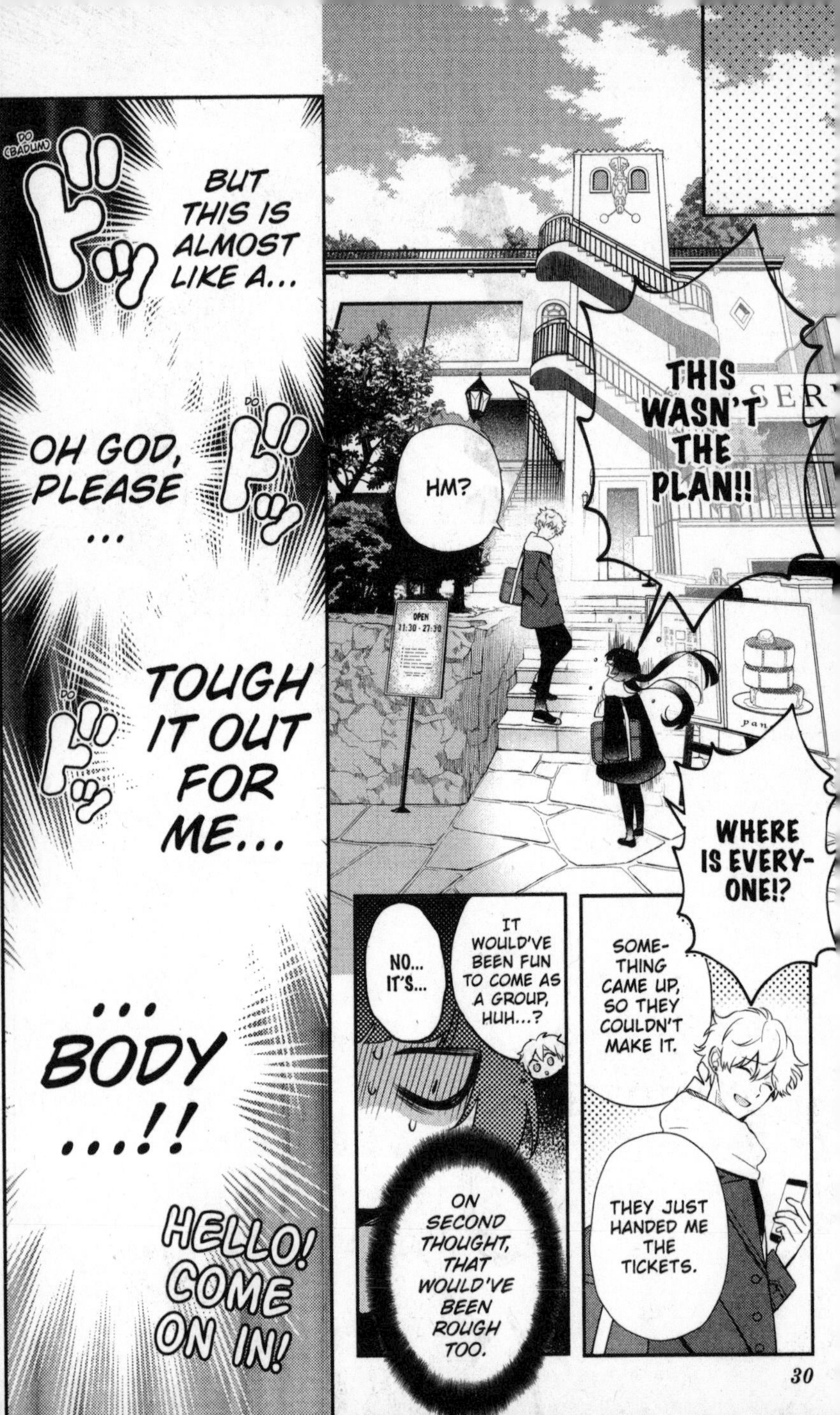
THIS WASN'T THE PLAN!!
HM?
WHERE IS EVERY-ONE!?
SOME-THING CAME UP, SO THEY COULDN'T MAKE IT.
THEY JUST HANDED ME THE TICKETS.
IT WOULD'VE BEEN FUN TO COME AS A GROUP, HUH...?
NO... IT'S...
ON SECOND THOUGHT, THAT WOULD'VE BEEN ROUGH TOO.
DO (BADUM)
BUT THIS IS ALMOST LIKE A...
DO
OH GOD, PLEASE ...
DO
TOUGH IT OUT FOR ME...
...BODY ...!!
HELLO! COME ON IN!

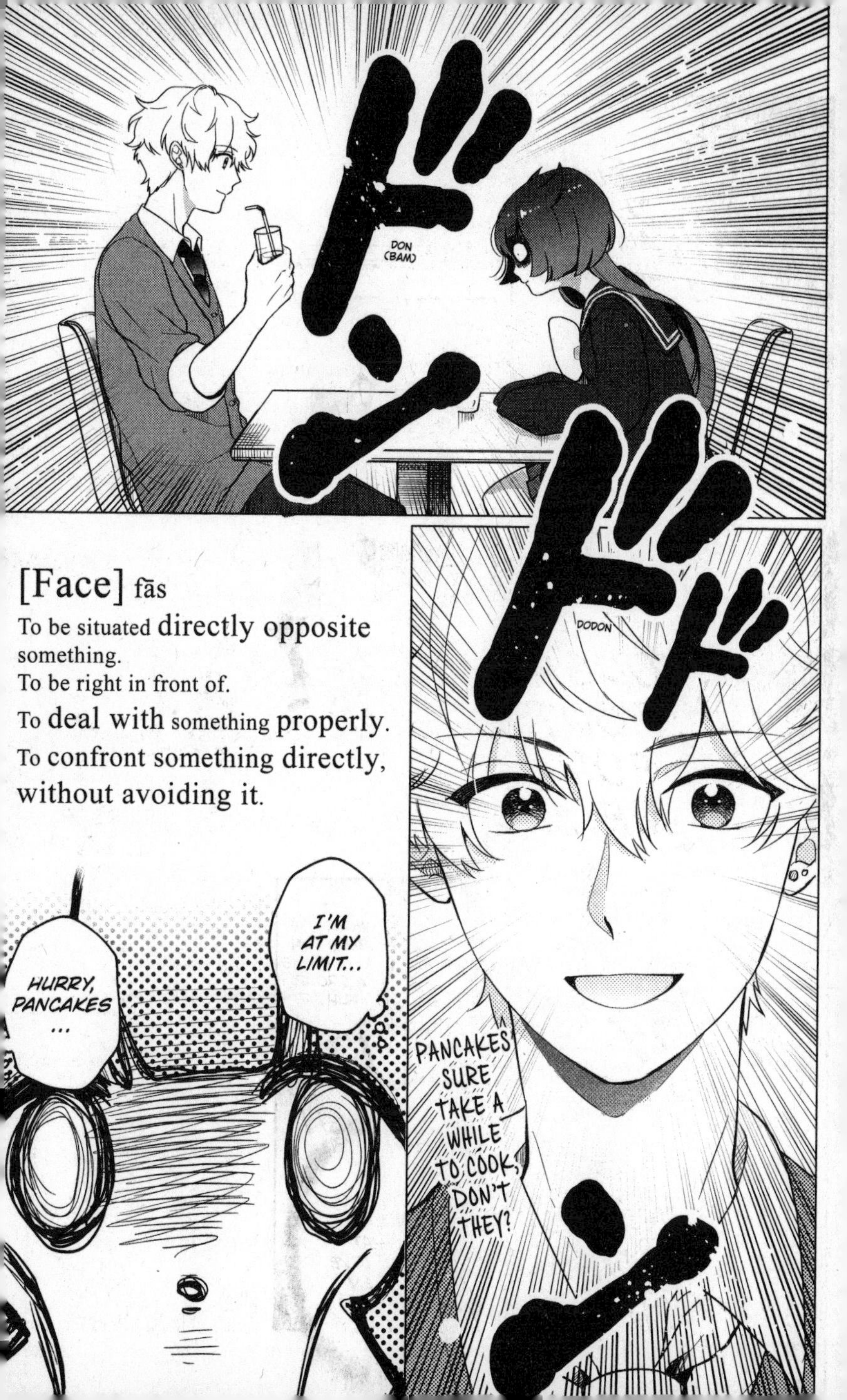
DON (BAM)
DODON
PANCAKES SURE TAKE A WHILE TO COOK, DON'T THEY?
[Face] fās
To be situated directly opposite something.
To be right in front of.
To deal with something properly.
To confront something directly, without avoiding it.
I'M AT MY LIMIT...
HURRY, PANCAKES...

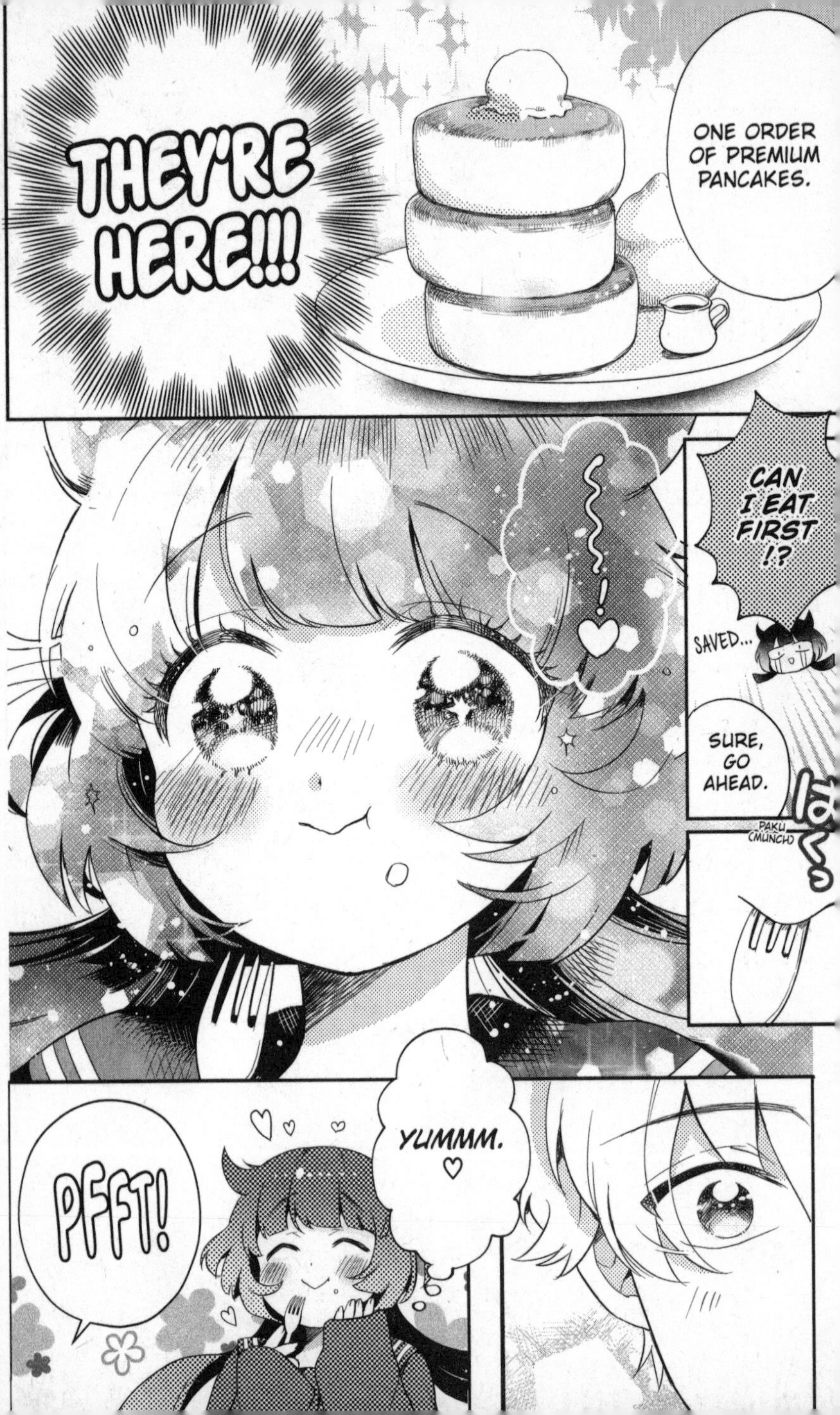
ONE ORDER OF PREMIUM PANCAKES.
THEY'RE HERE!!!
CAN I EAT FIRST!?
SAVED...
SURE, GO AHEAD.
PAKU (MUNCH)
YUMMM. ♡
PFFT!

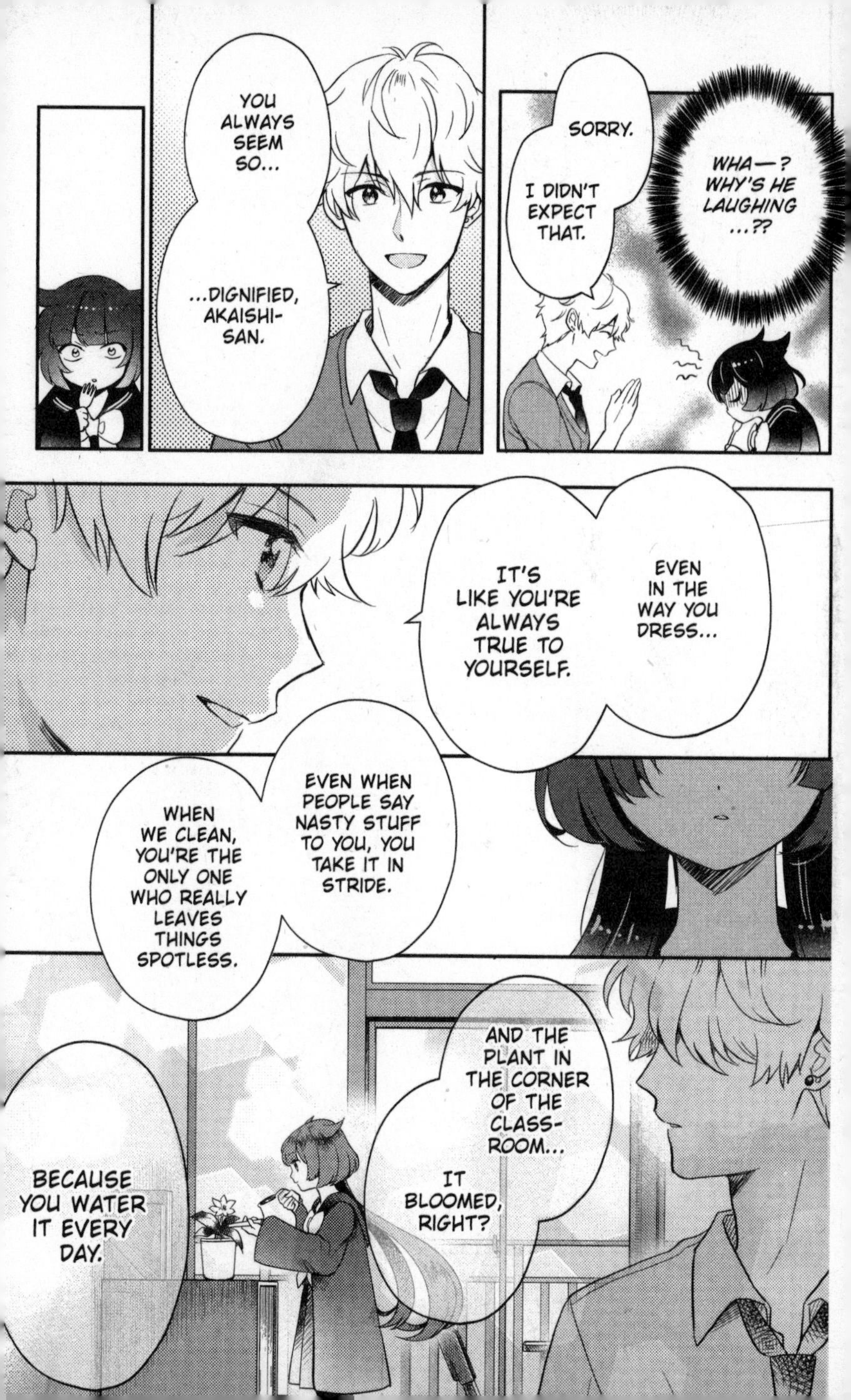
WHA—? WHY'S HE LAUGHING ...??
SORRY.
I DIDN'T EXPECT THAT.
YOU ALWAYS SEEM SO...
...DIGNIFIED, AKAISHI-SAN.
EVEN IN THE WAY YOU DRESS...
IT'S LIKE YOU'RE ALWAYS TRUE TO YOURSELF.
EVEN WHEN PEOPLE SAY NASTY STUFF TO YOU, YOU TAKE IT IN STRIDE.
WHEN WE CLEAN, YOU'RE THE ONLY ONE WHO REALLY LEAVES THINGS SPOTLESS.
AND THE PLANT IN THE CORNER OF THE CLASS-ROOM...
IT BLOOMED, RIGHT?
BECAUSE YOU WATER IT EVERY DAY.

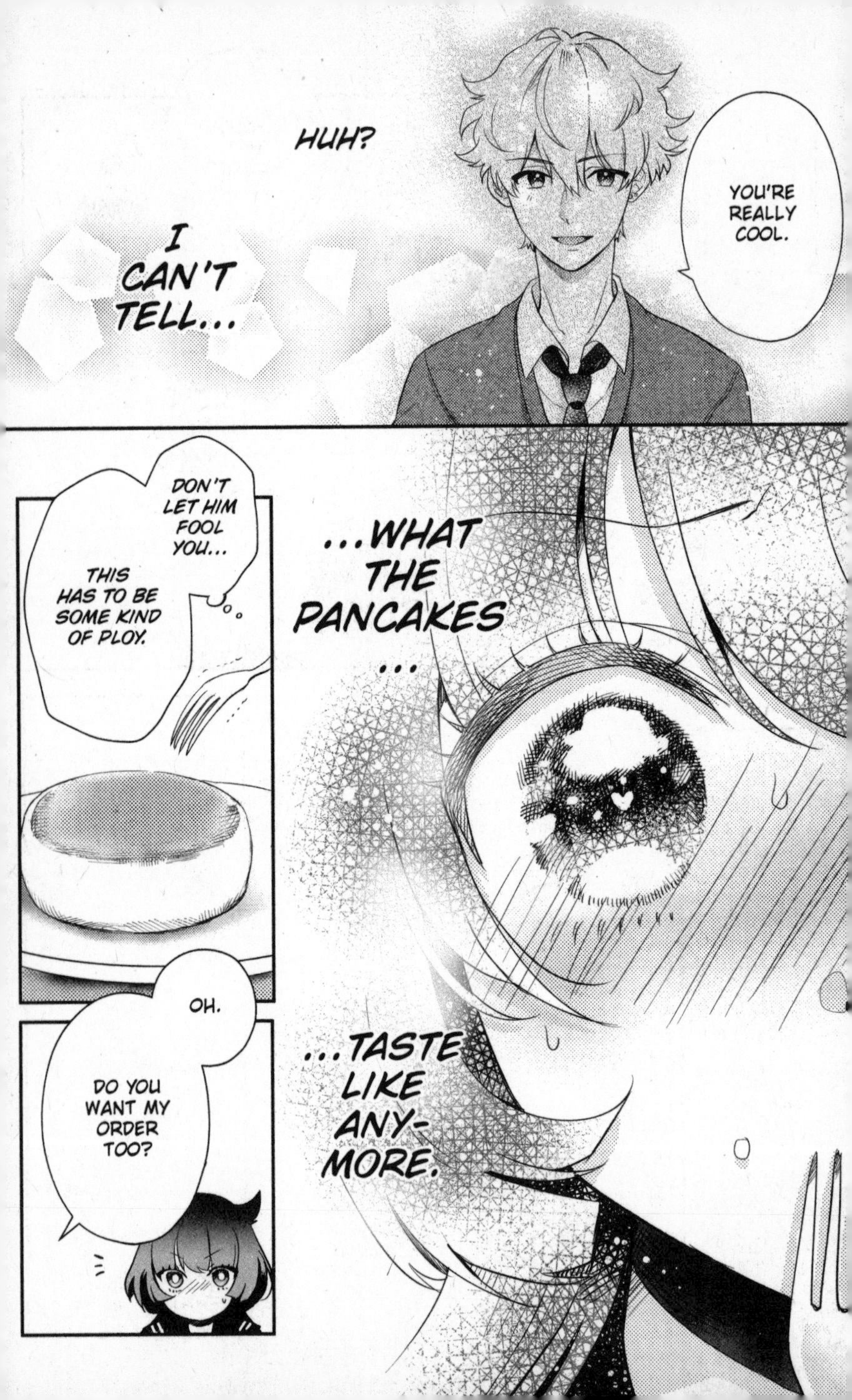
YOU'RE REALLY COOL.
HUH?
I CAN'T TELL...
...WHAT THE PANCAKES...
...TASTE LIKE ANY-MORE.
DON'T LET HIM FOOL YOU...
THIS HAS TO BE SOME KIND OF PLOY.
OH.
DO YOU WANT MY ORDER TOO?

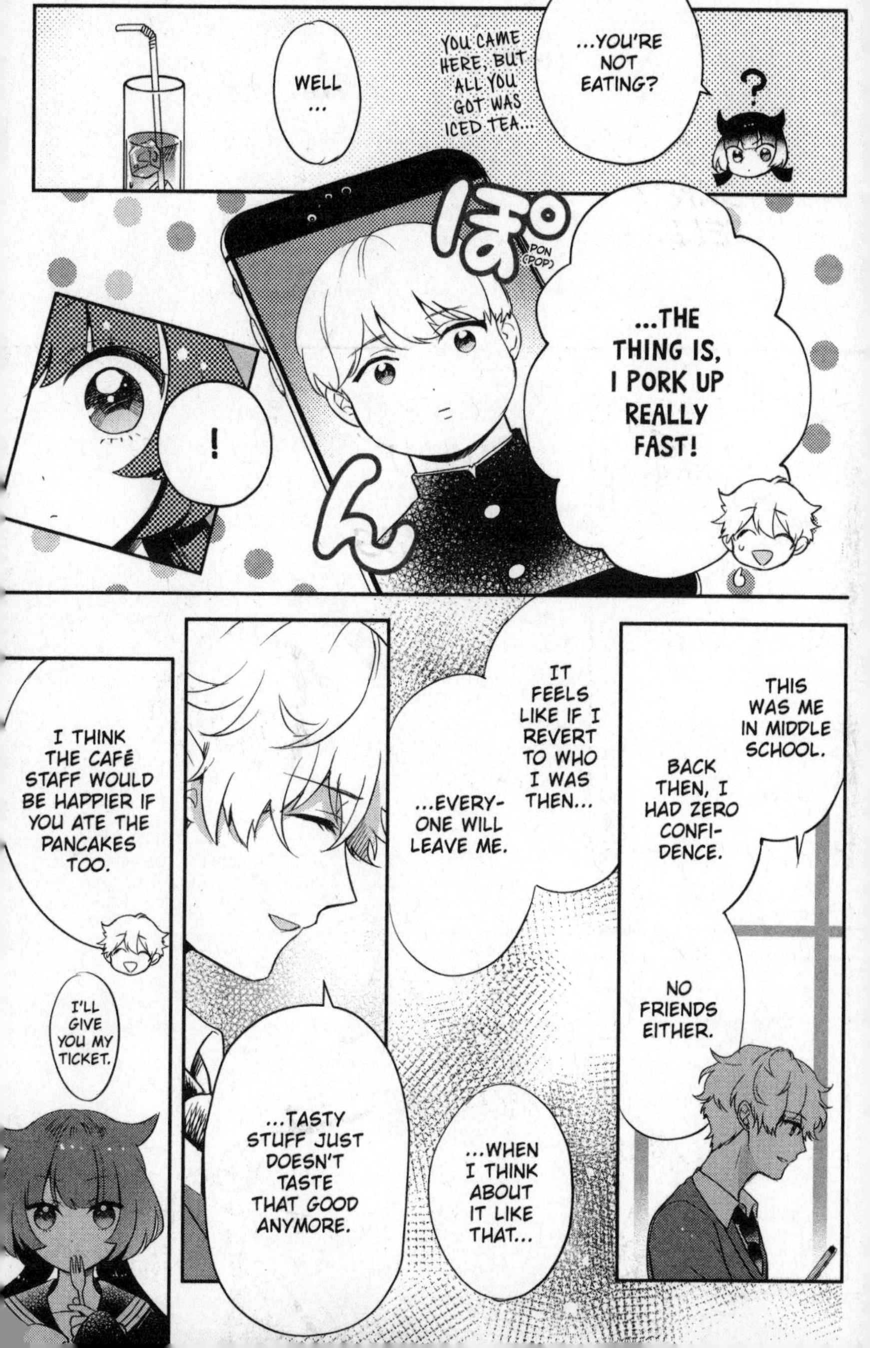
...YOU'RE NOT EATING?
YOU CAME HERE, BUT ALL YOU GOT WAS ICED TEA...
WELL...
ぽん
PON (POP)
...THE THING IS, I PORK UP REALLY FAST!
!
THIS WAS ME IN MIDDLE SCHOOL.
BACK THEN, I HAD ZERO CONFIDENCE.
NO FRIENDS EITHER.
IT FEELS LIKE IF I REVERT TO WHO I WAS THEN...
...EVERYONE WILL LEAVE ME.
...WHEN I THINK ABOUT IT LIKE THAT...
...TASTY STUFF JUST DOESN'T TASTE THAT GOOD ANYMORE.
I THINK THE CAFÉ STAFF WOULD BE HAPPIER IF YOU ATE THE PANCAKES TOO.
I'LL GIVE YOU MY TICKET.

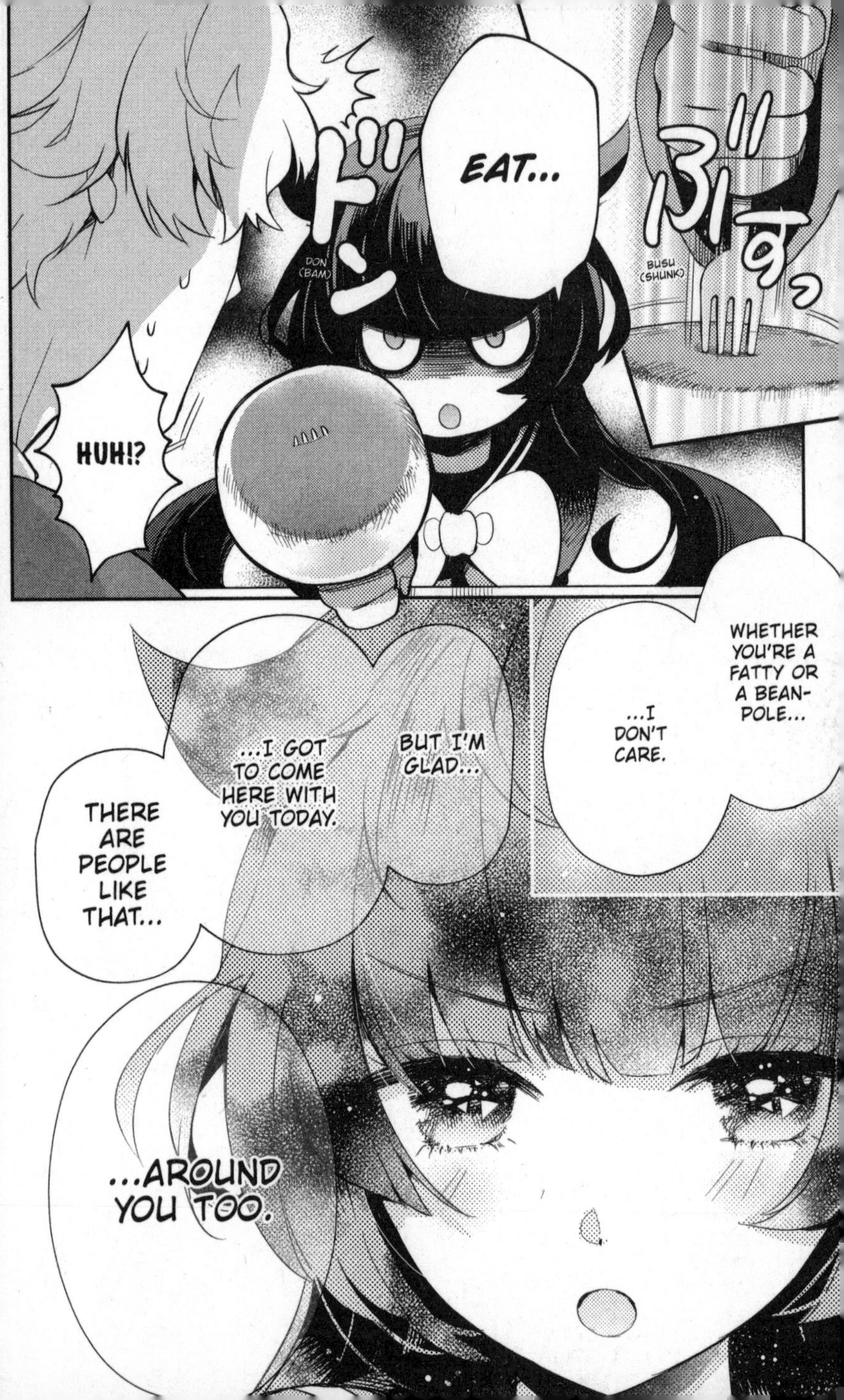
ぶすっ
BUSU (SHUNK)
EAT...
ドン
DON (BAM)
HUH!?
WHETHER YOU'RE A FATTY OR A BEAN-POLE...
...I DON'T CARE.
BUT I'M GLAD...
...I GOT TO COME HERE WITH YOU TODAY.
THERE ARE PEOPLE LIKE THAT...
...AROUND YOU TOO.

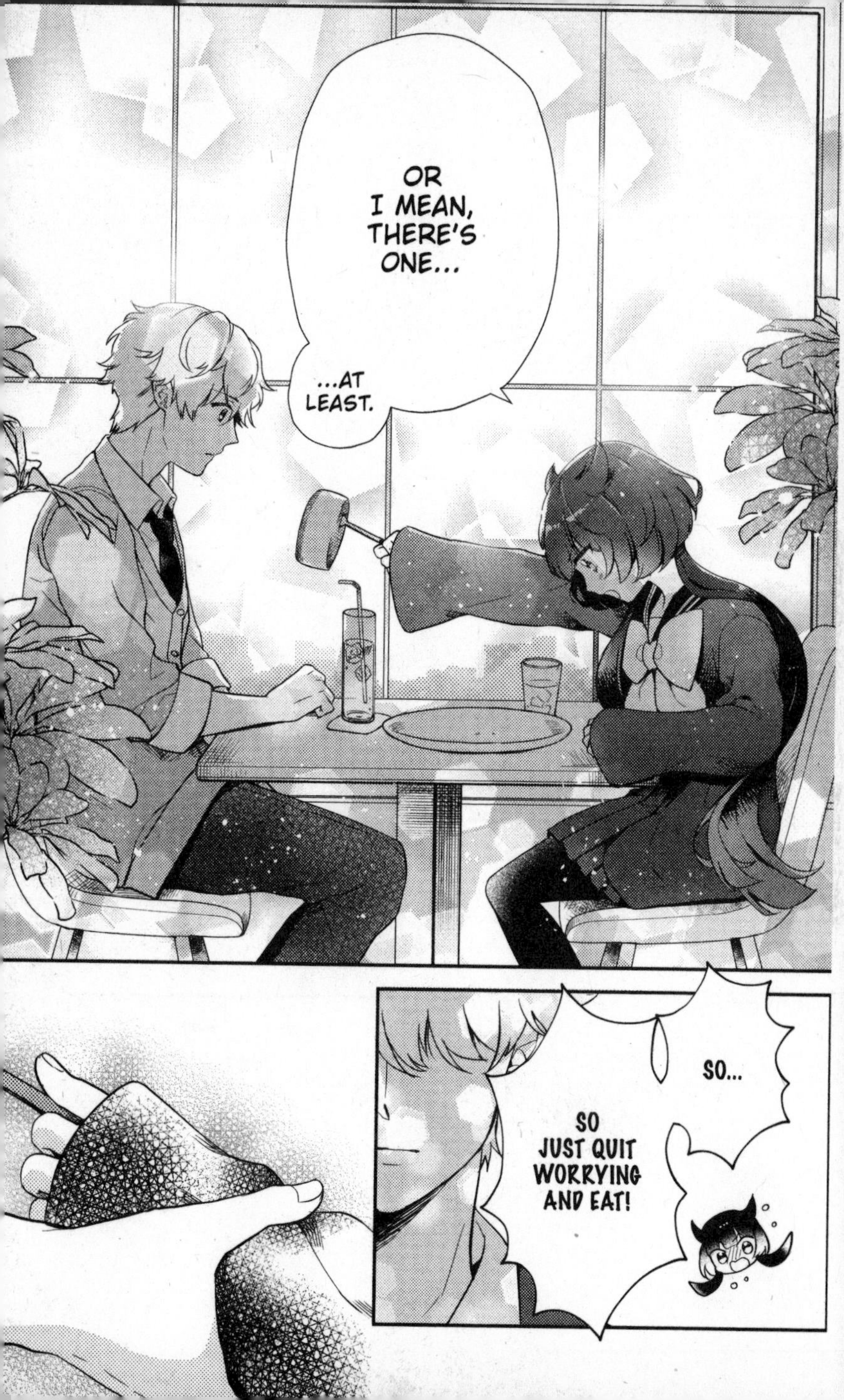
OR I MEAN, THERE'S ONE...
...AT LEAST.
SO...
SO JUST QUIT WORRYING AND EAT!

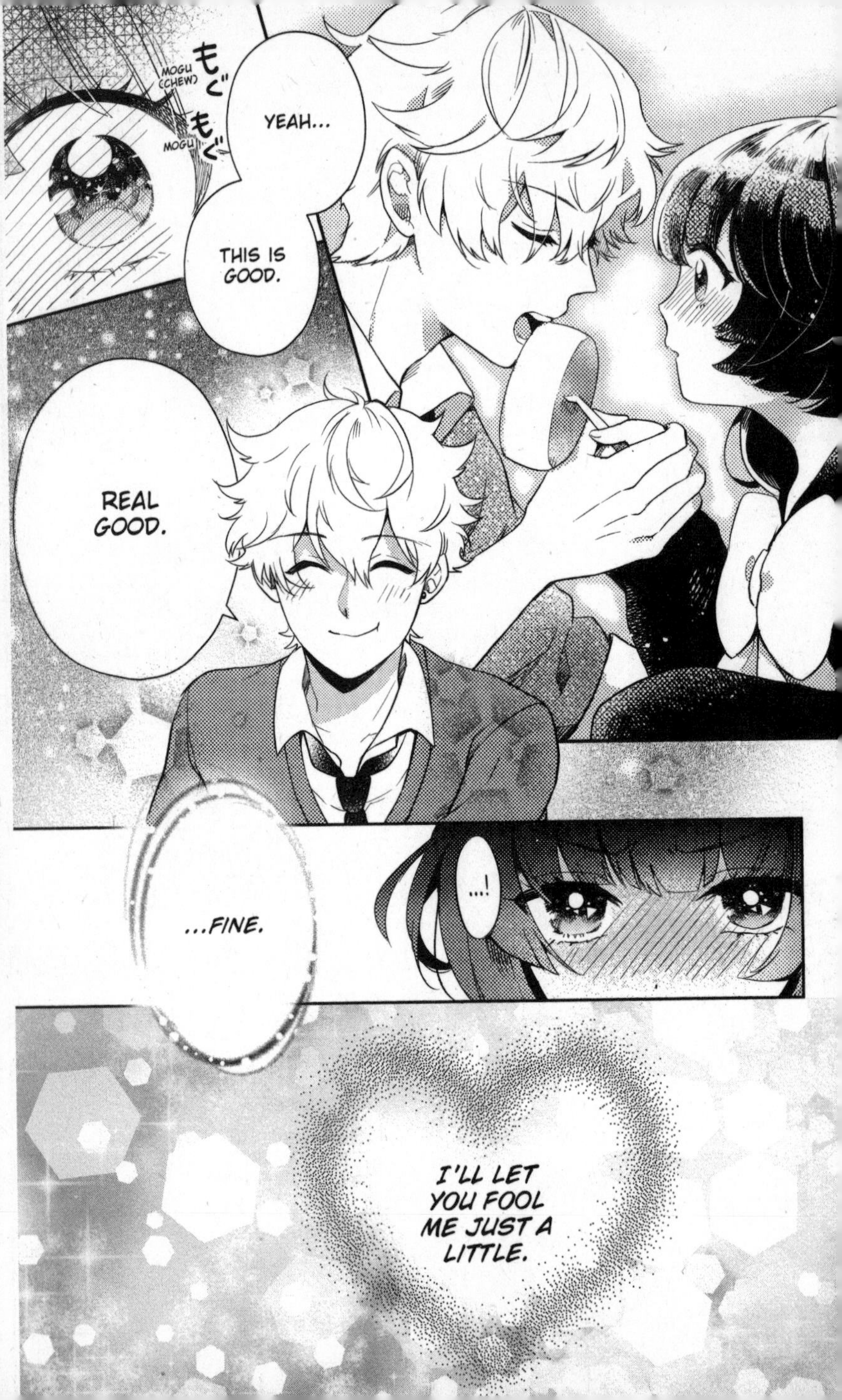
YEAH...
THIS IS GOOD.
もぐ MOGU (CHEW)
もぐ MOGU
REAL GOOD.
...!
...FINE.
I'LL LET YOU FOOL ME JUST A LITTLE.

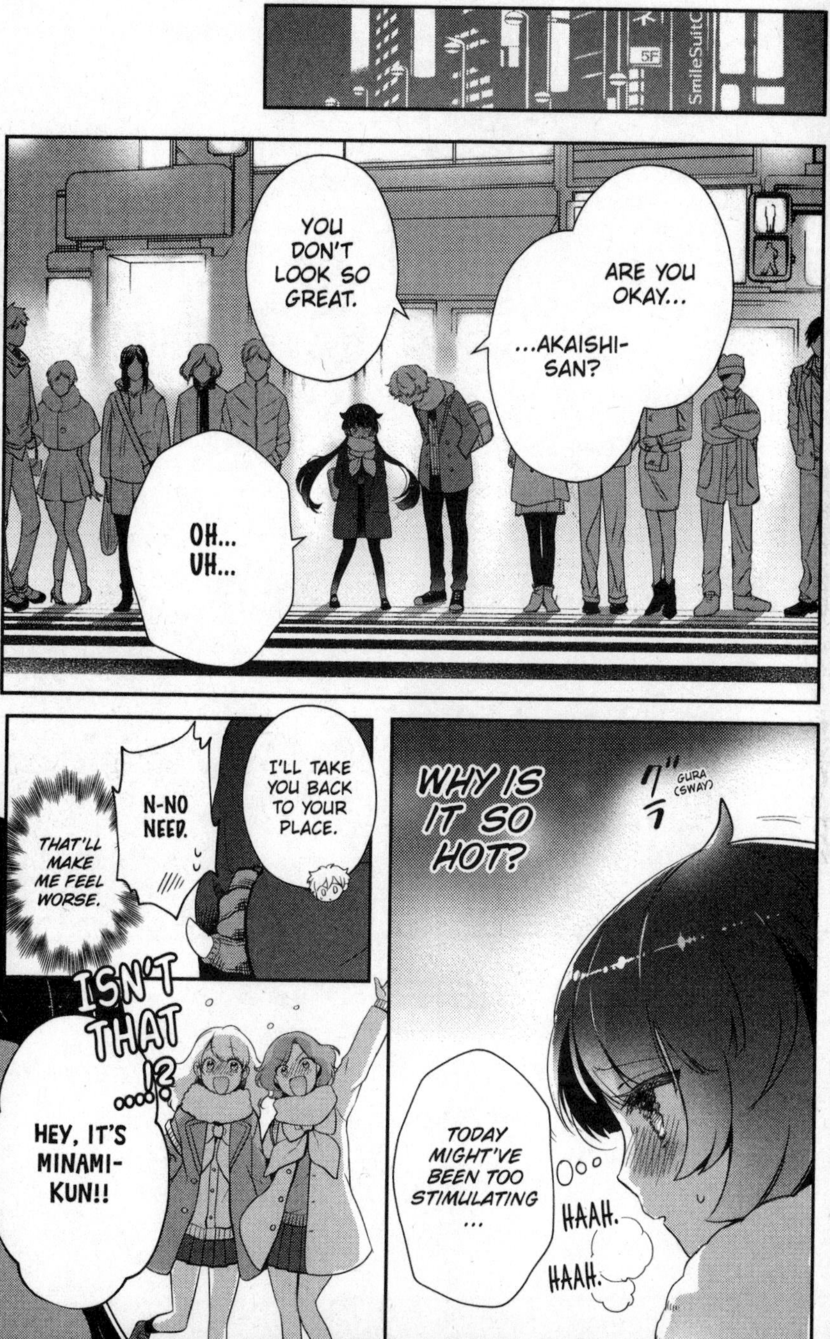
ARE YOU OKAY... ...AKAISHI-SAN?
YOU DON'T LOOK SO GREAT.
OH... UH...
GURA (SWAY)
WHY IS IT SO HOT?
HAAH. HAAH.
TODAY MIGHT'VE BEEN TOO STIMULATING...
I'LL TAKE YOU BACK TO YOUR PLACE.
N-NO NEED.
THAT'LL MAKE ME FEEL WORSE.
ISN'T THAT ...!?
HEY, IT'S MINAMI-KUN!!

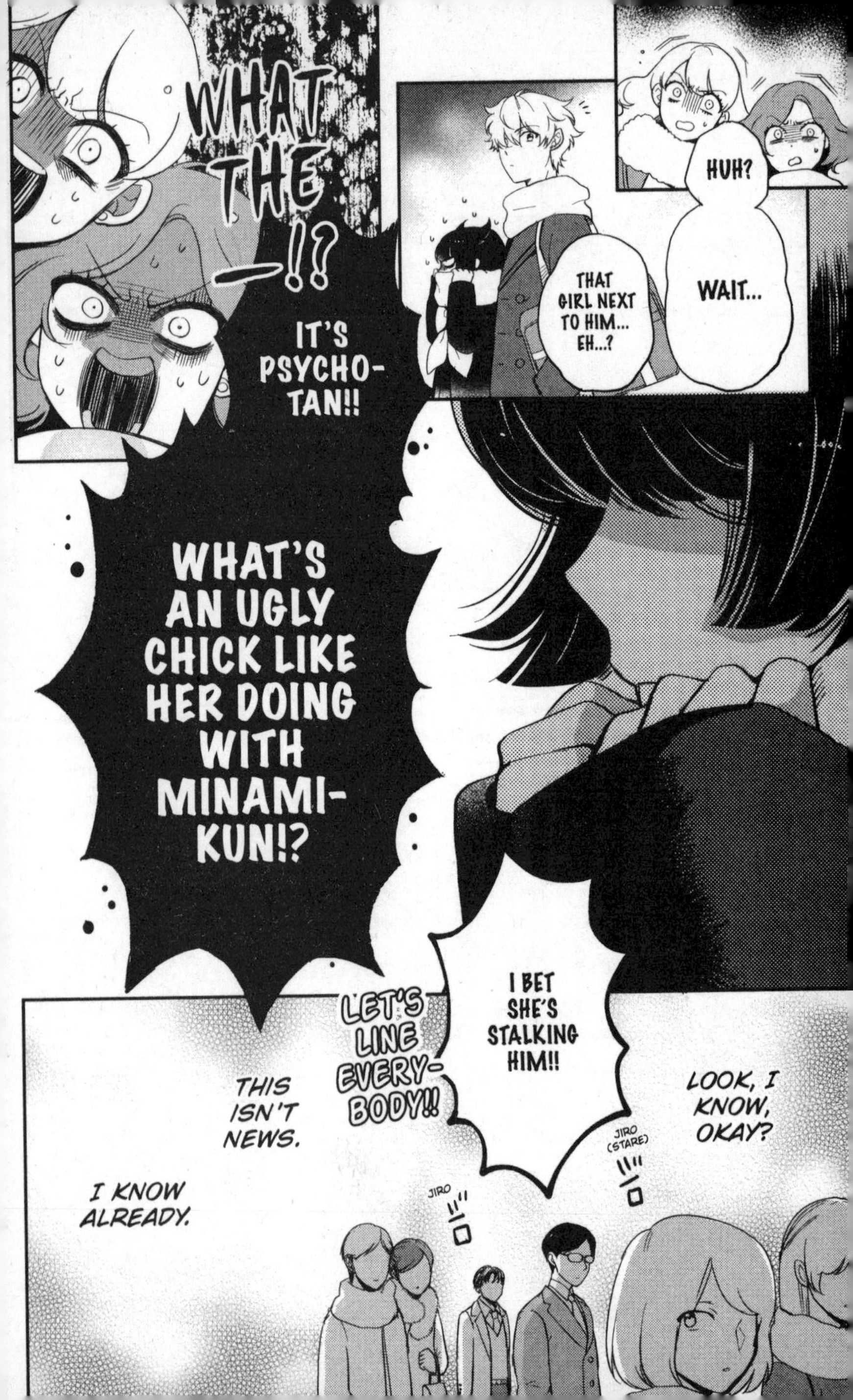

HUH?
WAIT...
THAT GIRL NEXT TO HIM... EH...?
WHAT THE—!?
IT'S PSYCHO-TAN!!
WHAT'S AN UGLY CHICK LIKE HER DOING WITH MINAMI-KUN!?
LOOK, I KNOW, OKAY?
JIRO (STARE)
I BET SHE'S STALKING HIM!!
LET'S LINE EVERY-BODY!!
JIRO
THIS ISN'T NEWS.
I KNOW ALREADY.

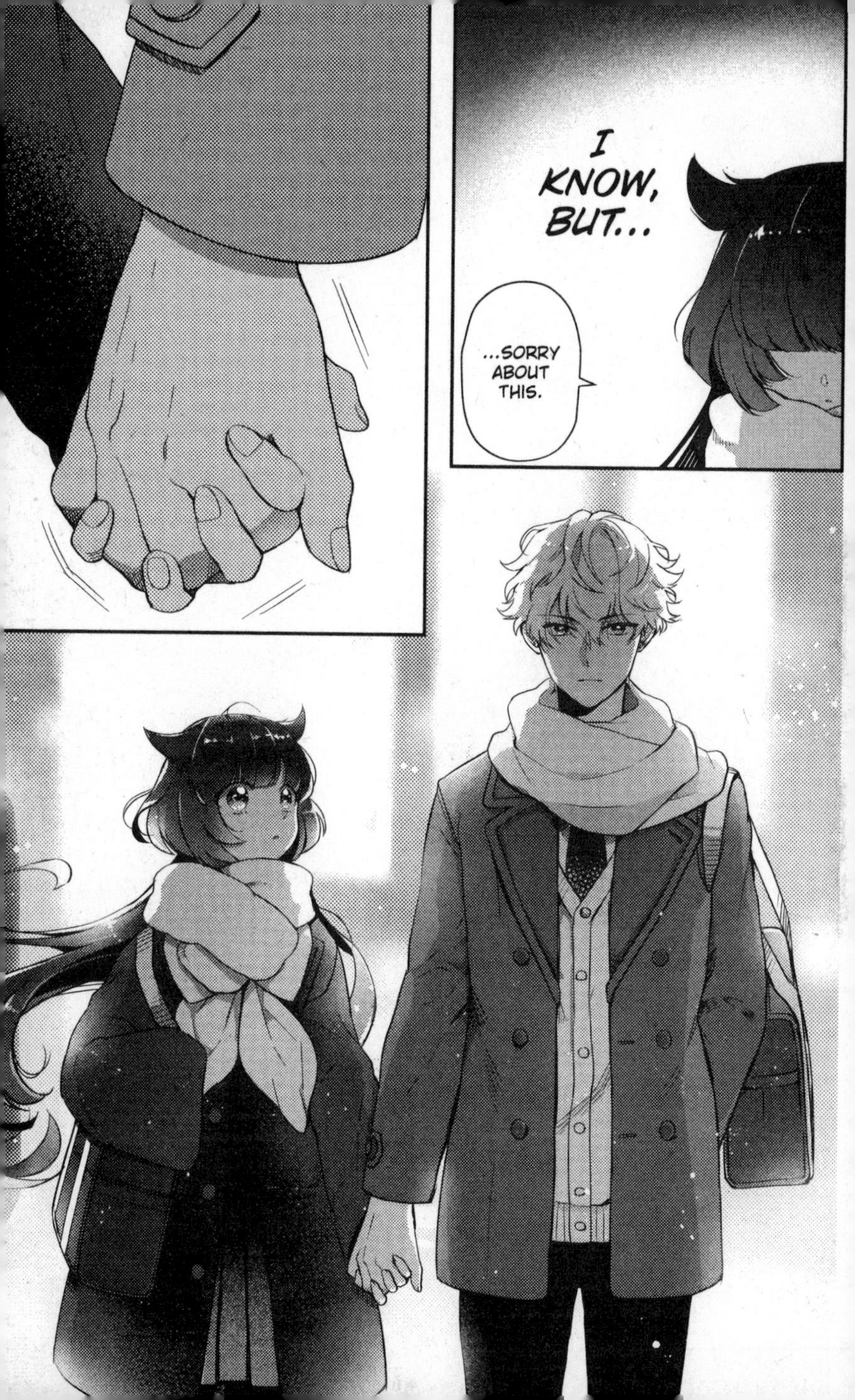
I KNOW, BUT...
...SORRY ABOUT THIS.

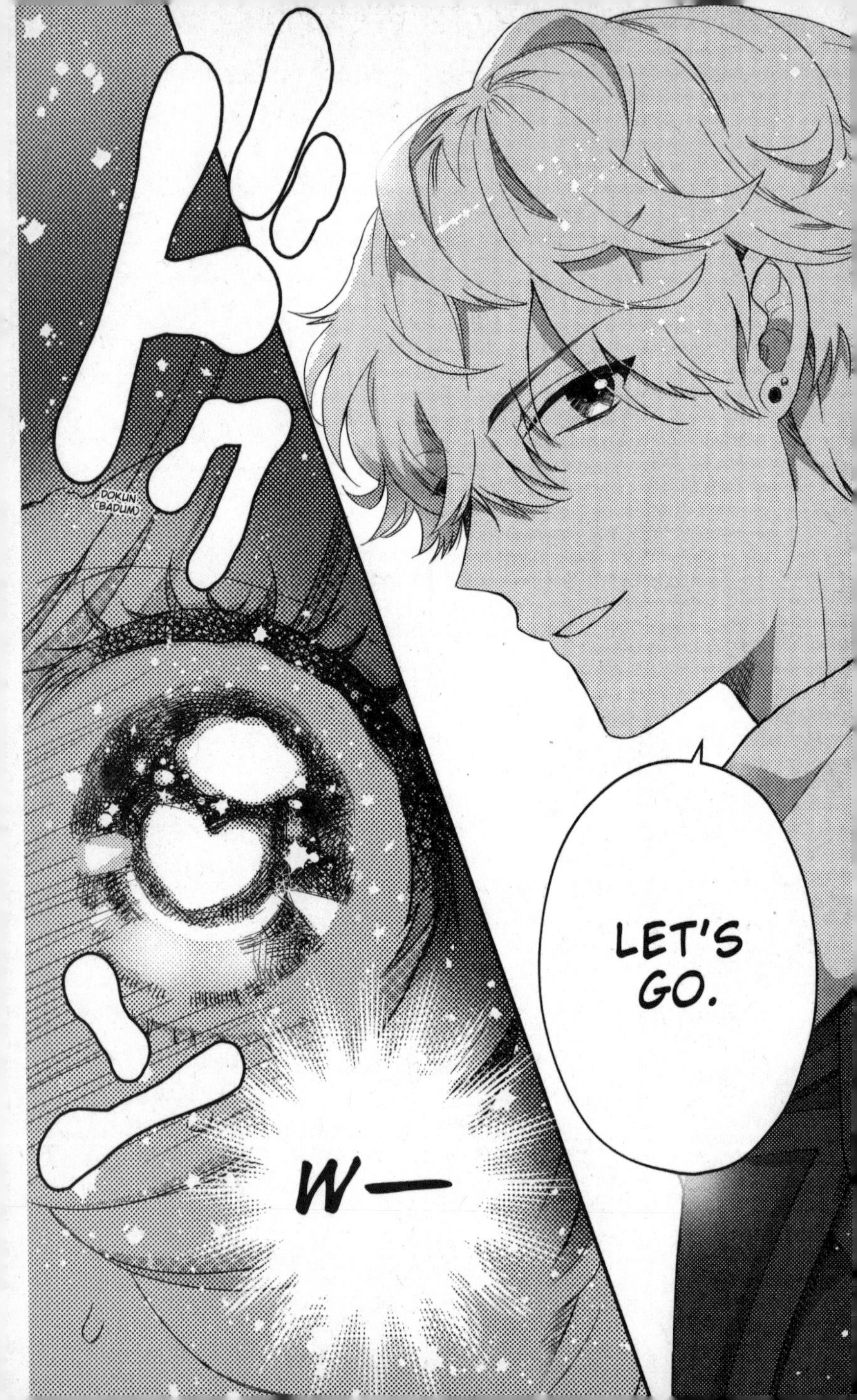
LET'S GO.
ドクン
DOKUN (BADUM)
W—

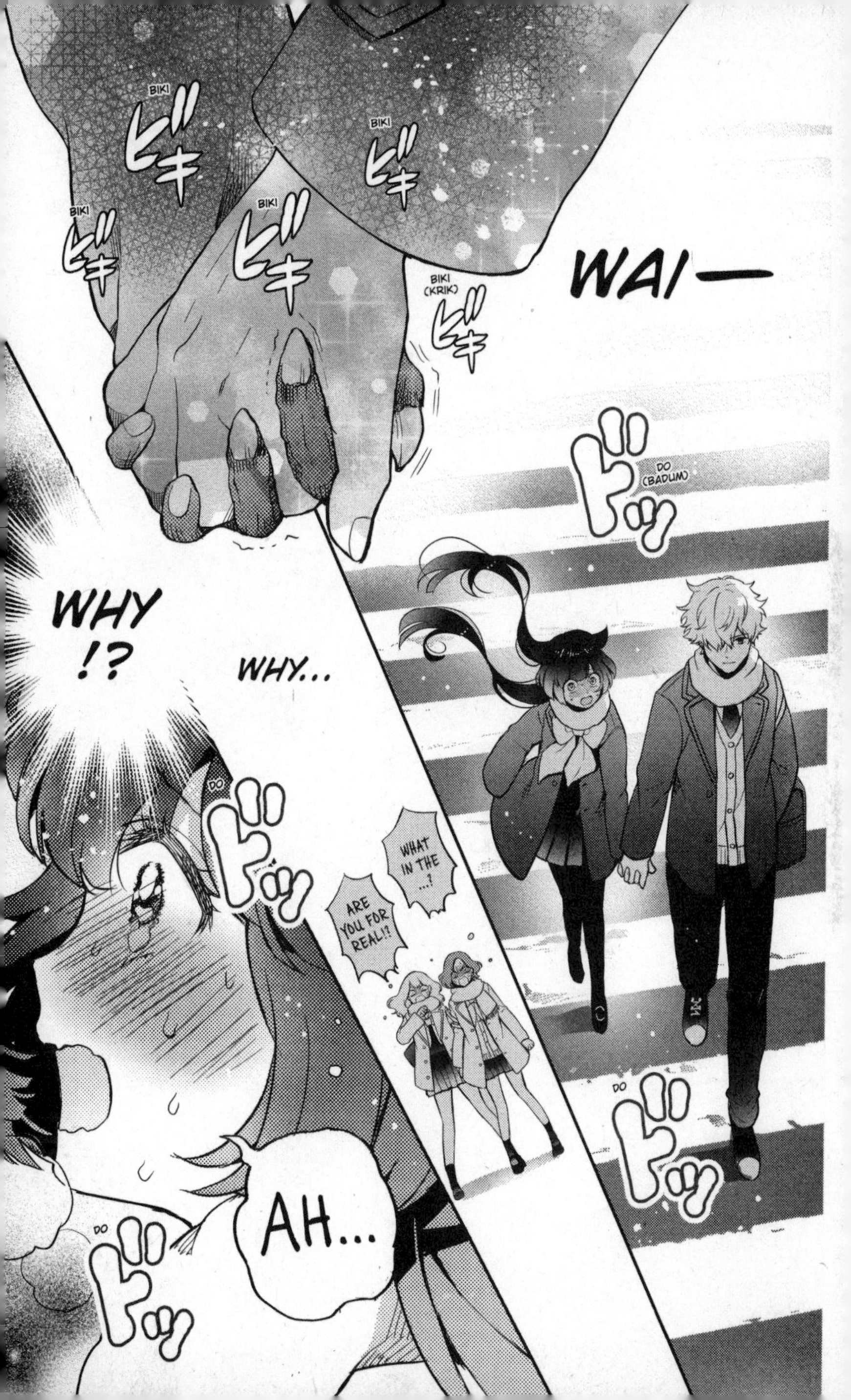
BIKI
BIKI
BIKI
BIKI
BIKI (KRIK)
WAI—
DO (BADUM)
DO
WHAT IN THE ...?
ARE YOU FOR REAL!?
WHY!?
WHY...
DO
AH...
DO

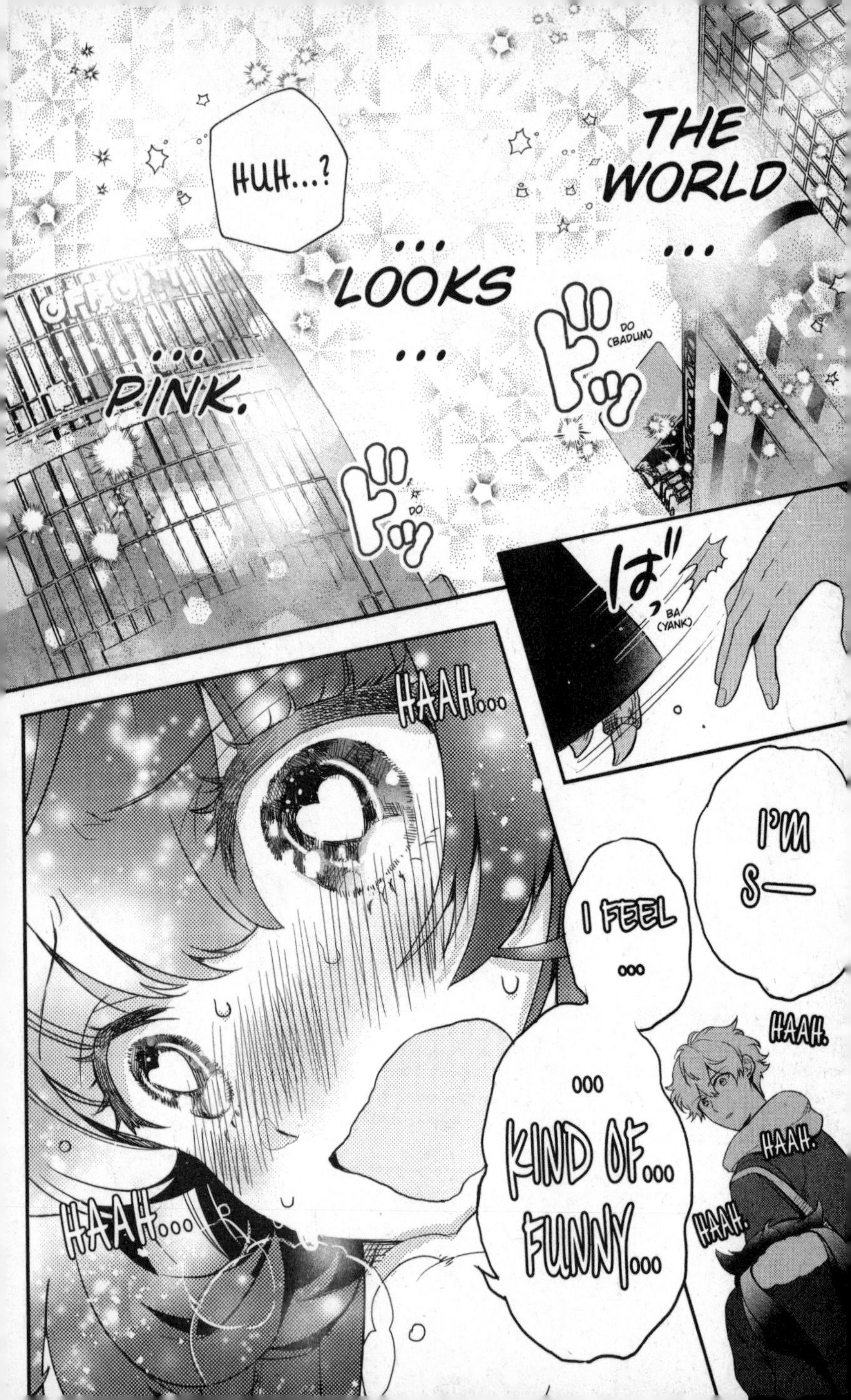
THE WORLD ...
HUH...?
... LOOKS ...
DO (BADUM)
... PINK.
DO
BA (YANK)
HAAH...
I'M S—
I FEEL ...
... KIND OF... FUNNY...
HAAH.
HAAH.
HAAH.
HAAH...

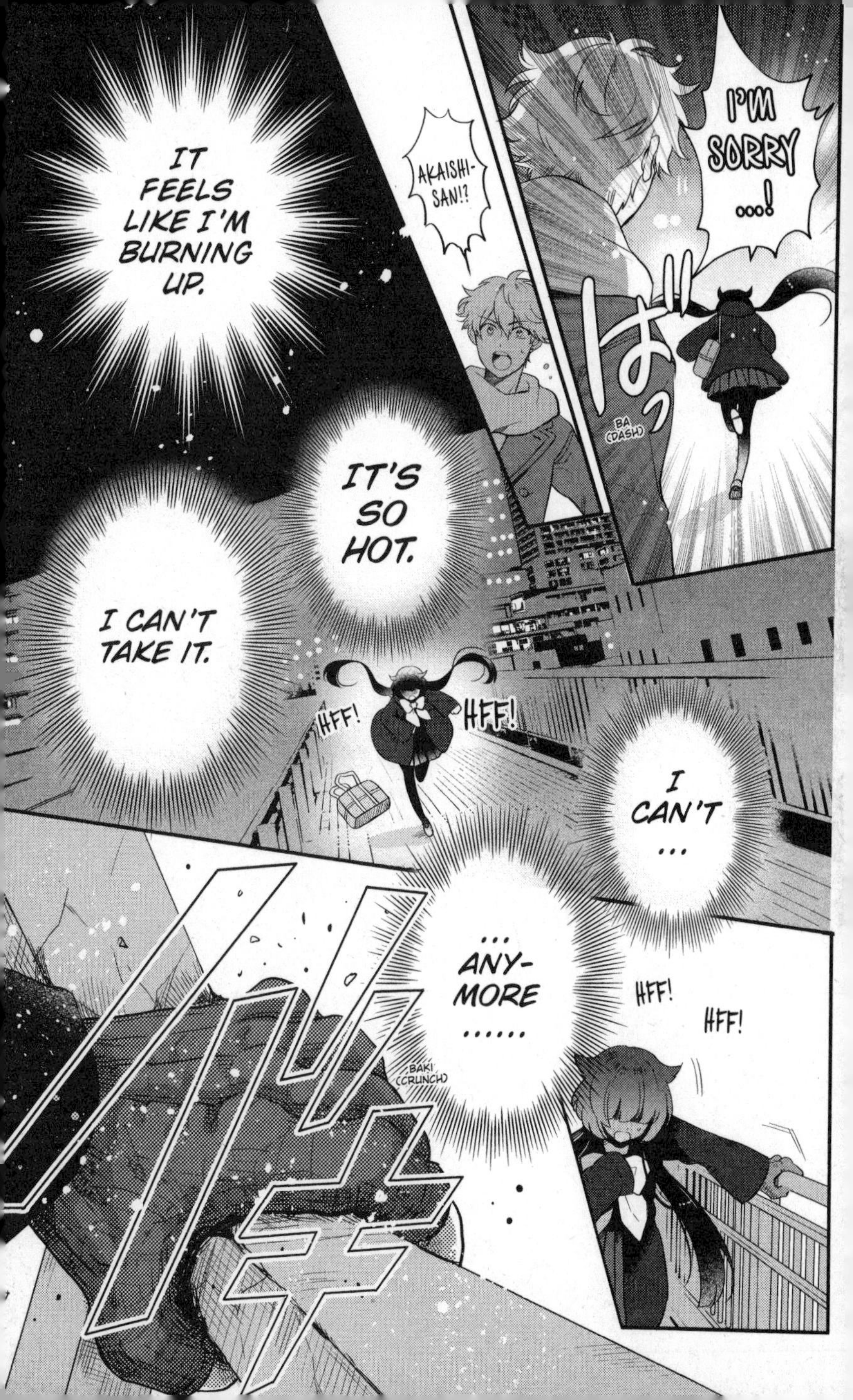
I'M SORRY ...!
BA (DASH)
AKAISHI-SAN!?
IT FEELS LIKE I'M BURNING UP.
IT'S SO HOT.
I CAN'T TAKE IT.
HFF!
HFF!
I CAN'T ...
... ANY-MORE ......
HFF!
HFF!
BAKI (CRUNCH)

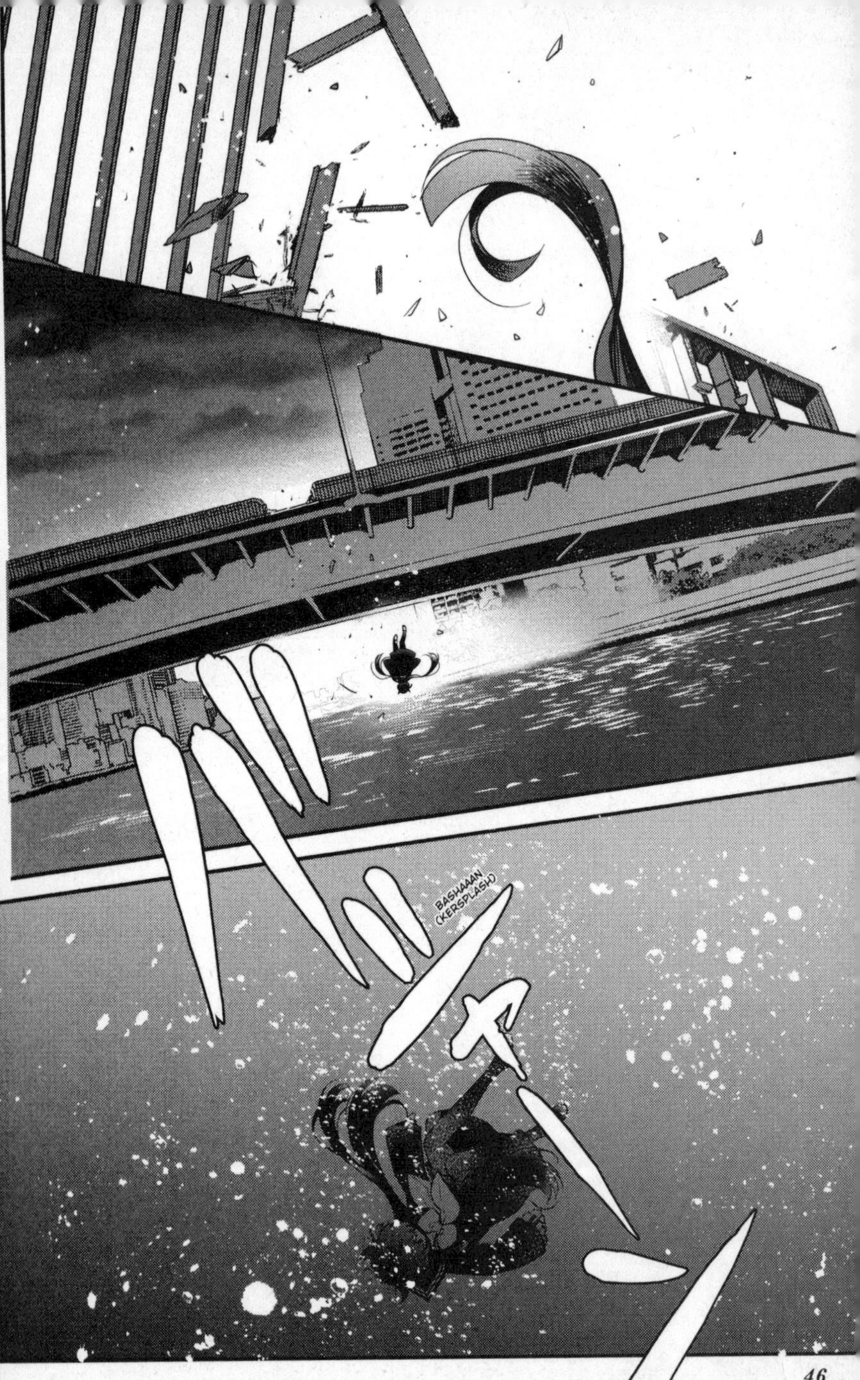
BASHAAAN
(KERSPLASH)

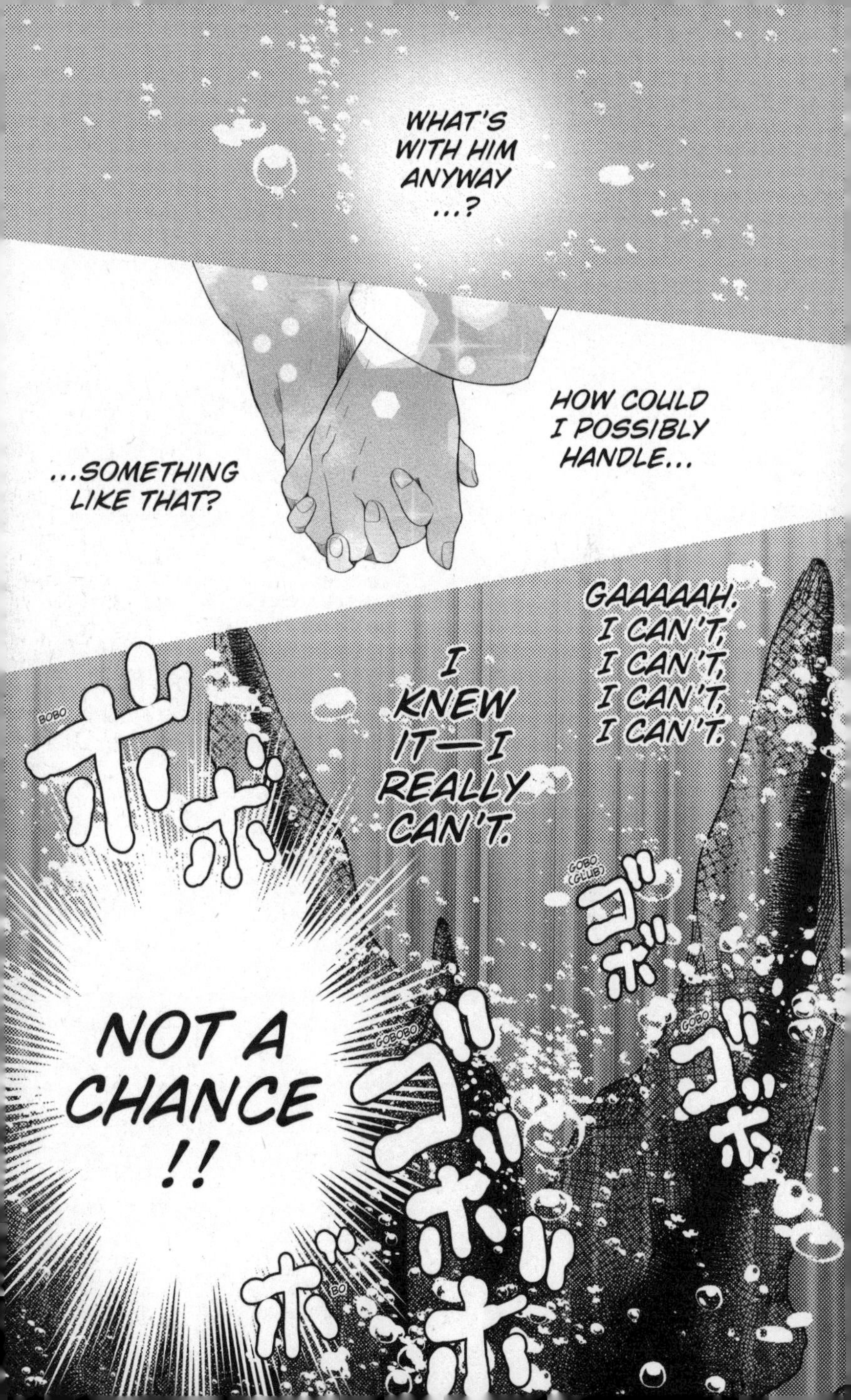
WHAT'S WITH HIM ANYWAY ...?
HOW COULD I POSSIBLY HANDLE...
...SOMETHING LIKE THAT?
GAAAAAH. I CAN'T, I CAN'T, I CAN'T, I CAN'T.
I KNEW IT—I REALLY CAN'T.
BOBO
GOBO (GLUB)
GOBO
GOBOBO
NOT A CHANCE!!
BO

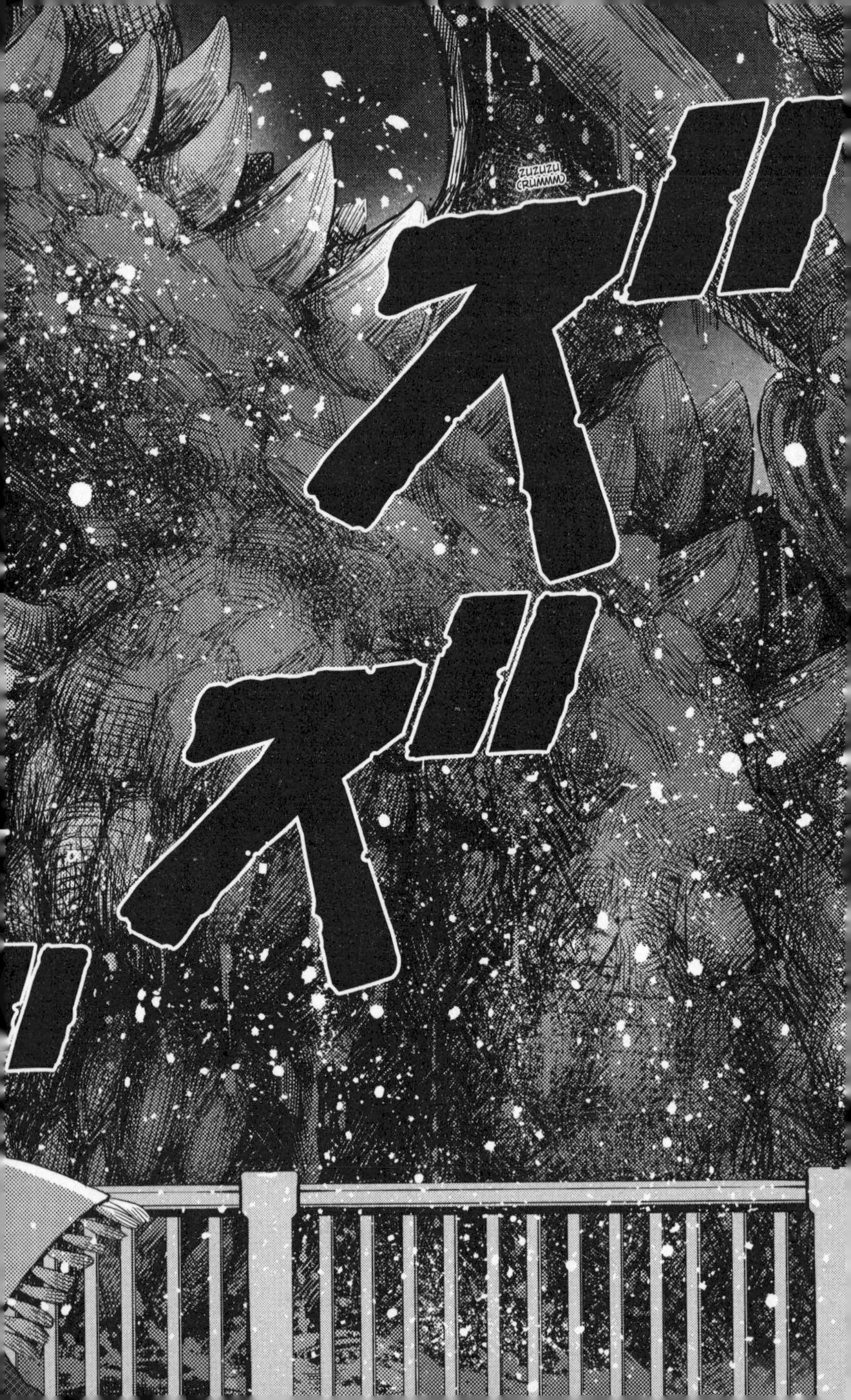
ズズズ
ZUZUZU (RUMMM)

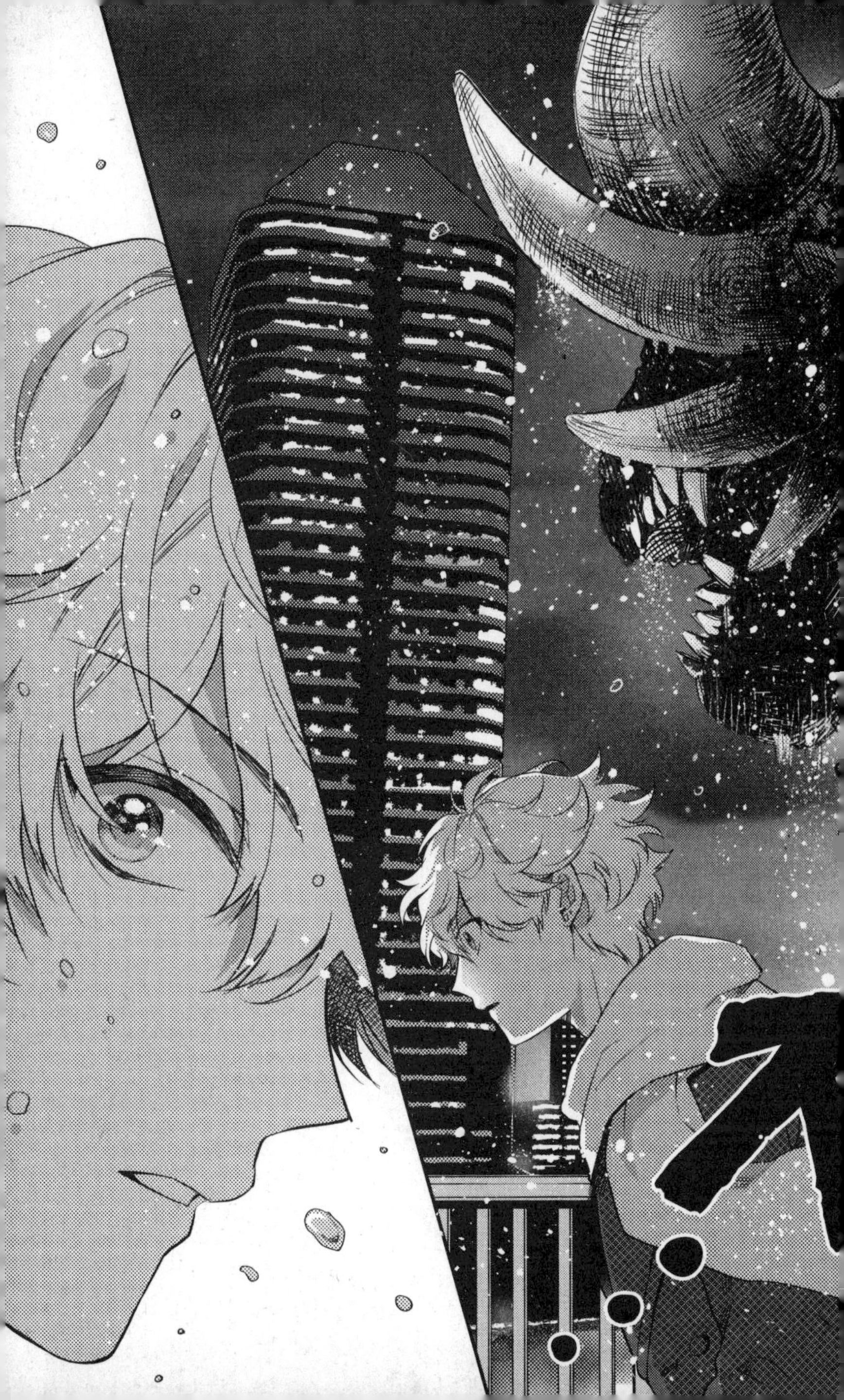

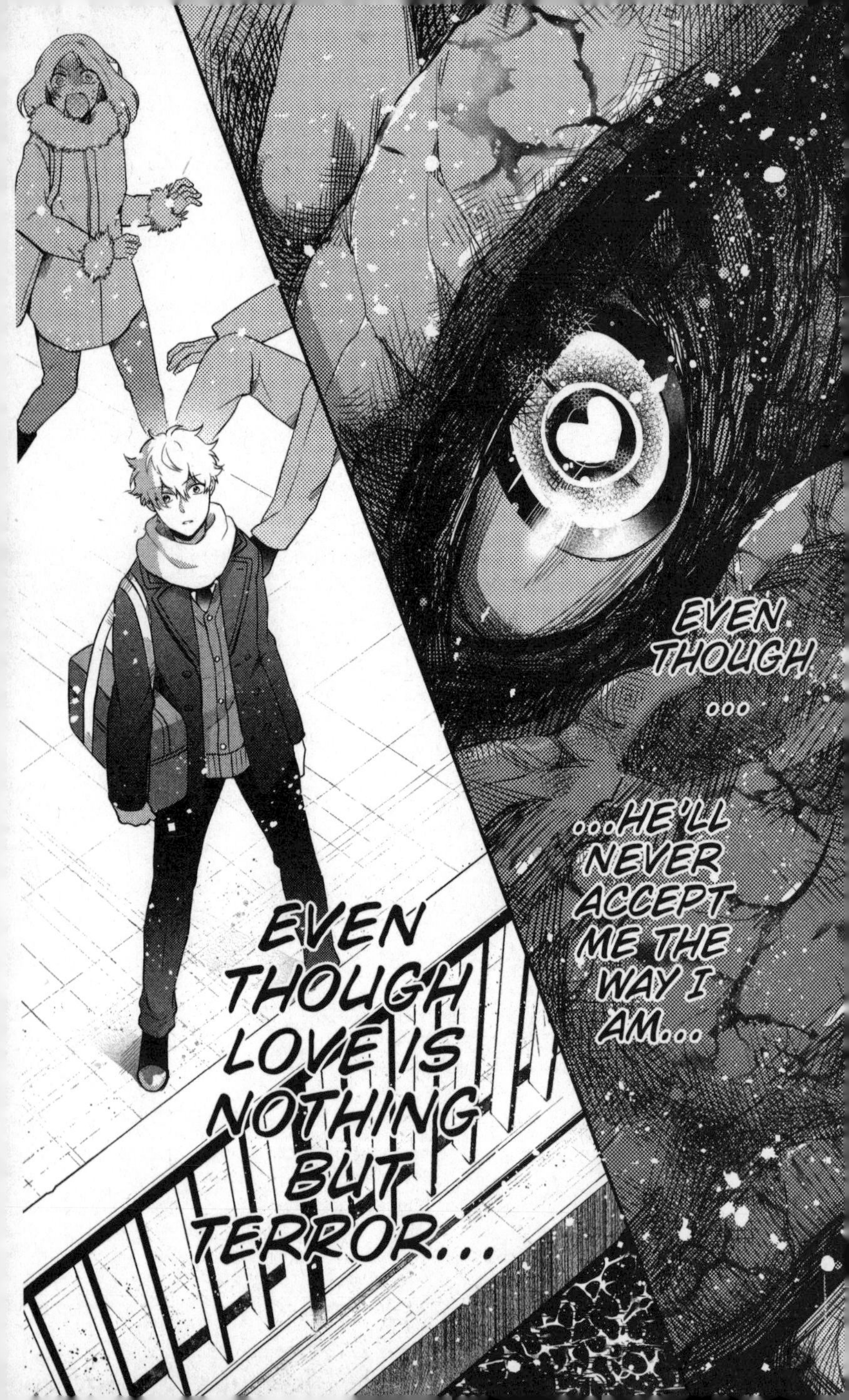
EVEN THOUGH...
...HE'LL NEVER ACCEPT ME THE WAY I AM...
EVEN THOUGH LOVE IS NOTHING BUT TERROR...

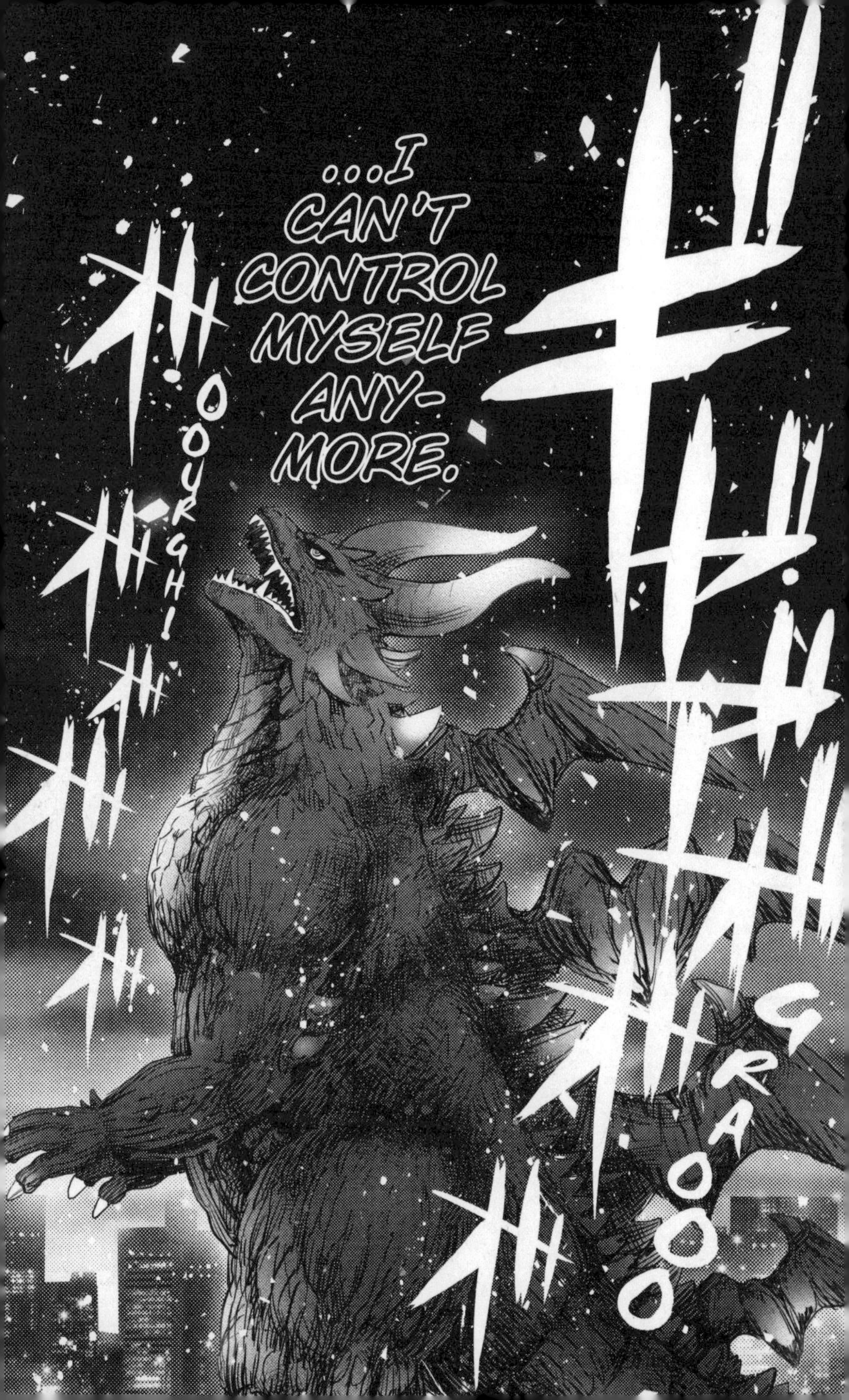
...I CAN'T CONTROL MYSELF ANY-MORE.
GRAOOOO
OOURGH!

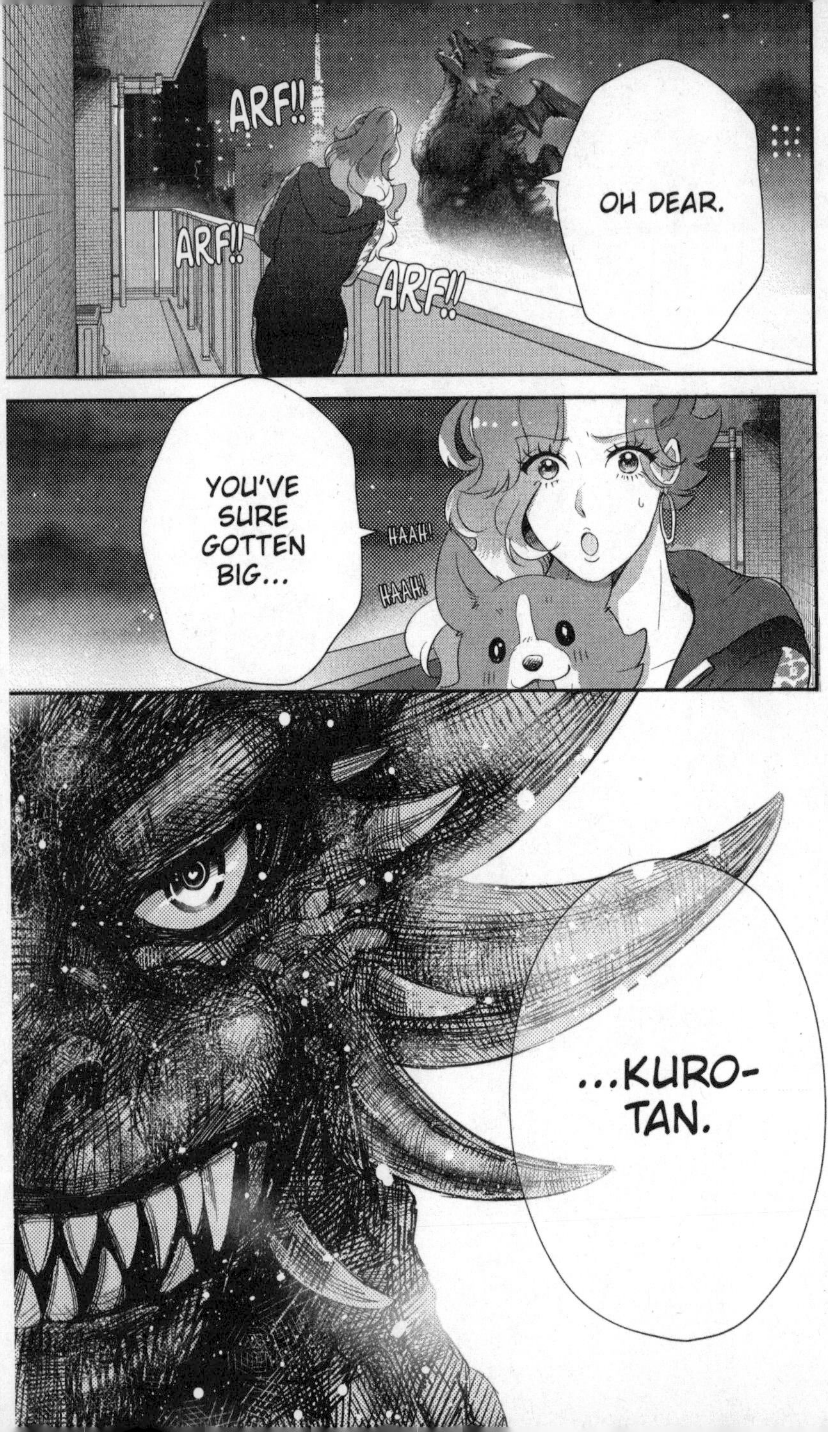
ARF!!
ARF!!
ARF!!
OH DEAR.
YOU'VE SURE GOTTEN BIG...
HAAH!
HAAH!
...KURO-TAN.

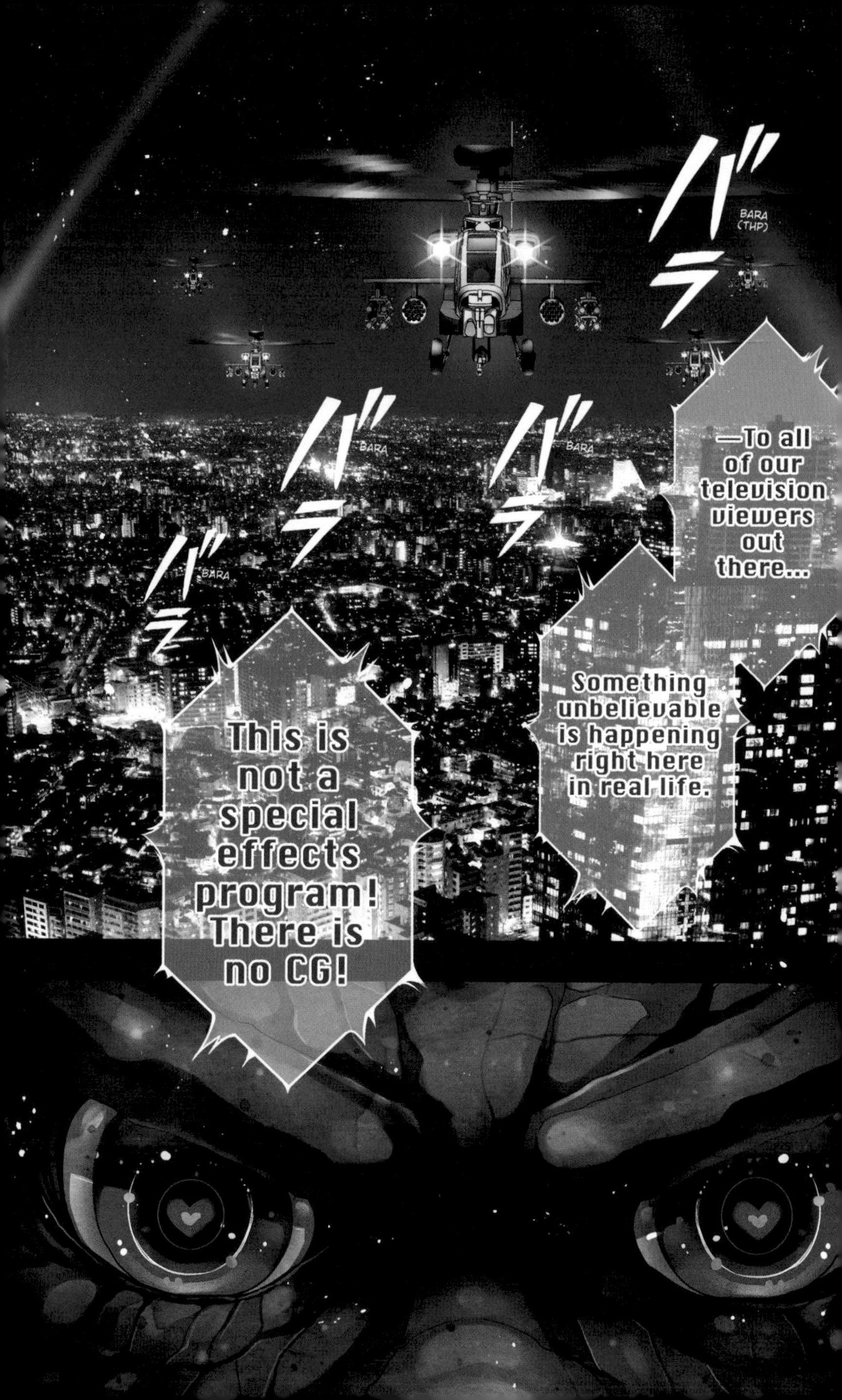

バラ
BARA (THP)
—To all of our television viewers out there...
バラ
BARA
バラ
BARA
Something unbelievable is happening right here in real life.
バラ
BARA
This is not a special effects program! There is no CG!

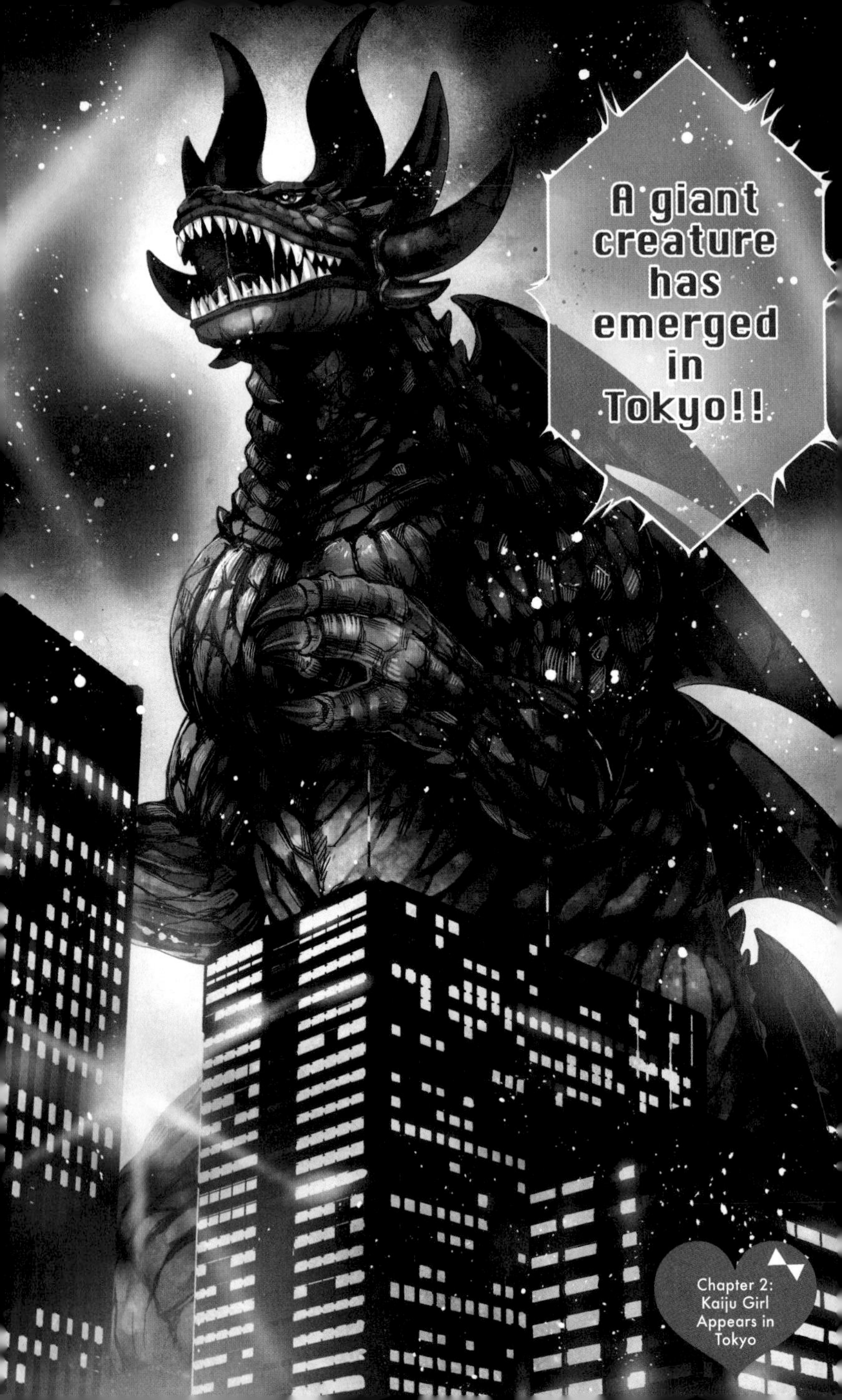
A giant creature has emerged in Tokyo!!
Chapter 2: Kaiju Girl Appears in Tokyo

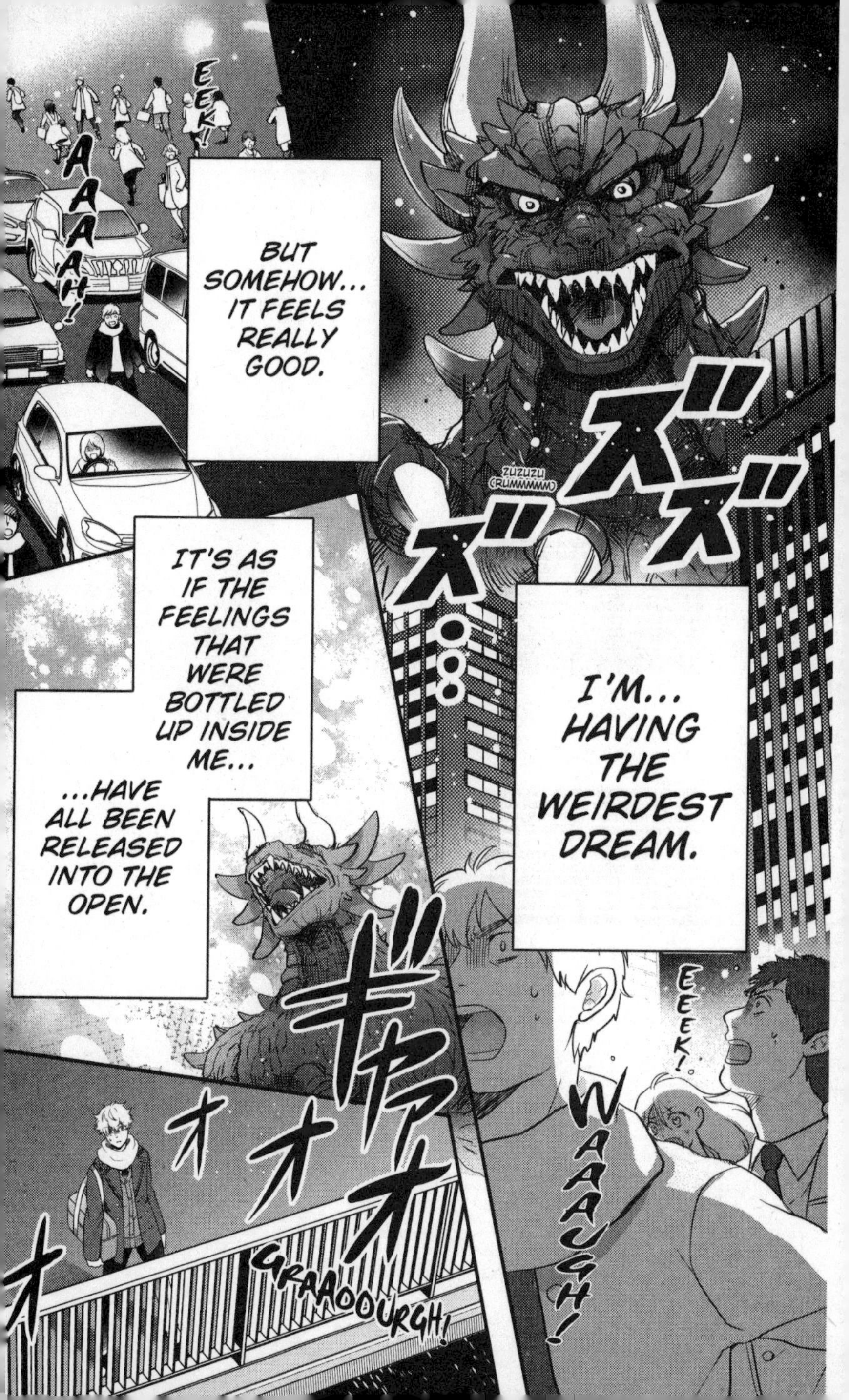
ズズズ
ZUZUZU
(RUMMMMM)
I'M... HAVING THE WEIRDEST DREAM.
EEEK!
AAAAAH!
BUT SOMEHOW... IT FEELS REALLY GOOD.
IT'S AS IF THE FEELINGS THAT WERE BOTTLED UP INSIDE ME...
...HAVE ALL BEEN RELEASED INTO THE OPEN.
EEEK!
WAAAUGH!
ギャアオオオ
GRAAAOOURGH!

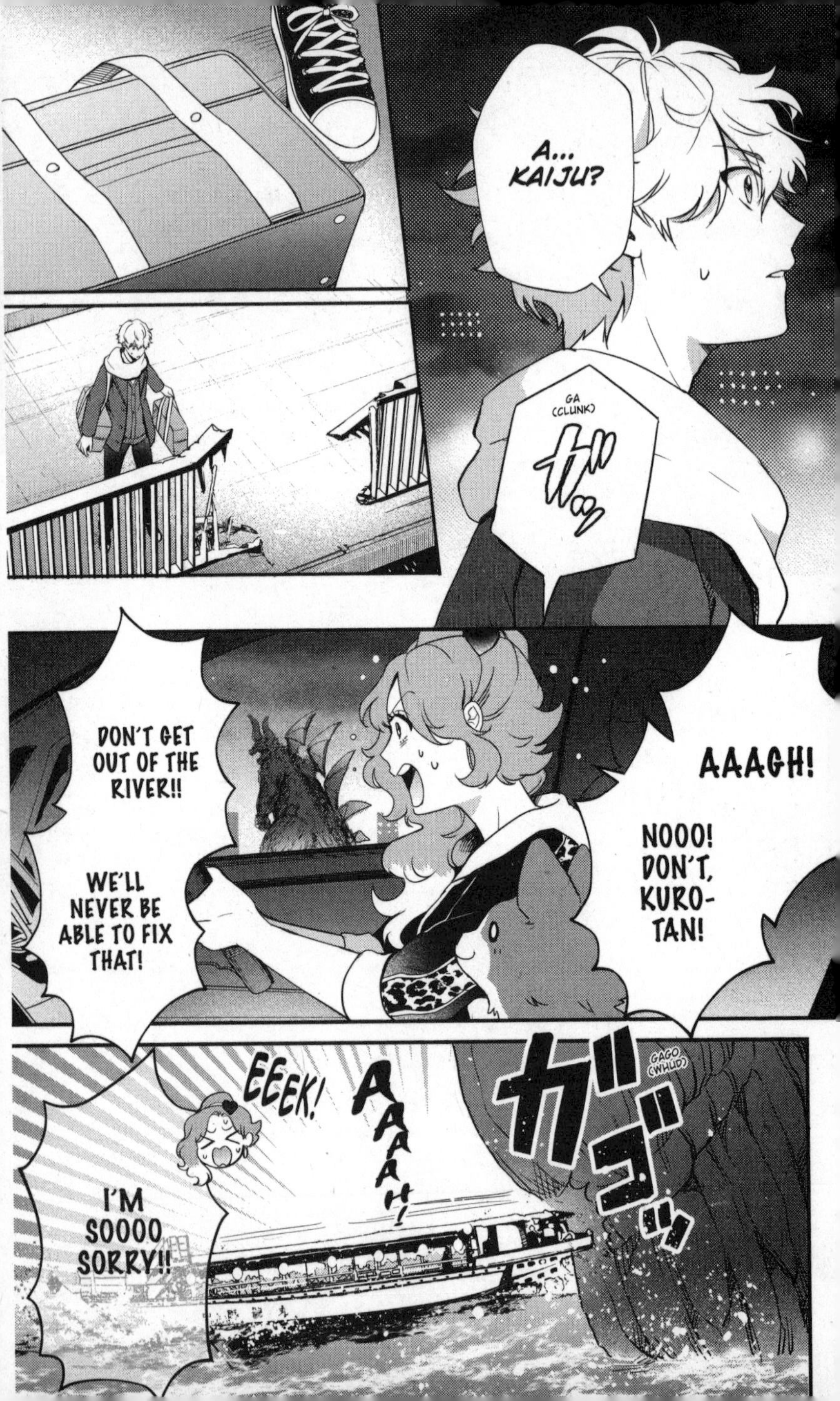
A... KAIJU?
GA (CLUNK)
AAAGH!
NOOO! DON'T, KURO-TAN!
DON'T GET OUT OF THE RIVER!!
WE'LL NEVER BE ABLE TO FIX THAT!
GAGO (WHUD)
AAAAH!
EEEK!
I'M SOOOO SORRY!!

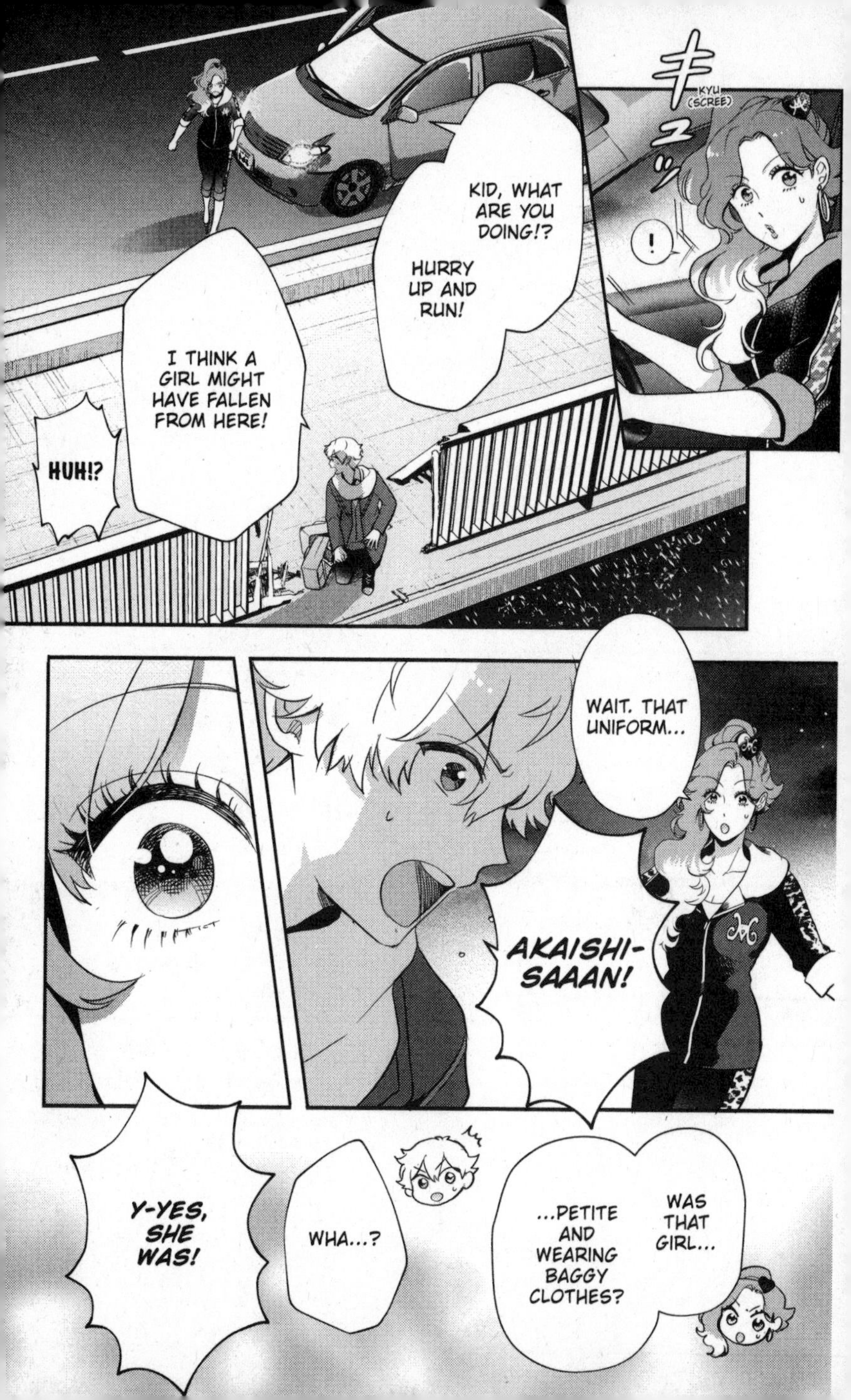

KYU (SCREE)
!
KID, WHAT ARE YOU DOING!?
HURRY UP AND RUN!
I THINK A GIRL MIGHT HAVE FALLEN FROM HERE!
HUH!?
WAIT. THAT UNIFORM...
AKAISHI-SAAAN!
WAS THAT GIRL...
...PETITE AND WEARING BAGGY CLOTHES?
WHA...?
Y-YES, SHE WAS!

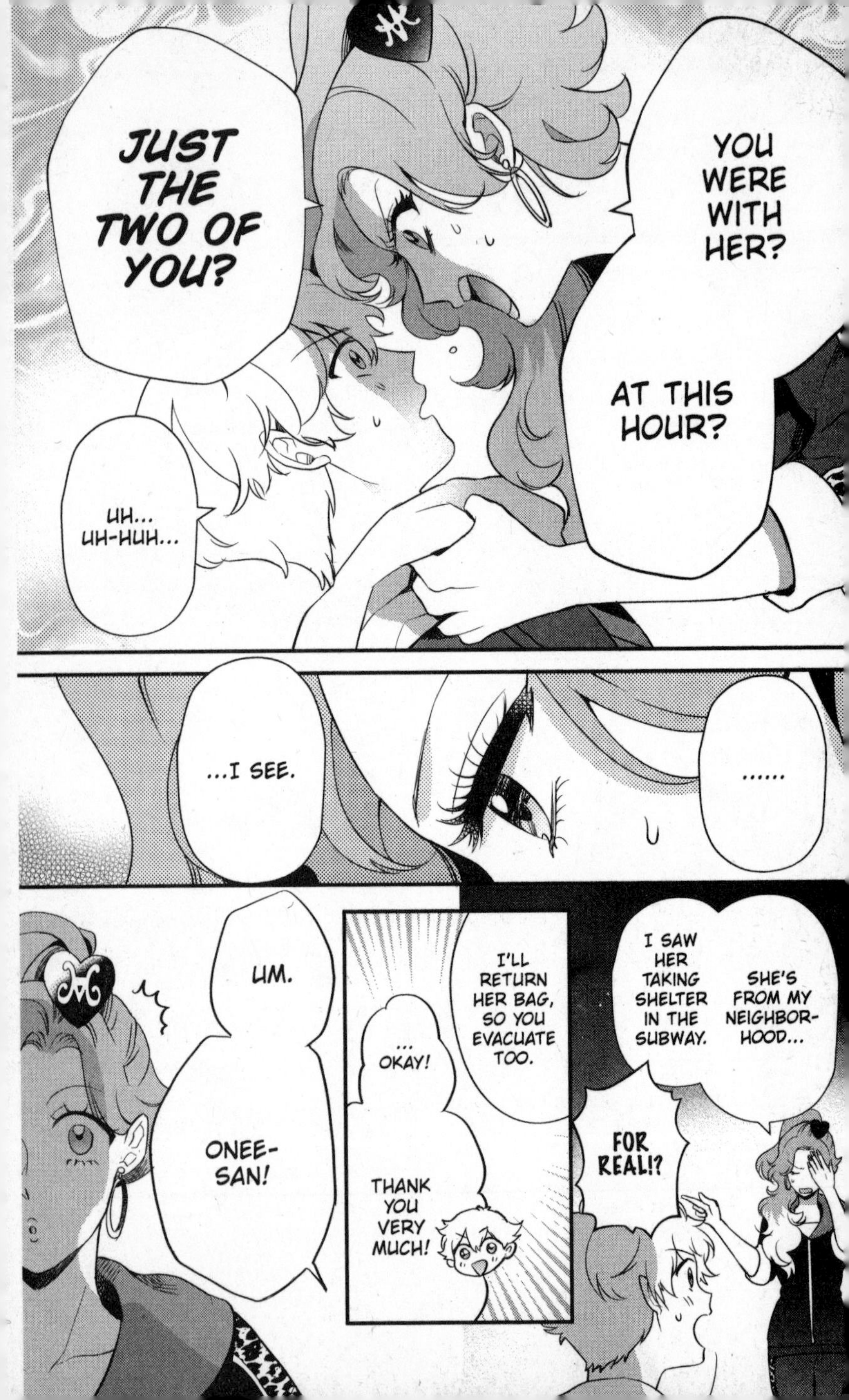
YOU WERE WITH HER?
AT THIS HOUR?
JUST THE TWO OF YOU?
UH... UH-HUH...
......
...I SEE.
SHE'S FROM MY NEIGHBOR-HOOD...
I SAW HER TAKING SHELTER IN THE SUBWAY.
FOR REAL!?
I'LL RETURN HER BAG, SO YOU EVACUATE TOO.
...OKAY!
THANK YOU VERY MUCH!
UM.
ONEE-SAN!

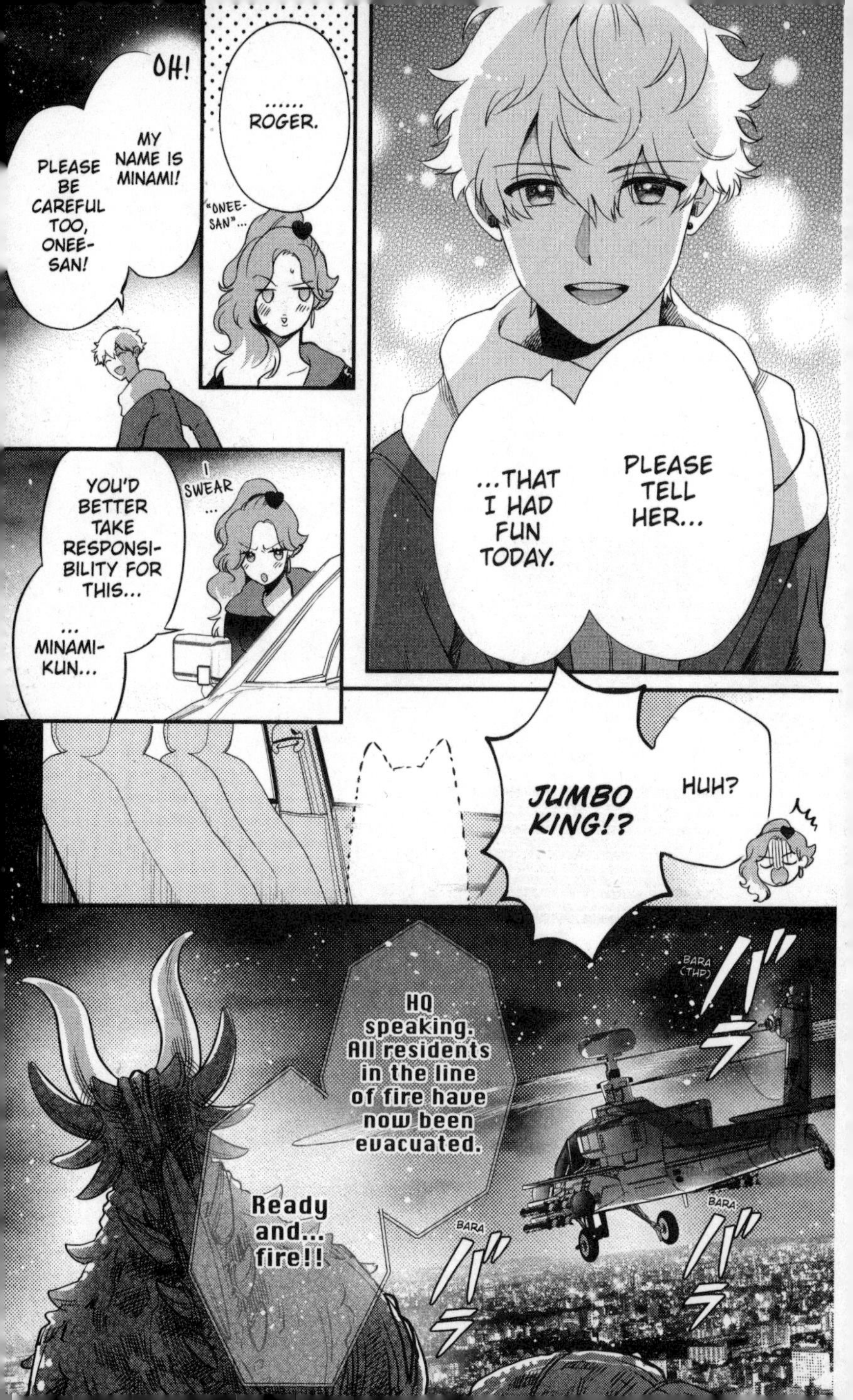
PLEASE TELL HER...
...THAT I HAD FUN TODAY.
......ROGER.
"ONEE-SAN"...
OH!
MY NAME IS MINAMI!
PLEASE BE CAREFUL TOO, ONEE-SAN!
I SWEAR...
YOU'D BETTER TAKE RESPONSIBILITY FOR THIS...
...MINAMI-KUN...
HUH?
JUMBO KING!?
BARA (THP)
HQ speaking. All residents in the line of fire have now been evacuated.
Ready and... fire!!
BARA
BARA

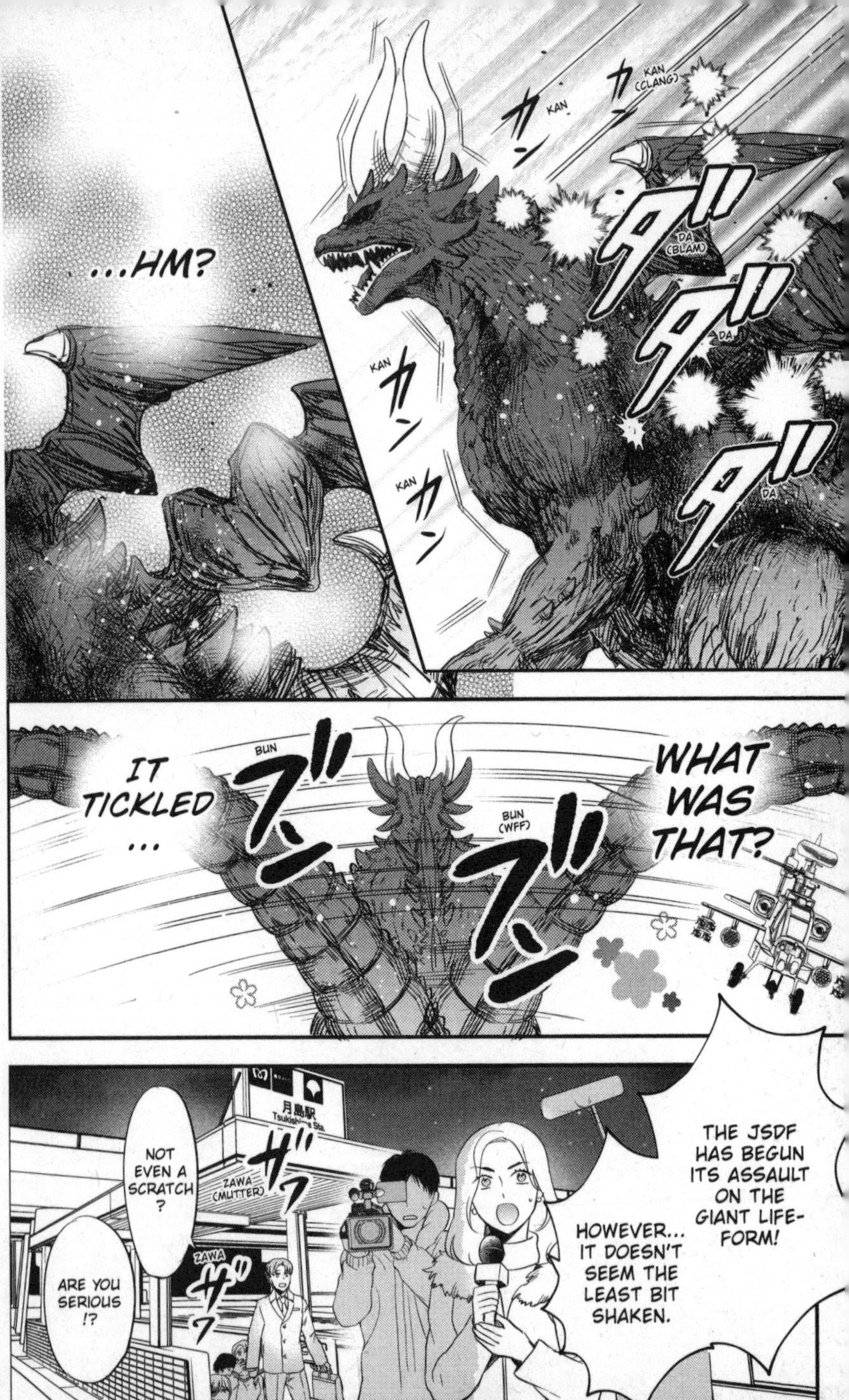
KAN (CLANG)
KAN
カンカン
DA (BLAM)
DA
DA
ダダダ
KAN
KAN
カンカン
...HM?
WHAT WAS THAT?
BUN (WFF)
BUN
ブンブン
IT TICKLED...
THE JSDF HAS BEGUN ITS ASSAULT ON THE GIANT LIFE-FORM!
HOWEVER... IT DOESN'T SEEM THE LEAST BIT SHAKEN.
月島駅
ZAWA (MUTTER)
ZAWA
ザワザワ
NOT EVEN A SCRATCH?
ARE YOU SERIOUS!?

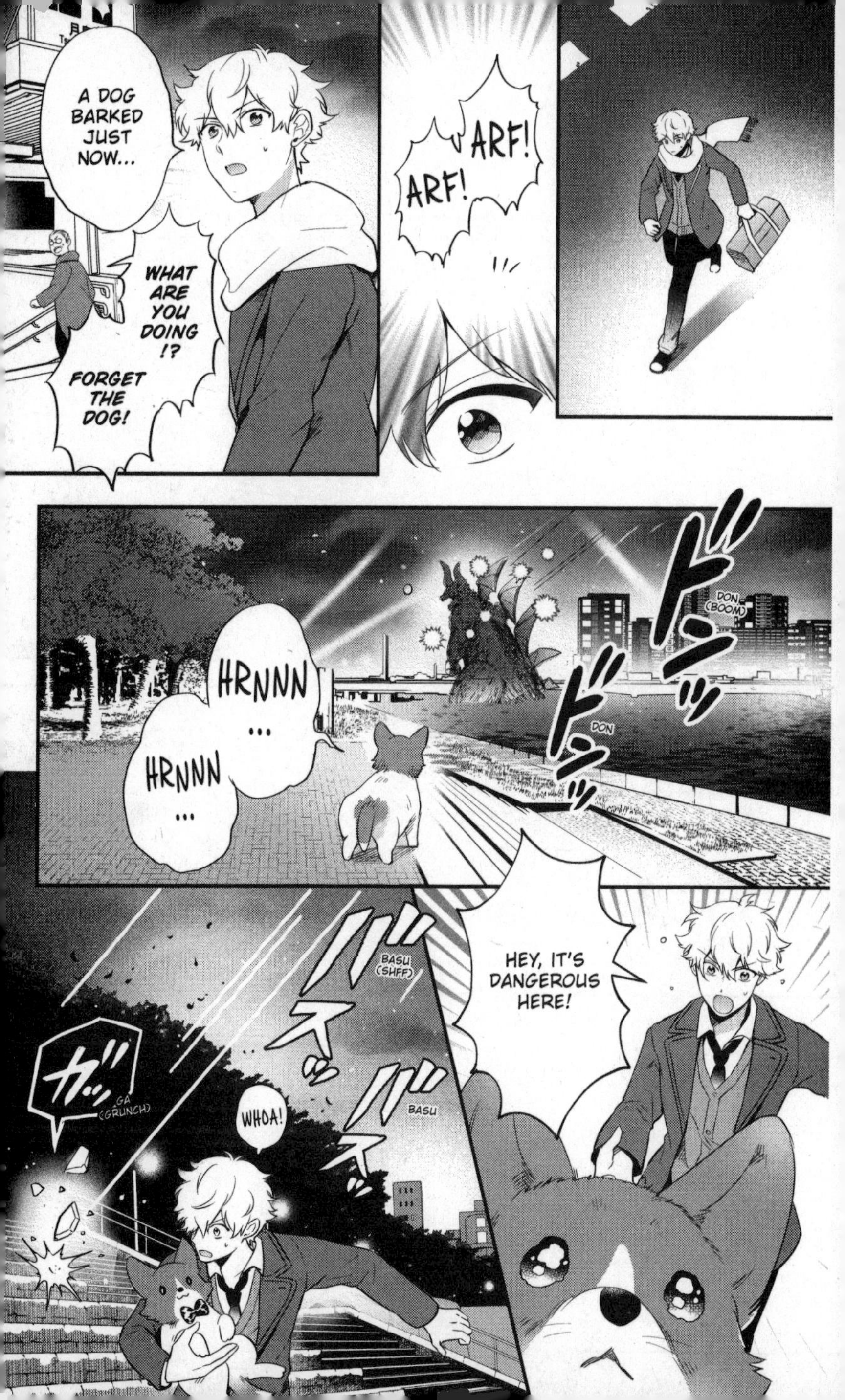
ARF!
ARF!
A DOG BARKED JUST NOW...
WHAT ARE YOU DOING!? FORGET THE DOG!
DON (BOOM)
DON
HRNNN...
HRNNN...
HEY, IT'S DANGEROUS HERE!
BASU (SHFF)
BASU
GA (GRUNCH)
WHOA!

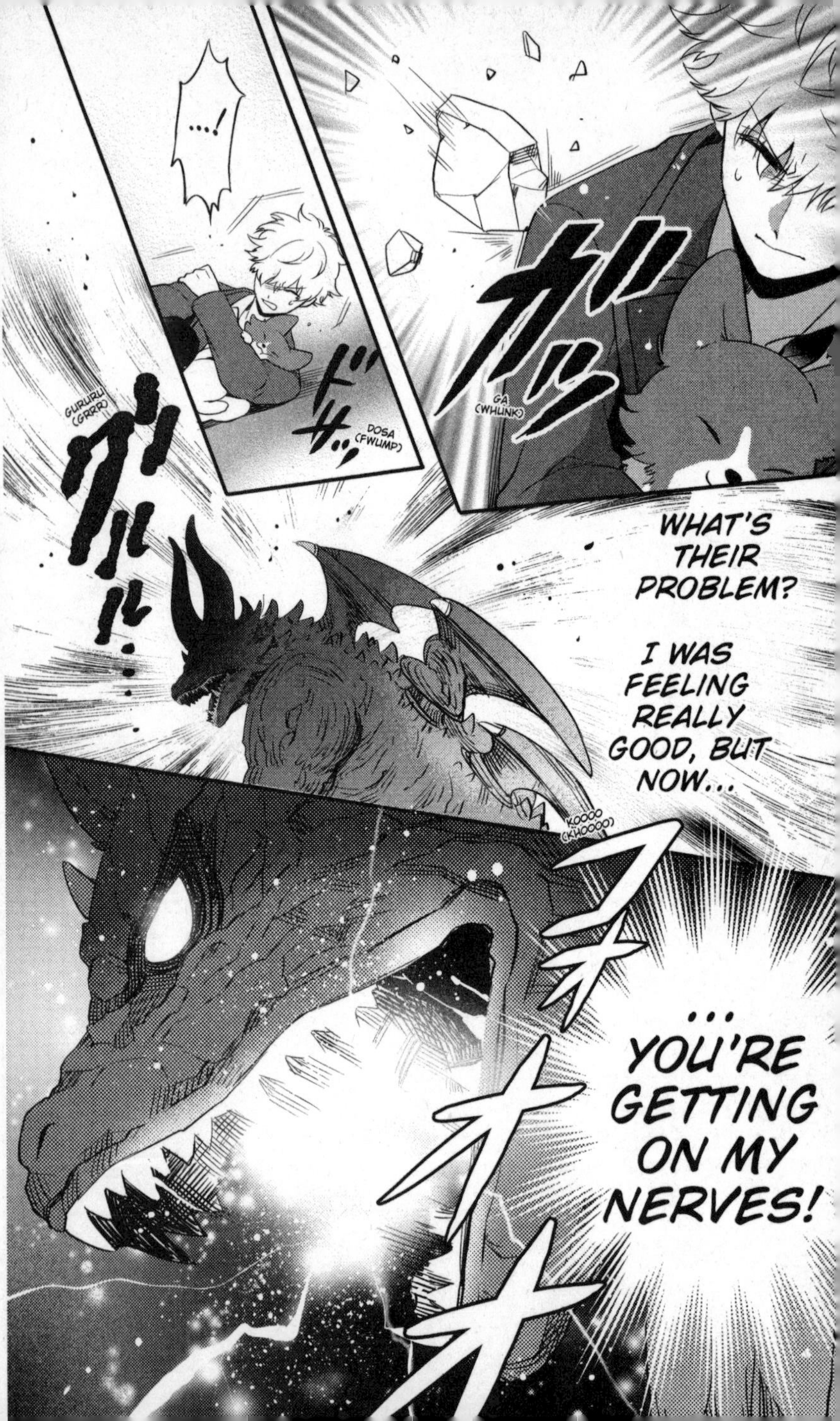

GA (WHLINK)
...!
DOSA (FWUMP)
WHAT'S THEIR PROBLEM?
I WAS FEELING REALLY GOOD, BUT NOW...
GURURU (GRRR)
KOOOO (KHOOOO)
...YOU'RE GETTING ON MY NERVES!

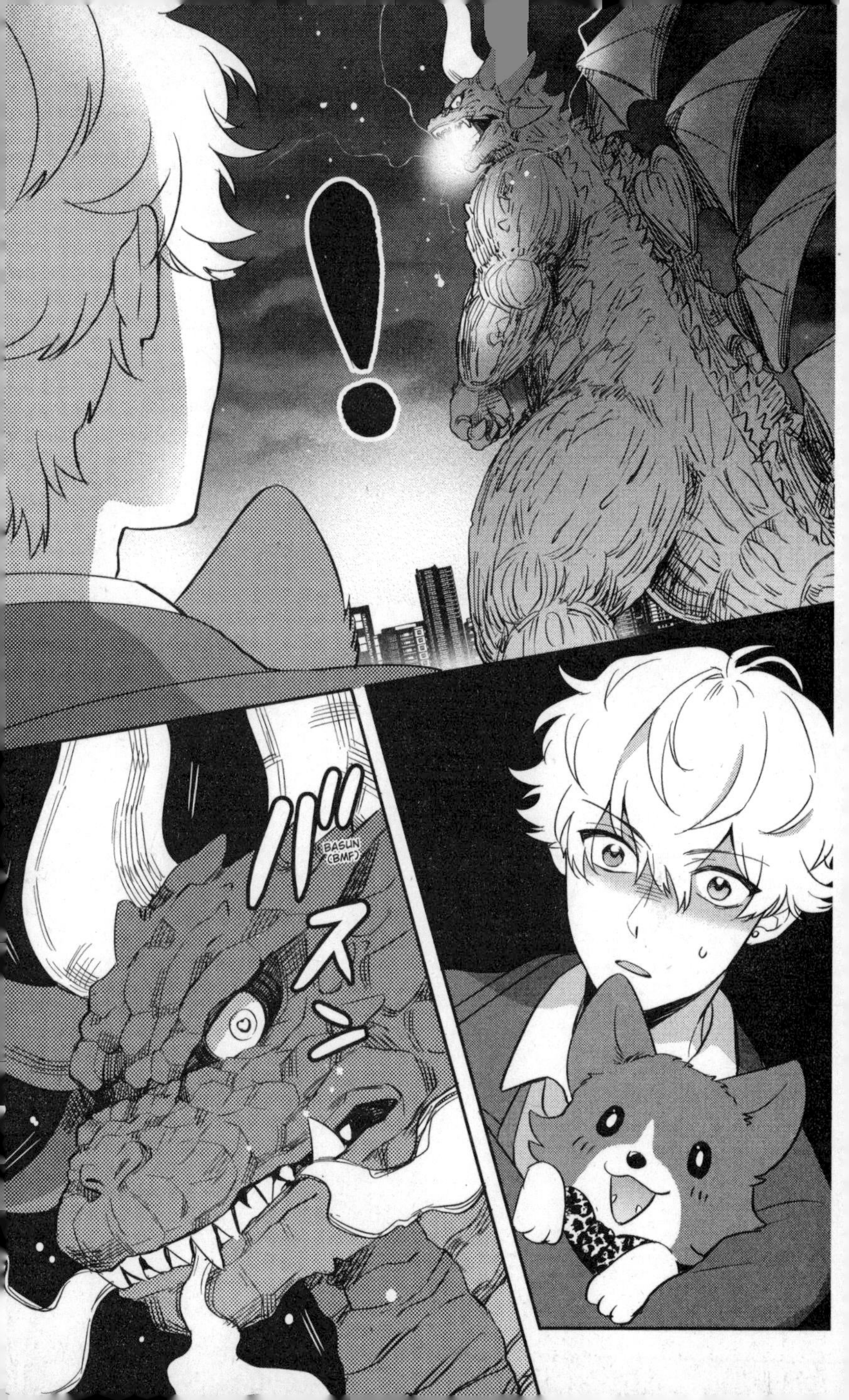
!
バスン
BASUN (BMF)

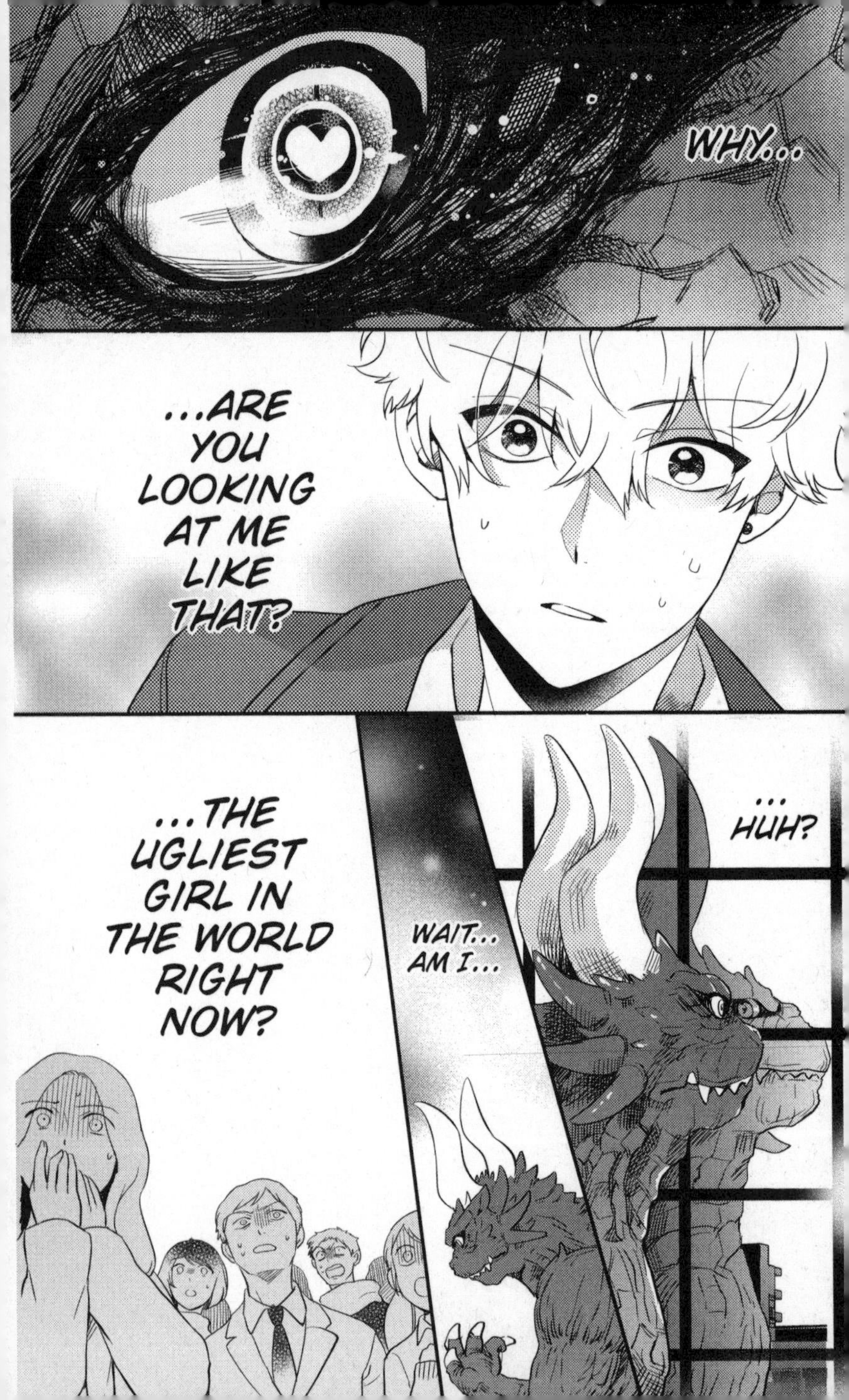
WHY...
...ARE YOU LOOKING AT ME LIKE THAT?
...HUH?
WAIT... AM I...
...THE UGLIEST GIRL IN THE WORLD RIGHT NOW?

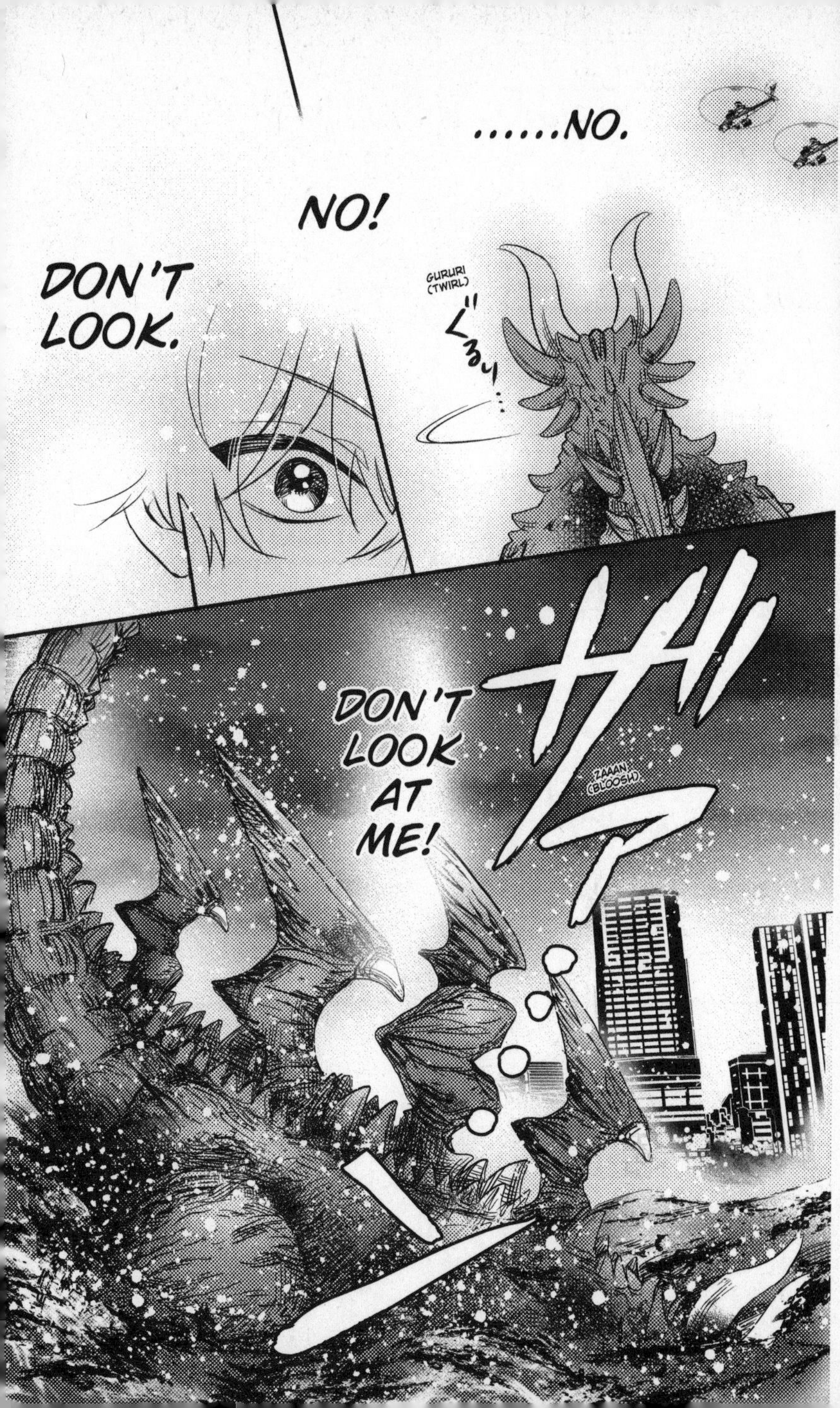

......NO.
GURURI (TWIRL)
NO!
DON'T LOOK.
ZAAAN (BLOOSH)
DON'T LOOK AT ME!

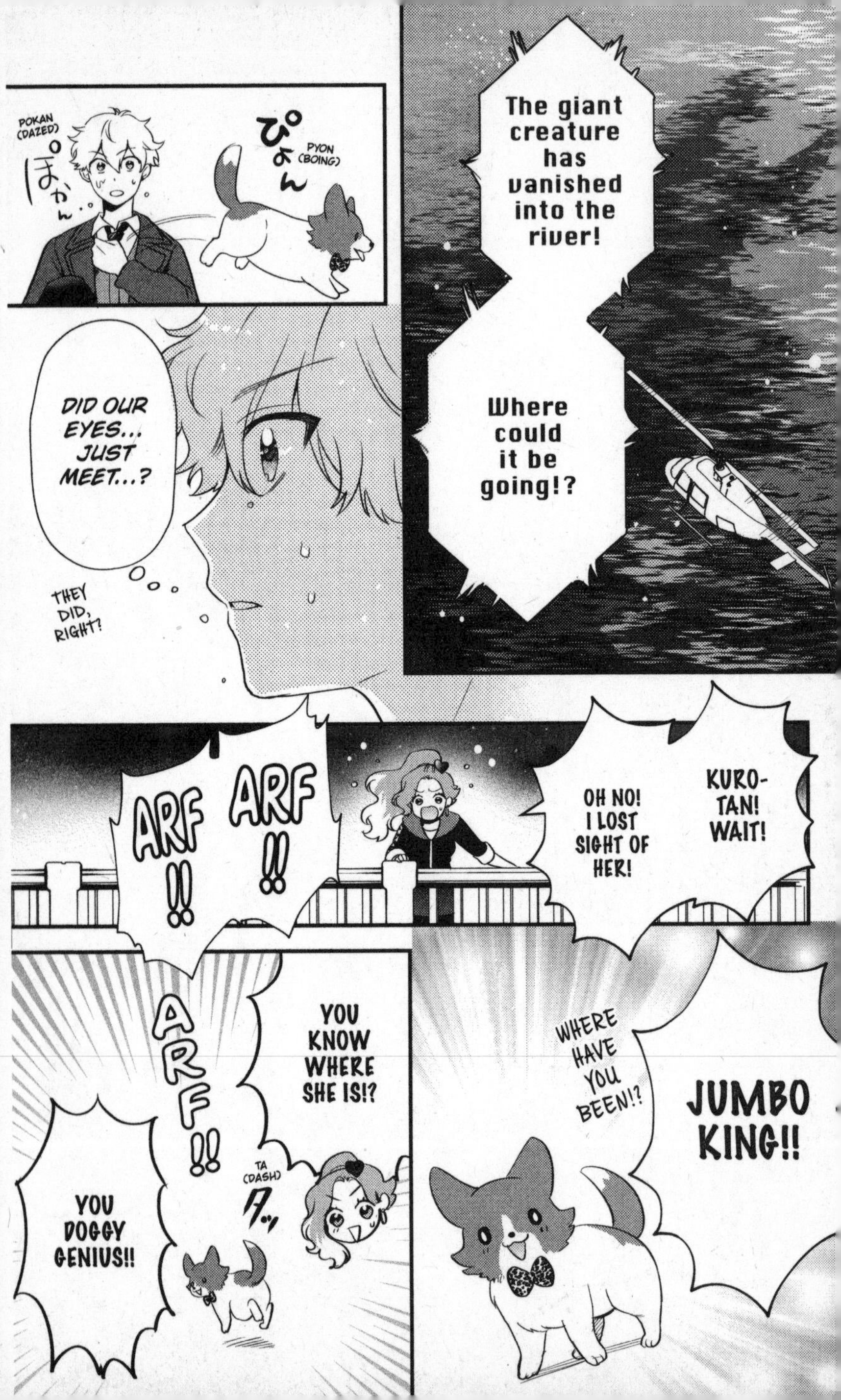

The giant creature has vanished into the river!
Where could it be going!?
ぴょん
PYON (BOING)
POKAN (DAZED)
ぽかん…
DID OUR EYES... JUST MEET...?
THEY DID, RIGHT?
KURO-TAN! WAIT!
OH NO! I LOST SIGHT OF HER!
ARF!!
ARF!!
JUMBO KING!!
WHERE HAVE YOU BEEN!?
YOU KNOW WHERE SHE IS!?
ARF!!
TA (DASH)
タッ
YOU DOGGY GENIUS!!

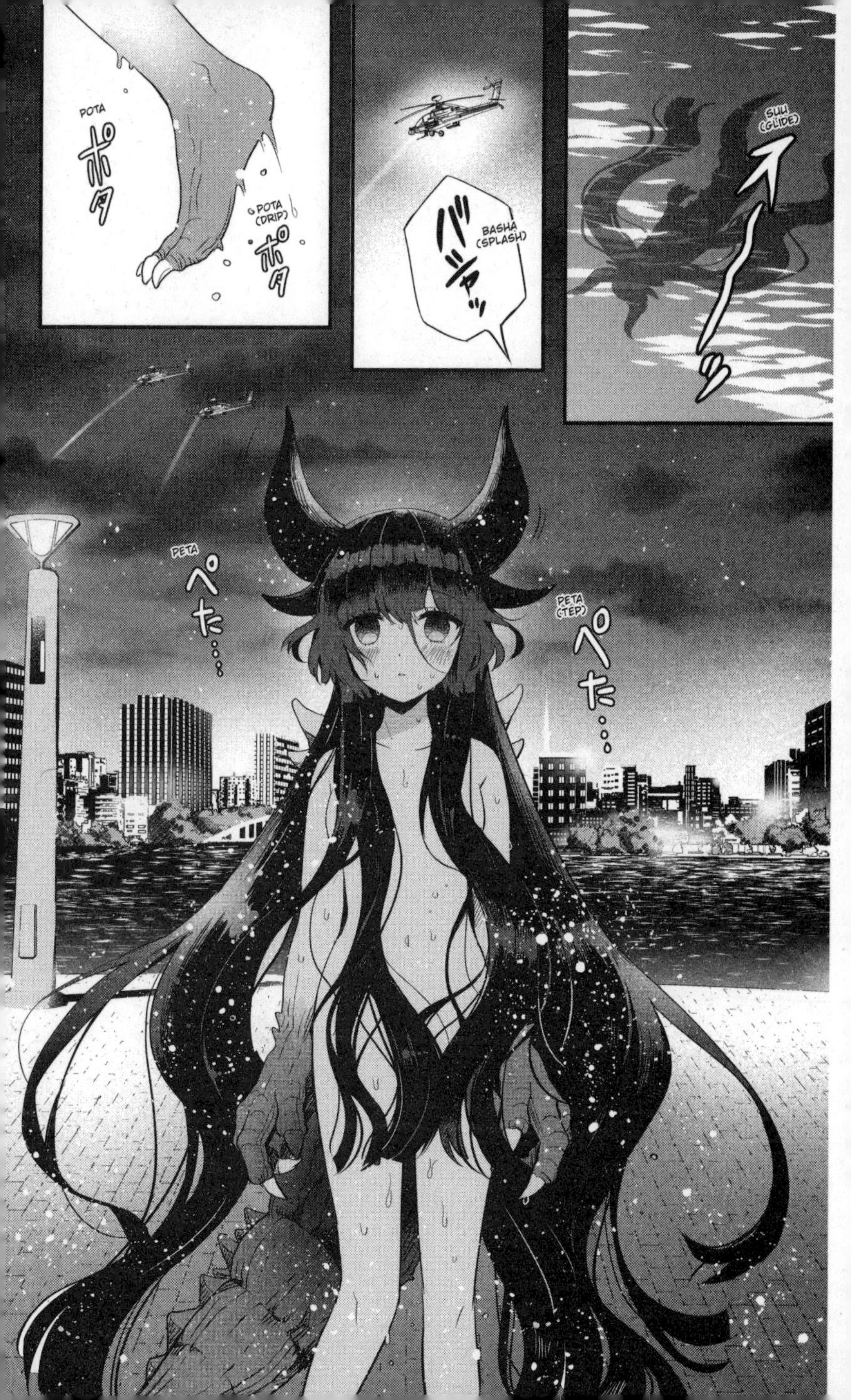

SUU (GLIDE)
BASHA (SPLASH)
バシャッ
POTA
ポタ
POTA (DRIP)
ポタ
PETA (STEP)
ぺた…
PETA
ぺた…

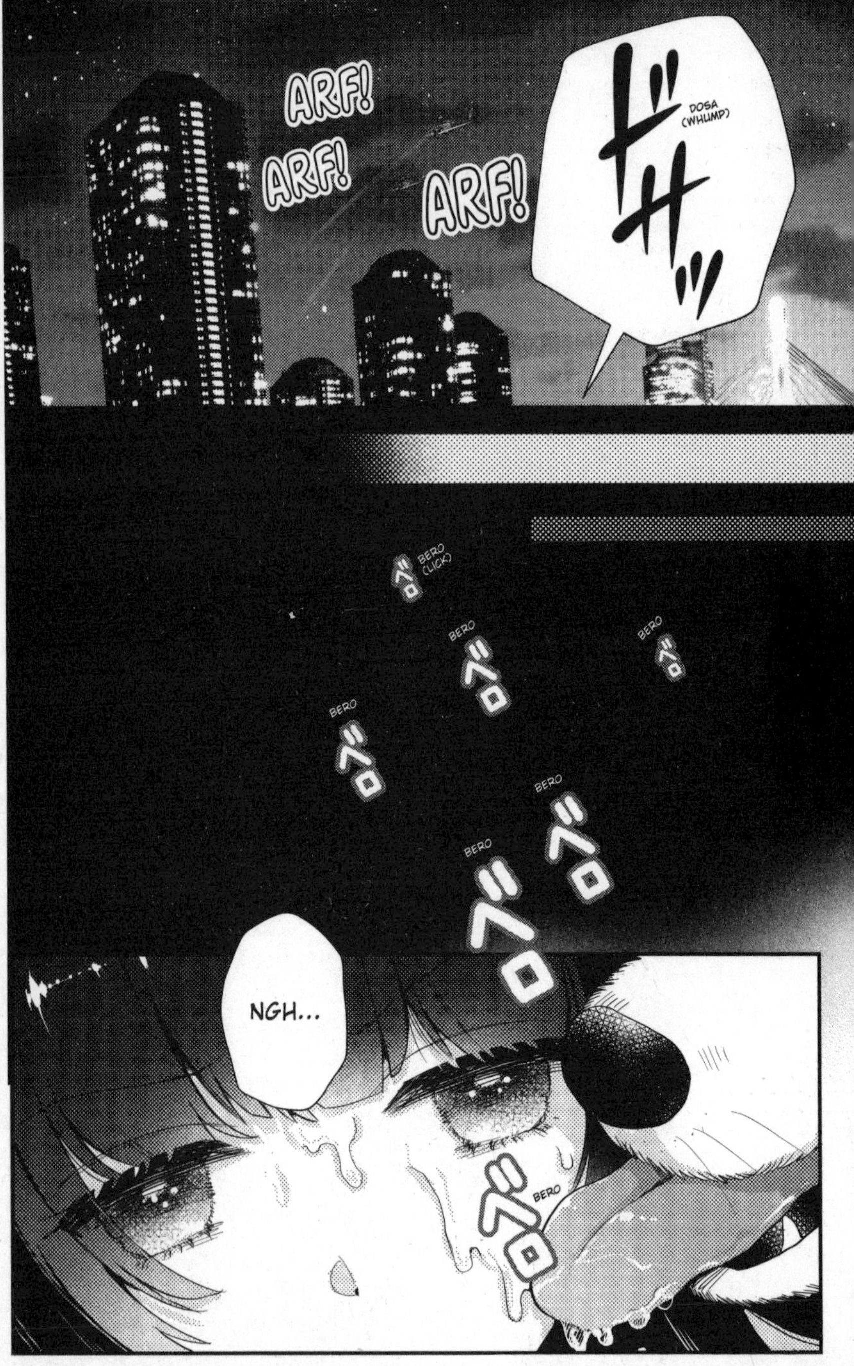
ドサッ
DOSA (WHUMP)
ARF!
ARF!
ARF!
ベロ
BERO (LICK)
ベロ
BERO
ベロ
BERO
ベロ
BERO
ベロ
BERO
ベロ
BERO
NGH...
ベロ
BERO

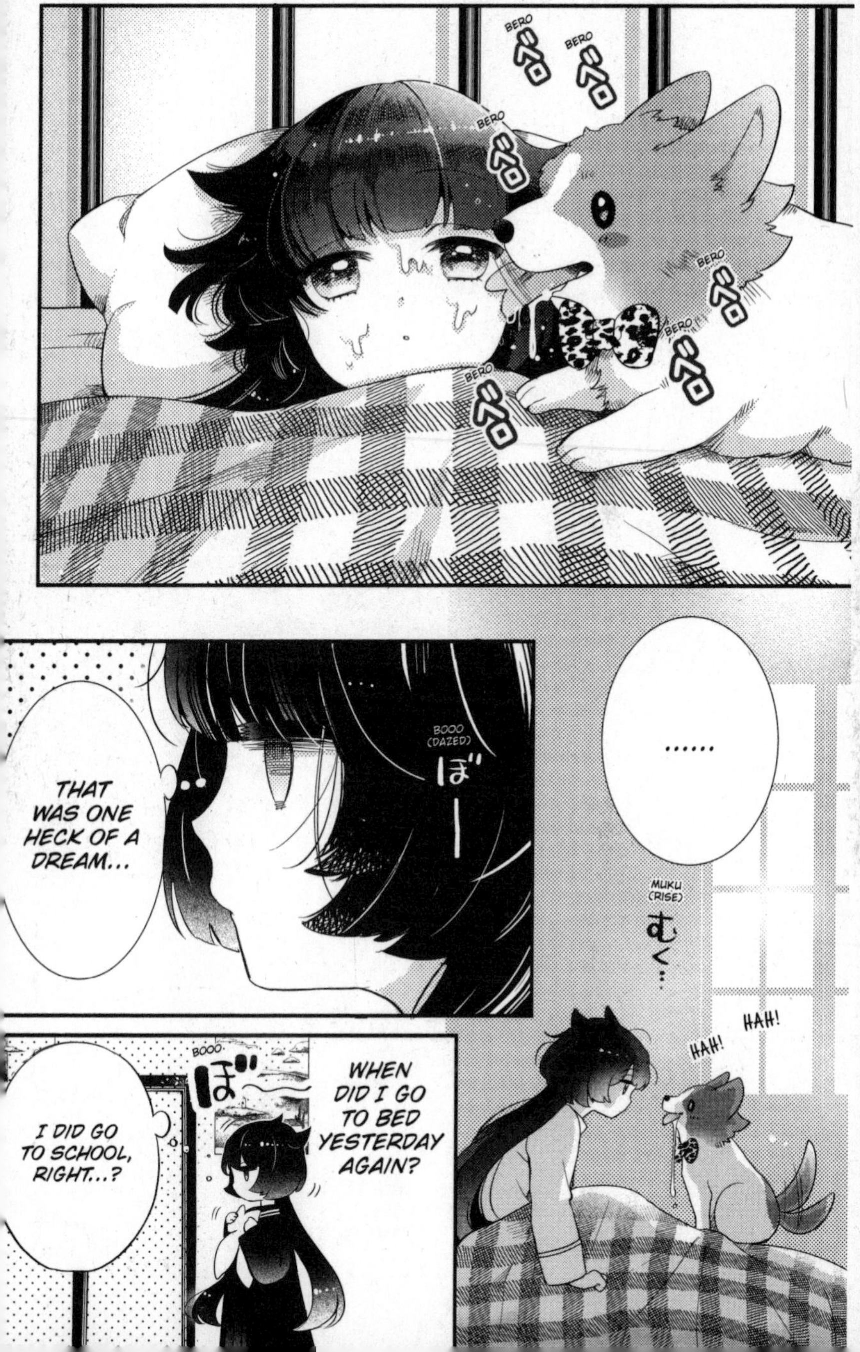
BERO ベロ
BERO ベロ
BERO ベロ
BERO ベロ
BERO ベロ
BERO ベロ
......
MUKU (RISE) むく…
HAH!
HAH!
BOOO (DAZED) ぼー
THAT WAS ONE HECK OF A DREAM...
WHEN DID I GO TO BED YESTERDAY AGAIN?
BOOO ぼ～
I DID GO TO SCHOOL, RIGHT...?

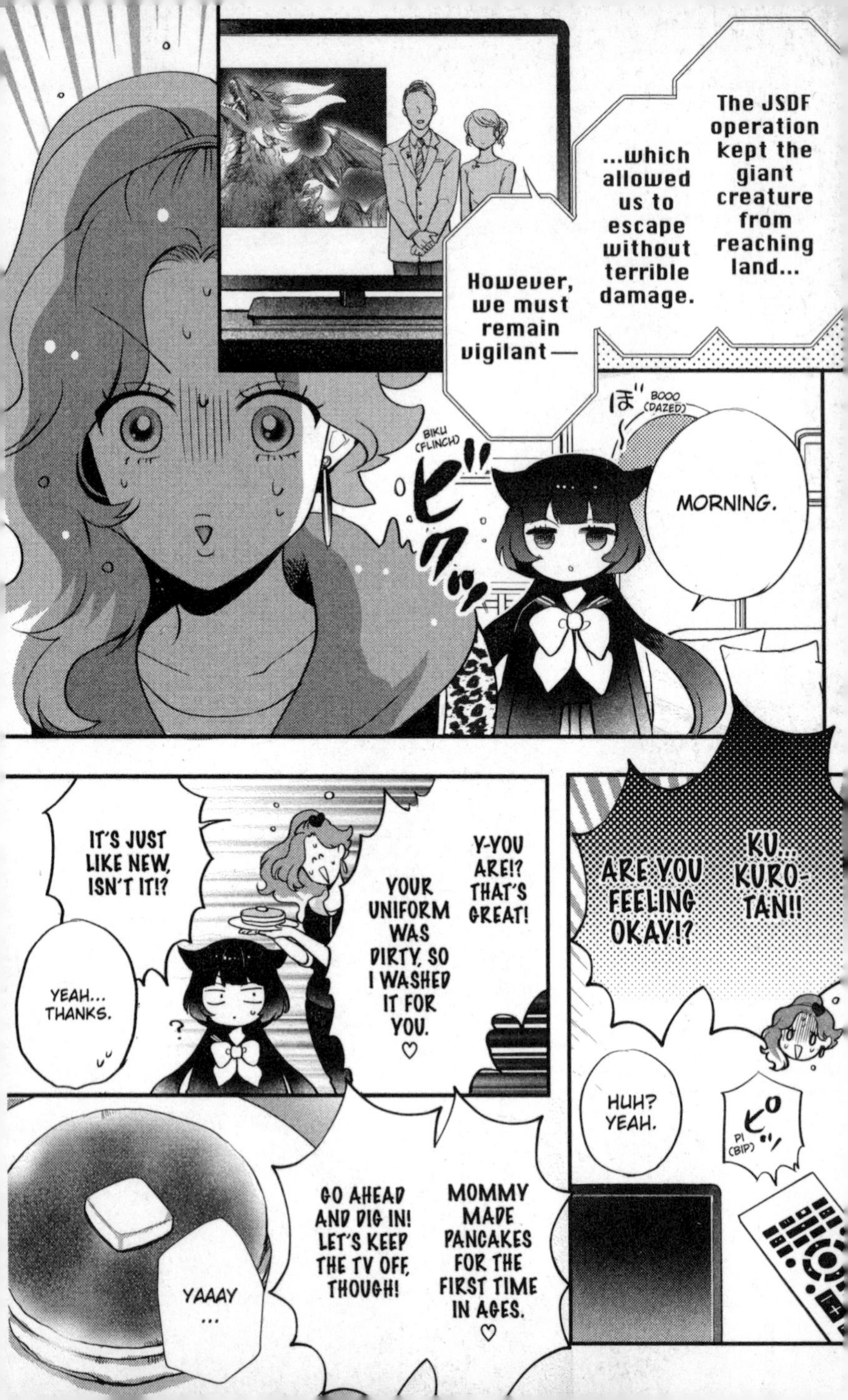
The JSDF operation kept the giant creature from reaching land...
...which allowed us to escape without terrible damage.
However, we must remain vigilant—
ぼ BOOO (DAZED)
MORNING.
ビクッ BIKU (FLINCH)
KU... KURO-TAN!!
ARE YOU FEELING OKAY!?
HUH? YEAH.
ピッ PI (BIP)
Y-YOU ARE!? THAT'S GREAT!
YOUR UNIFORM WAS DIRTY, SO I WASHED IT FOR YOU. ♡
IT'S JUST LIKE NEW, ISN'T IT!?
YEAH... THANKS.
MOMMY MADE PANCAKES FOR THE FIRST TIME IN AGES. ♡
GO AHEAD AND DIG IN! LET'S KEEP THE TV OFF, THOUGH!
YAAAY ...

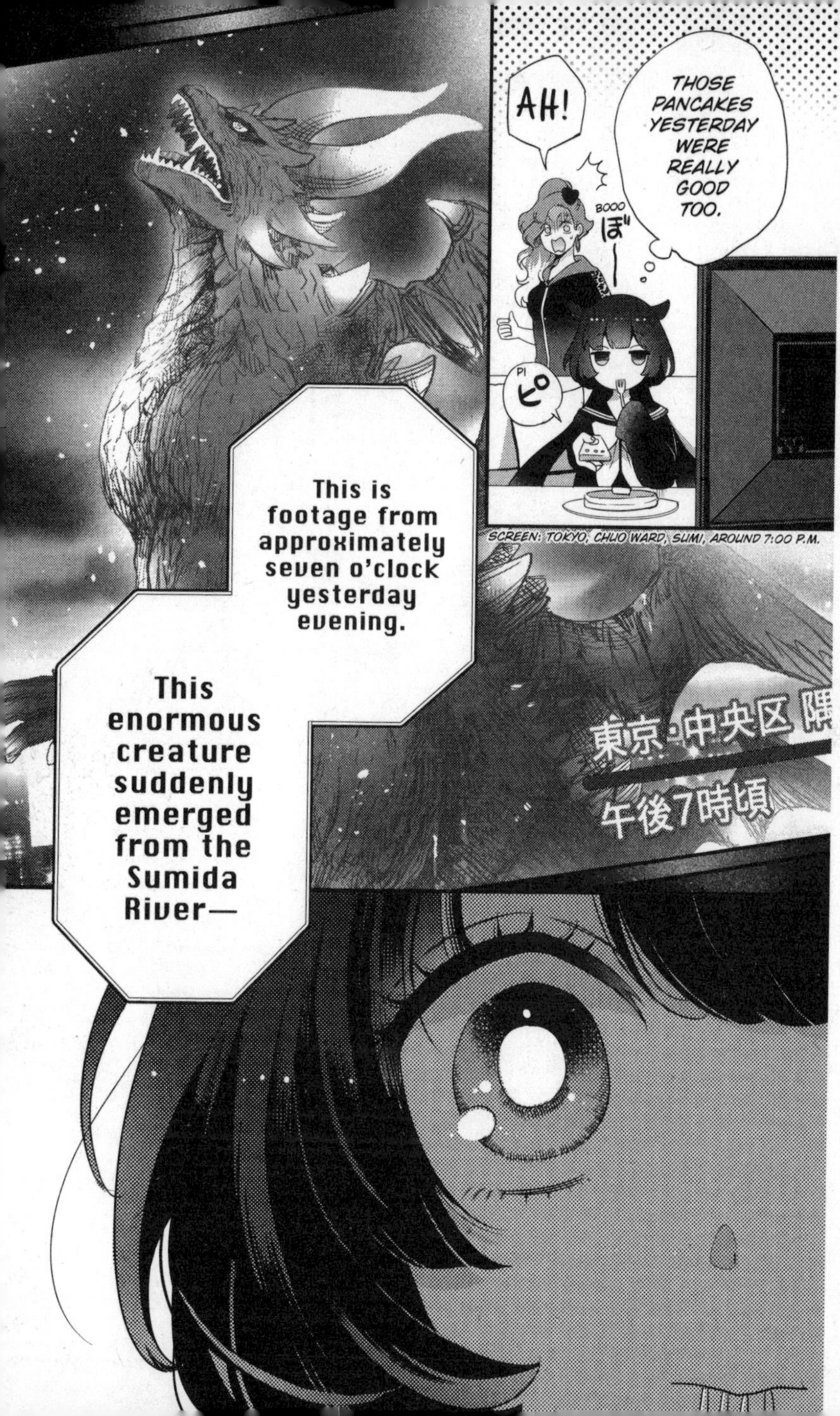
THOSE PANCAKES YESTERDAY WERE REALLY GOOD TOO.
AH!
BOOO ぼー
PI ピ
SCREEN: TOKYO, CHUO WARD, SUMI, AROUND 7:00 P.M.
東京・中央区 隅
午後7時頃
This is footage from approximately seven o'clock yesterday evening.
This enormous creature suddenly emerged from the Sumida River—

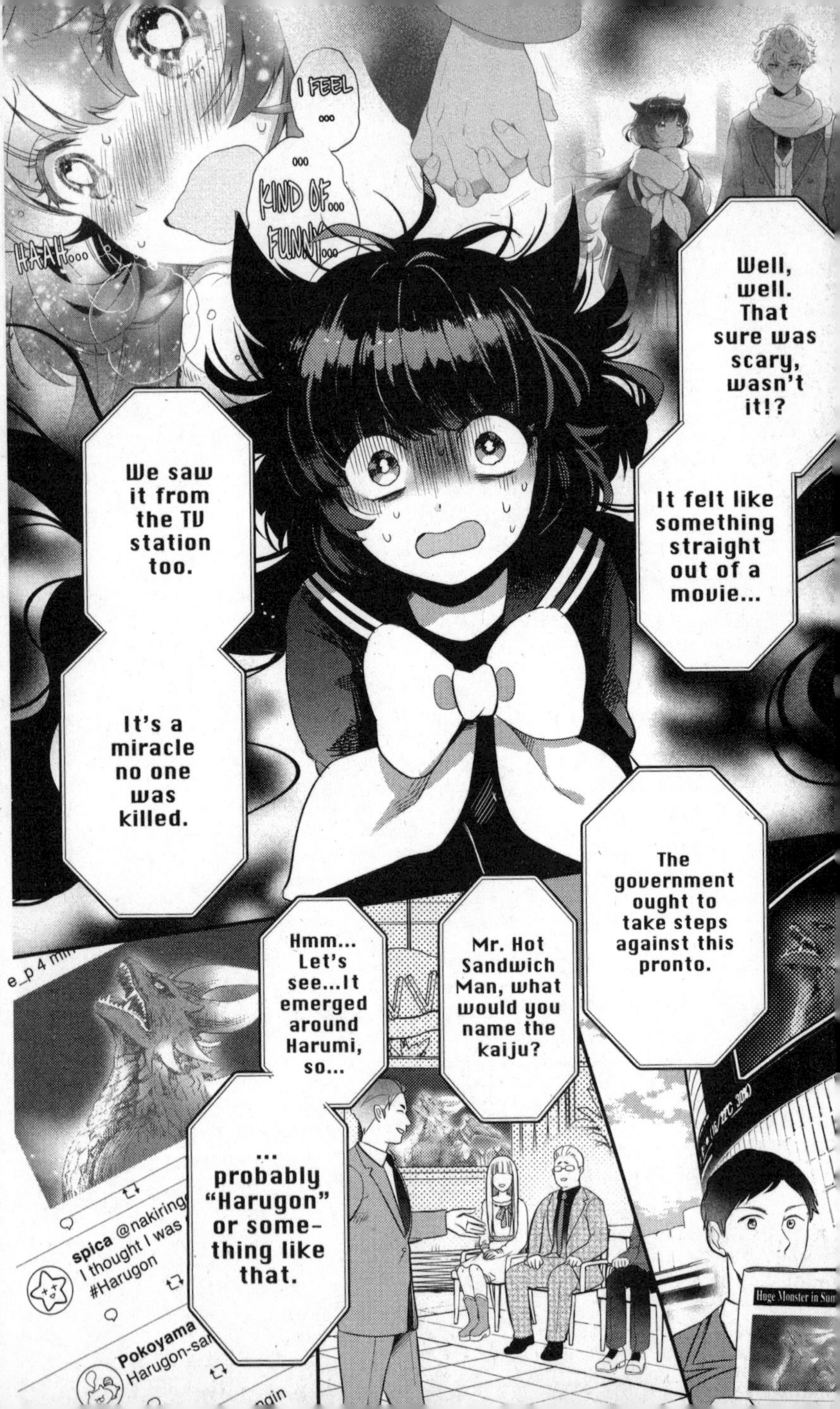
Well, well. That sure was scary, wasn't it!?
It felt like something straight out of a movie...
I FEEL ... ... KIND OF... FUNNY...
HAAH...
We saw it from the TV station too.
It's a miracle no one was killed.
The government ought to take steps against this pronto.
Mr. Hot Sandwich Man, what would you name the kaiju?
Hmm... Let's see...It emerged around Harumi, so...
... probably "Harugon" or some-thing like that.
spica @nakiring
I thought I was
#Harugon
Pokoyama
Huge Monster in Sun

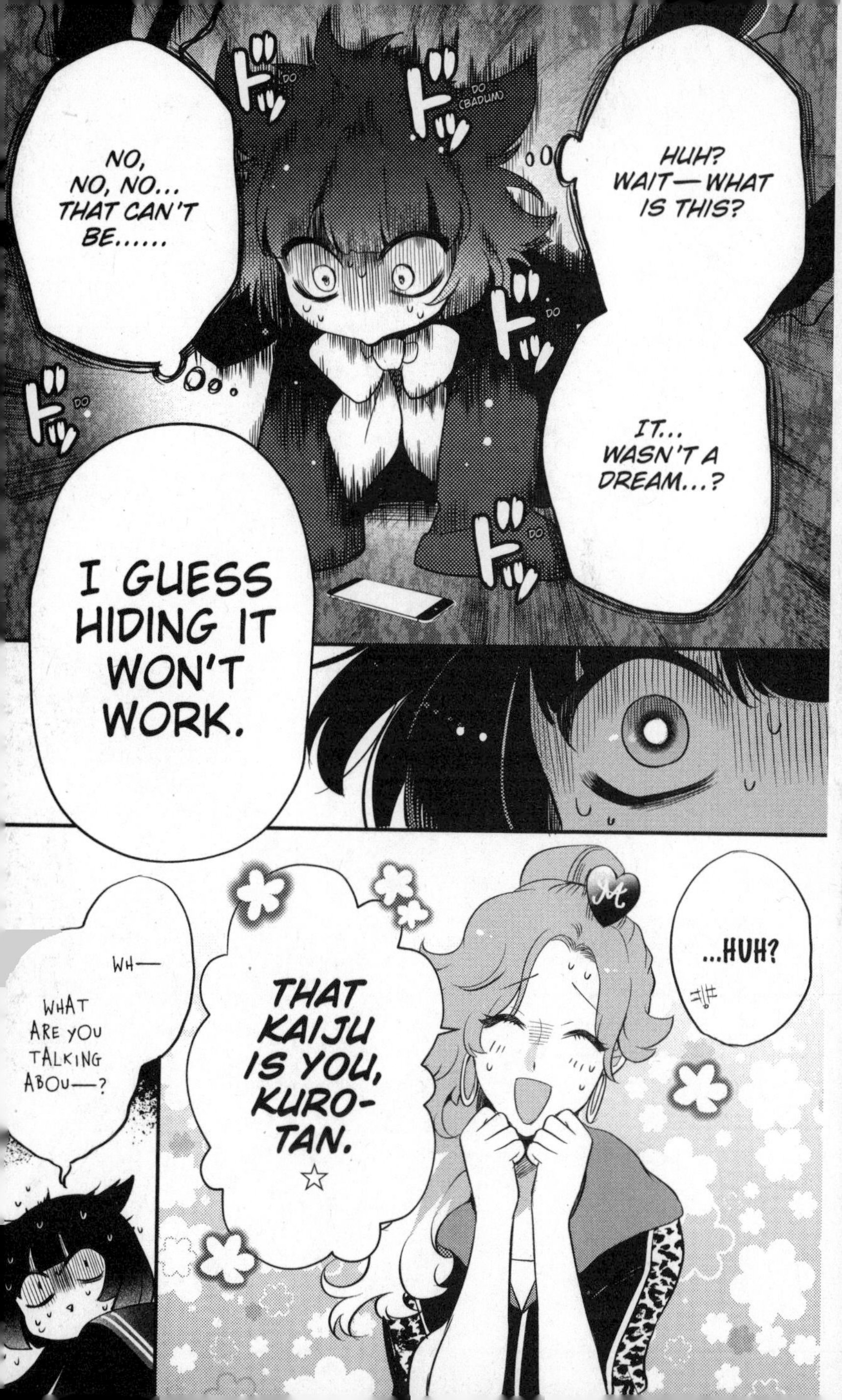
DO
DO (BADUM)
HUH? WAIT—WHAT IS THIS?
IT... WASN'T A DREAM...?
DO
DO
NO, NO, NO... THAT CAN'T BE......
DO
I GUESS HIDING IT WON'T WORK.
...HUH?
THAT KAIJU IS YOU, KURO-TAN. ☆
WH—
WHAT ARE YOU TALKING ABOU—?

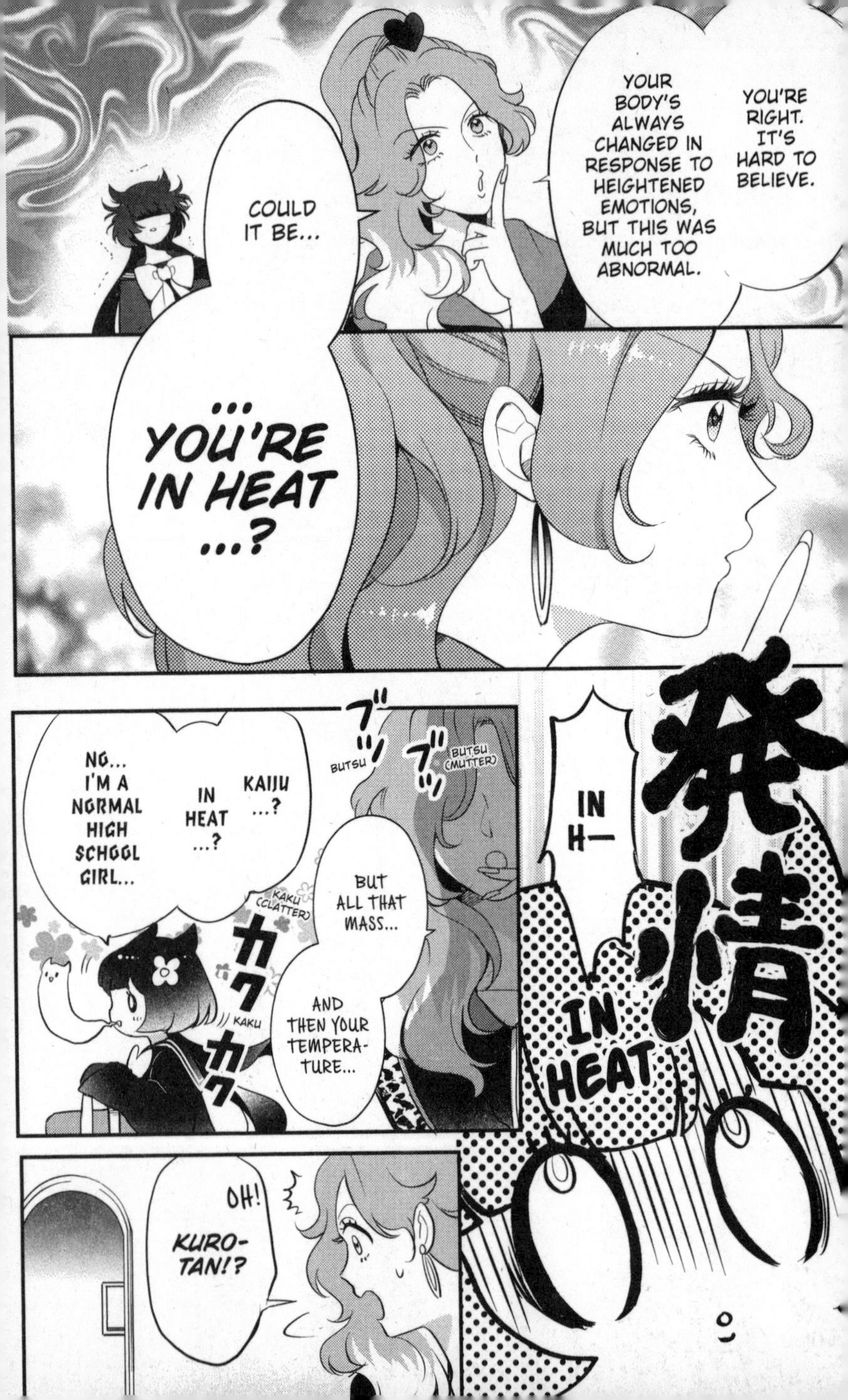
YOU'RE RIGHT. IT'S HARD TO BELIEVE.
YOUR BODY'S ALWAYS CHANGED IN RESPONSE TO HEIGHTENED EMOTIONS, BUT THIS WAS MUCH TOO ABNORMAL.
COULD IT BE...
...YOU'RE IN HEAT...?
発情
IN HEAT
IN H—
ブツ BUTSU
ブツ BUTSU (MUTTER)
BUT ALL THAT MASS...
AND THEN YOUR TEMPERA-TURE...
KAIJU...?
IN HEAT...?
NO... I'M A NORMAL HIGH SCHOOL GIRL...
カク KAKU (CLATTER)
カク KAKU
OH!
KURO-TAN!?

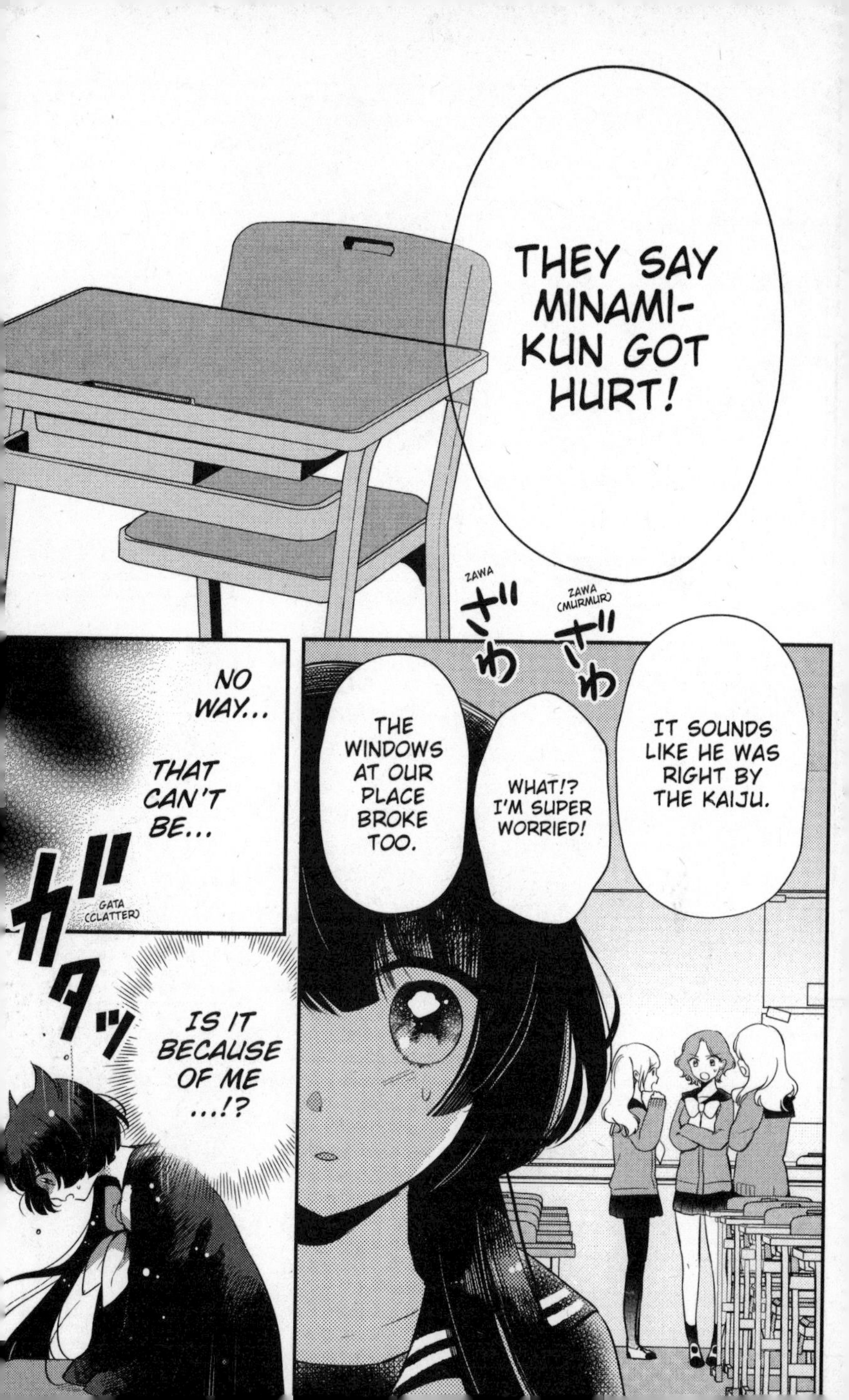
THEY SAY MINAMI-KUN GOT HURT!
ZAWA
ZAWA (MURMUR)
IT SOUNDS LIKE HE WAS RIGHT BY THE KAIJU.
WHAT!? I'M SUPER WORRIED!
THE WINDOWS AT OUR PLACE BROKE TOO.
NO WAY...
THAT CAN'T BE...
GATA (CLATTER)
IS IT BECAUSE OF ME ...!?

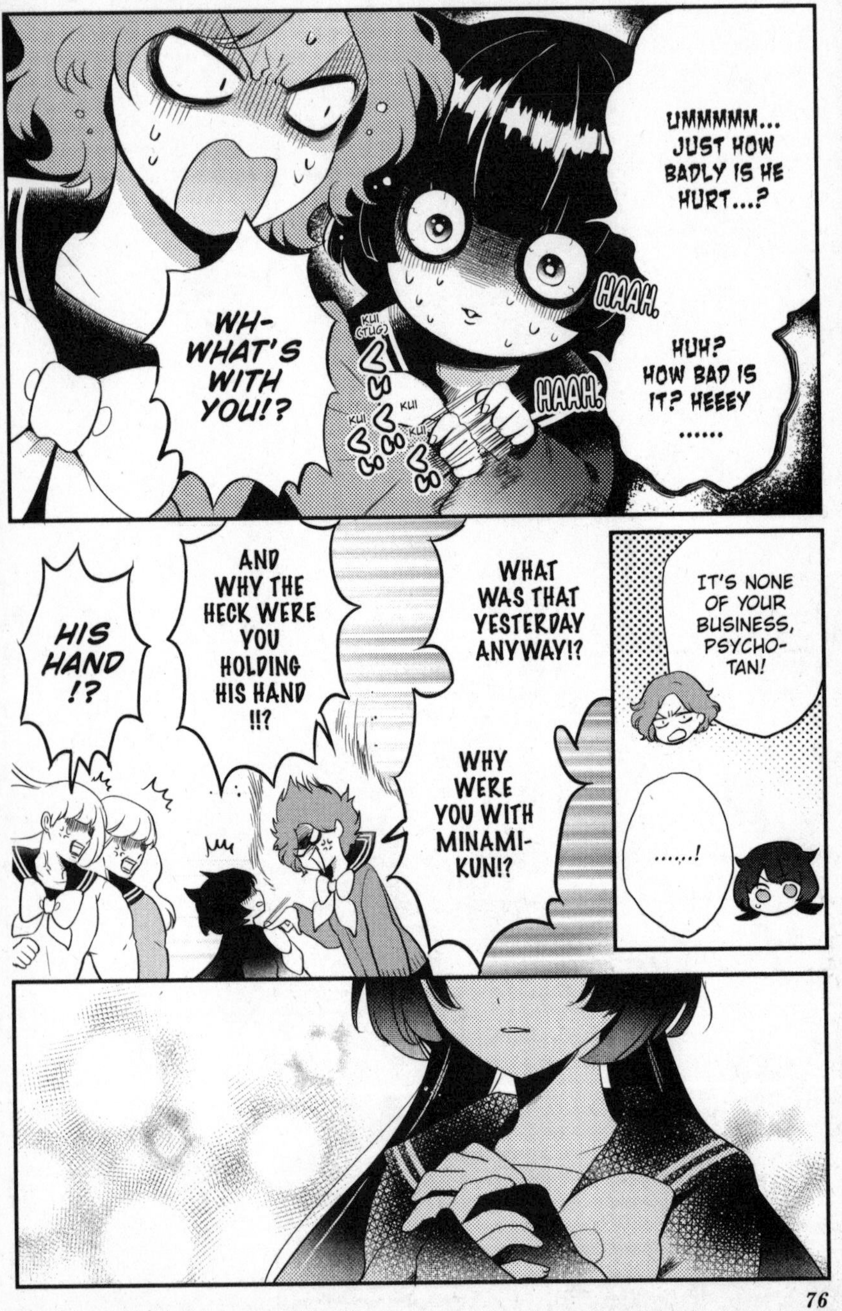
UMMMMM... JUST HOW BADLY IS HE HURT...?
HAAH.
HAAH.
HUH? HOW BAD IS IT? HEEEY ......
WH-WHAT'S WITH YOU!?
KUI (TUG)
KUI
KUI
KUI
IT'S NONE OF YOUR BUSINESS, PSYCHO-TAN!
......!
WHAT WAS THAT YESTERDAY ANYWAY!?
WHY WERE YOU WITH MINAMI-KUN!?
AND WHY THE HECK WERE YOU HOLDING HIS HAND!!?
HIS HAND!?

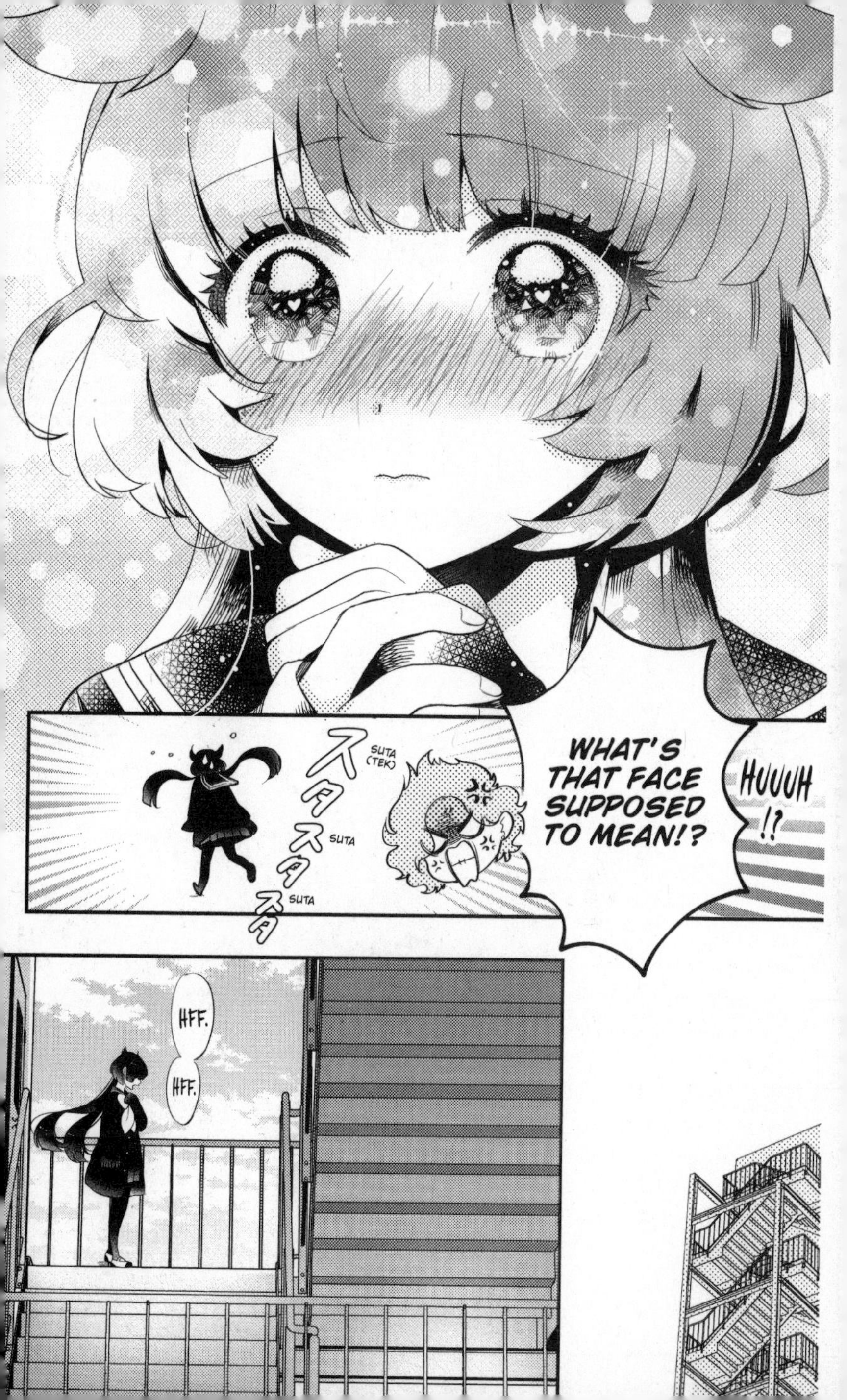
HUUUH !?
WHAT'S THAT FACE SUPPOSED TO MEAN!?
スタ
SUTA (TEK)
スタ
SUTA
スタ
SUTA
HFF.
HFF.

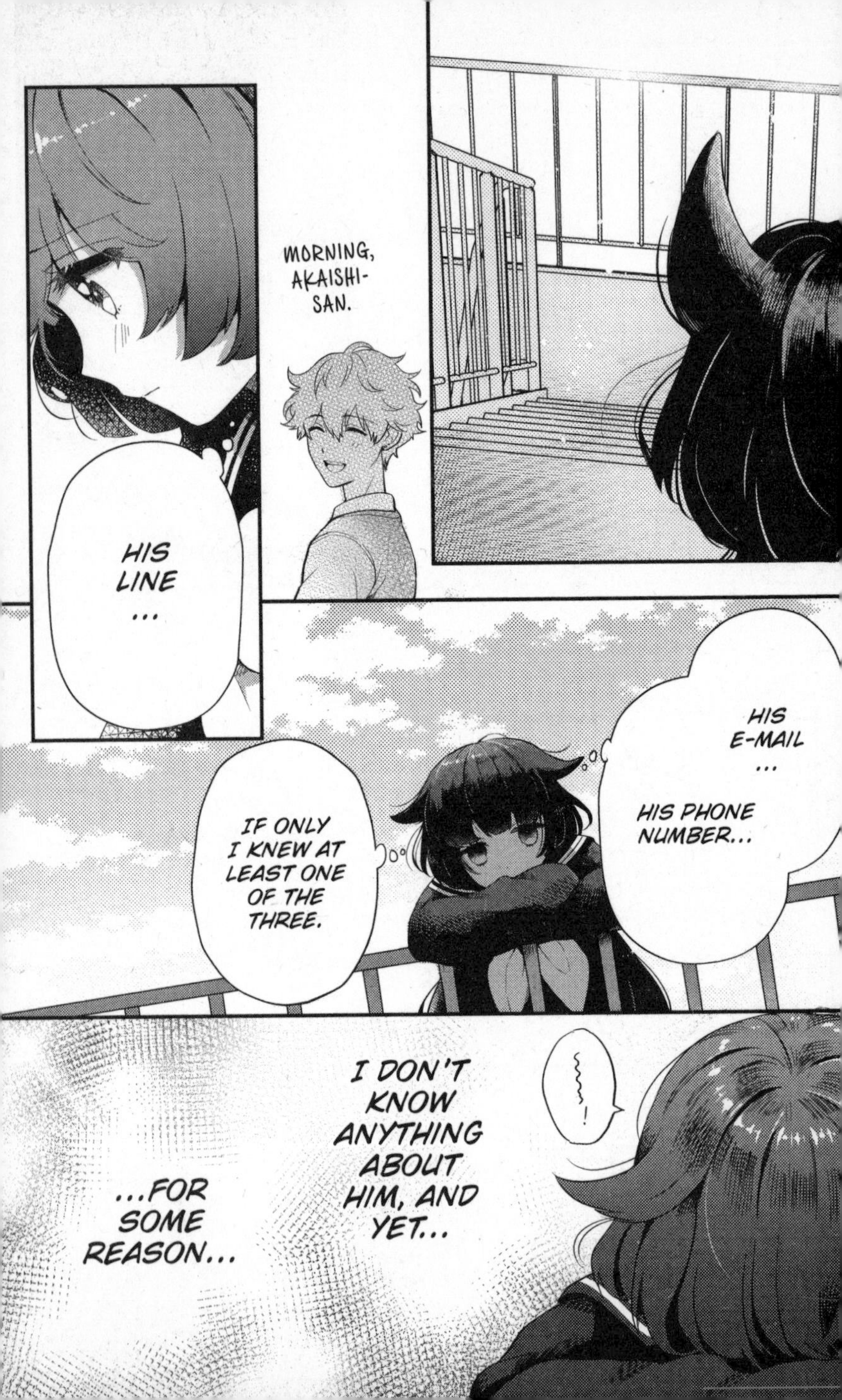
MORNING, AKAISHI-SAN.
HIS LINE...
HIS E-MAIL... HIS PHONE NUMBER...
IF ONLY I KNEW AT LEAST ONE OF THE THREE.
I DON'T KNOW ANYTHING ABOUT HIM, AND YET...
...FOR SOME REASON...

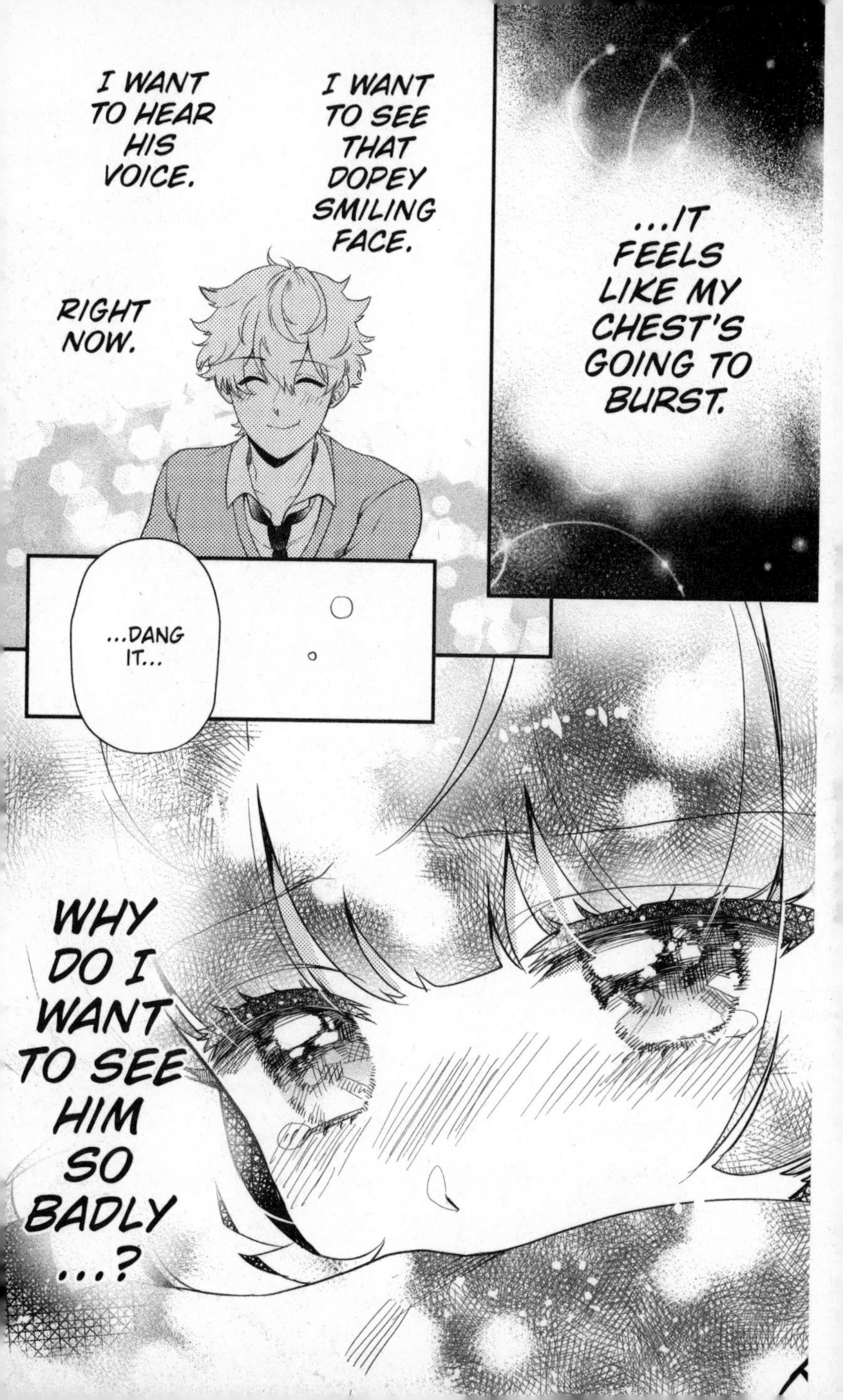
...IT FEELS LIKE MY CHEST'S GOING TO BURST.
I WANT TO SEE THAT DOPEY SMILING FACE.
I WANT TO HEAR HIS VOICE.
RIGHT NOW.
...DANG IT...
WHY DO I WANT TO SEE HIM SO BADLY ...?

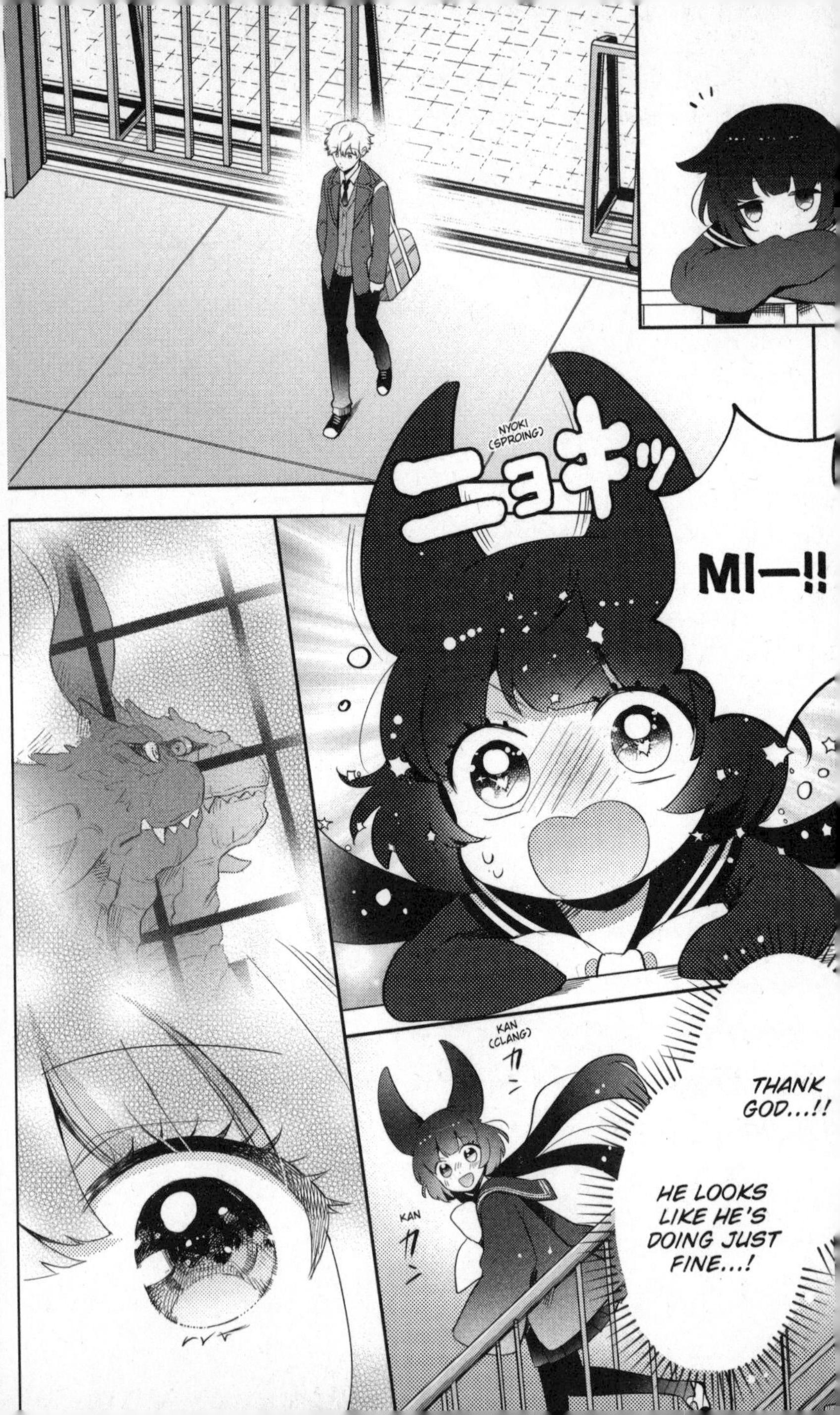
NYOKI (SPROING)
ニョキッ
MI—!!
KAN (CLANG)
カン
KAN
カン
THANK GOD...!!
HE LOOKS LIKE HE'S DOING JUST FINE...!

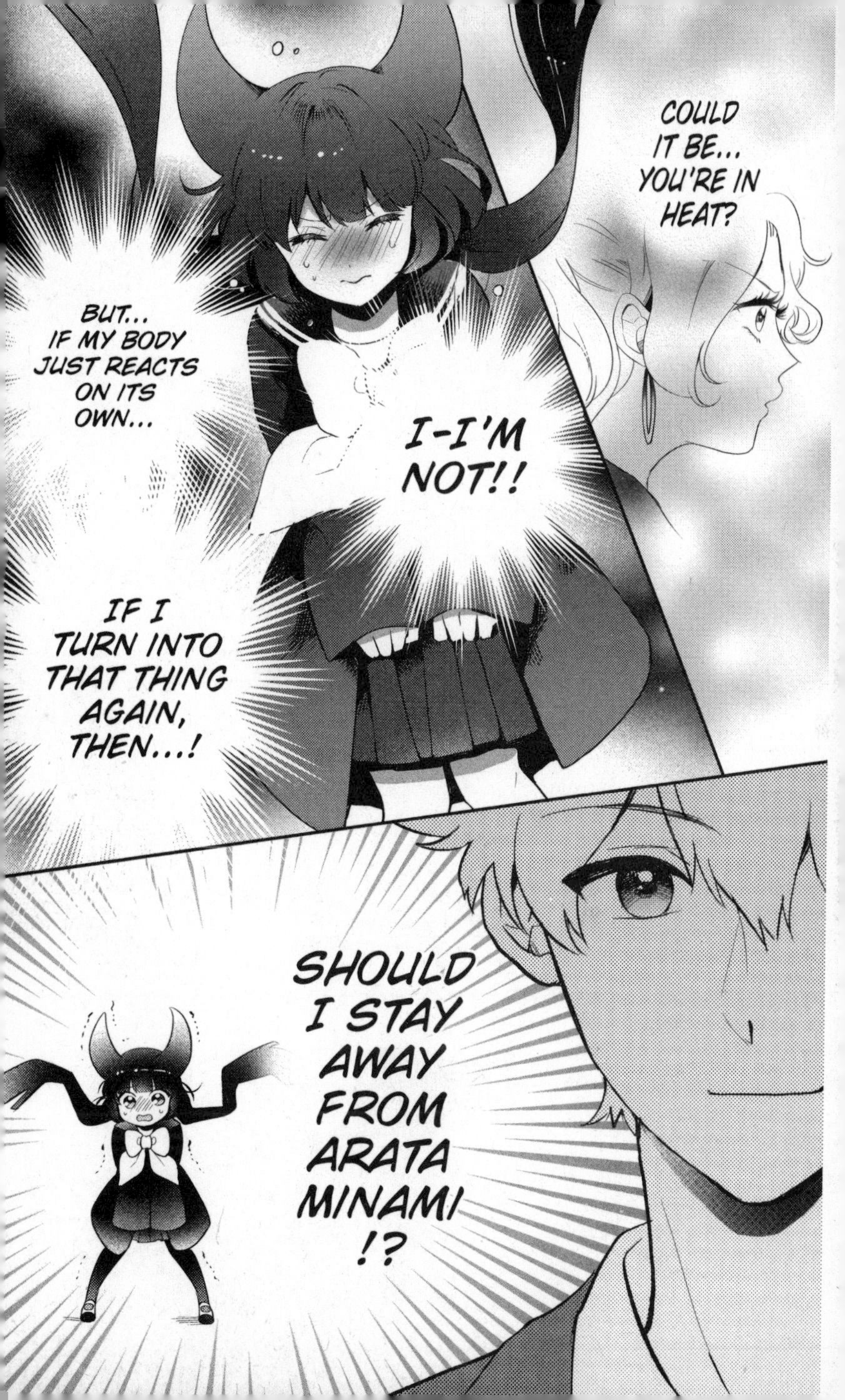
COULD IT BE... YOU'RE IN HEAT?
I-I'M NOT!!
BUT... IF MY BODY JUST REACTS ON ITS OWN...
IF I TURN INTO THAT THING AGAIN, THEN...!
SHOULD I STAY AWAY FROM ARATA MINAMI!?

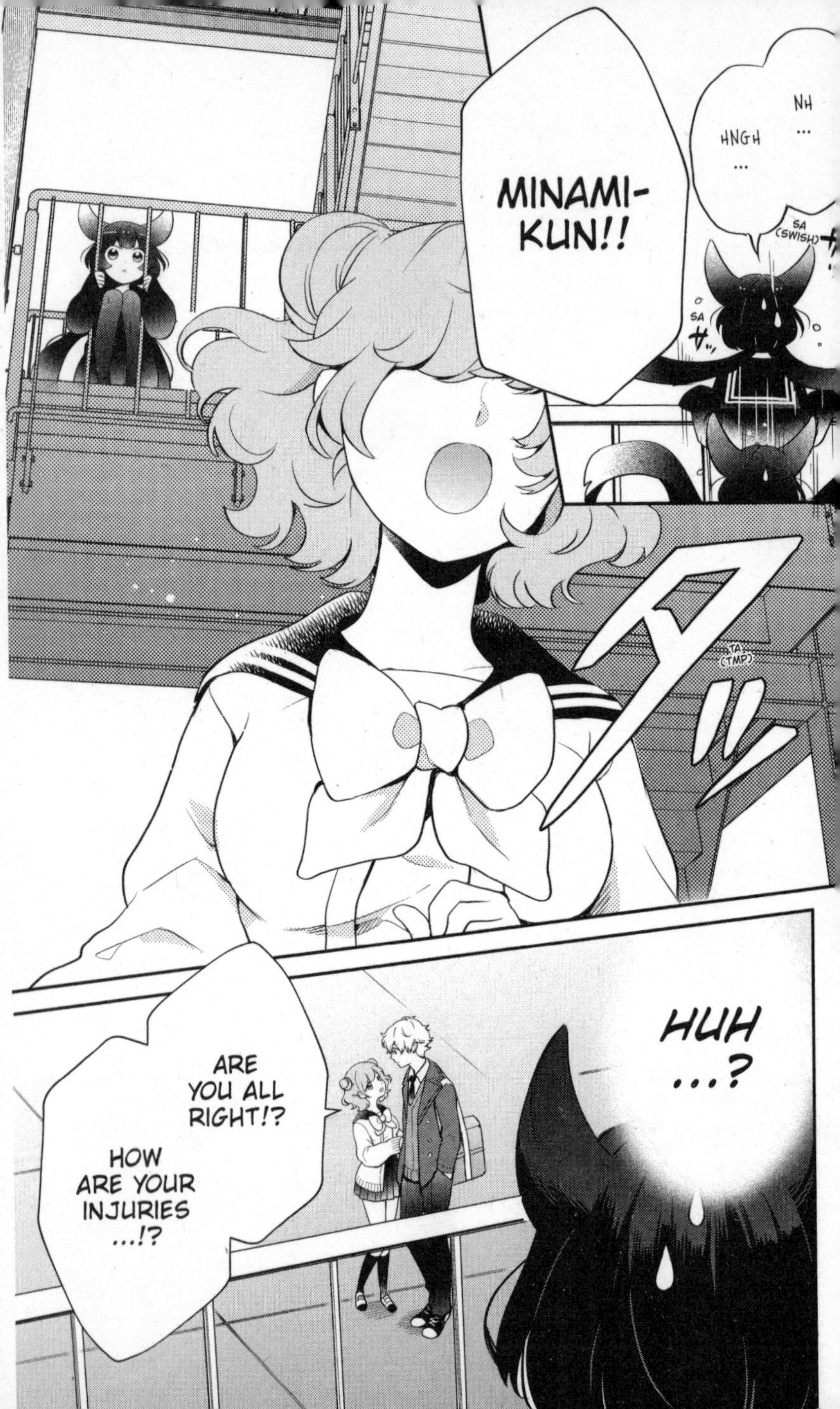
NH ... HNGH ...
SA (SWISH)
SA
MINAMI-KUN!!
TA (TMP)
HUH ...?
ARE YOU ALL RIGHT!?
HOW ARE YOUR INJURIES ...!?

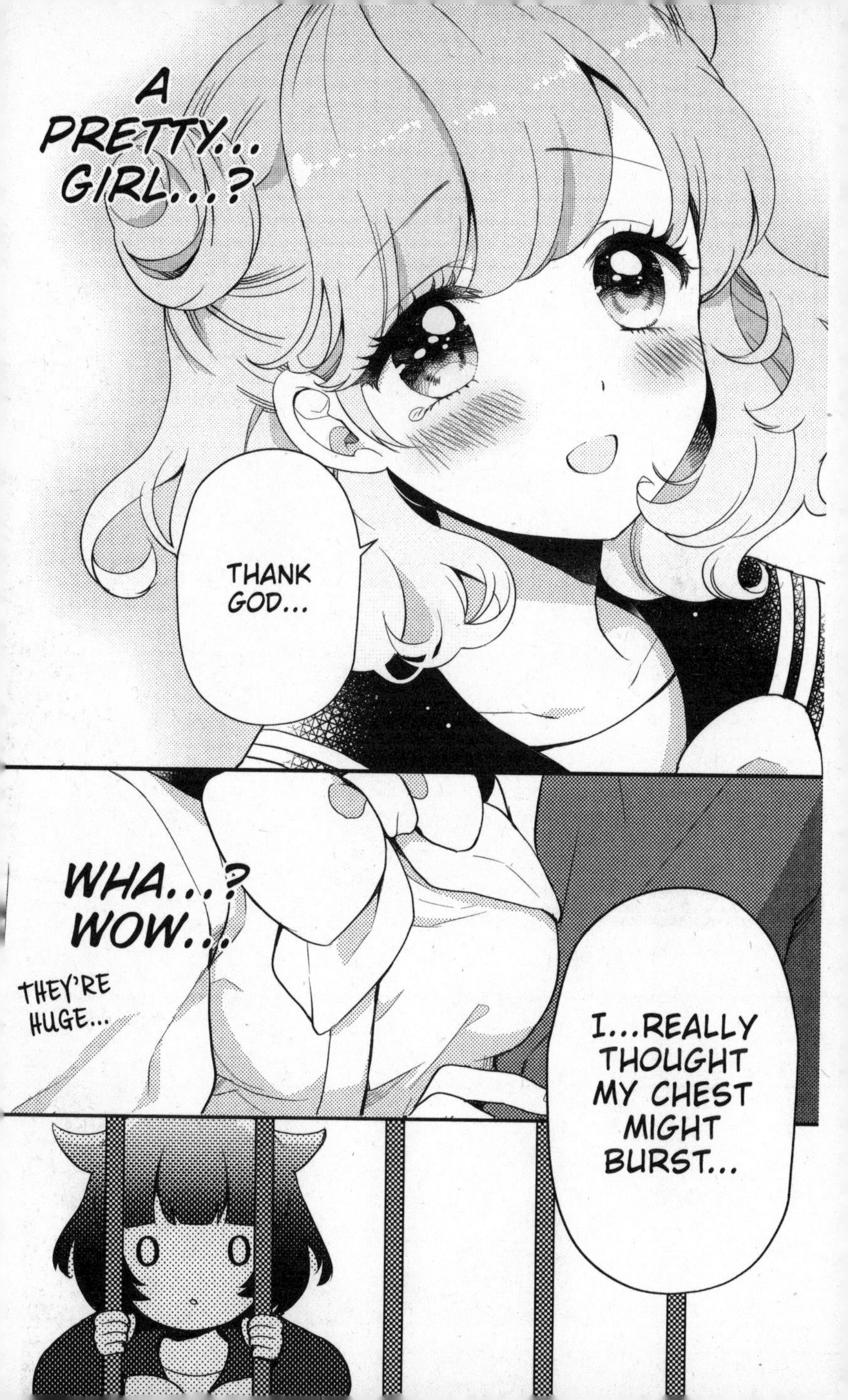
A PRETTY... GIRL...?
THANK GOD...
I...REALLY THOUGHT MY CHEST MIGHT BURST...
WHA...? WOW...
THEY'RE HUGE...

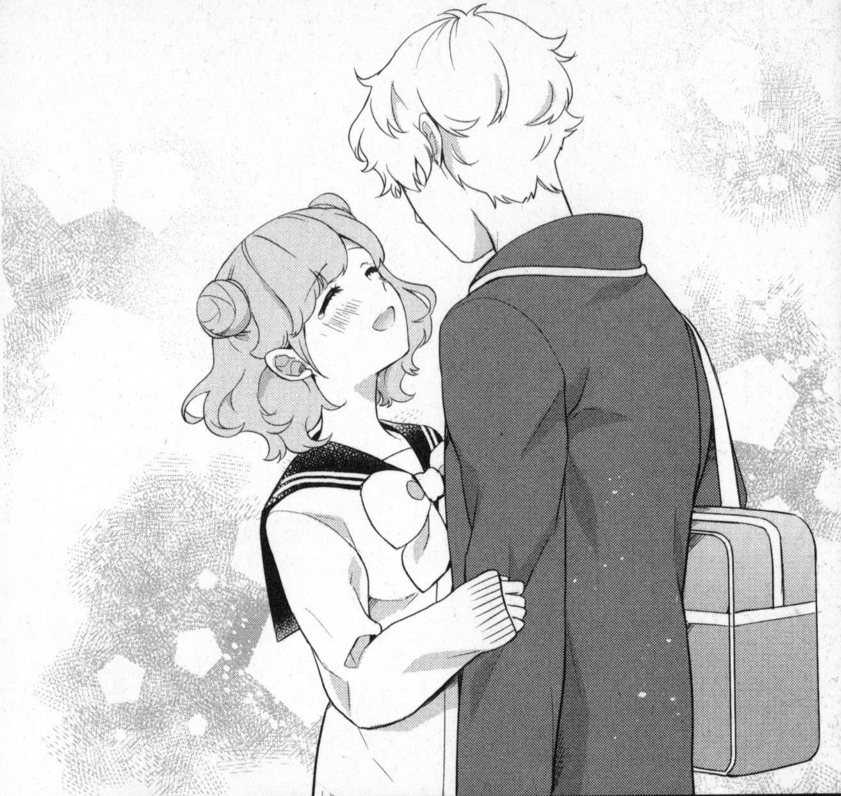
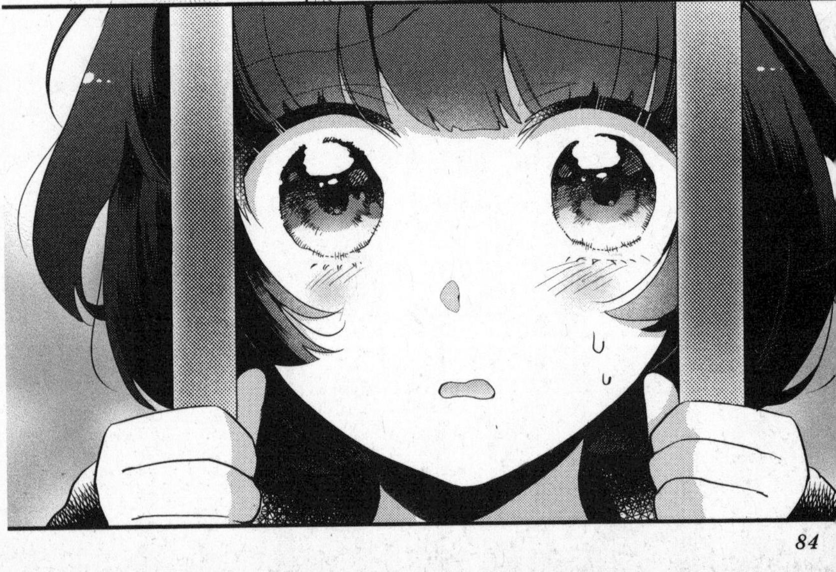

KAIJU♥GIRL
CARAMELISE

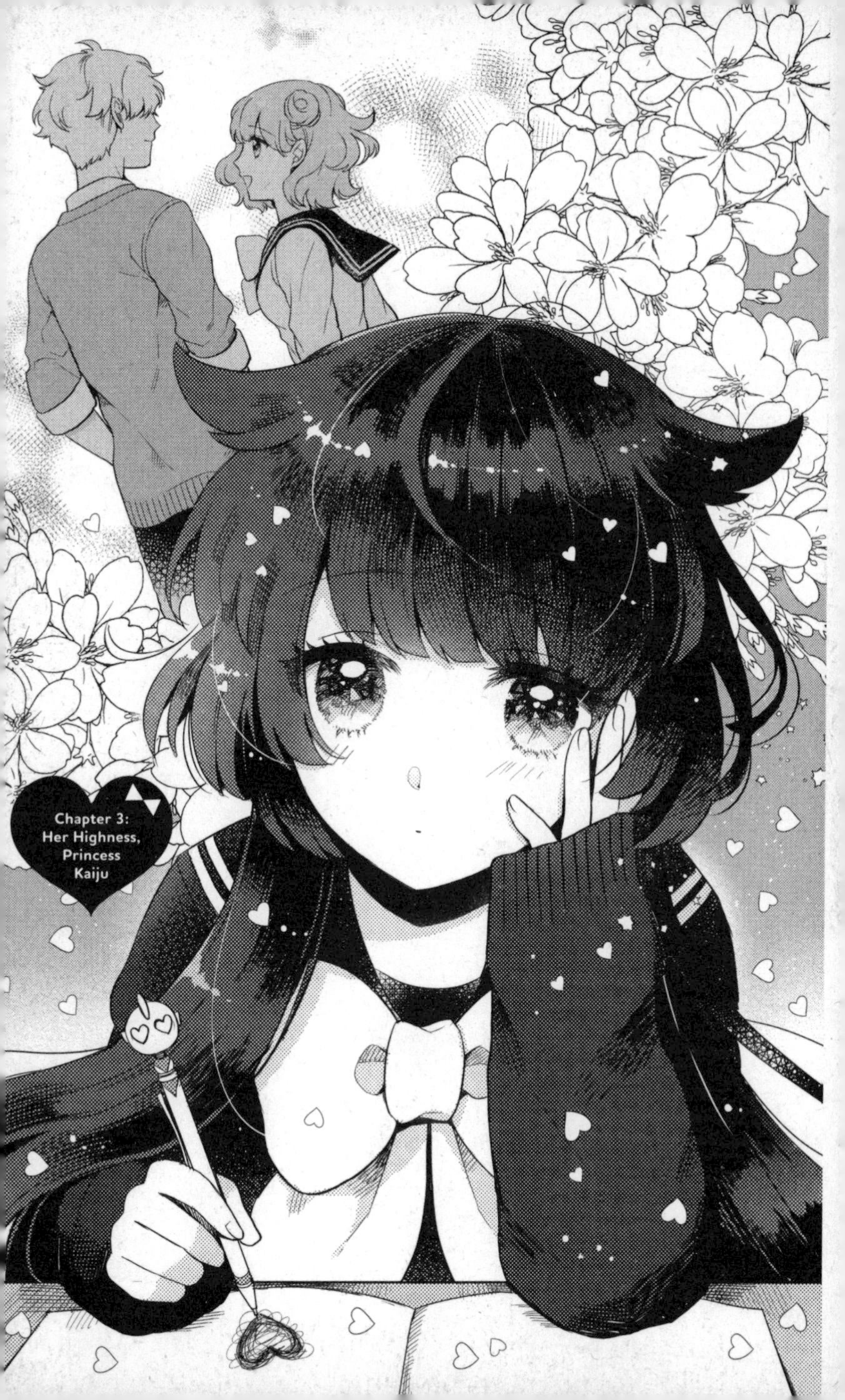
Chapter 3:
Her Highness,
Princess
Kaiju

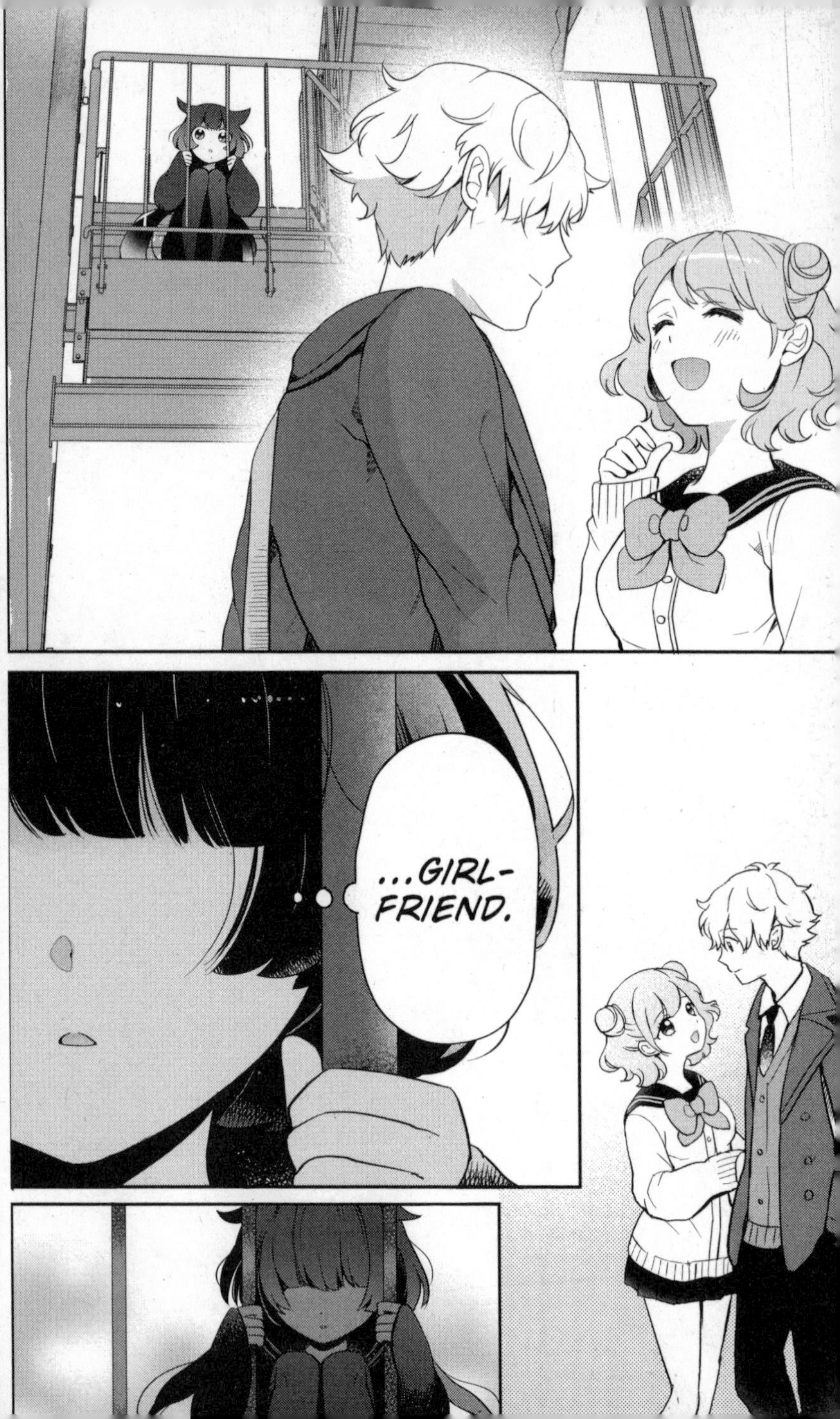
...GIRL-
FRIEND.

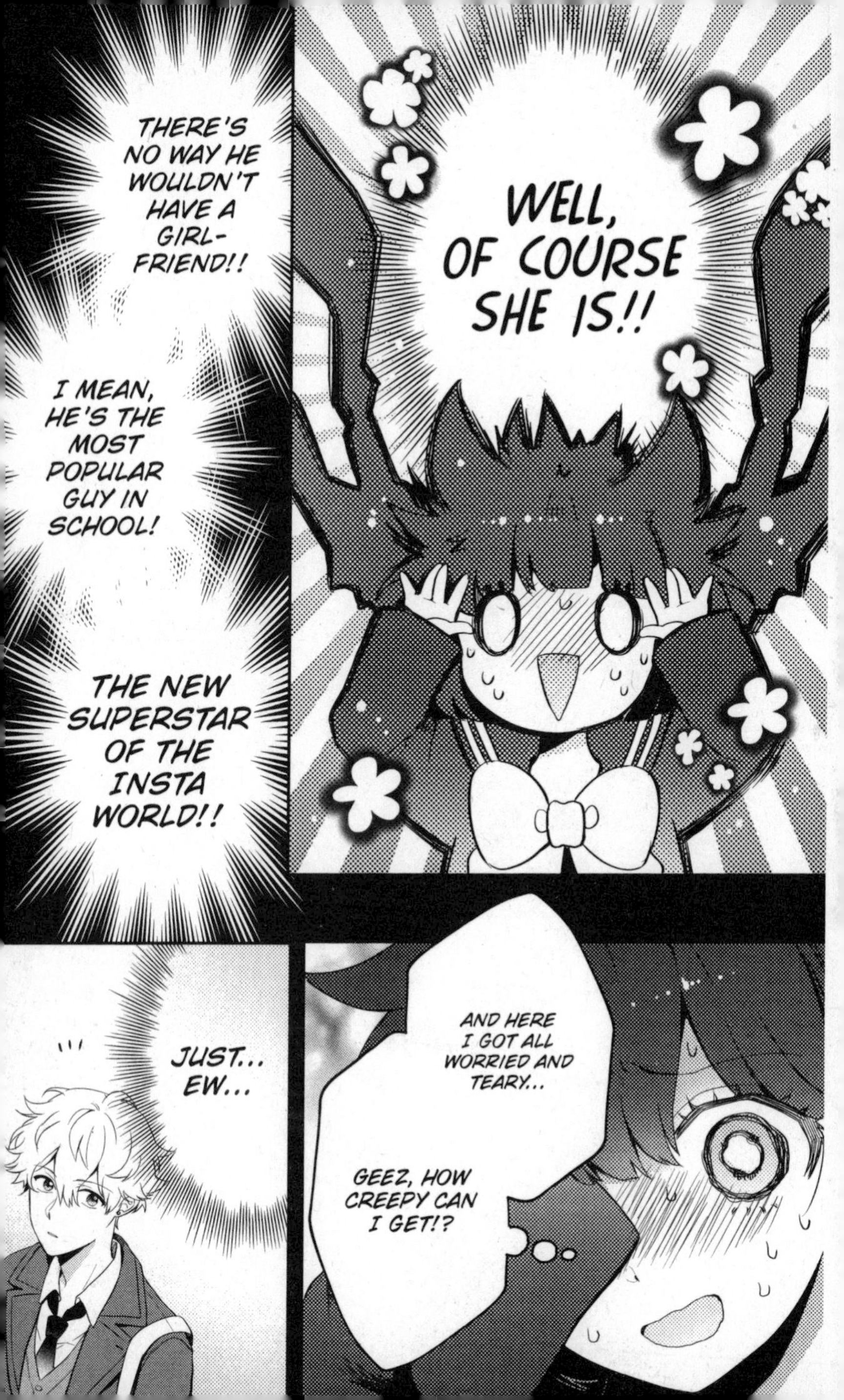
WELL, OF COURSE SHE IS!!
THERE'S NO WAY HE WOULDN'T HAVE A GIRL-FRIEND!!
I MEAN, HE'S THE MOST POPULAR GUY IN SCHOOL!
THE NEW SUPERSTAR OF THE INSTA WORLD!!
AND HERE I GOT ALL WORRIED AND TEARY...
GEEZ, HOW CREEPY CAN I GET!?
JUST... EW...

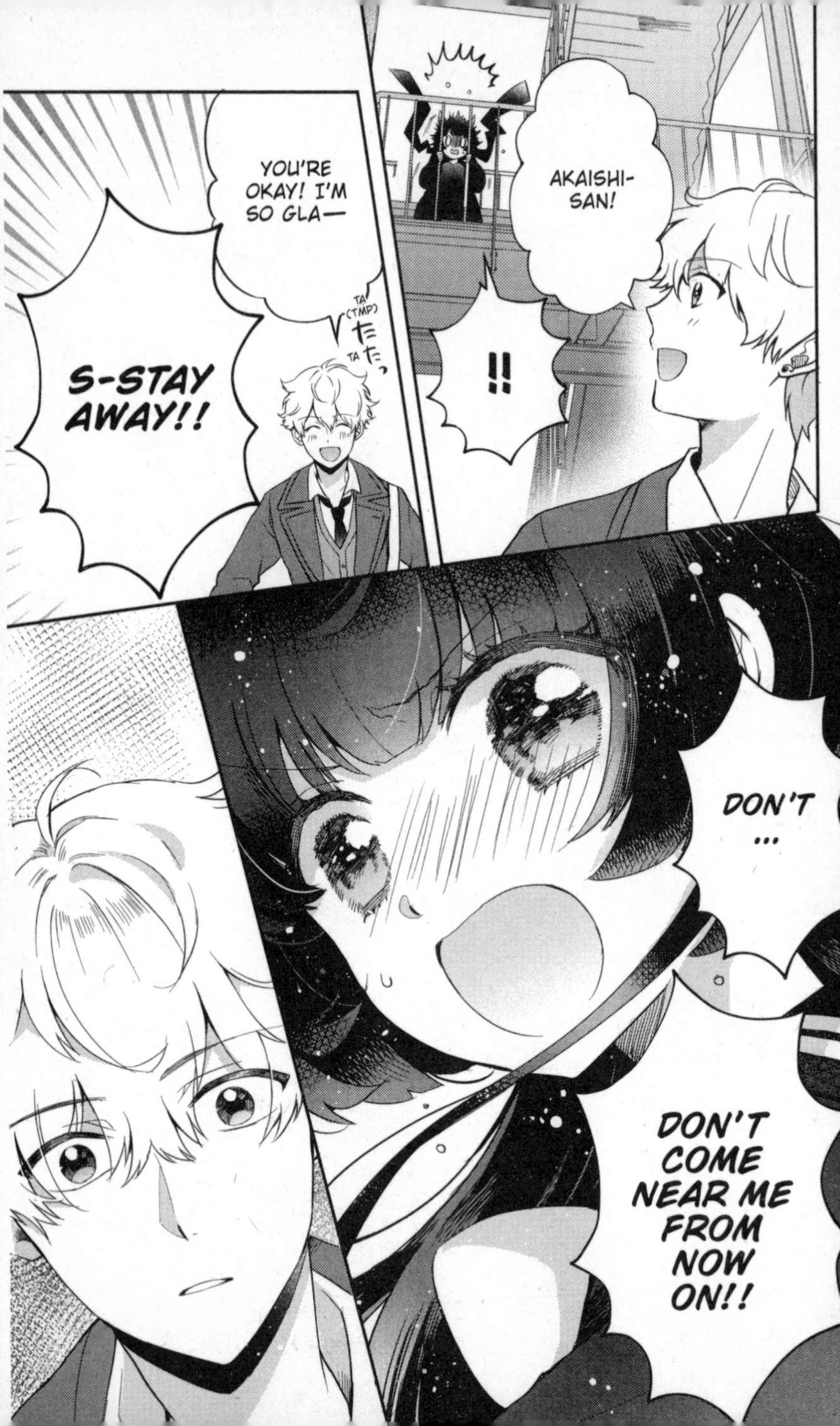
AKAISHI-SAN!
!!
YOU'RE OKAY! I'M SO GLA—
TA (TMP) たたっ TA
S-STAY AWAY!!
DON'T ...
DON'T COME NEAR ME FROM NOW ON!!

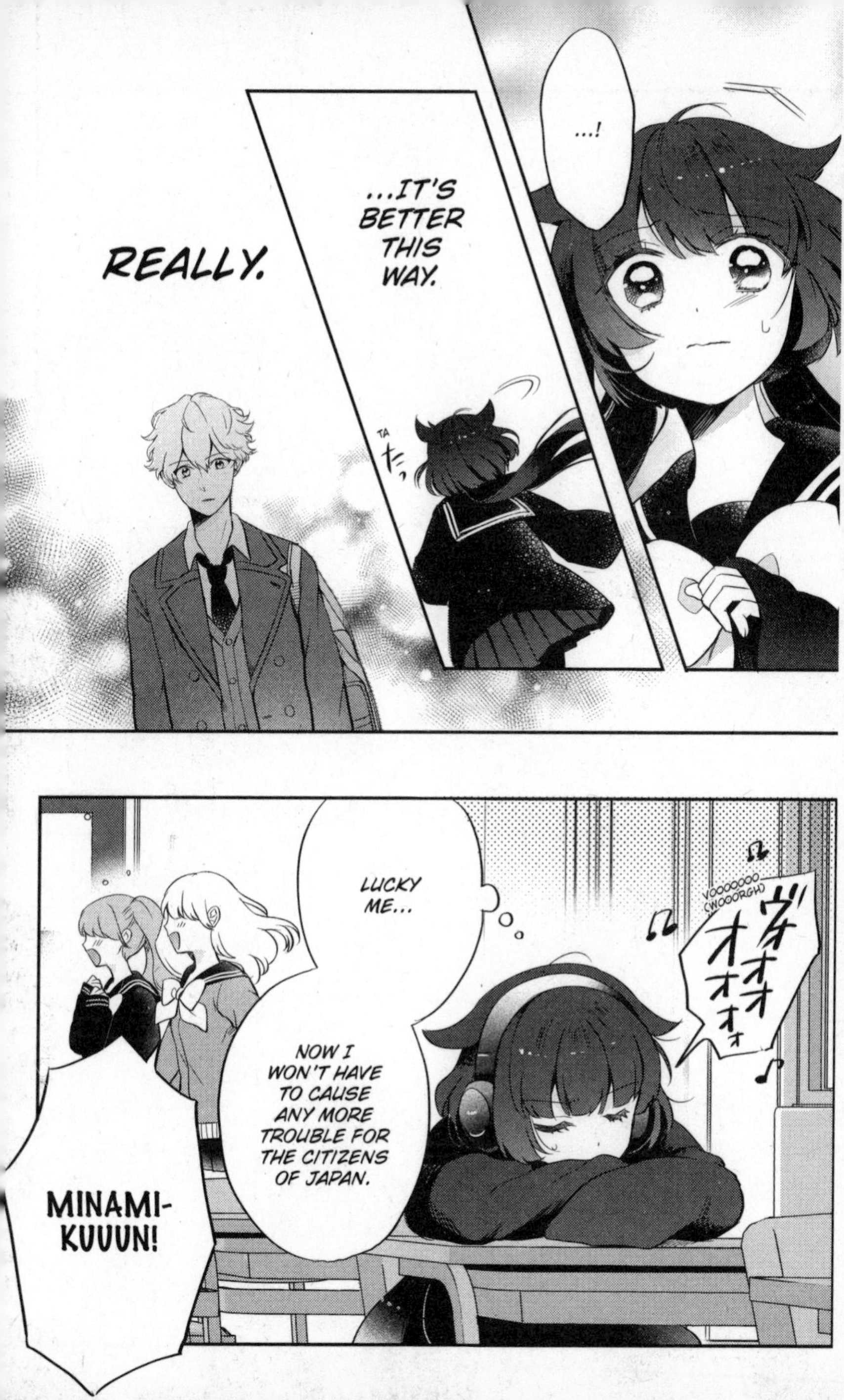
...!
...IT'S BETTER THIS WAY.
TA
たっ
REALLY.
ヴォオオオオオォ
VOOOOOOO (WOOORGH)
LUCKY ME...
NOW I WON'T HAVE TO CAUSE ANY MORE TROUBLE FOR THE CITIZENS OF JAPAN.
MINAMI-KUUUN!

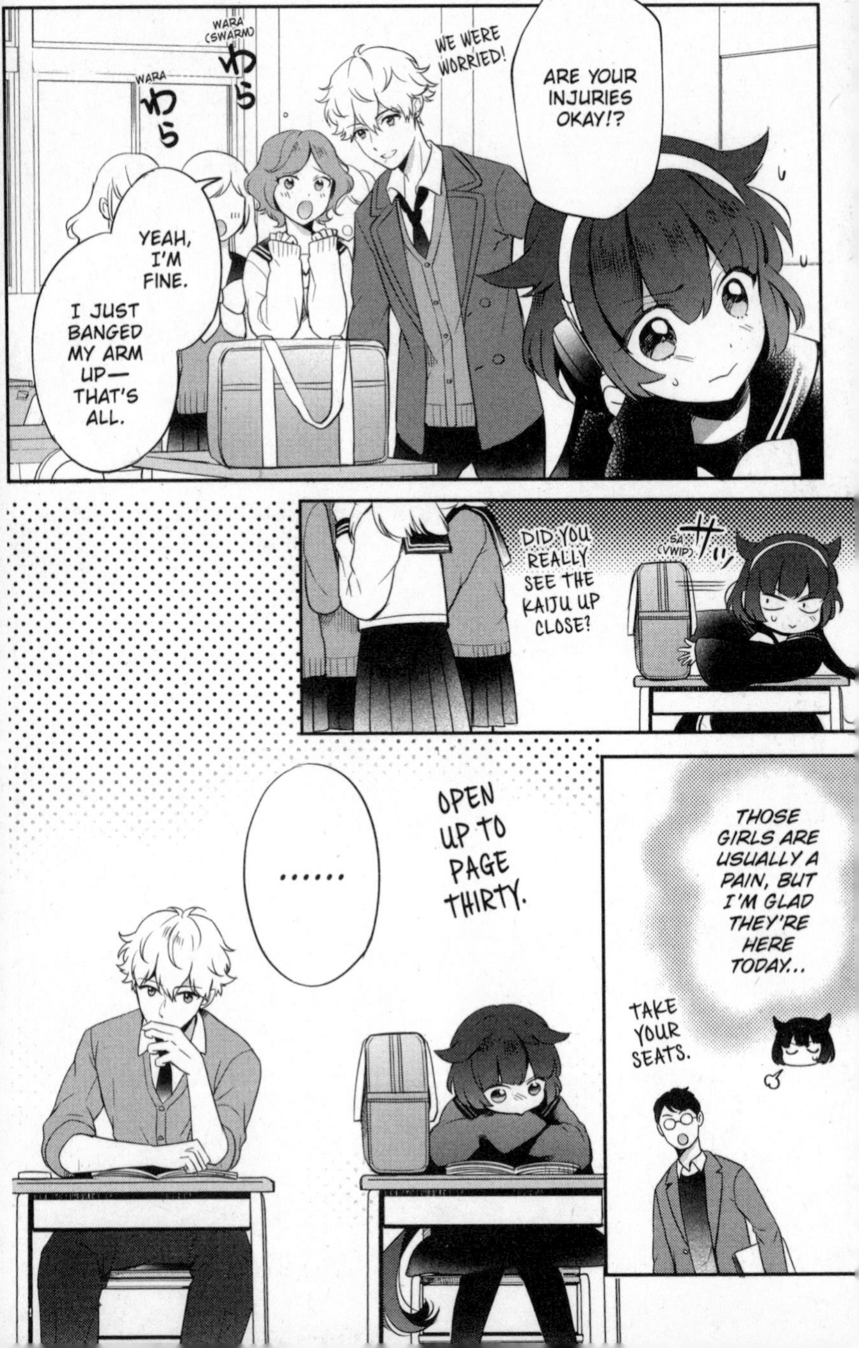
ARE YOUR INJURIES OKAY!?
WE WERE WORRIED!
WARA (SWARM) わら
WARA わら
YEAH, I'M FINE.
I JUST BANGED MY ARM UP— THAT'S ALL.
SA (VWIP) サッ
DID YOU REALLY SEE THE KAIJU UP CLOSE?
THOSE GIRLS ARE USUALLY A PAIN, BUT I'M GLAD THEY'RE HERE TODAY...
TAKE YOUR SEATS.
OPEN UP TO PAGE THIRTY.
......

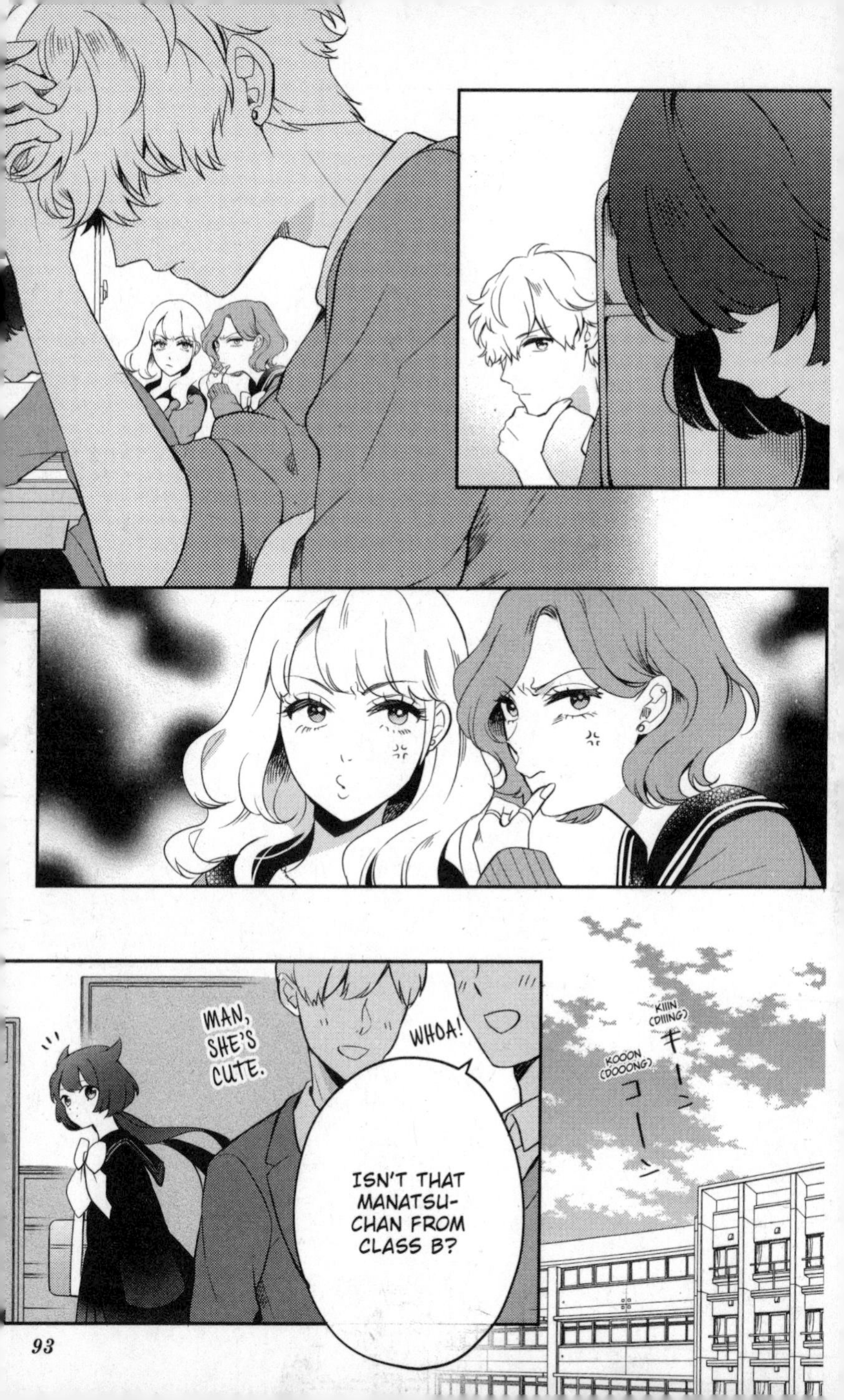
KIIIN (DIIING)
キーン
KOOON (DOOONG)
コーン
ISN'T THAT MANATSU-CHAN FROM CLASS B?
WHOA!
MAN, SHE'S CUTE.

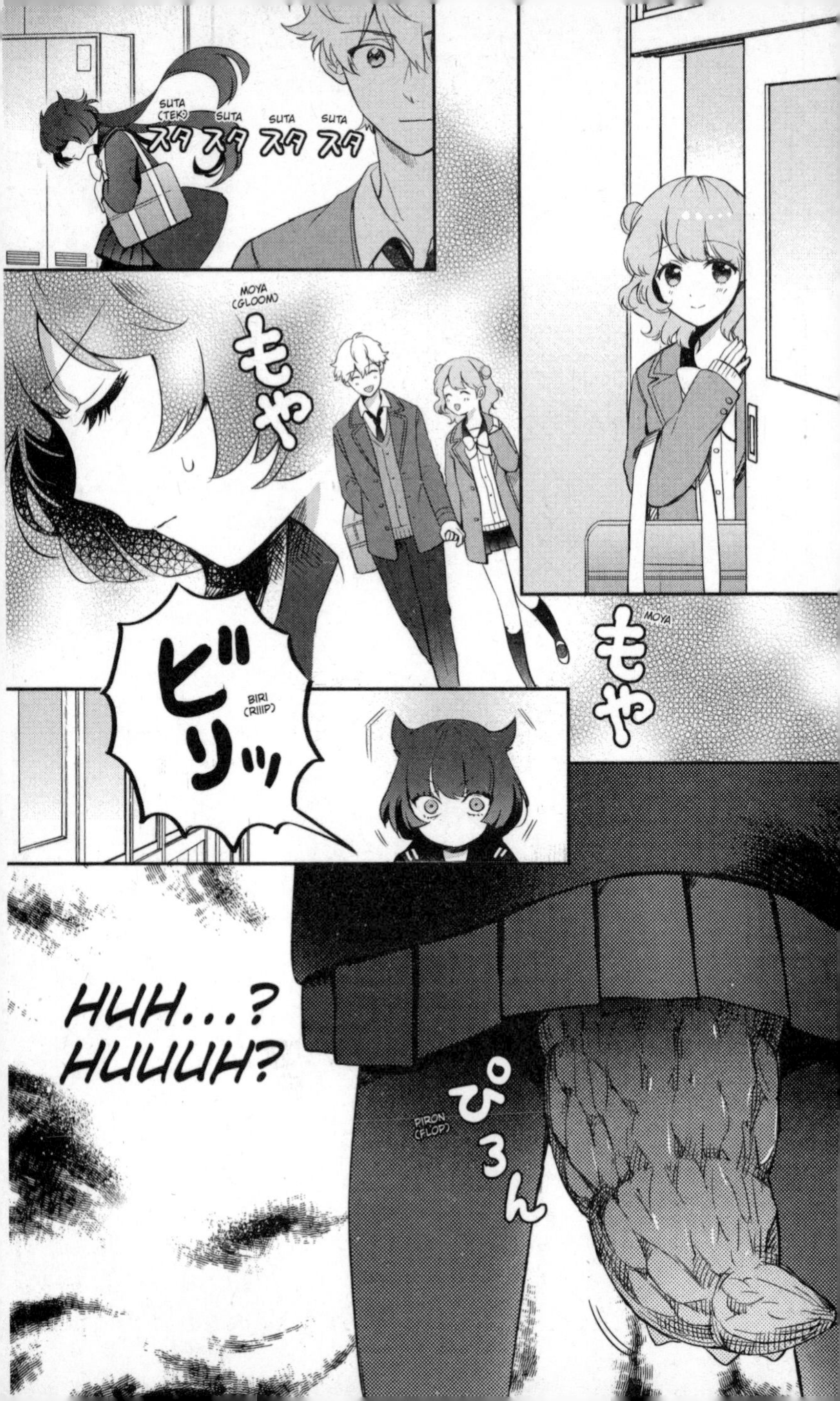
SUTA (TEK)
スタ
SUTA
スタ
SUTA
スタ
SUTA
スタ
MOYA (GLOOM)
もや
MOYA
もや
ビリッ
BIRI (RIIIP)
HUH...? HUUUH?
ぴろん
PIRON (FLOP)

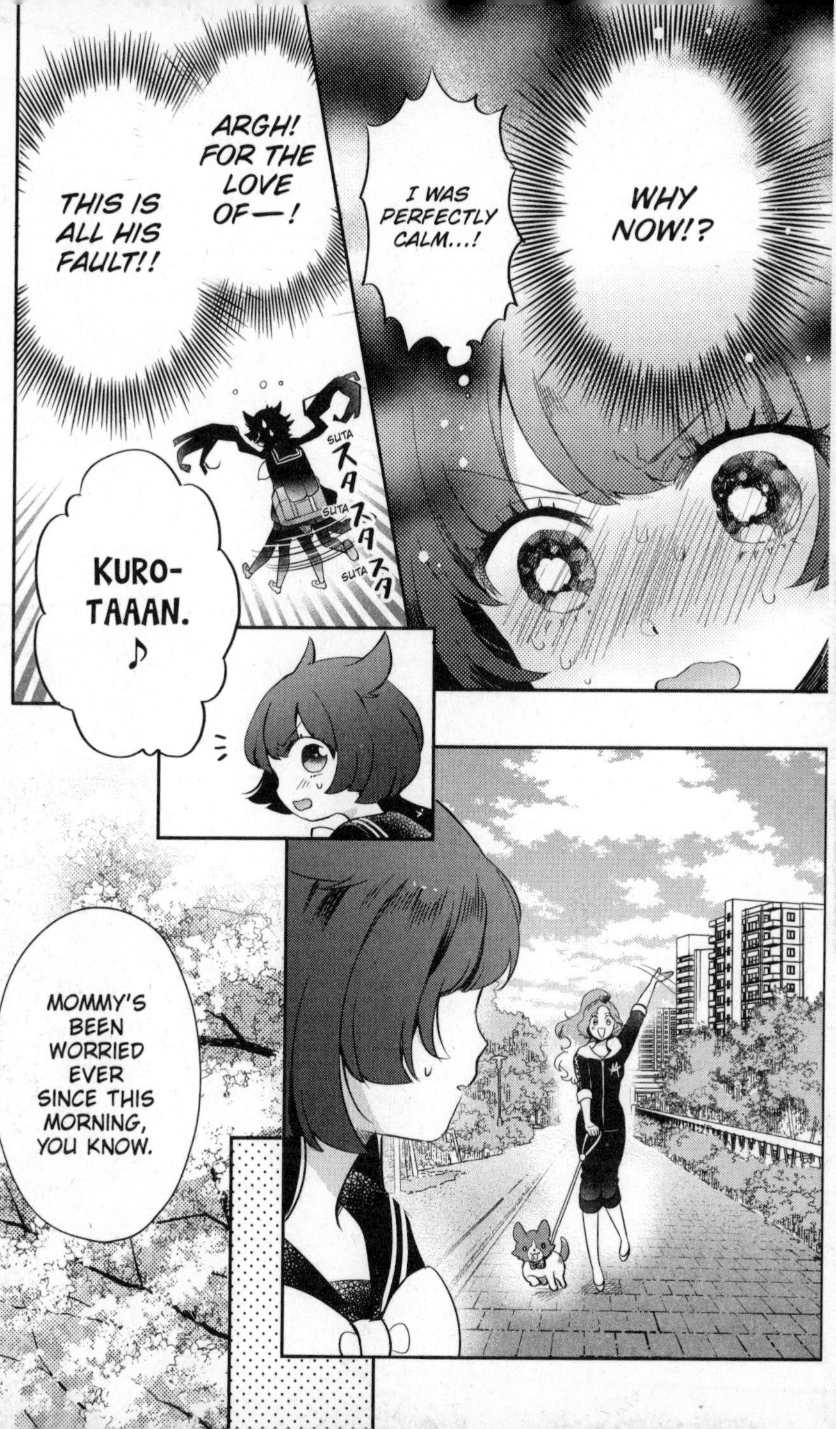
WHY NOW!?
I WAS PERFECTLY CALM...!
ARGH! FOR THE LOVE OF—!
THIS IS ALL HIS FAULT!!
SUTA
SUTA
SUTA
KURO-TAAAN. ♪
MOMMY'S BEEN WORRIED EVER SINCE THIS MORNING, YOU KNOW.

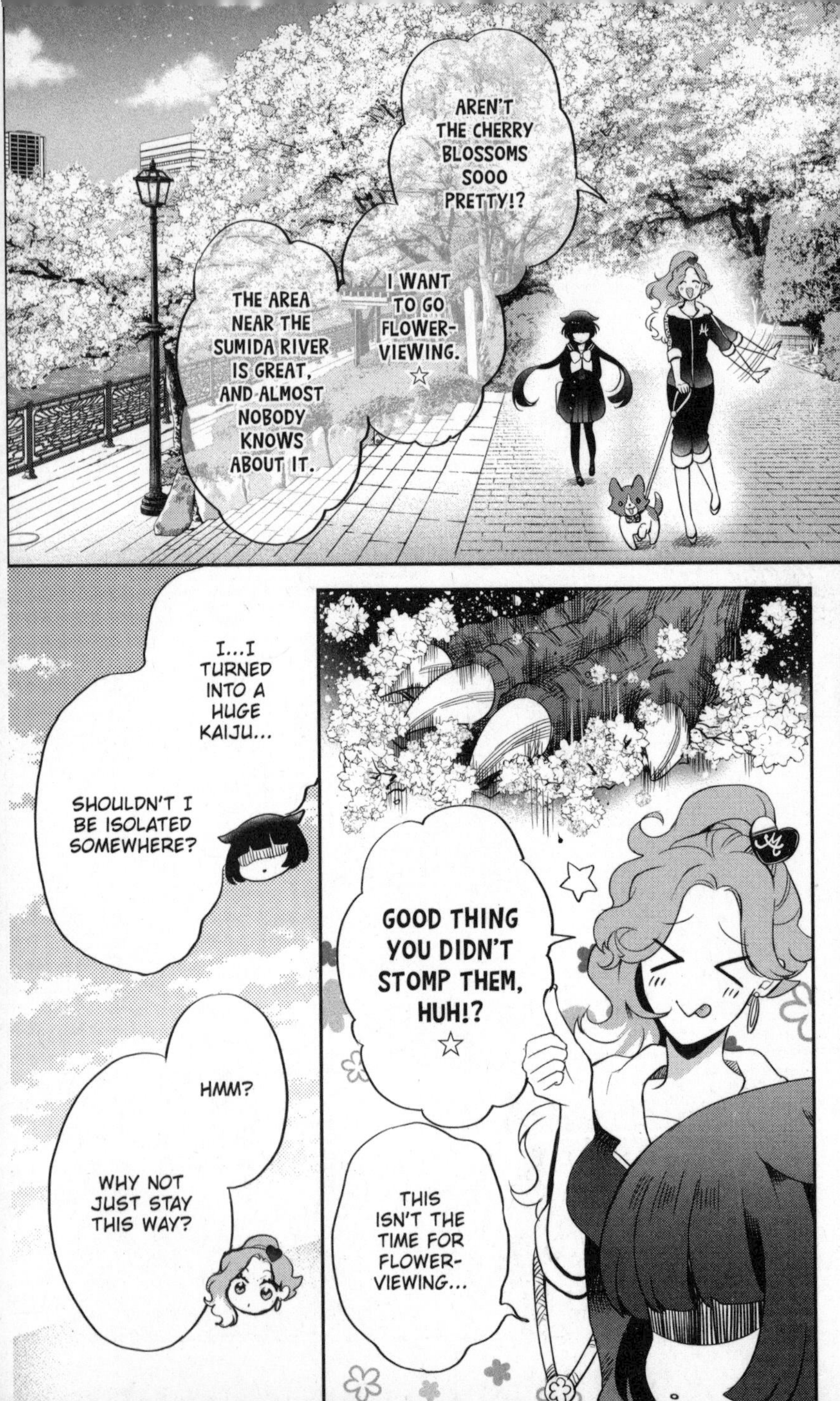
AREN'T THE CHERRY BLOSSOMS SOOO PRETTY!?
I WANT TO GO FLOWER-VIEWING. ☆
THE AREA NEAR THE SUMIDA RIVER IS GREAT, AND ALMOST NOBODY KNOWS ABOUT IT.
GOOD THING YOU DIDN'T STOMP THEM, HUH!? ☆
THIS ISN'T THE TIME FOR FLOWER-VIEWING...
I...I TURNED INTO A HUGE KAIJU...
SHOULDN'T I BE ISOLATED SOMEWHERE?
HMM?
WHY NOT JUST STAY THIS WAY?

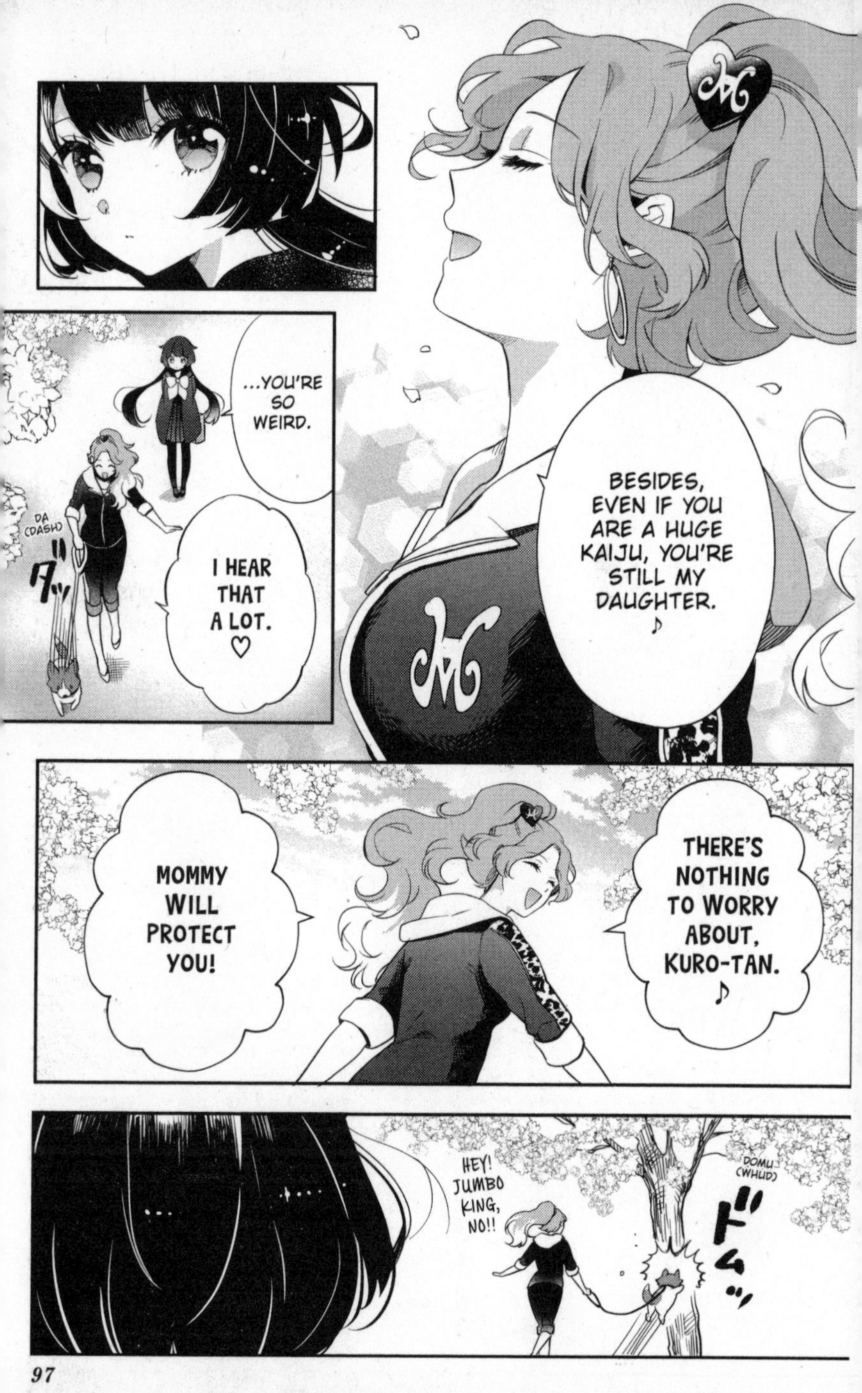
BESIDES, EVEN IF YOU ARE A HUGE KAIJU, YOU'RE STILL MY DAUGHTER. ♪
...YOU'RE SO WEIRD.
I HEAR THAT A LOT. ♡
DA (DASH)
THERE'S NOTHING TO WORRY ABOUT, KURO-TAN. ♪
MOMMY WILL PROTECT YOU!
DOMU (WHUD)
HEY! JUMBO KING, NO!!

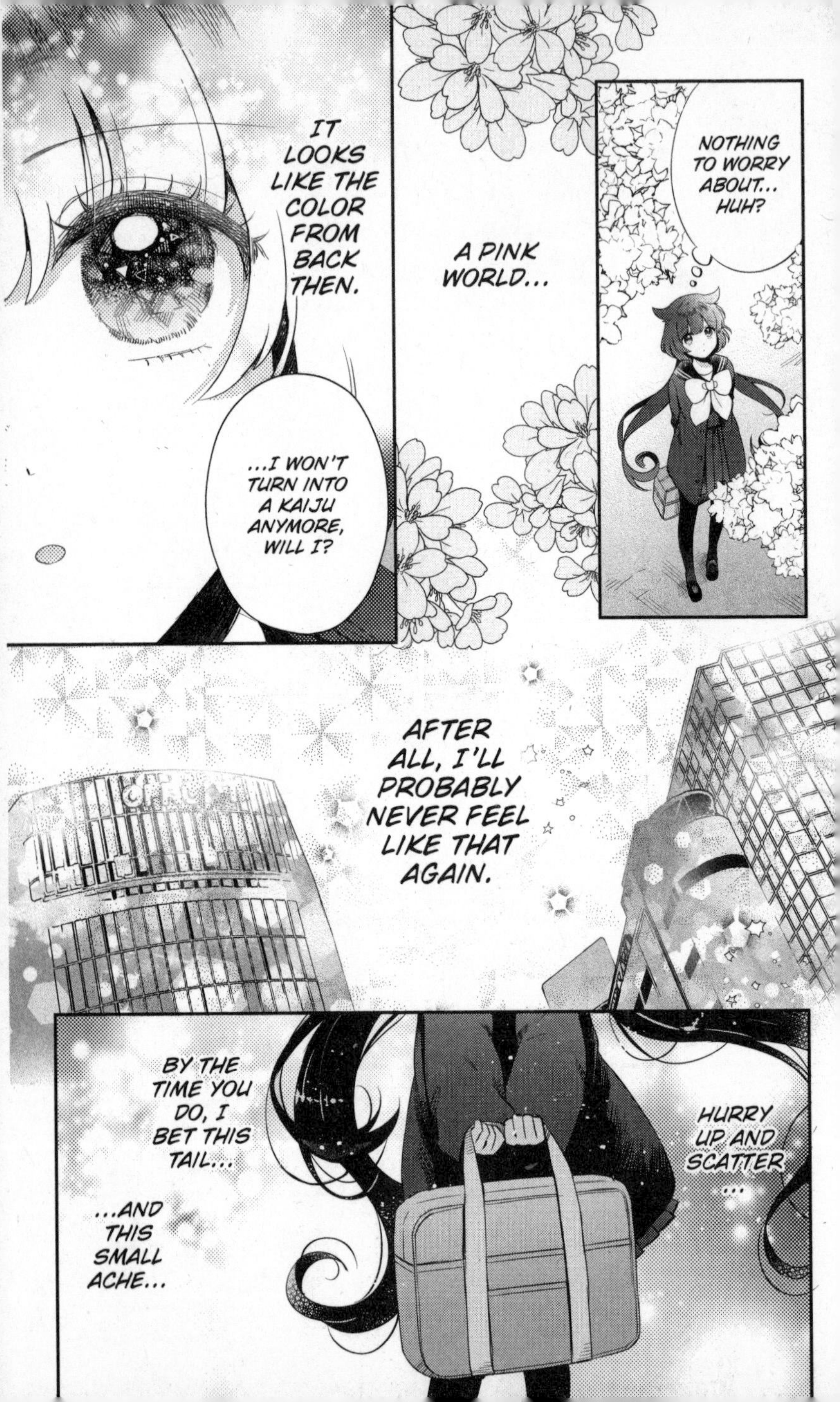
NOTHING TO WORRY ABOUT... HUH?
A PINK WORLD...
IT LOOKS LIKE THE COLOR FROM BACK THEN.
...I WON'T TURN INTO A KAIJU ANYMORE, WILL I?
AFTER ALL, I'LL PROBABLY NEVER FEEL LIKE THAT AGAIN.
HURRY UP AND SCATTER...
BY THE TIME YOU DO, I BET THIS TAIL...
...AND THIS SMALL ACHE...

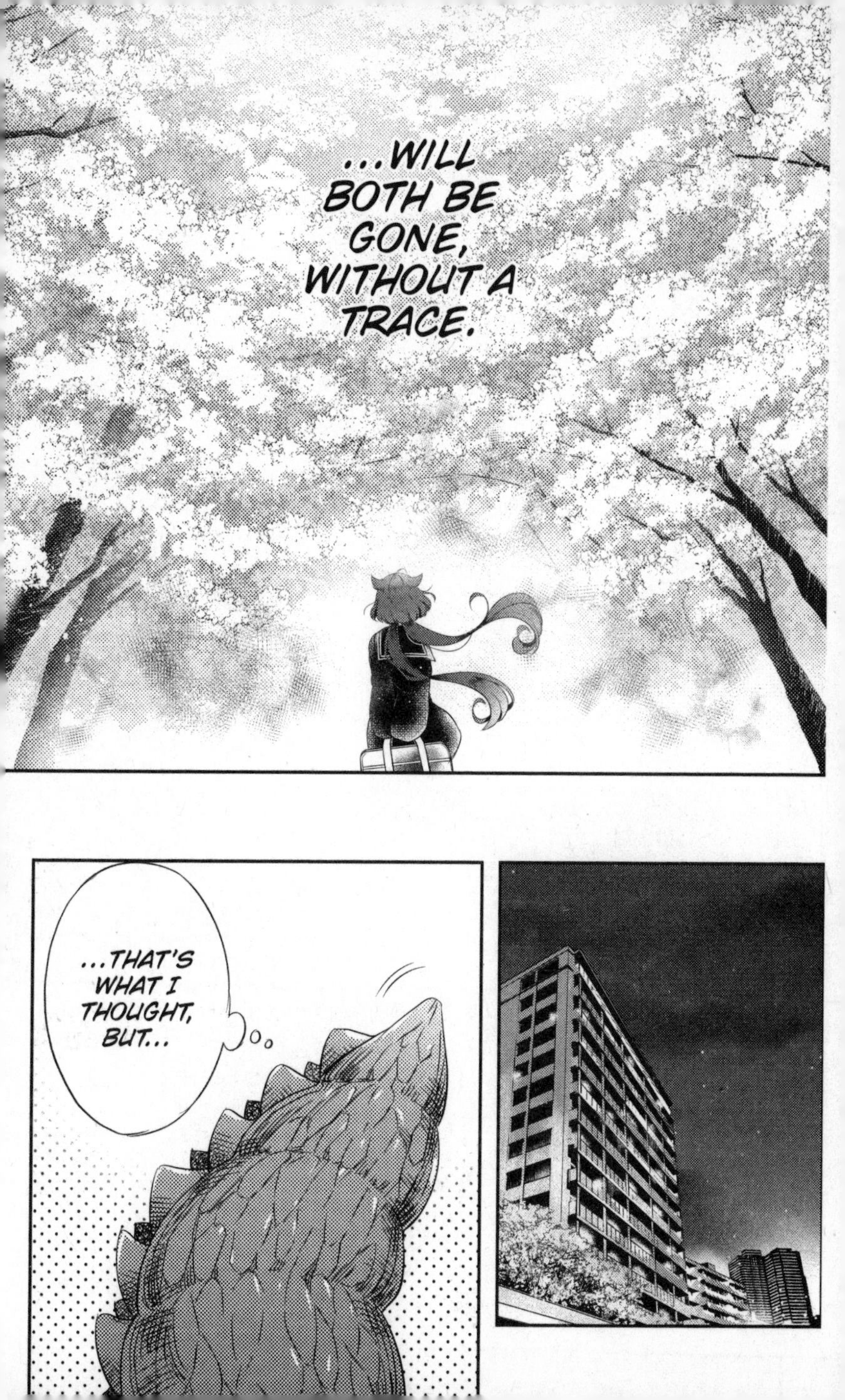
...WILL BOTH BE GONE, WITHOUT A TRACE.
...THAT'S WHAT I THOUGHT, BUT...

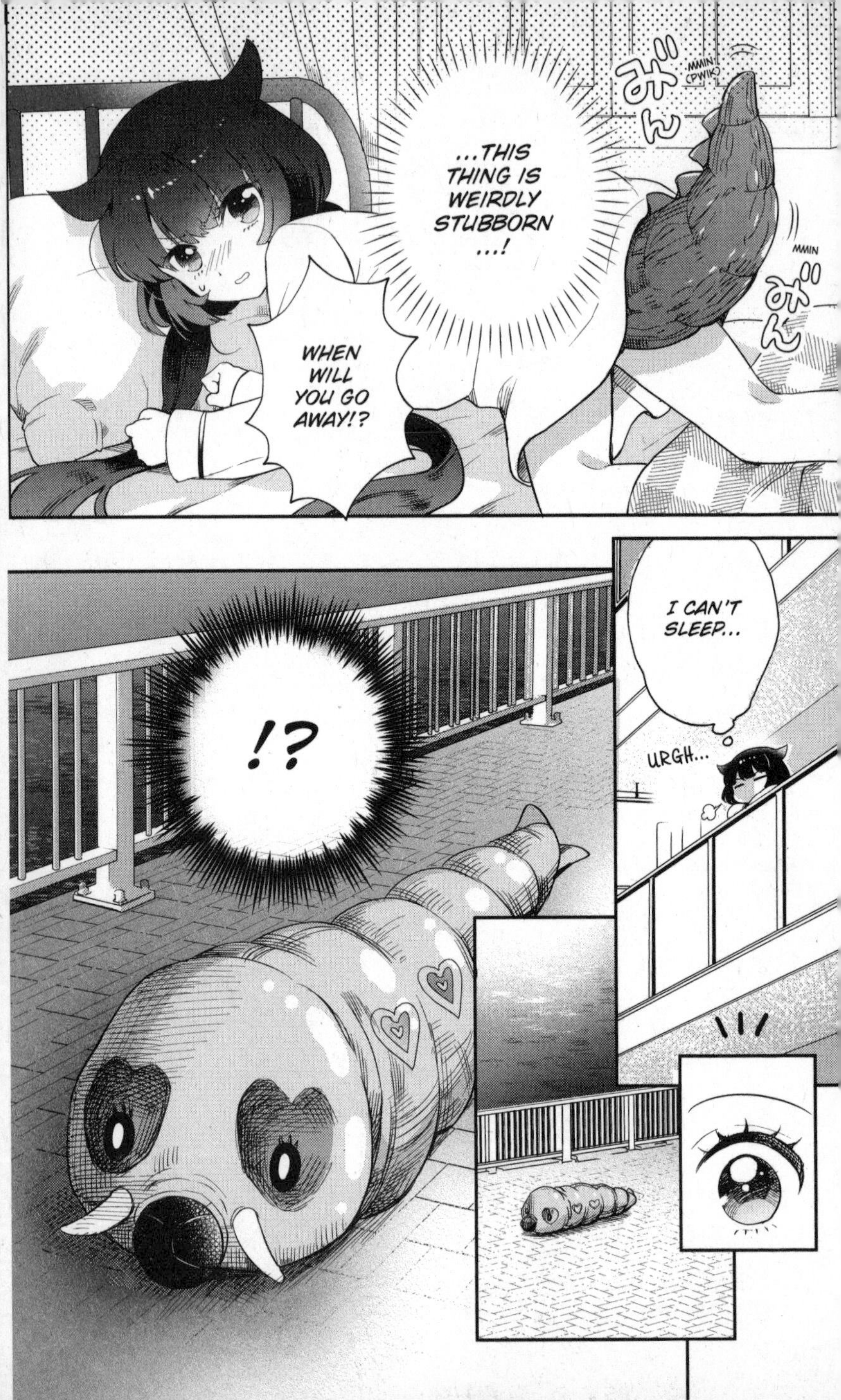
みん
MMIN (PWIK)
...THIS THING IS WEIRDLY STUBBORN ...!
MMIN
みん
WHEN WILL YOU GO AWAY!?
I CAN'T SLEEP...
URGH...
!?

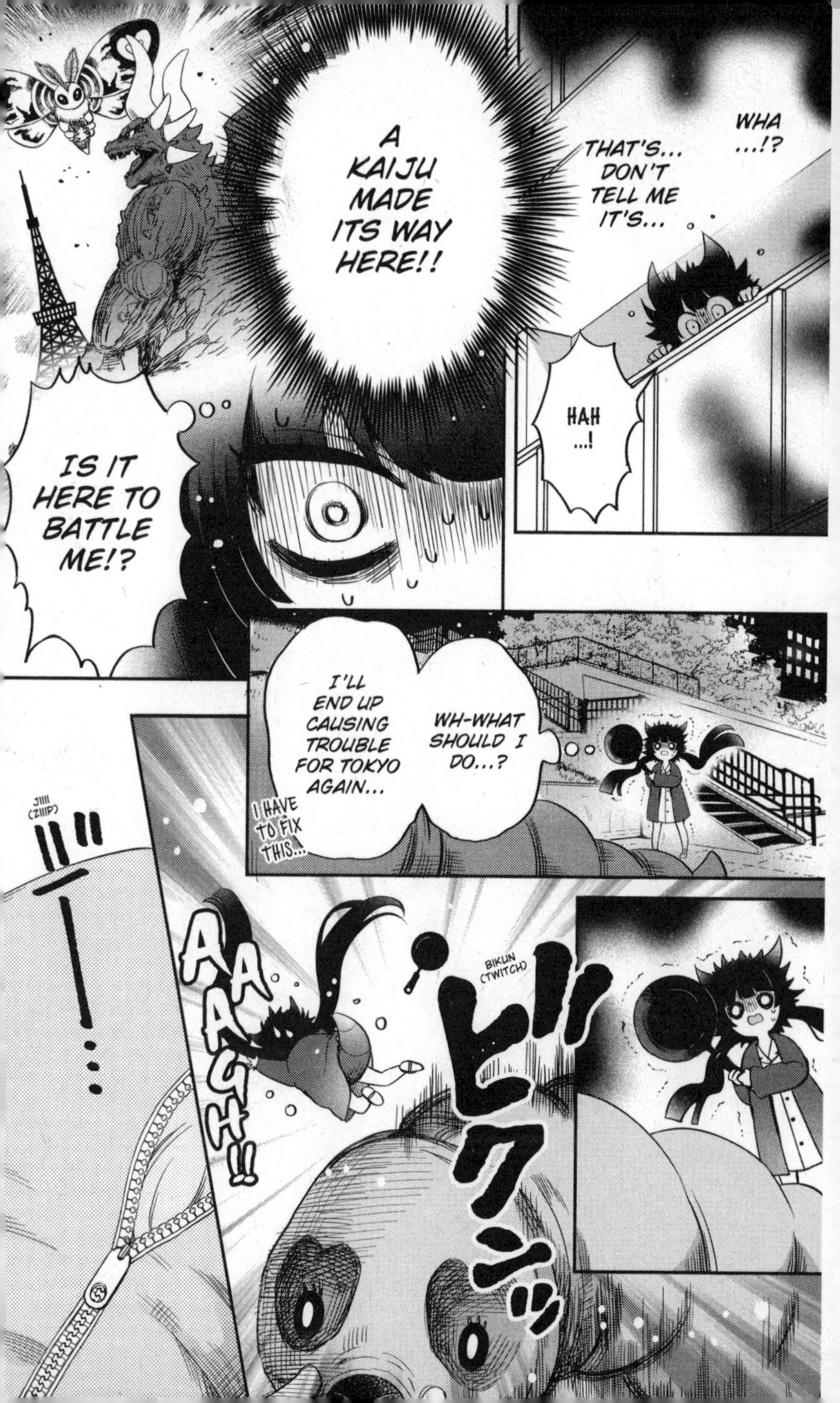
WHA ...!?
THAT'S... DON'T TELL ME IT'S...
HAH ...!
A KAIJU MADE ITS WAY HERE!!
IS IT HERE TO BATTLE ME!?
WH-WHAT SHOULD I DO...?
I'LL END UP CAUSING TROUBLE FOR TOKYO AGAIN...
I HAVE TO FIX THIS...
BIKUN (TWITCH)
AAAUGH!!
JIIII (ZIIIP)

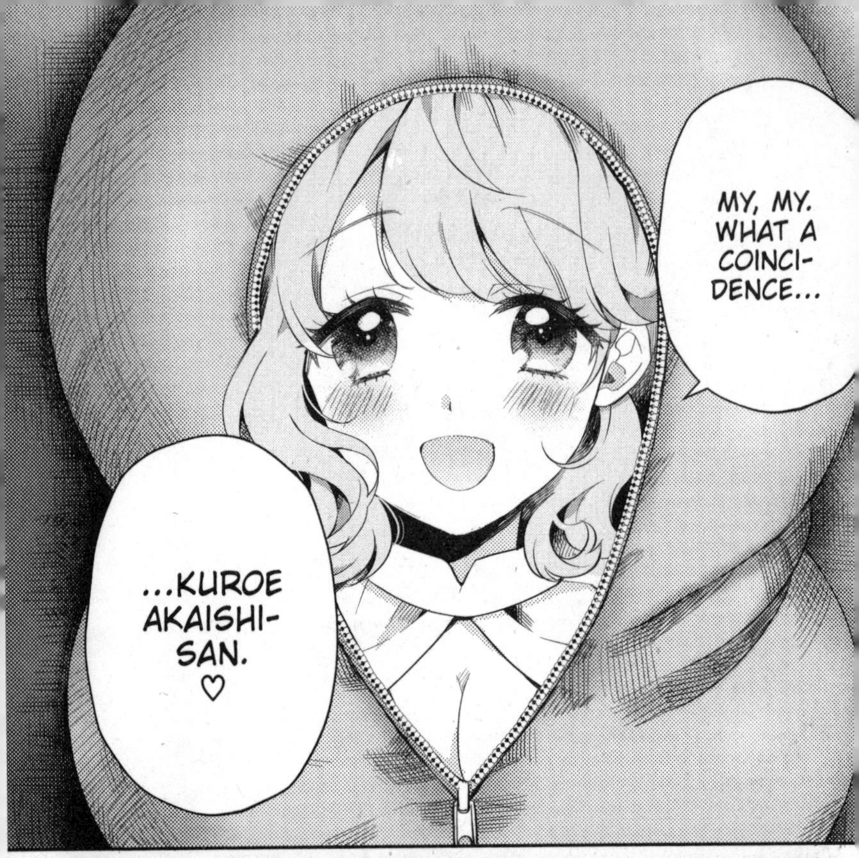
MY, MY. WHAT A COINCI-DENCE...
...KUROE AKAISHI-SAN. ♡
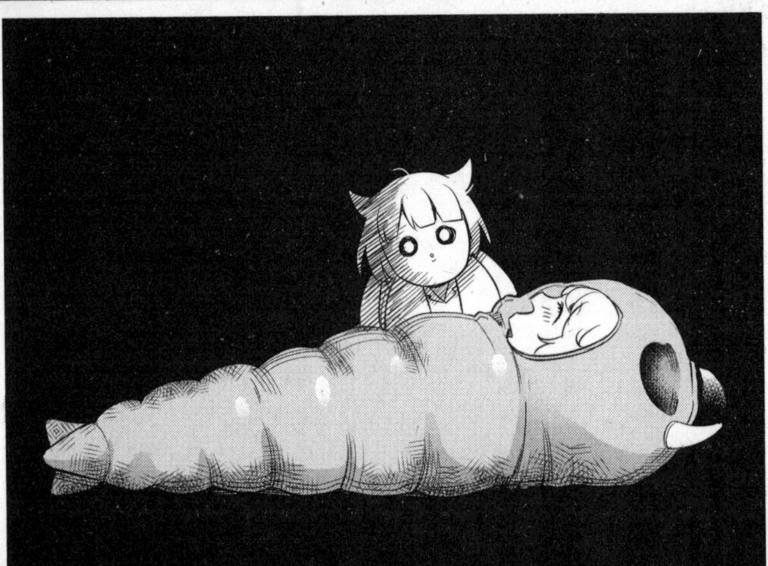

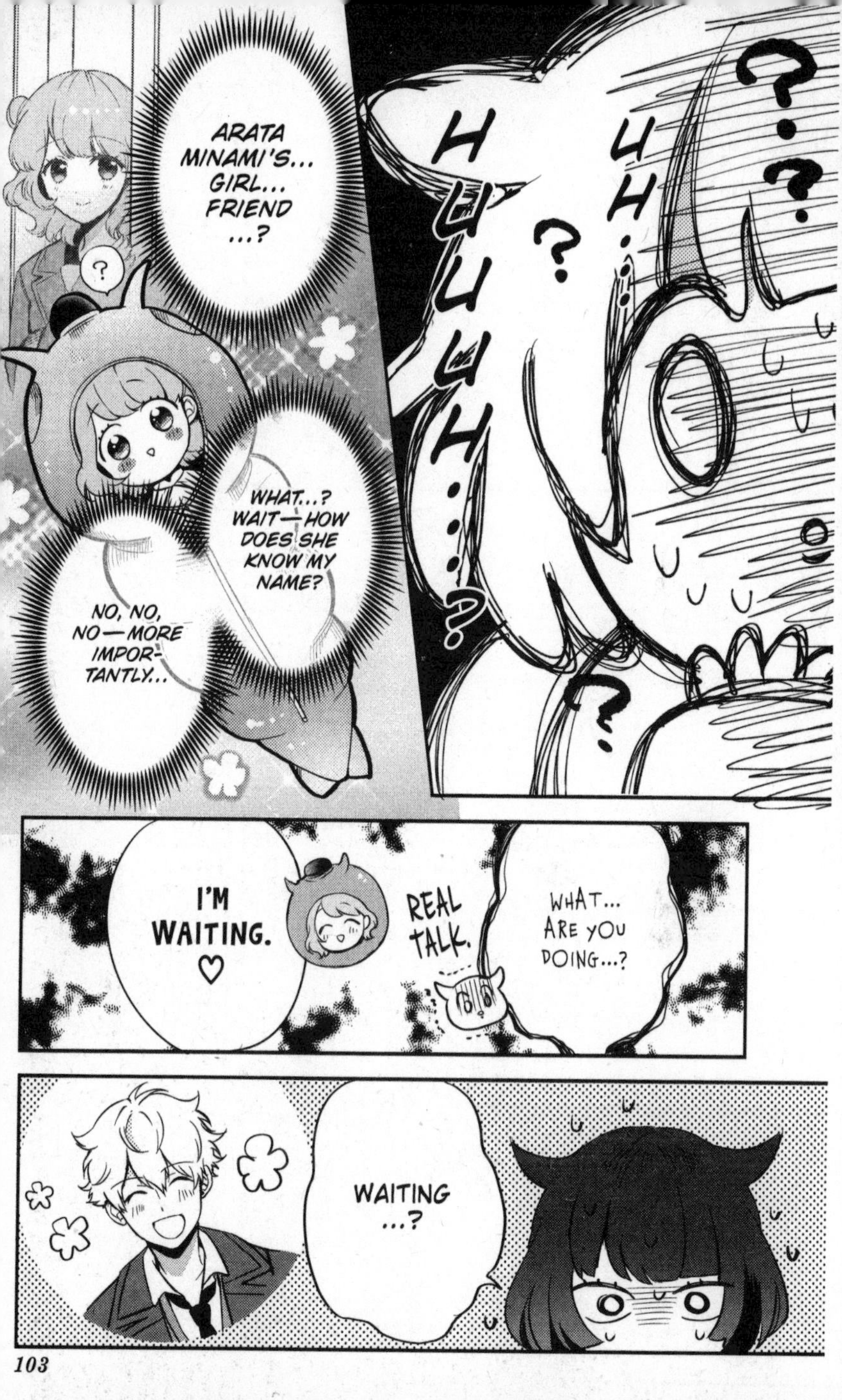
??
UHH...
?
HUUUUH...?
?
ARATA MINAMI'S... GIRL... FRIEND ...?
?
WHAT...? WAIT—HOW DOES SHE KNOW MY NAME?
NO, NO, NO—MORE IMPOR-TANTLY...
WHAT... ARE YOU DOING...?
REAL TALK.
I'M WAITING. ♡
WAITING ...?

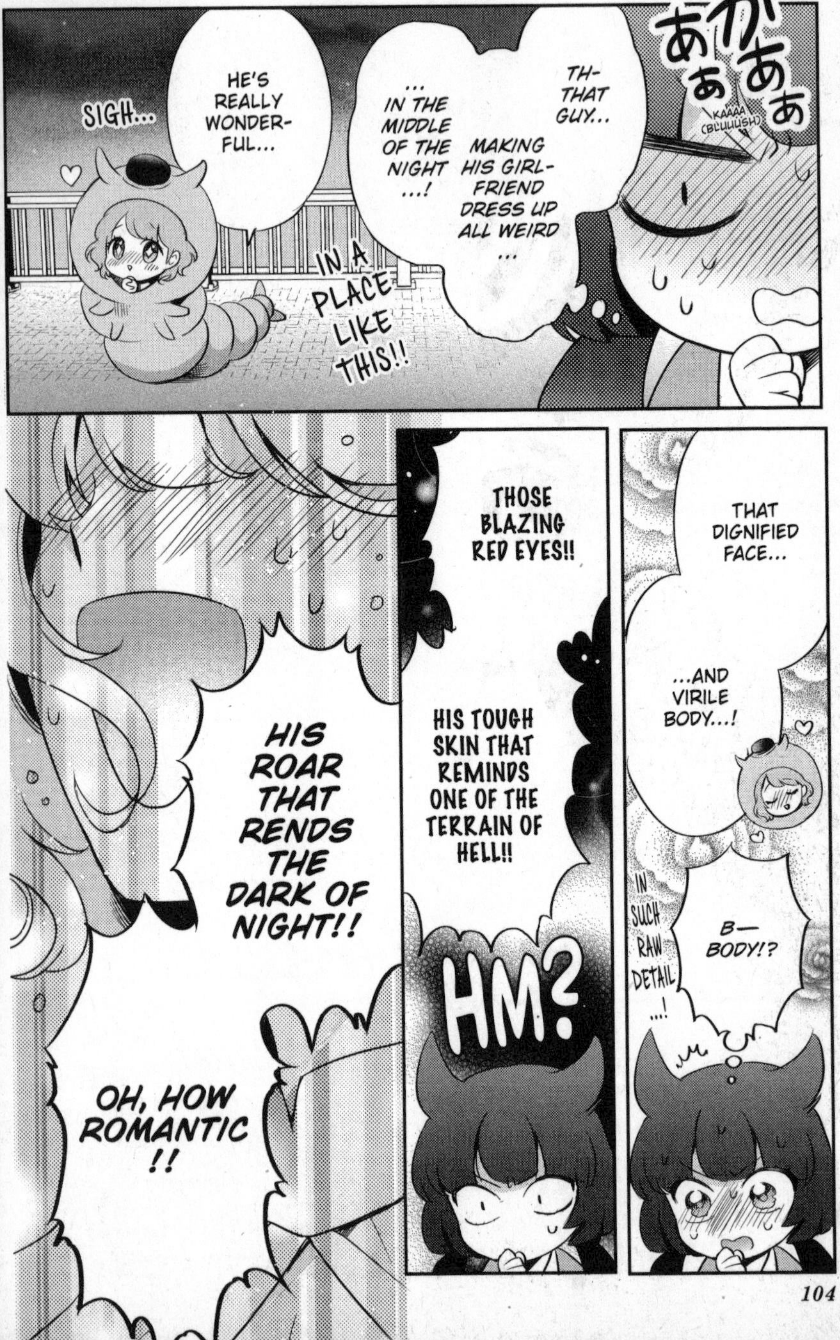
あかぁあぁ
KAAAA (BLUUUSH)
TH- THAT GUY...
MAKING HIS GIRL-FRIEND DRESS UP ALL WEIRD ...
... IN THE MIDDLE OF THE NIGHT ...!
IN A PLACE LIKE THIS!!
HE'S REALLY WONDER-FUL...
SIGH...
THAT DIGNIFIED FACE...
...AND VIRILE BODY...!
B— BODY!?
IN SUCH RAW DETAIL ...!
THOSE BLAZING RED EYES!!
HIS TOUGH SKIN THAT REMINDS ONE OF THE TERRAIN OF HELL!!
HM?
HIS ROAR THAT RENDS THE DARK OF NIGHT!!
OH, HOW ROMANTIC !!

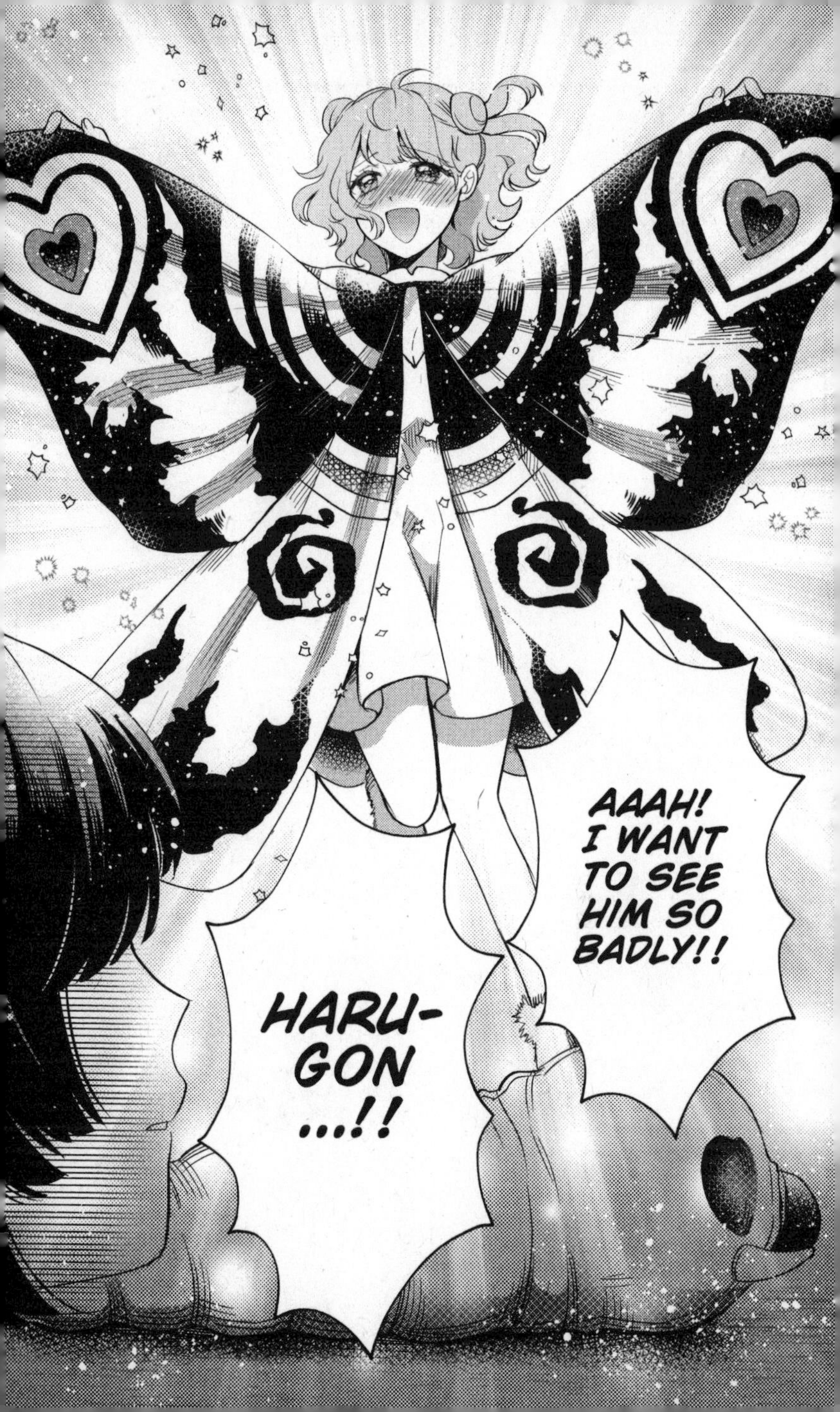
AAAH! I WANT TO SEE HIM SO BADLY!!
HARU-GON ...!!

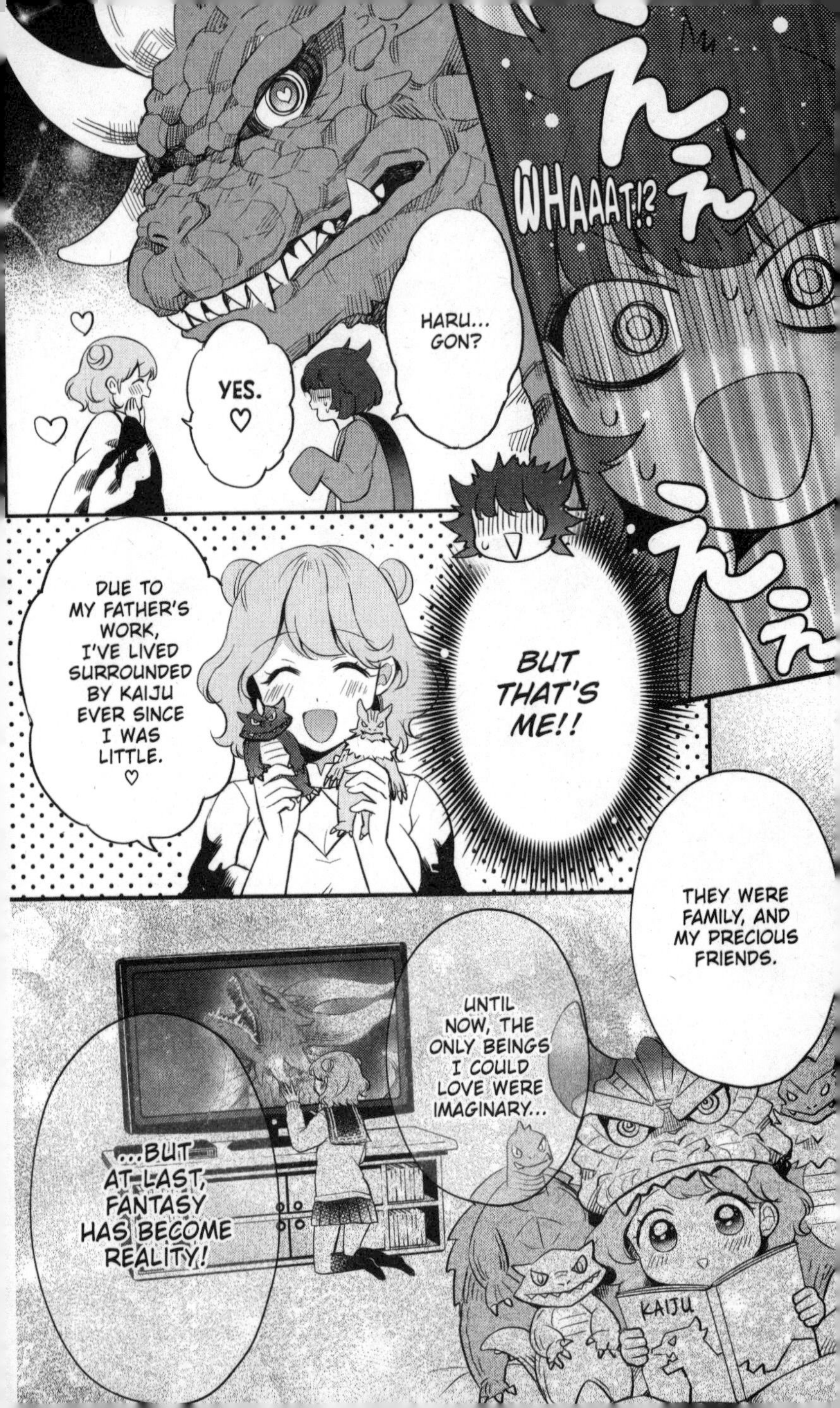
HARU... GON?
YES. ♡
WHAAAT!?
BUT THAT'S ME!!
DUE TO MY FATHER'S WORK, I'VE LIVED SURROUNDED BY KAIJU EVER SINCE I WAS LITTLE. ♡
THEY WERE FAMILY, AND MY PRECIOUS FRIENDS.
UNTIL NOW, THE ONLY BEINGS I COULD LOVE WERE IMAGINARY...
...BUT AT LAST, FANTASY HAS BECOME REALITY!
KAIJU

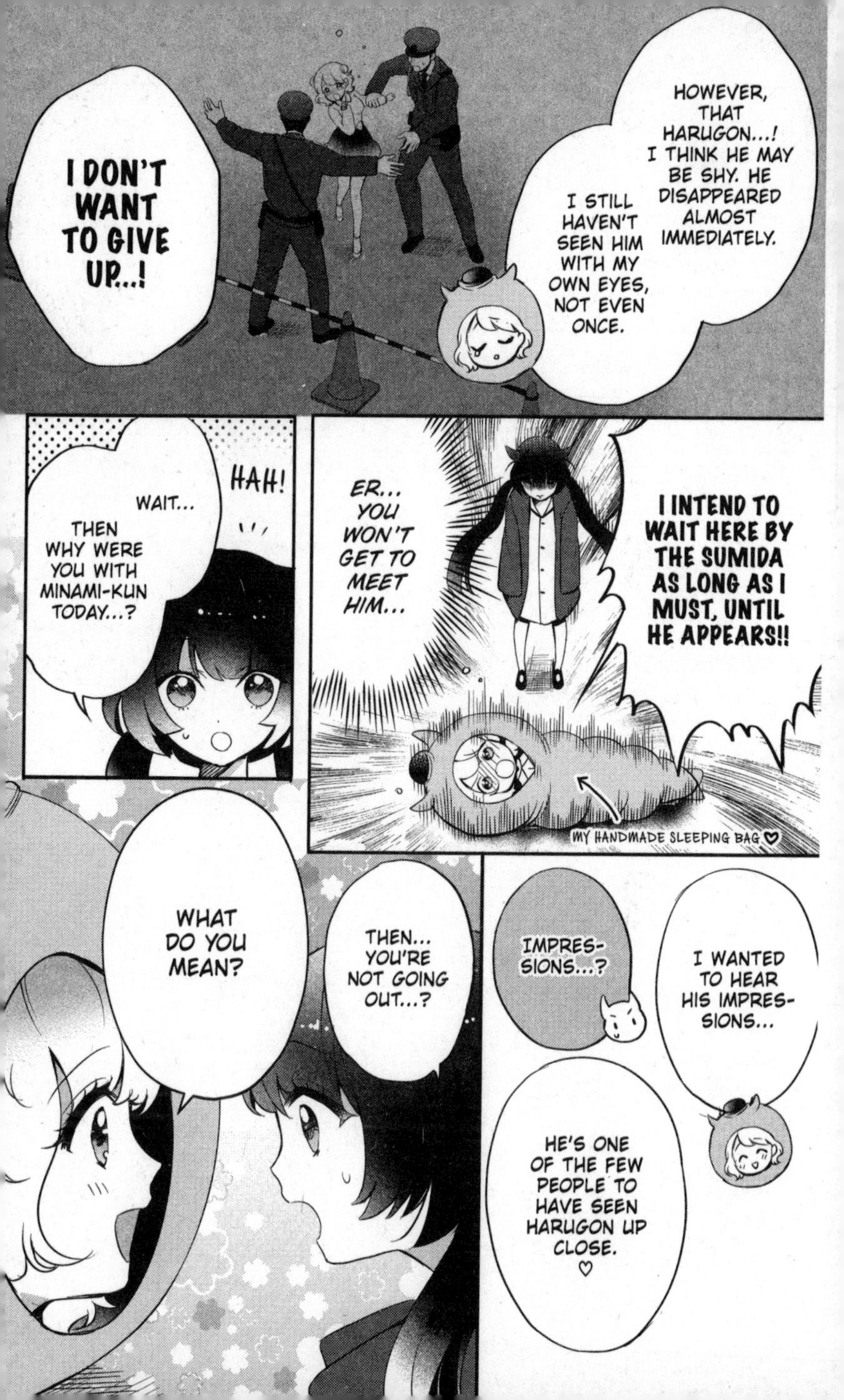
HOWEVER, THAT HARUGON...! I THINK HE MAY BE SHY. HE DISAPPEARED ALMOST IMMEDIATELY.
I STILL HAVEN'T SEEN HIM WITH MY OWN EYES, NOT EVEN ONCE.
I DON'T WANT TO GIVE UP...!
I INTEND TO WAIT HERE BY THE SUMIDA AS LONG AS I MUST, UNTIL HE APPEARS!!
ER... YOU WON'T GET TO MEET HIM...
MY HANDMADE SLEEPING BAG ♡
HAH!
WAIT... THEN WHY WERE YOU WITH MINAMI-KUN TODAY...?
I WANTED TO HEAR HIS IMPRESSIONS...
IMPRES-SIONS...?
HE'S ONE OF THE FEW PEOPLE TO HAVE SEEN HARUGON UP CLOSE. ♡
THEN... YOU'RE NOT GOING OUT...?
WHAT DO YOU MEAN?

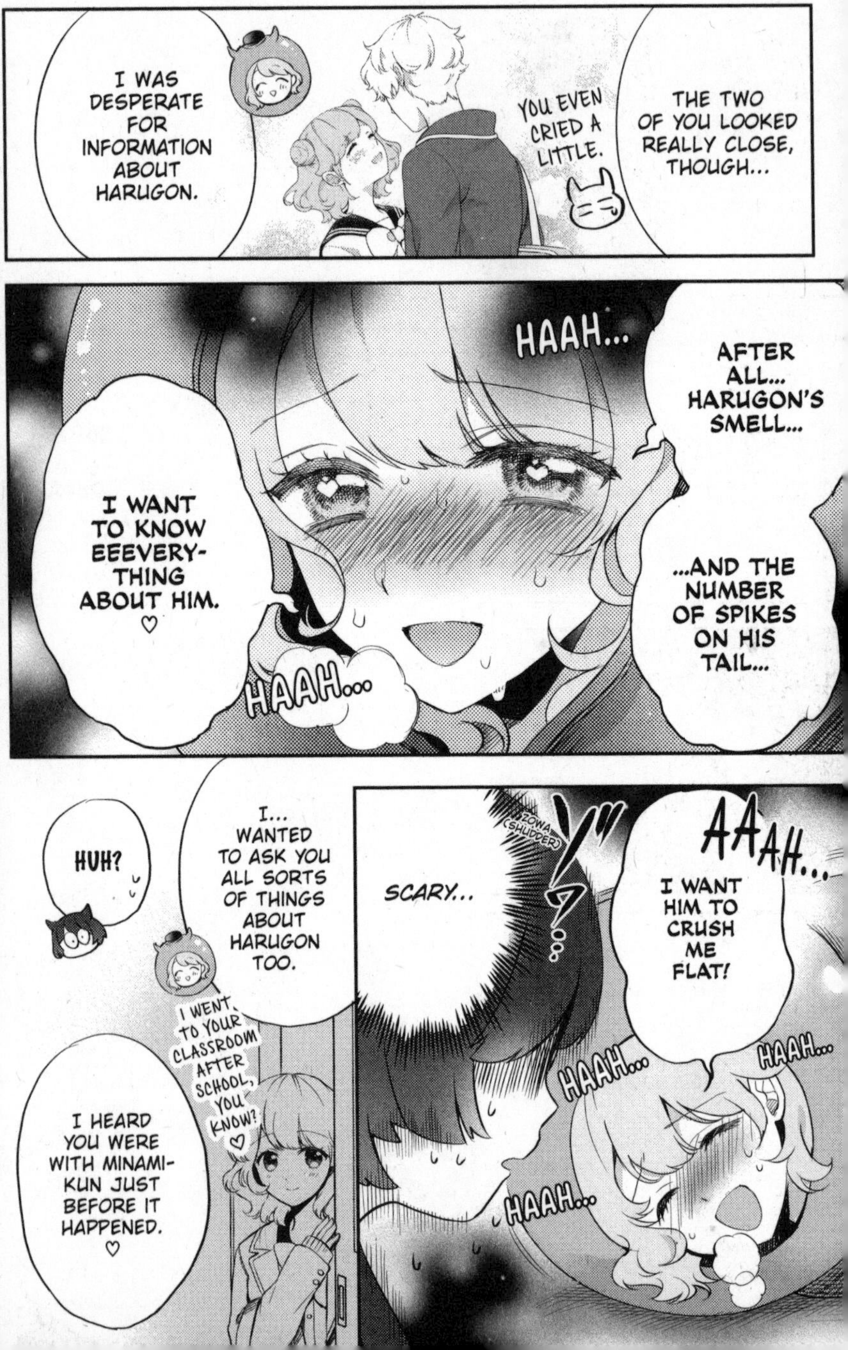
THE TWO OF YOU LOOKED REALLY CLOSE, THOUGH...
YOU EVEN CRIED A LITTLE.
I WAS DESPERATE FOR INFORMATION ABOUT HARUGON.
HAAH...
AFTER ALL... HARUGON'S SMELL...
...AND THE NUMBER OF SPIKES ON HIS TAIL...
I WANT TO KNOW EEEVERY-THING ABOUT HIM. ♡
HAAH...
AAAH...
I WANT HIM TO CRUSH ME FLAT!
ZOWA (SHUDDER)
SCARY...
HAAH...
HAAH...
HAAH...
I... WANTED TO ASK YOU ALL SORTS OF THINGS ABOUT HARUGON TOO.
HUH?
I WENT TO YOUR CLASSROOM AFTER SCHOOL, YOU KNOW? ♡
I HEARD YOU WERE WITH MINAMI-KUN JUST BEFORE IT HAPPENED. ♡

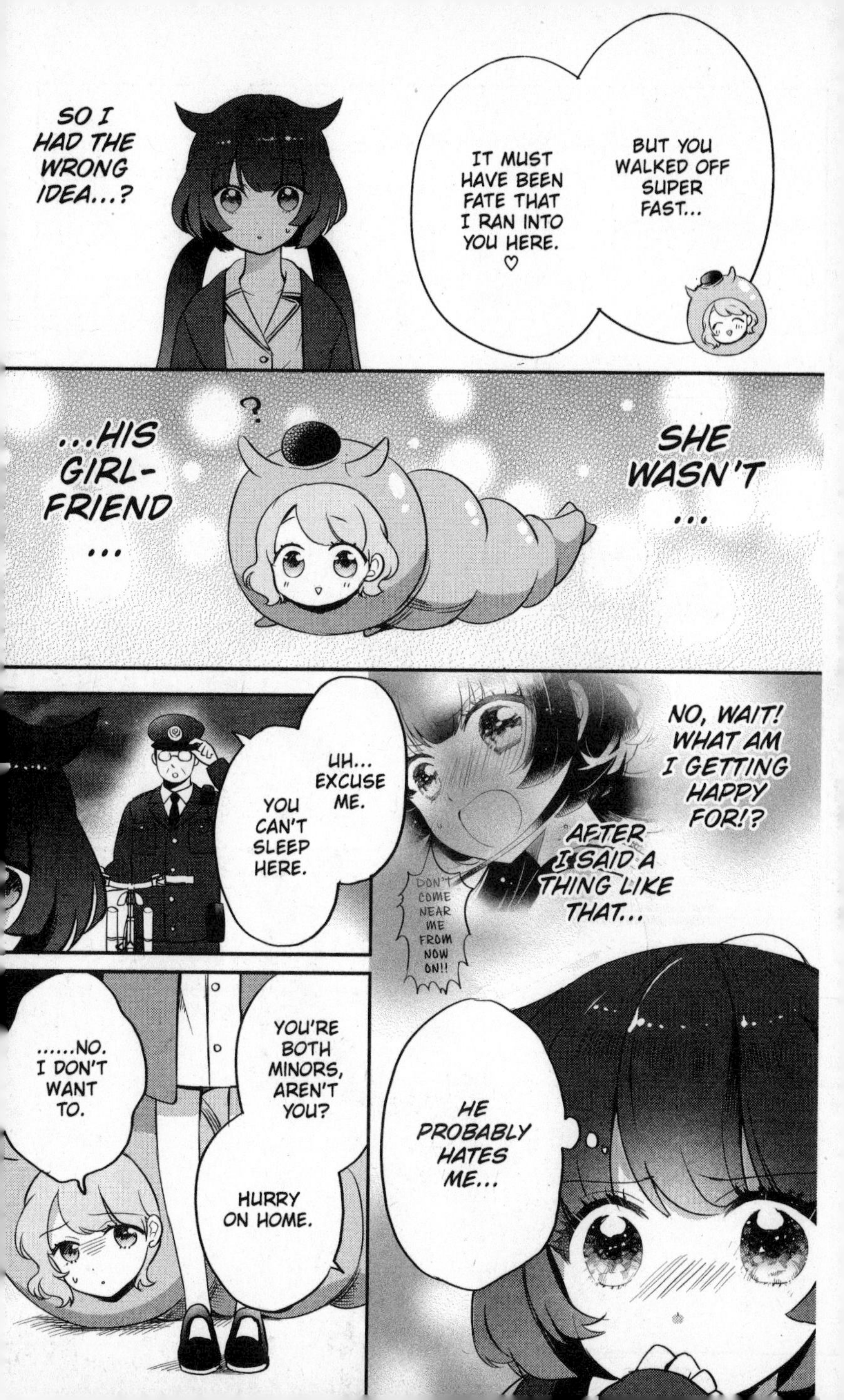
BUT YOU WALKED OFF SUPER FAST...
IT MUST HAVE BEEN FATE THAT I RAN INTO YOU HERE. ♡
SO I HAD THE WRONG IDEA...?
SHE WASN'T ...
...HIS GIRL-FRIEND ...
NO, WAIT! WHAT AM I GETTING HAPPY FOR!?
AFTER I SAID A THING LIKE THAT...
DON'T COME NEAR ME FROM NOW ON!!
UH... EXCUSE ME.
YOU CAN'T SLEEP HERE.
HE PROBABLY HATES ME...
YOU'RE BOTH MINORS, AREN'T YOU?
HURRY ON HOME.
......NO. I DON'T WANT TO.

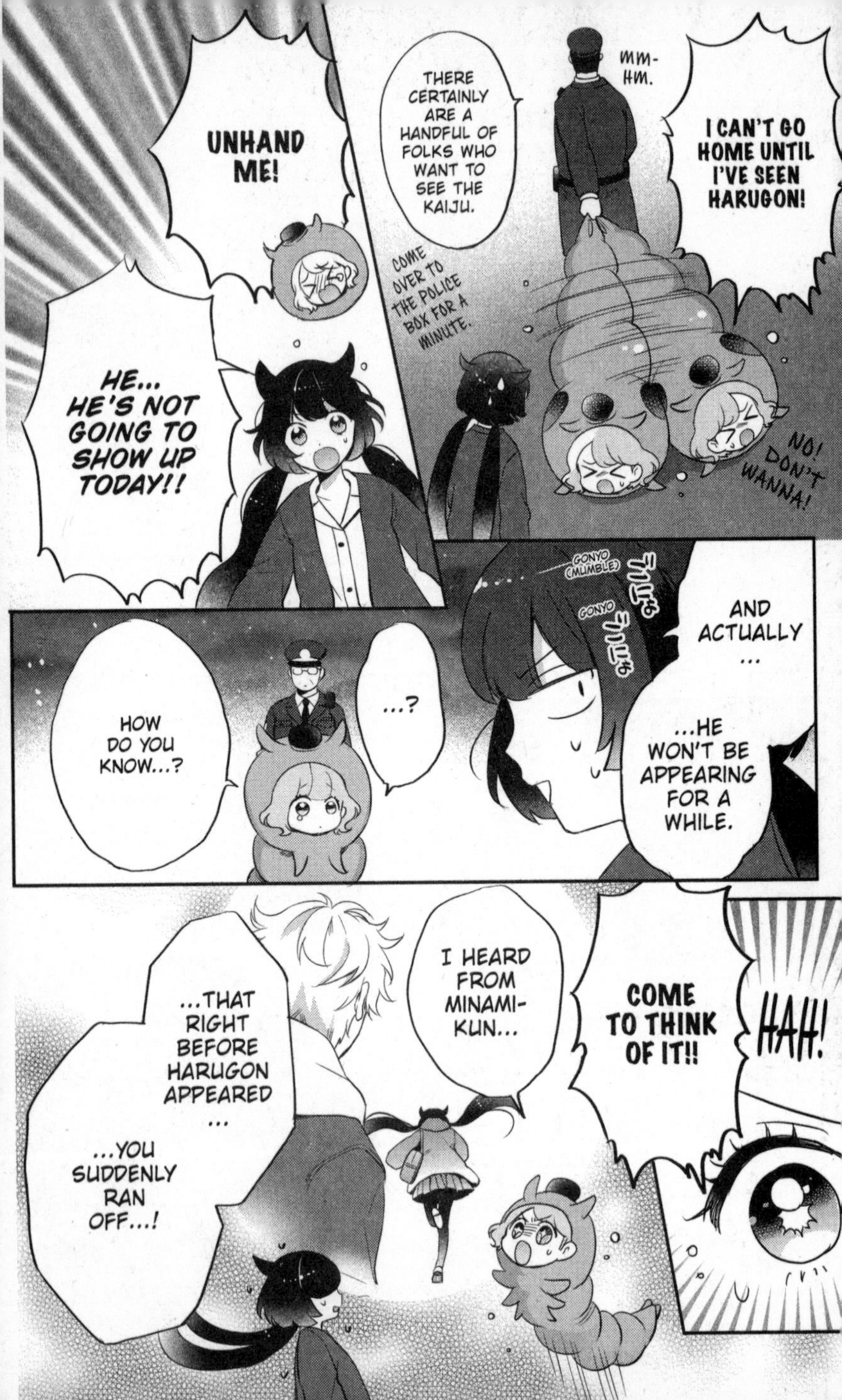
I CAN'T GO HOME UNTIL I'VE SEEN HARUGON!
MM-HM.
THERE CERTAINLY ARE A HANDFUL OF FOLKS WHO WANT TO SEE THE KAIJU.
COME OVER TO THE POLICE BOX FOR A MINUTE.
NO! DON'T WANNA!
UNHAND ME!
HE... HE'S NOT GOING TO SHOW UP TODAY!!
GONYO (MUMBLE)
GONYO
AND ACTUALLY ...
...HE WON'T BE APPEARING FOR A WHILE.
...?
HOW DO YOU KNOW...?
HAH!
COME TO THINK OF IT!!
I HEARD FROM MINAMI-KUN...
...THAT RIGHT BEFORE HARUGON APPEARED ...
...YOU SUDDENLY RAN OFF...!

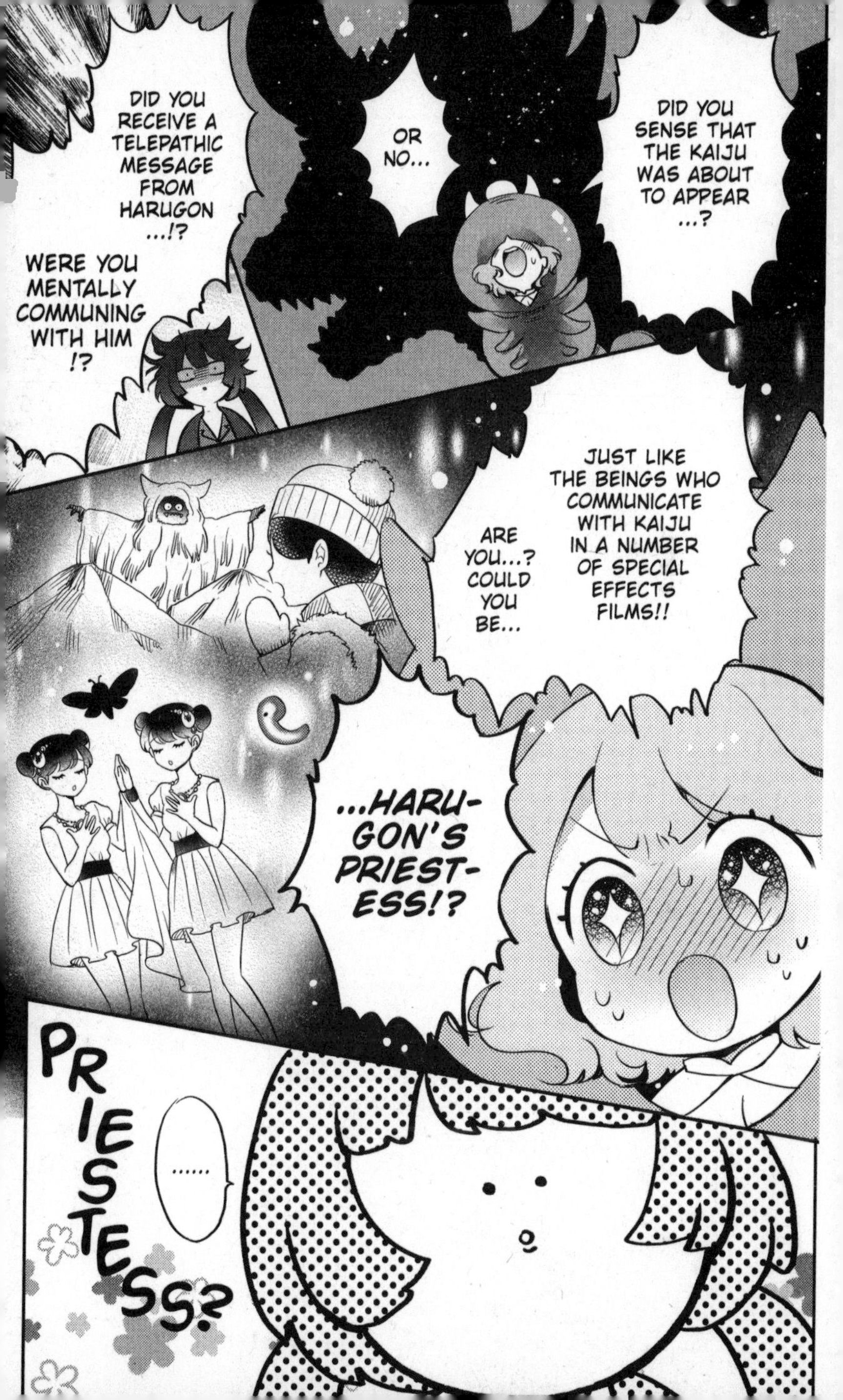
DID YOU SENSE THAT THE KAIJU WAS ABOUT TO APPEAR ...?
OR NO...
DID YOU RECEIVE A TELEPATHIC MESSAGE FROM HARUGON ...!?
WERE YOU MENTALLY COMMUNING WITH HIM !?
JUST LIKE THE BEINGS WHO COMMUNICATE WITH KAIJU IN A NUMBER OF SPECIAL EFFECTS FILMS!!
ARE YOU...? COULD YOU BE...
...HARU-GON'S PRIEST-ESS!?
......
PRIESTESS?

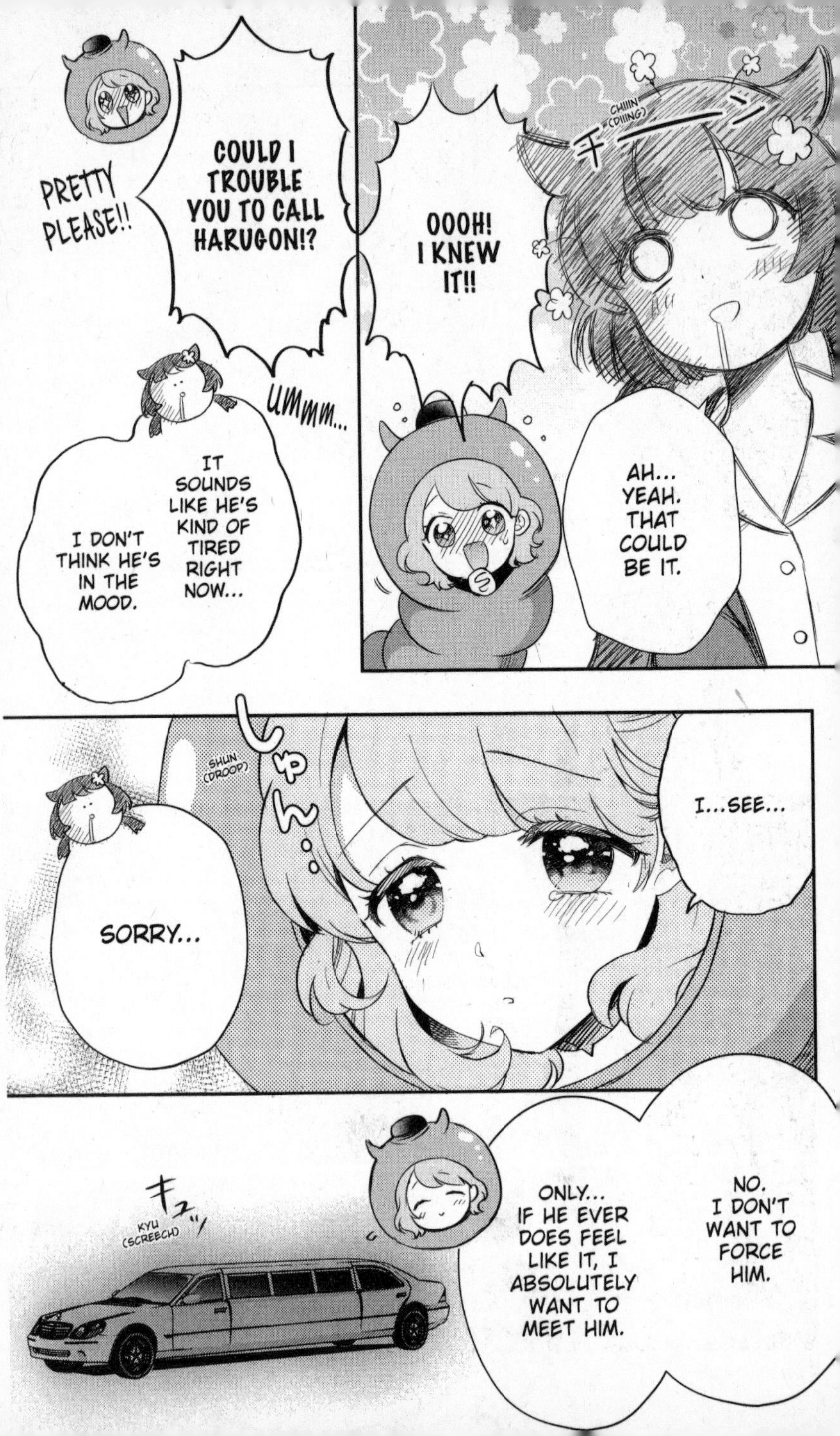
CHIIIN (DIIING)
OOOH! I KNEW IT!!
AH... YEAH. THAT COULD BE IT.
COULD I TROUBLE YOU TO CALL HARUGON!?
PRETTY PLEASE!!
UMMM...
IT SOUNDS LIKE HE'S KIND OF TIRED RIGHT NOW...
I DON'T THINK HE'S IN THE MOOD.
SHUN (DROOP)
I...SEE...
SORRY...
NO. I DON'T WANT TO FORCE HIM.
ONLY... IF HE EVER DOES FEEL LIKE IT, I ABSOLUTELY WANT TO MEET HIM.
KYU (SCREECH)

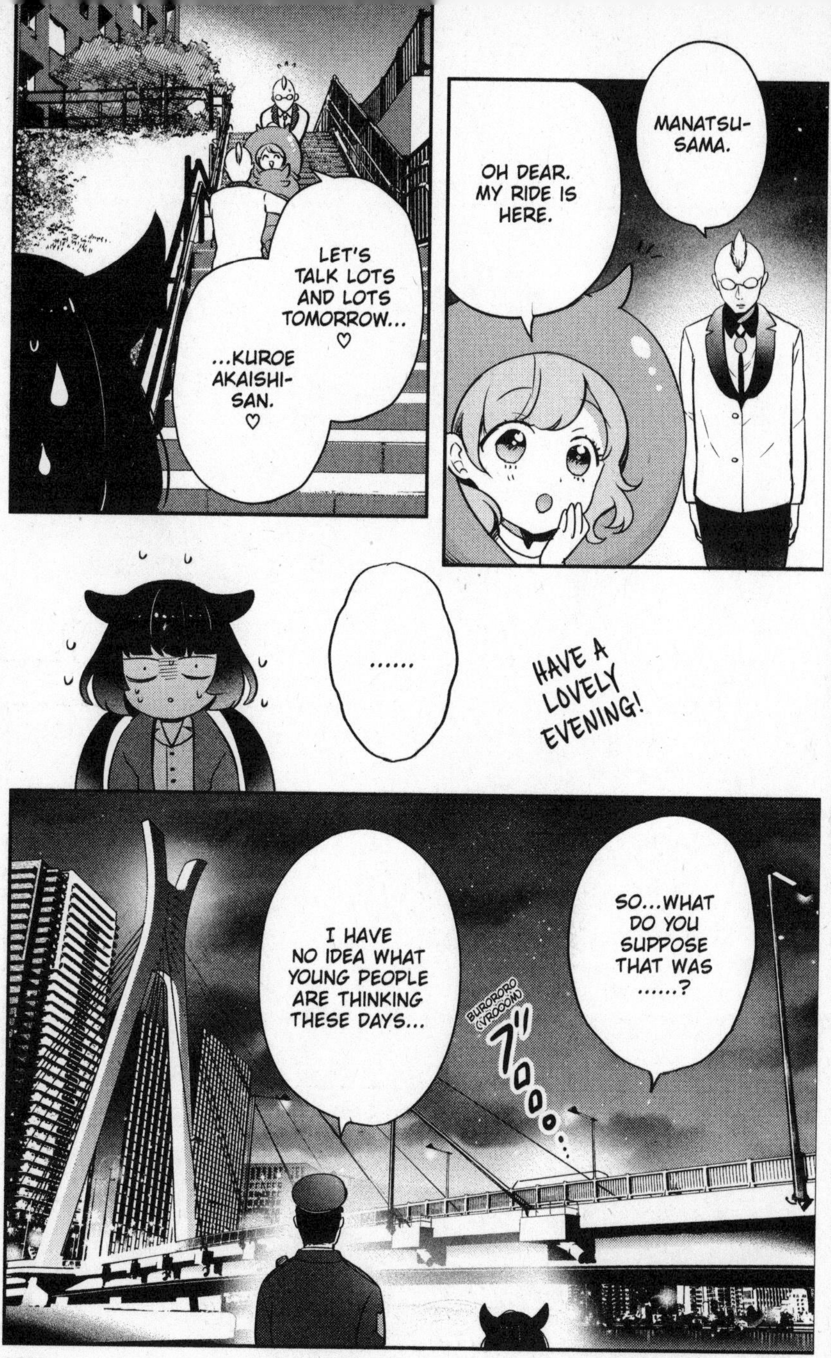
MANATSU-SAMA.
OH DEAR. MY RIDE IS HERE.
LET'S TALK LOTS AND LOTS TOMORROW... ♡
...KUROE AKAISHI-SAN. ♡
HAVE A LOVELY EVENING!
......
SO...WHAT DO YOU SUPPOSE THAT WAS......?
BUROROROR (VROOOM)
I HAVE NO IDEA WHAT YOUNG PEOPLE ARE THINKING THESE DAYS...

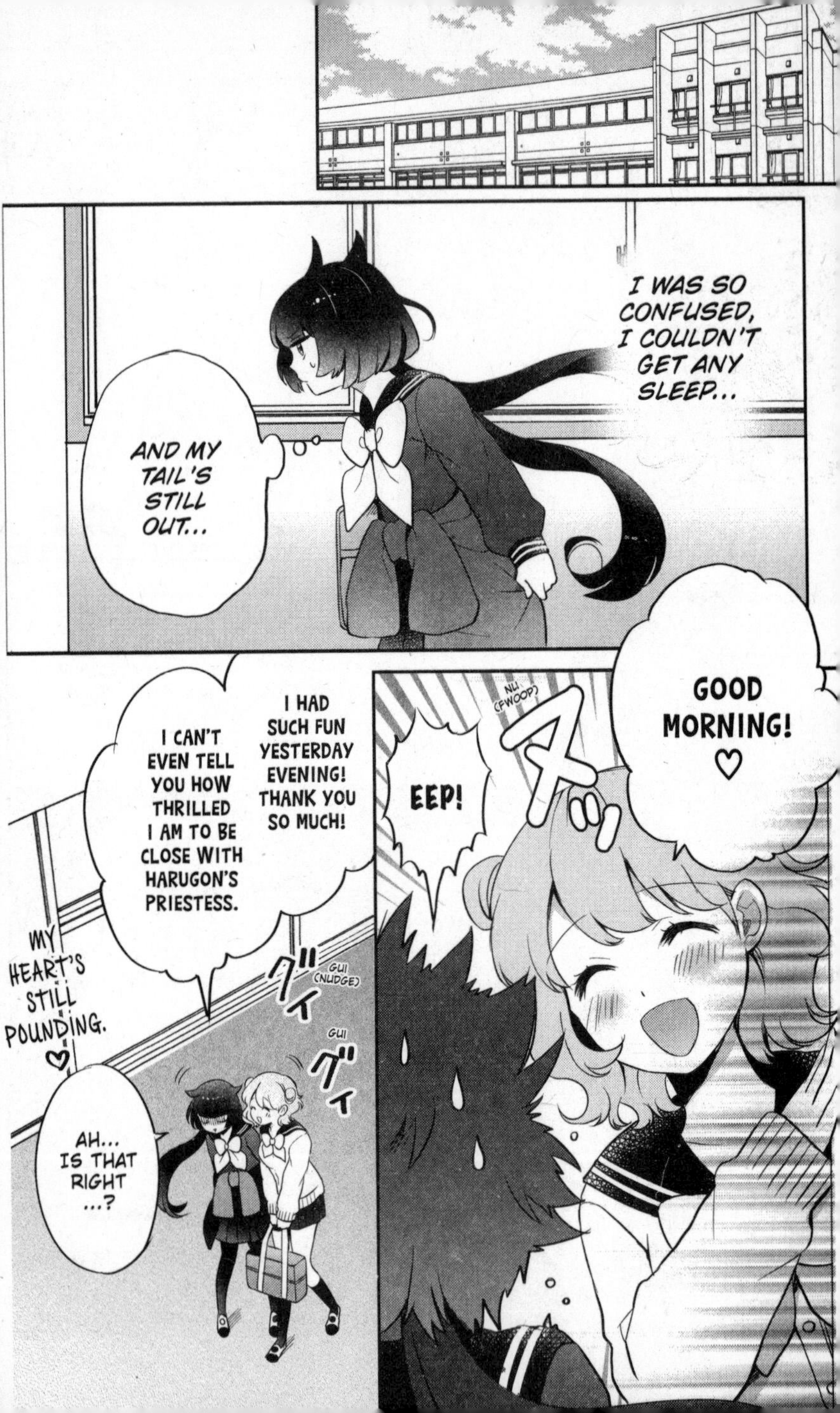
I WAS SO CONFUSED, I COULDN'T GET ANY SLEEP...
AND MY TAIL'S STILL OUT...
GOOD MORNING! ♡
NU (FWOOP)
EEP!
I HAD SUCH FUN YESTERDAY EVENING! THANK YOU SO MUCH!
I CAN'T EVEN TELL YOU HOW THRILLED I AM TO BE CLOSE WITH HARUGON'S PRIESTESS.
GUI (NUDGE)
GUI
MY HEART'S STILL POUNDING. ♡
AH... IS THAT RIGHT ...?

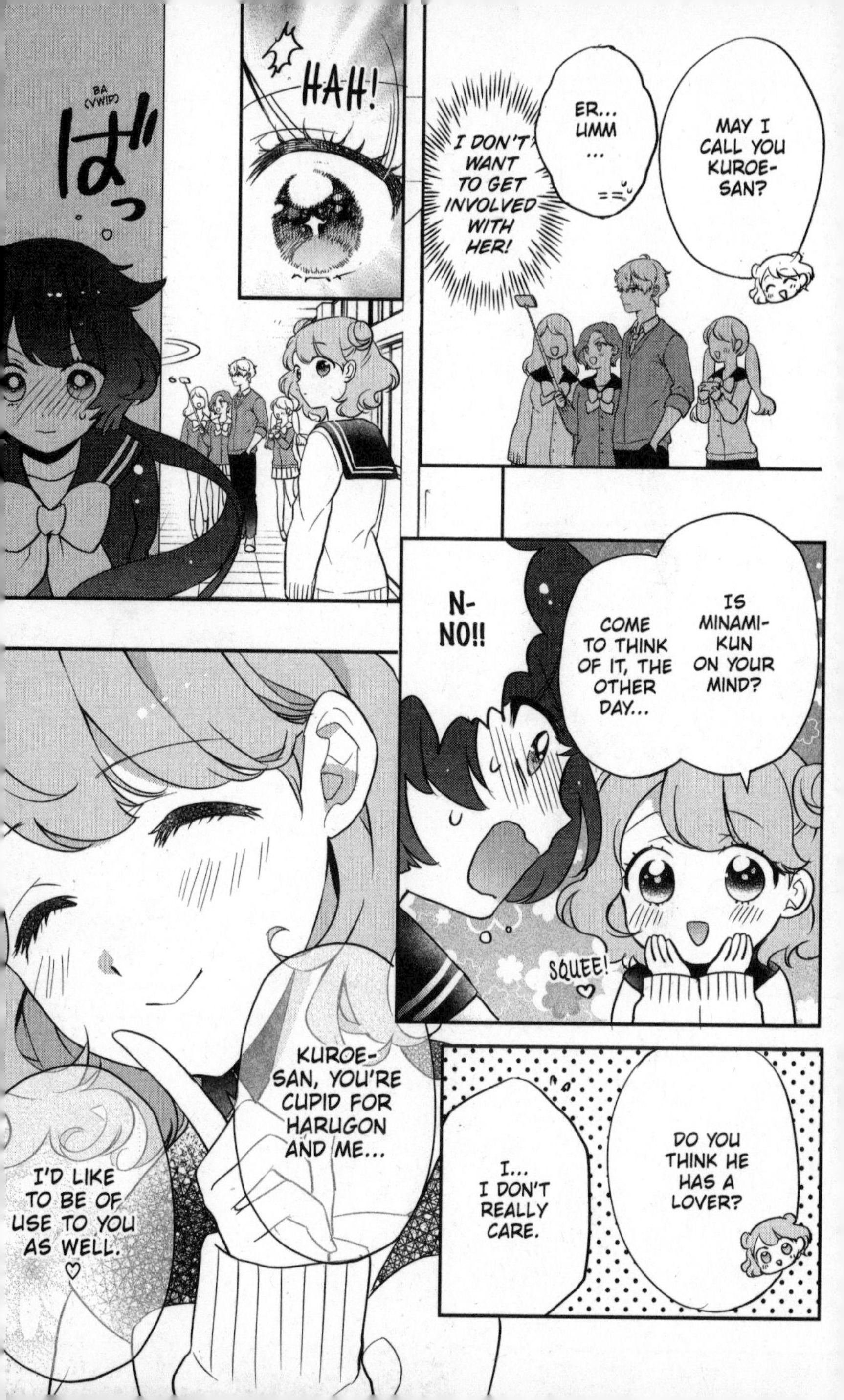
MAY I CALL YOU KUROE-SAN?
ER... UMM ...
I DON'T WANT TO GET INVOLVED WITH HER!
HAH!
BA (VWIP)
ばっ
IS MINAMI-KUN ON YOUR MIND?
COME TO THINK OF IT, THE OTHER DAY...
N-NO!!
SQUEE! ♡
DO YOU THINK HE HAS A LOVER?
I... I DON'T REALLY CARE.
KUROE-SAN, YOU'RE CUPID FOR HARUGON AND ME...
I'D LIKE TO BE OF USE TO YOU AS WELL. ♡

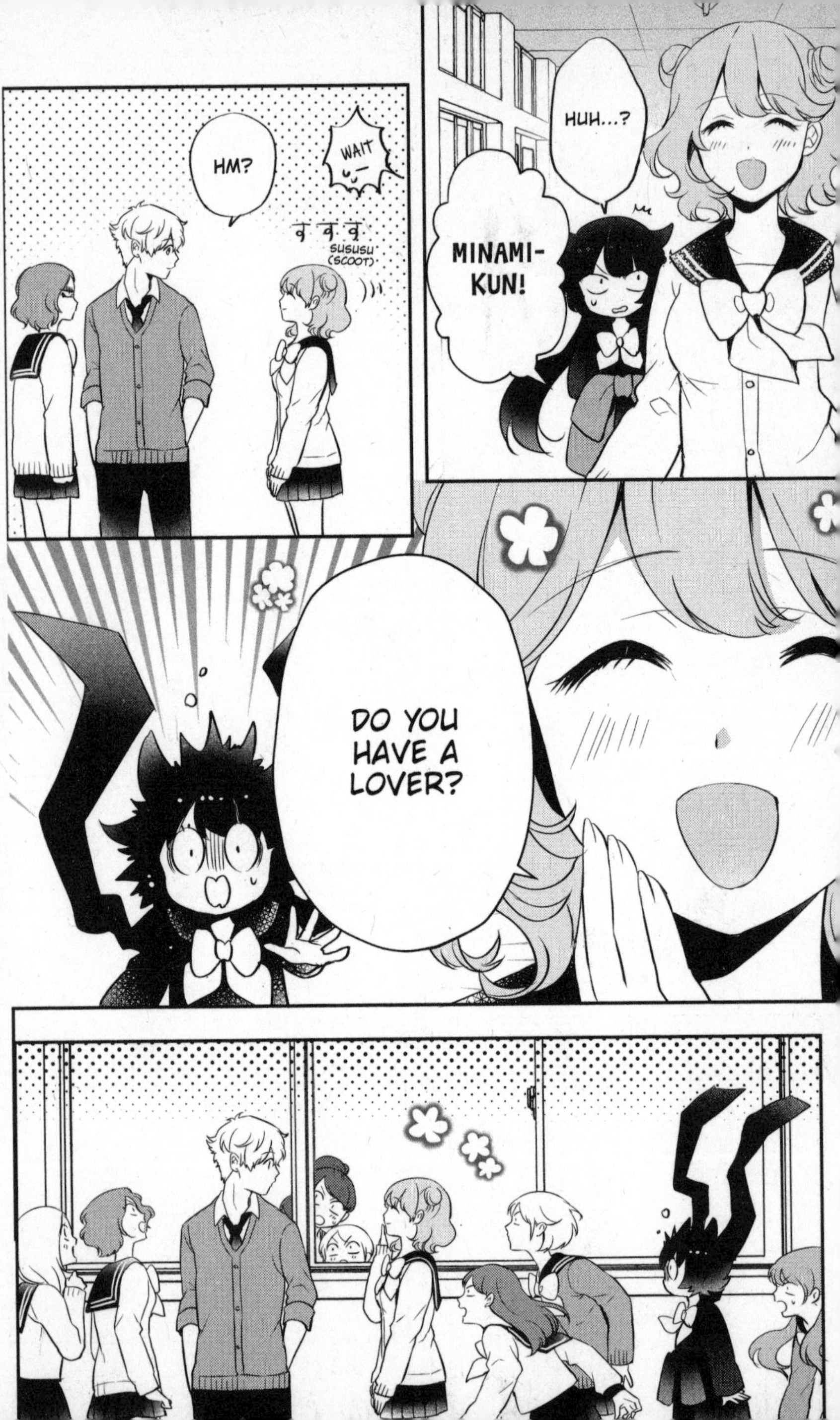
HUH...?
MINAMI-KUN!
WAIT
HM?
すすす
SUSUSU (SCOOT)
DO YOU HAVE A LOVER?

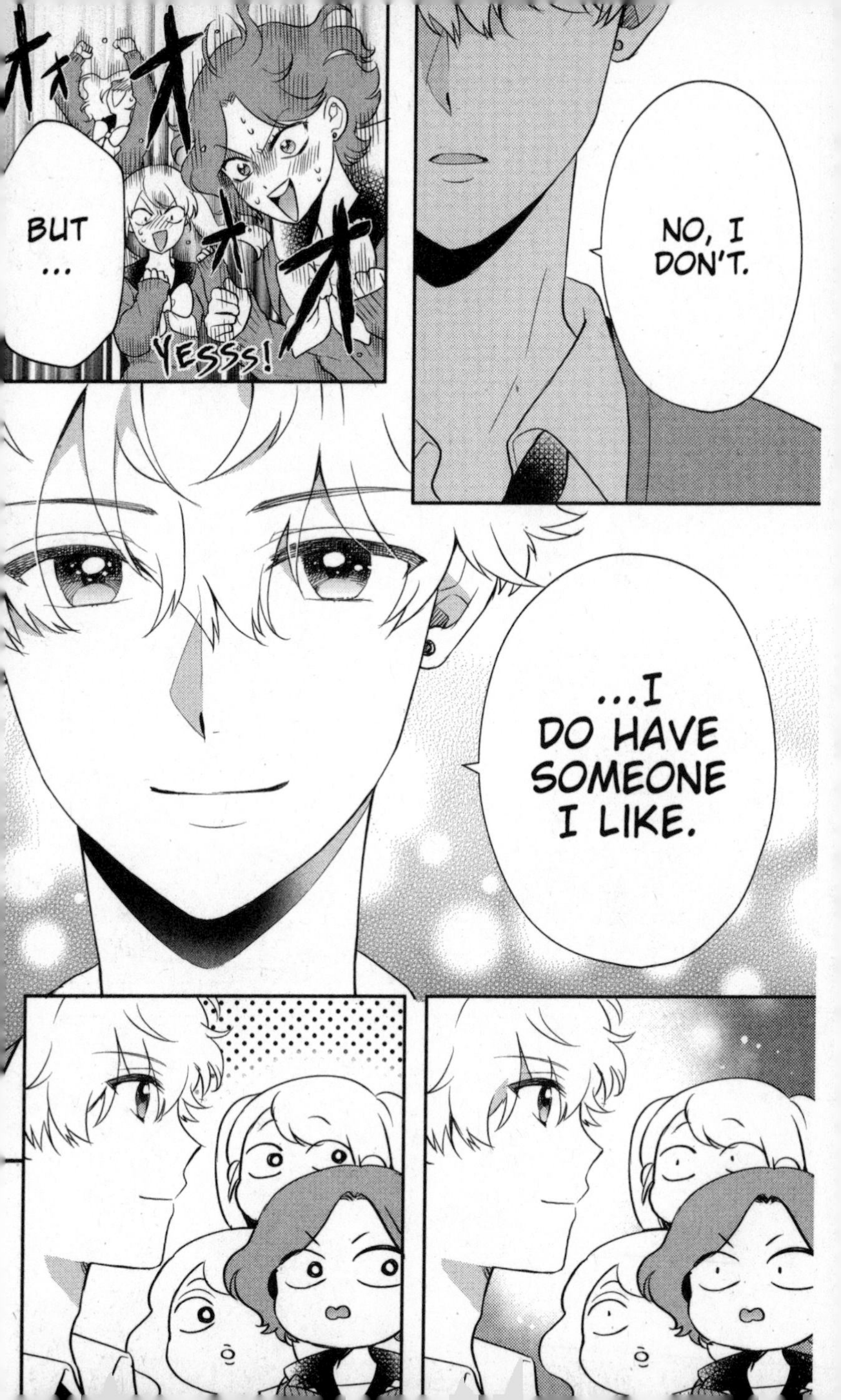
NO, I DON'T.
BUT ...
YESSS!
...I DO HAVE SOMEONE I LIKE.

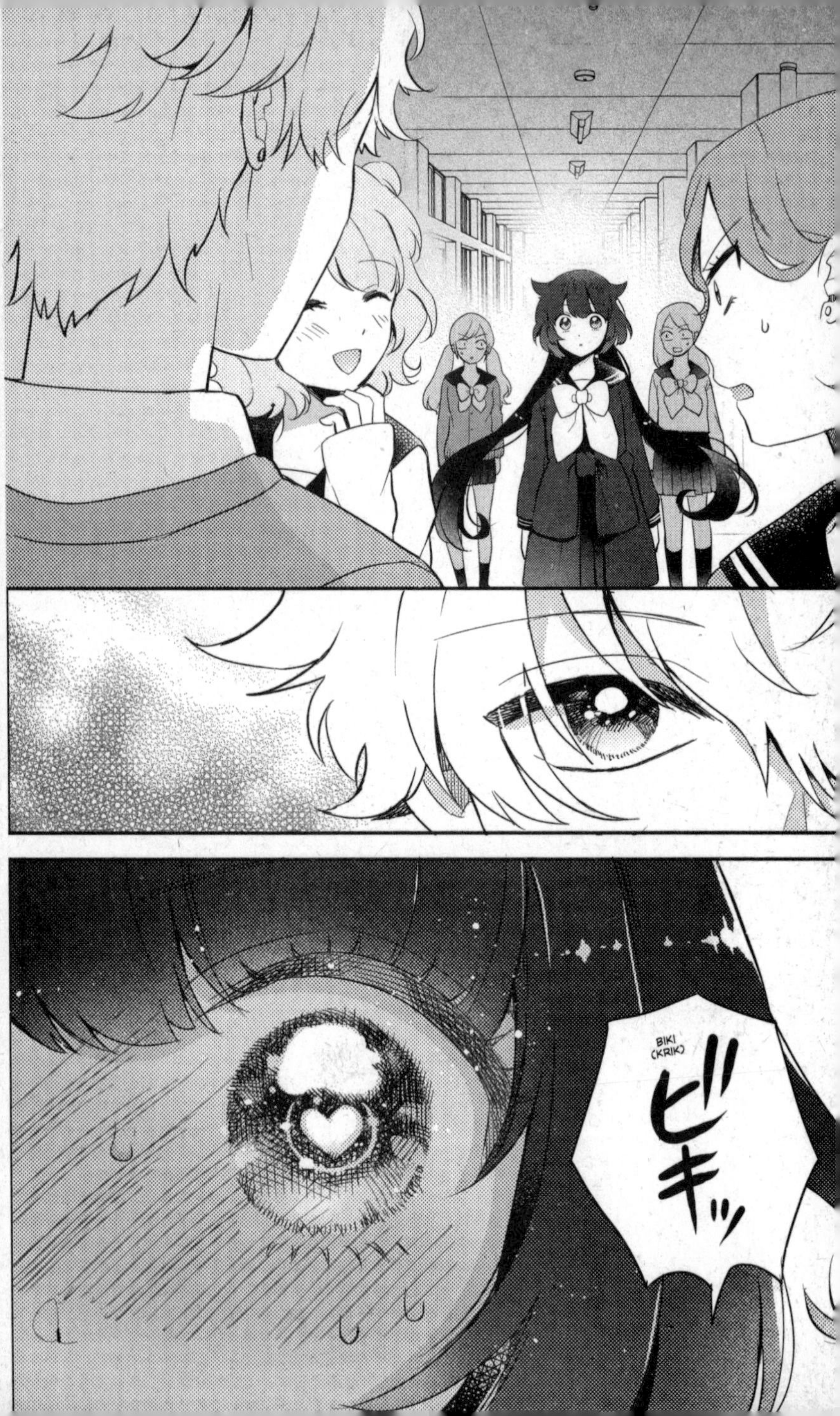
BIKI (KRIK)
ビキッ

KAIJU GIRL
CARAMELISE

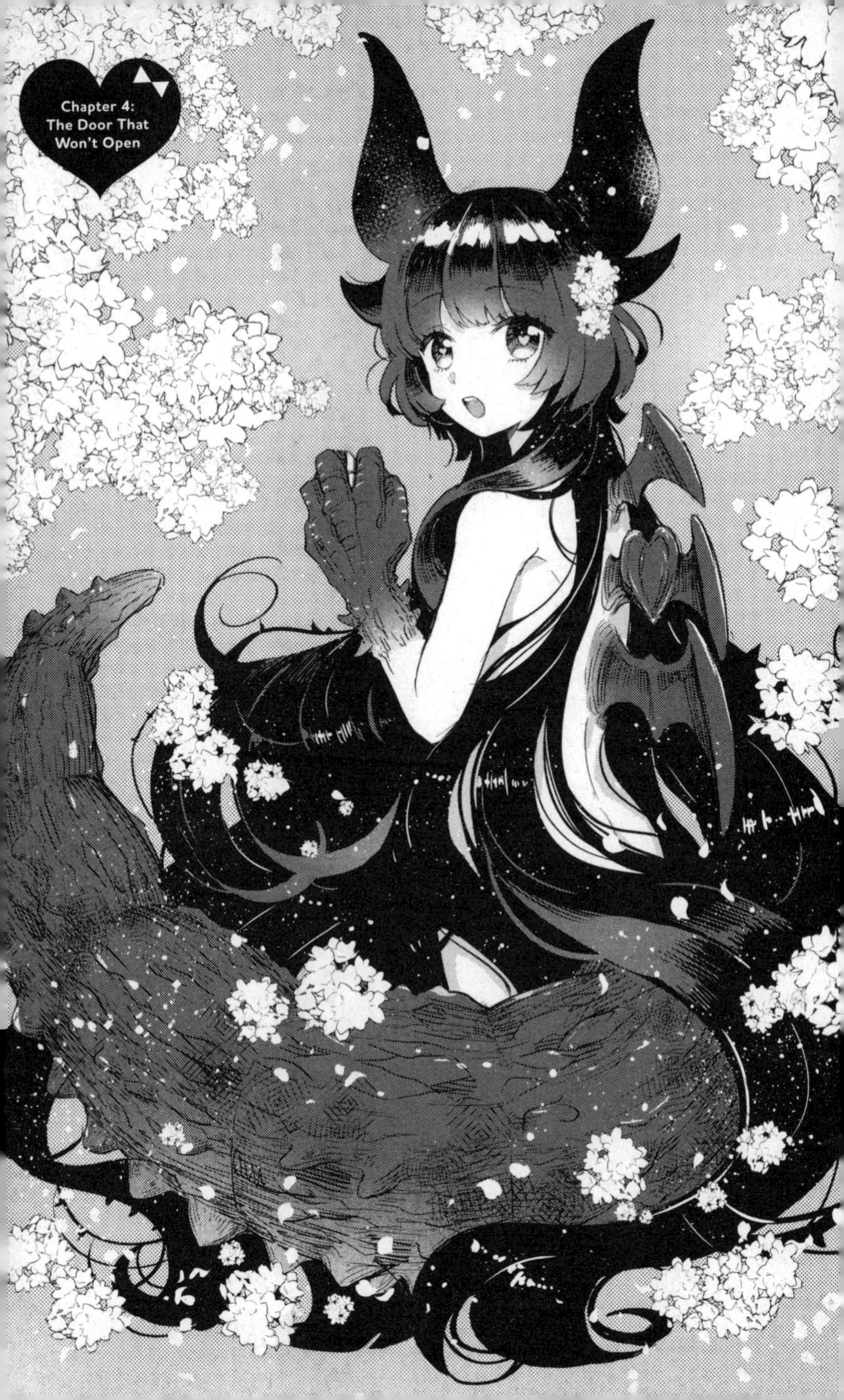
Chapter 4:
The Door That
Won't Open

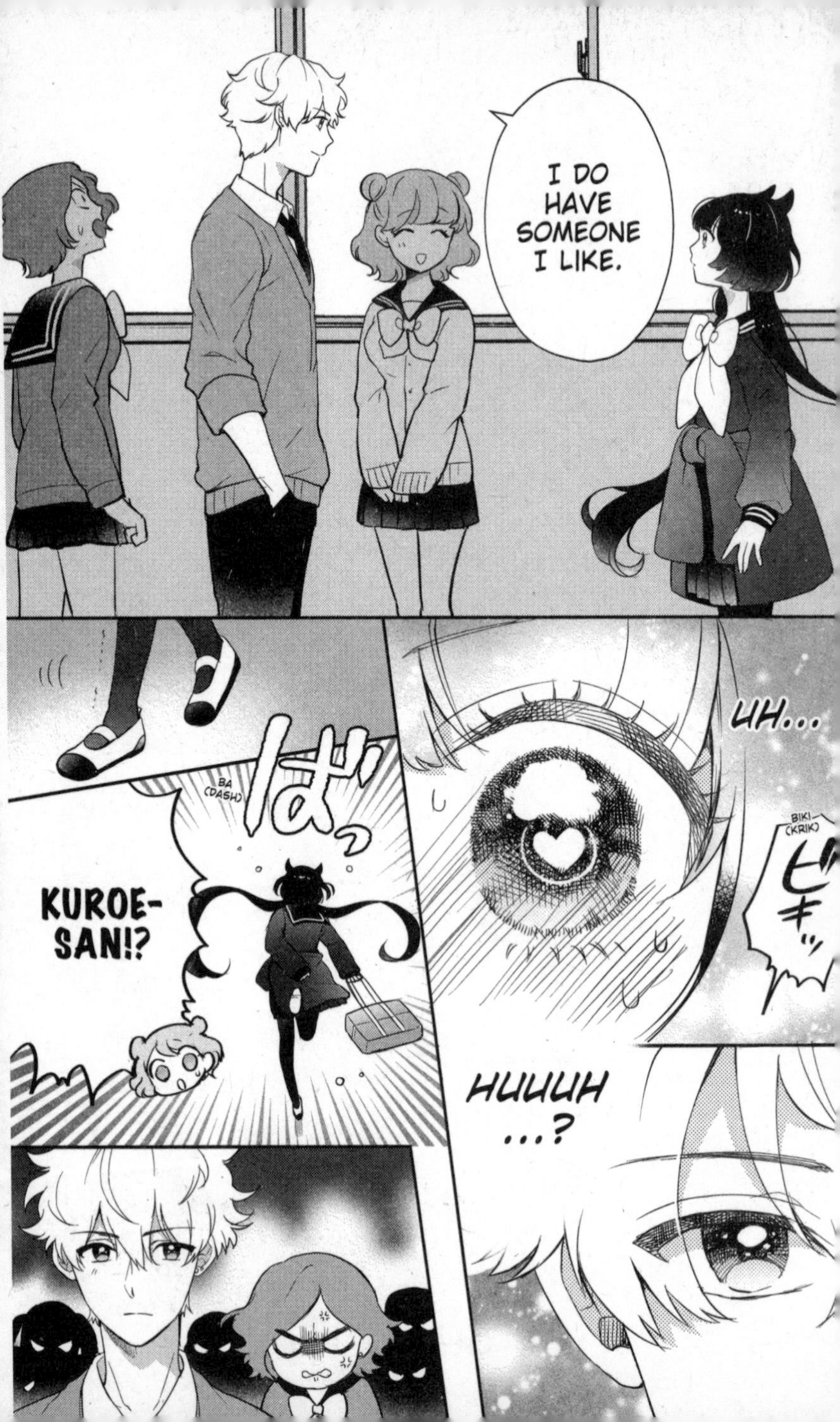

I DO HAVE SOMEONE I LIKE.
UH...
BIKI (KRIK)
ビキッ
HUUUH ...?
BA (DASH)
ばっ
KUROE-SAN!?

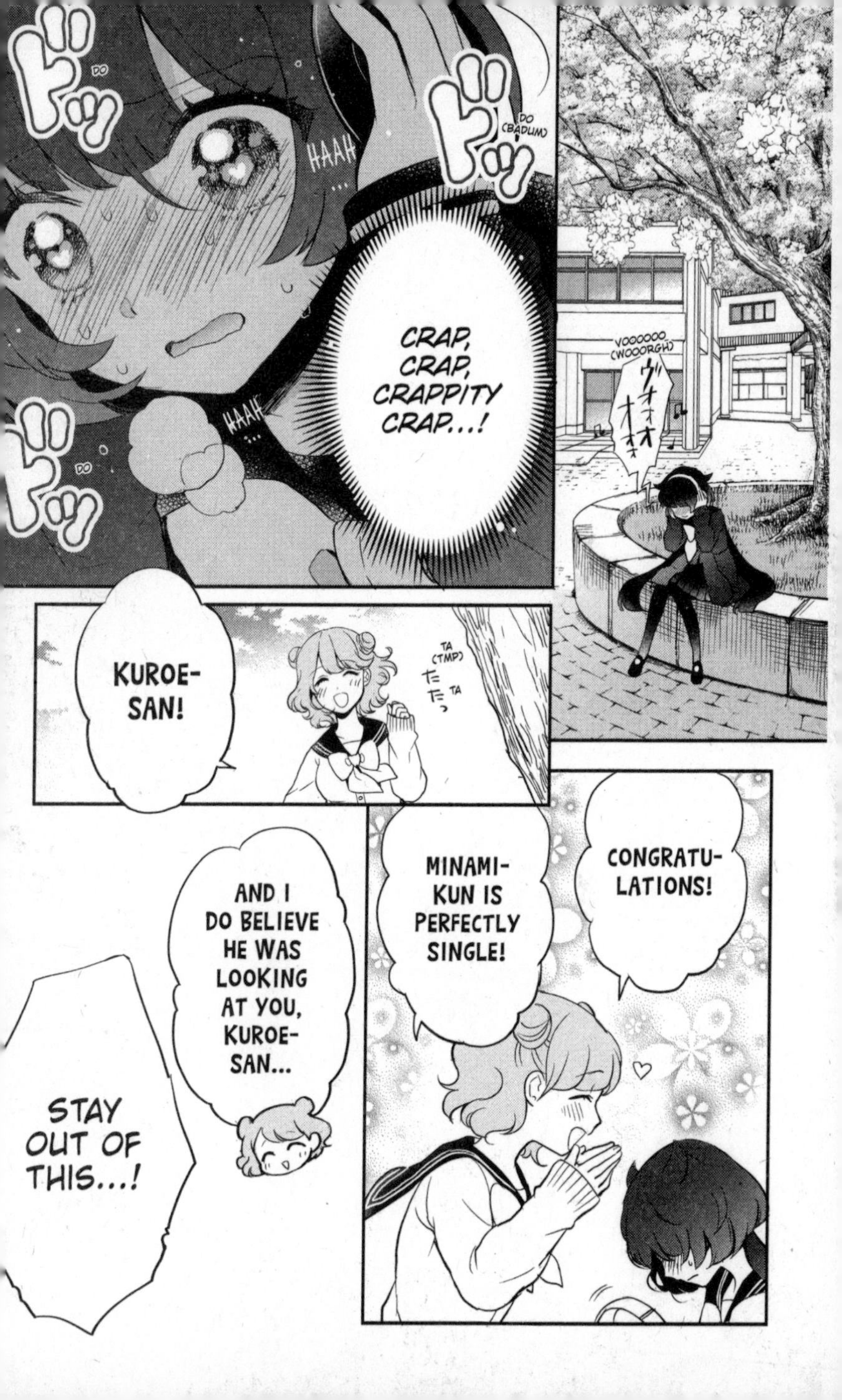
VOOOOOO (WOOORGH)
ヴォオオオォ
DO (BADUM)
DO
HAAH...
CRAP, CRAP, CRAPPITY CRAP...!
HAAH...
DO
KUROE-SAN!
TA (TMP)
たたっ
TA
CONGRATU-LATIONS!
MINAMI-KUN IS PERFECTLY SINGLE!
AND I DO BELIEVE HE WAS LOOKING AT YOU, KUROE-SAN...
STAY OUT OF THIS...!

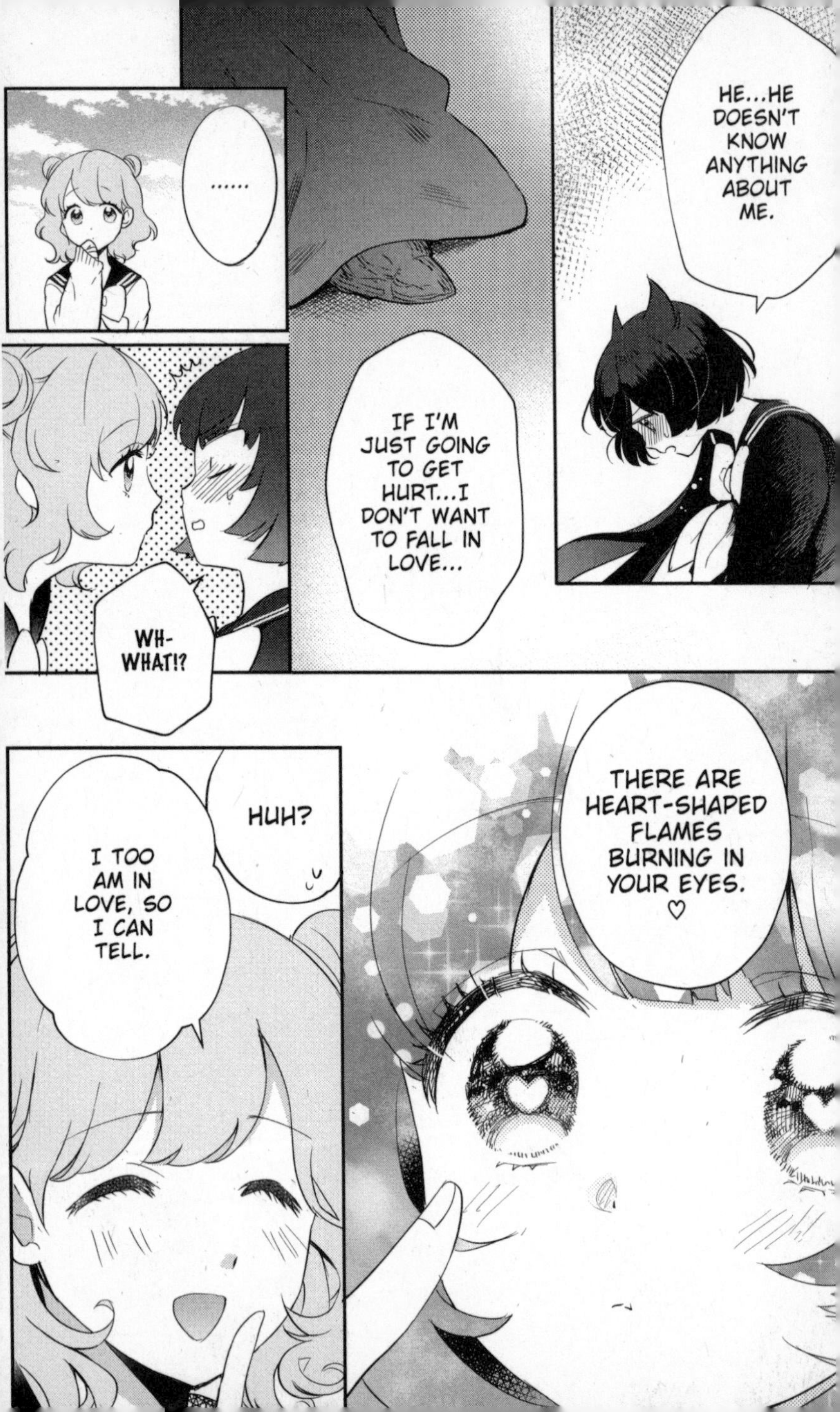
HE...HE DOESN'T KNOW ANYTHING ABOUT ME.
IF I'M JUST GOING TO GET HURT...I DON'T WANT TO FALL IN LOVE...
......
WH- WHAT!?
THERE ARE HEART-SHAPED FLAMES BURNING IN YOUR EYES. ♡
HUH?
I TOO AM IN LOVE, SO I CAN TELL.

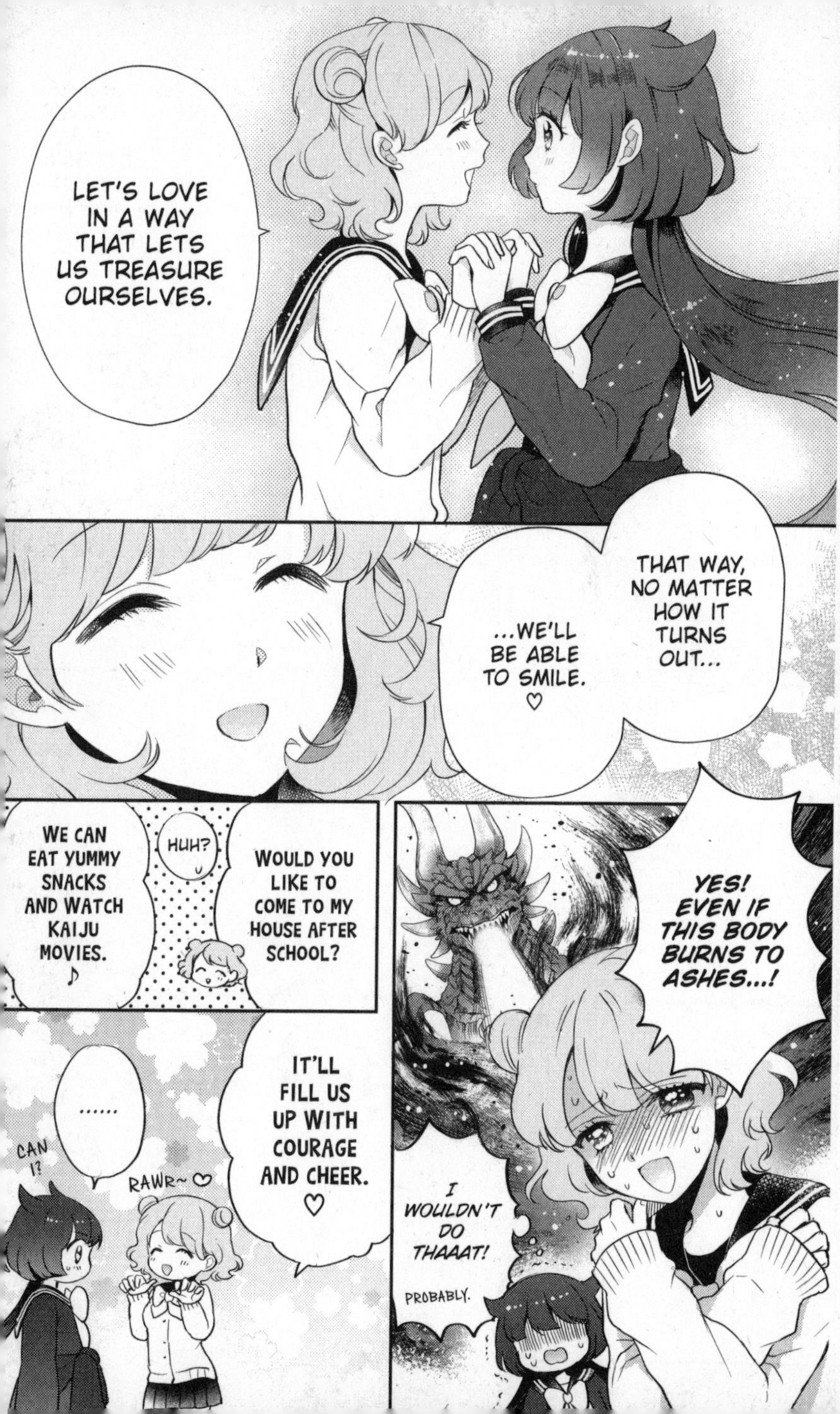
LET'S LOVE IN A WAY THAT LETS US TREASURE OURSELVES.
THAT WAY, NO MATTER HOW IT TURNS OUT...
...WE'LL BE ABLE TO SMILE. ♡
YES! EVEN IF THIS BODY BURNS TO ASHES...!
I WOULDN'T DO THAAAT!
PROBABLY.
WOULD YOU LIKE TO COME TO MY HOUSE AFTER SCHOOL?
HUH?
WE CAN EAT YUMMY SNACKS AND WATCH KAIJU MOVIES. ♪
IT'LL FILL US UP WITH COURAGE AND CHEER. ♡
RAWR~ ♡
......
CAN I?

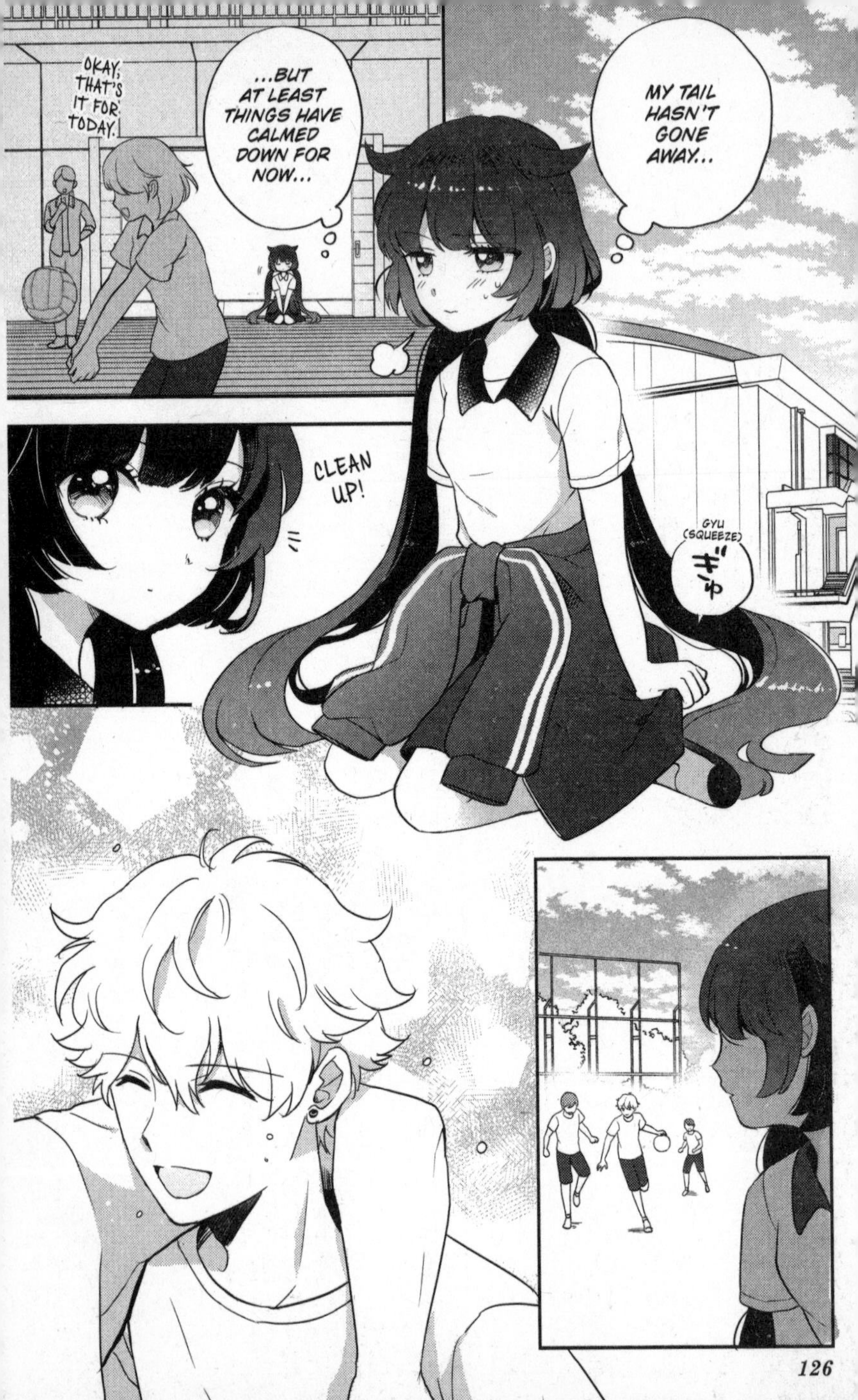
MY TAIL HASN'T GONE AWAY...
...BUT AT LEAST THINGS HAVE CALMED DOWN FOR NOW...
OKAY, THAT'S IT FOR TODAY.
GYU (SQUEEZE)
ぎゅ
CLEAN UP!

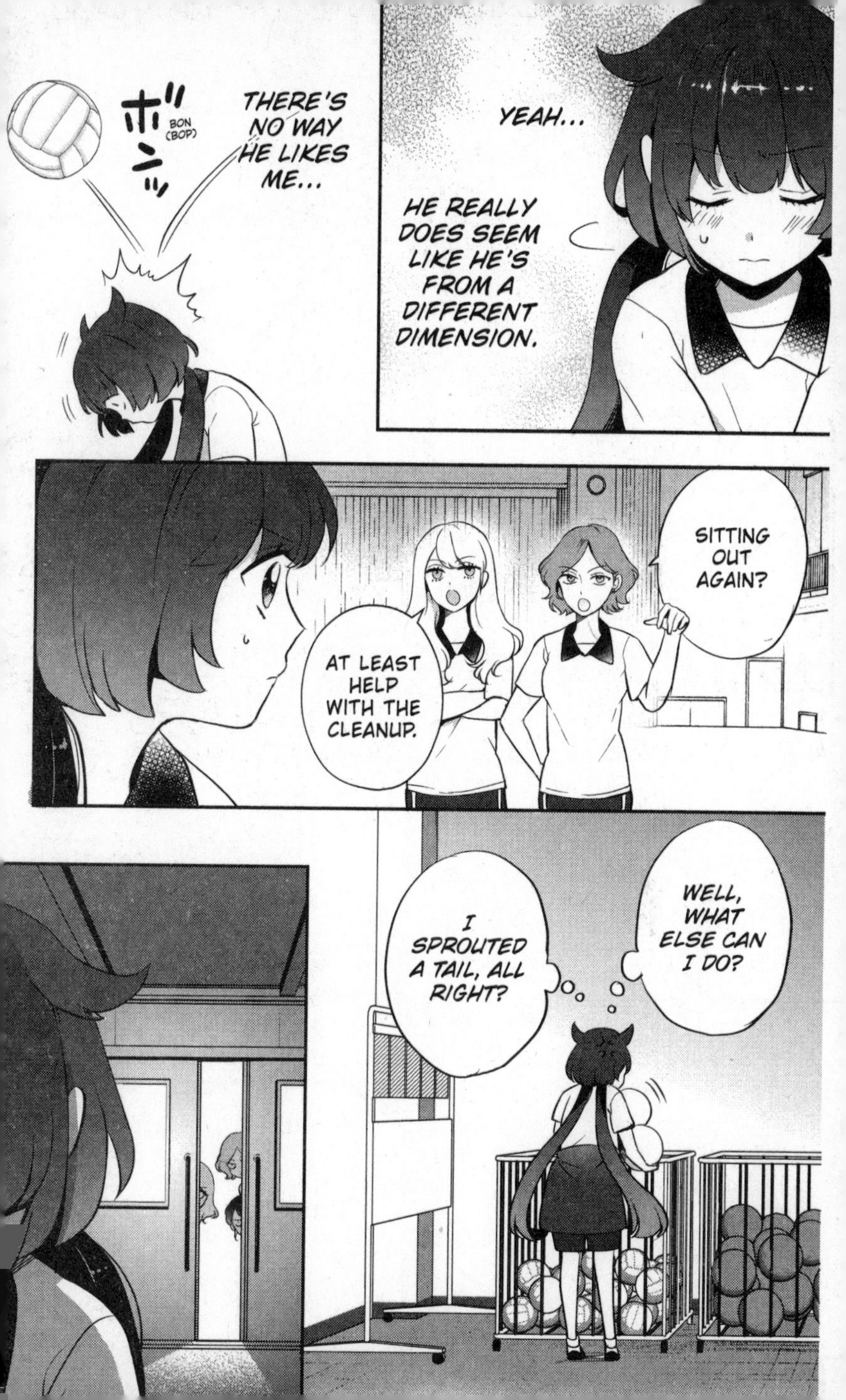
YEAH...
HE REALLY DOES SEEM LIKE HE'S FROM A DIFFERENT DIMENSION.
THERE'S NO WAY HE LIKES ME...
ボンッ
BON (BOP)
SITTING OUT AGAIN?
AT LEAST HELP WITH THE CLEANUP.
WELL, WHAT ELSE CAN I DO?
I SPROUTED A TAIL, ALL RIGHT?

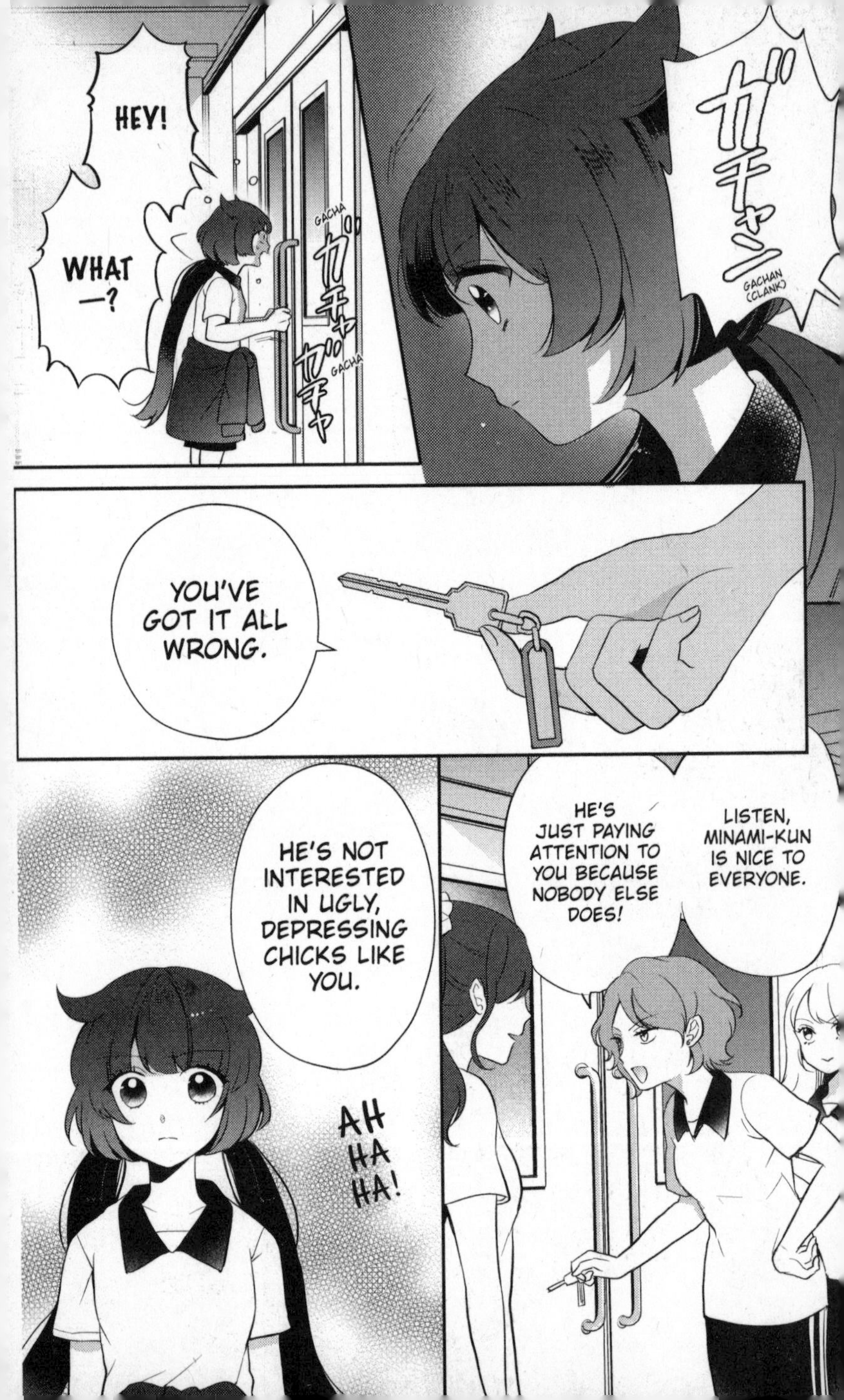
ガチャン
GACHAN (CLANK)
HEY!
WHAT—?
ガチャ
GACHA
ガチャ
GACHA
YOU'VE GOT IT ALL WRONG.
LISTEN, MINAMI-KUN IS NICE TO EVERYONE.
HE'S JUST PAYING ATTENTION TO YOU BECAUSE NOBODY ELSE DOES!
HE'S NOT INTERESTED IN UGLY, DEPRESSING CHICKS LIKE YOU.
AH HA HA!

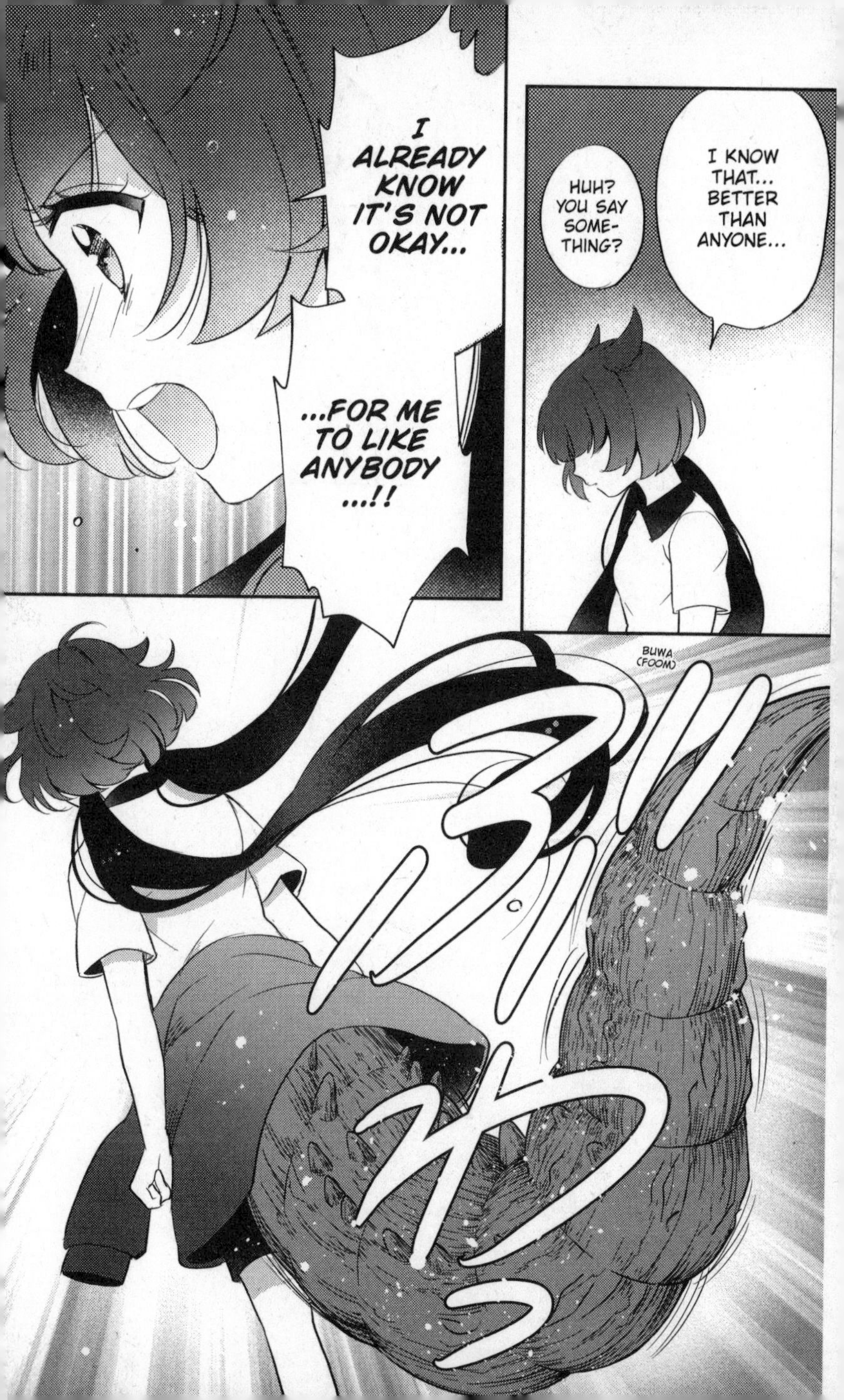
I KNOW THAT... BETTER THAN ANYONE...
HUH? YOU SAY SOME-THING?
I ALREADY KNOW IT'S NOT OKAY...
...FOR ME TO LIKE ANYBODY ...!!
BUWA (FOOM)

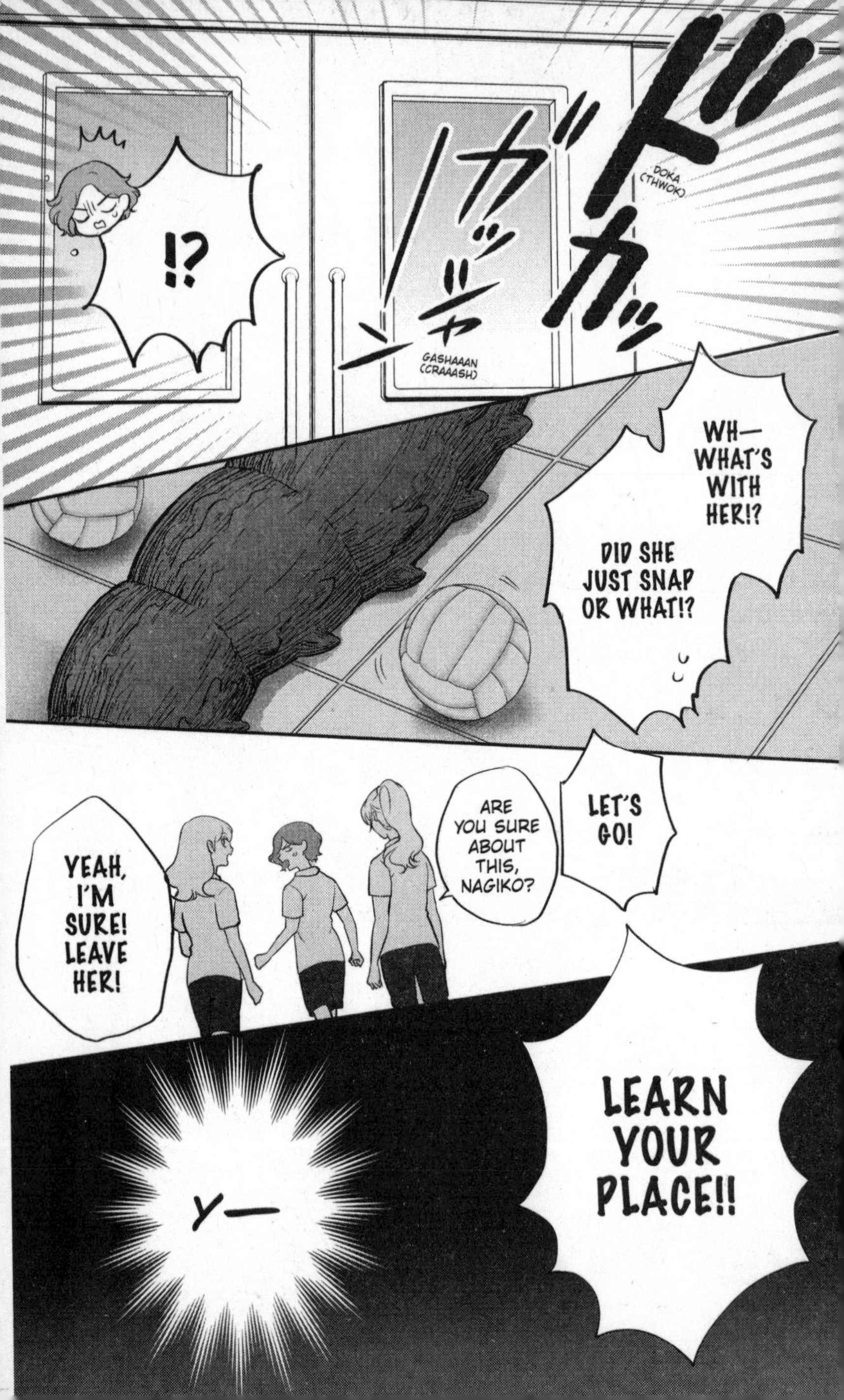
DOKA (THWOK)
GASHAAAN (CRAAASH)
!?
WH— WHAT'S WITH HER!?
DID SHE JUST SNAP OR WHAT!?
LET'S GO!
ARE YOU SURE ABOUT THIS, NAGIKO?
YEAH, I'M SURE! LEAVE HER!
LEARN YOUR PLACE!!
Y—

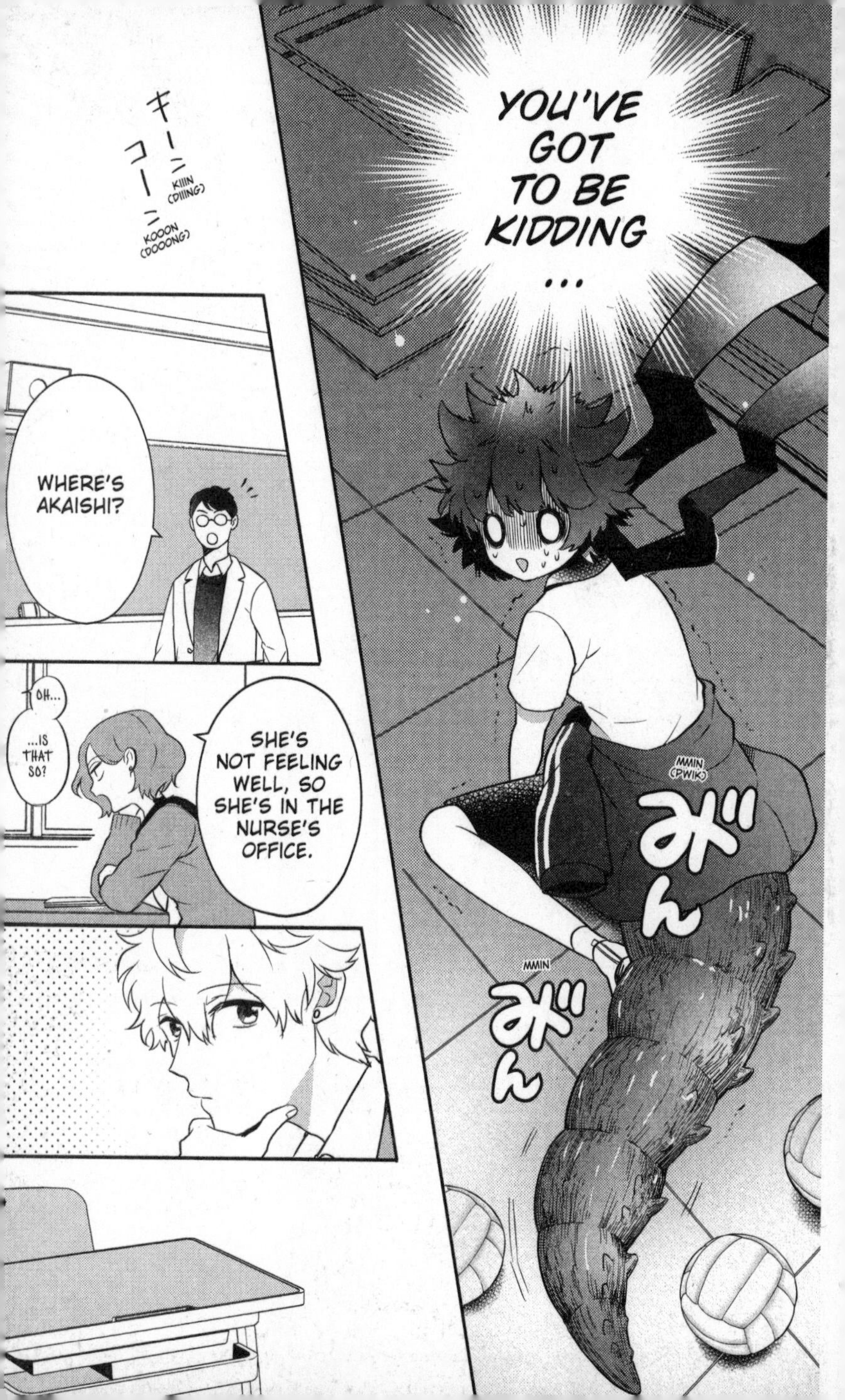
YOU'VE GOT TO BE KIDDING...
みﾞん
MMIN (PWIK)
みﾞん
MMIN
キーンコーン
KIIN (DIIING)
KOOON (DOOONG)
WHERE'S AKAISHI?
SHE'S NOT FEELING WELL, SO SHE'S IN THE NURSE'S OFFICE.
OH...
...IS THAT SO?

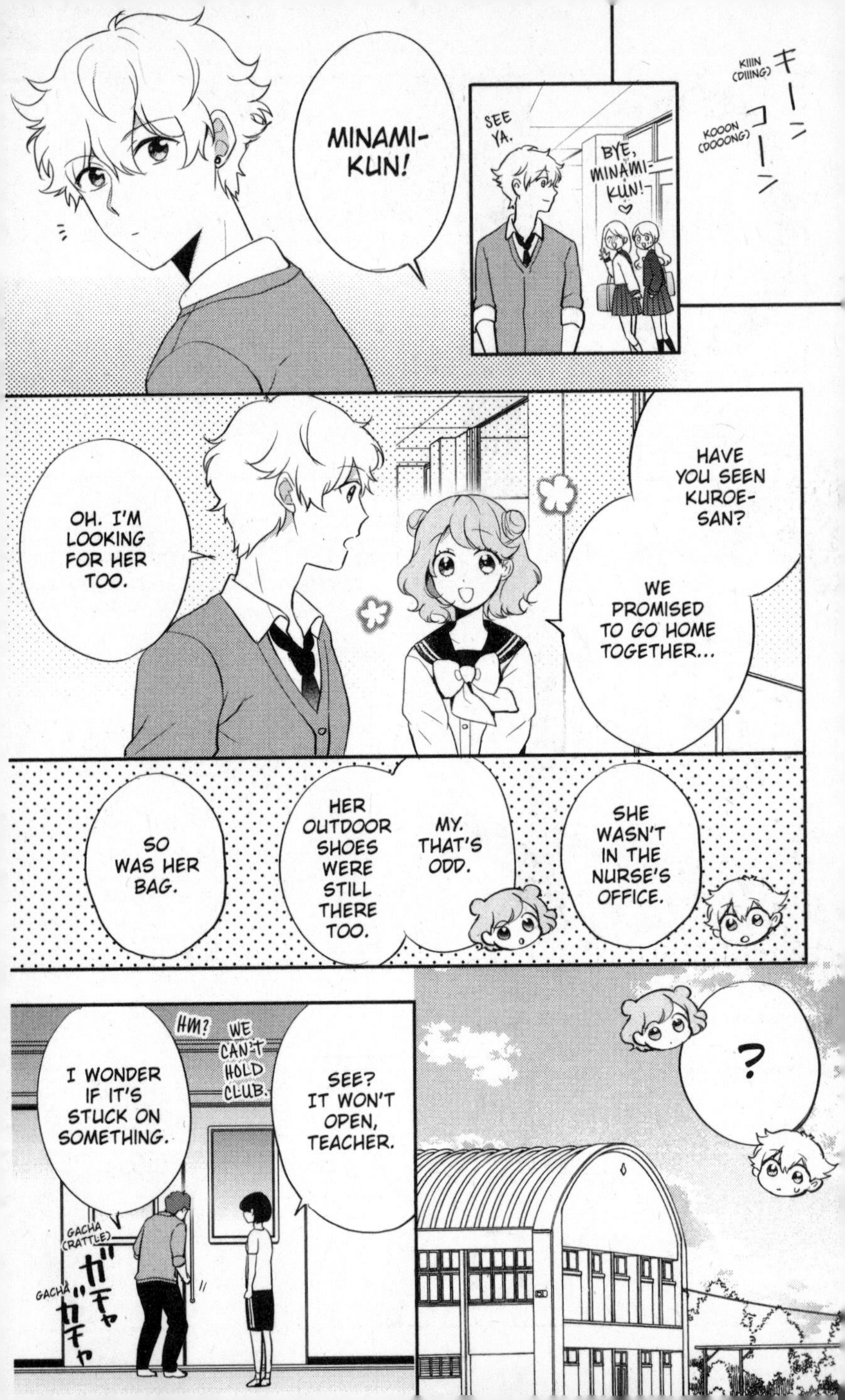
キーン
KIIIN (DIIING)
コーン
KOOON (DOOONG)
BYE, MINAMI-KUN!
SEE YA.
MINAMI-KUN!
HAVE YOU SEEN KUROE-SAN?
WE PROMISED TO GO HOME TOGETHER...
OH. I'M LOOKING FOR HER TOO.
SHE WASN'T IN THE NURSE'S OFFICE.
MY. THAT'S ODD.
HER OUTDOOR SHOES WERE STILL THERE TOO.
SO WAS HER BAG.
?
SEE? IT WON'T OPEN, TEACHER.
WE CAN'T HOLD CLUB.
HM?
I WONDER IF IT'S STUCK ON SOMETHING.
ガチャ
GACHA (RATTLE)
ガチャ
GACHA

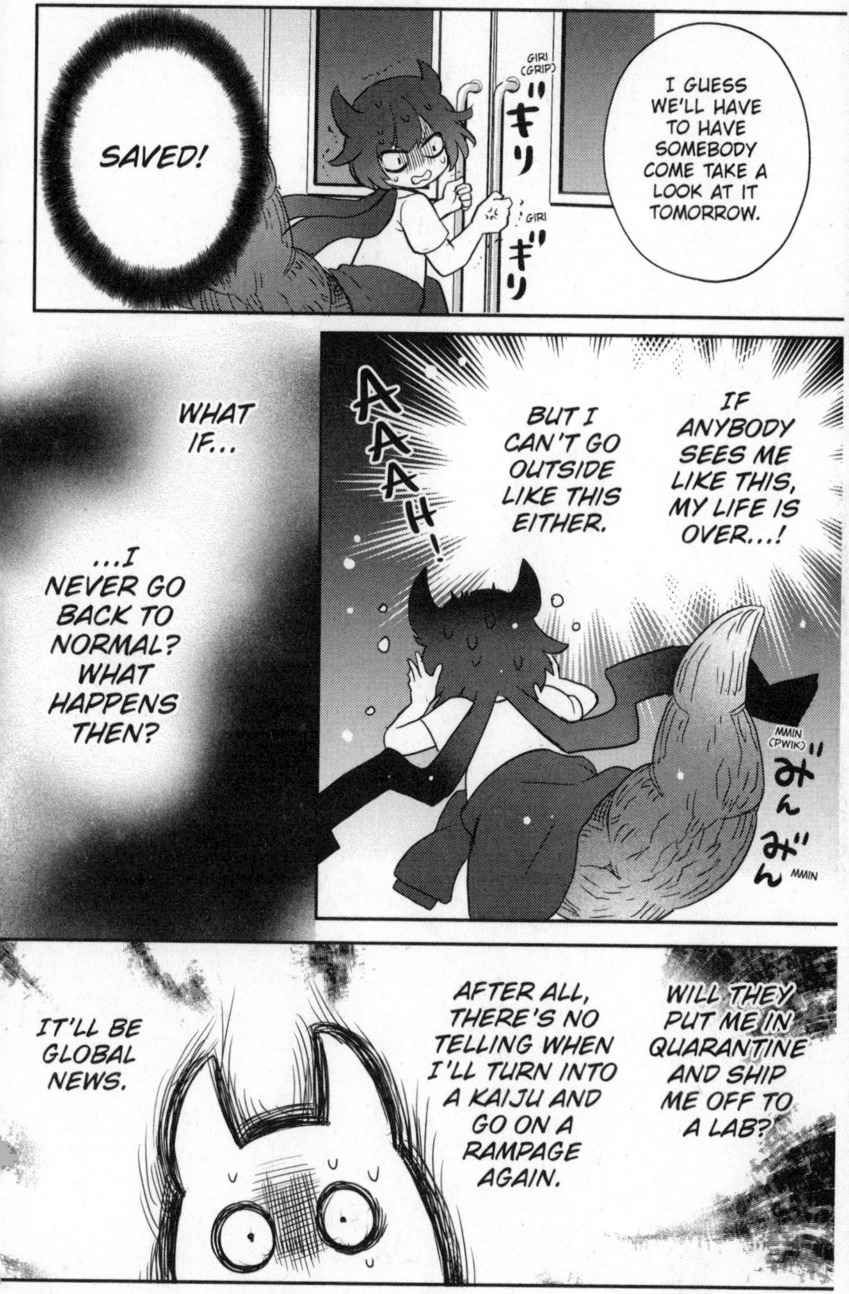
I GUESS WE'LL HAVE TO HAVE SOMEBODY COME TAKE A LOOK AT IT TOMORROW.
GIRI (GRIP)
ギリ
GIRI
ギリ
SAVED!
IF ANYBODY SEES ME LIKE THIS, MY LIFE IS OVER...!
BUT I CAN'T GO OUTSIDE LIKE THIS EITHER.
AAAH!
MMIN (PWIK)
みん
MMIN
みん
WHAT IF...
...I NEVER GO BACK TO NORMAL? WHAT HAPPENS THEN?
WILL THEY PUT ME IN QUARANTINE AND SHIP ME OFF TO A LAB?
AFTER ALL, THERE'S NO TELLING WHEN I'LL TURN INTO A KAIJU AND GO ON A RAMPAGE AGAIN.
IT'LL BE GLOBAL NEWS.

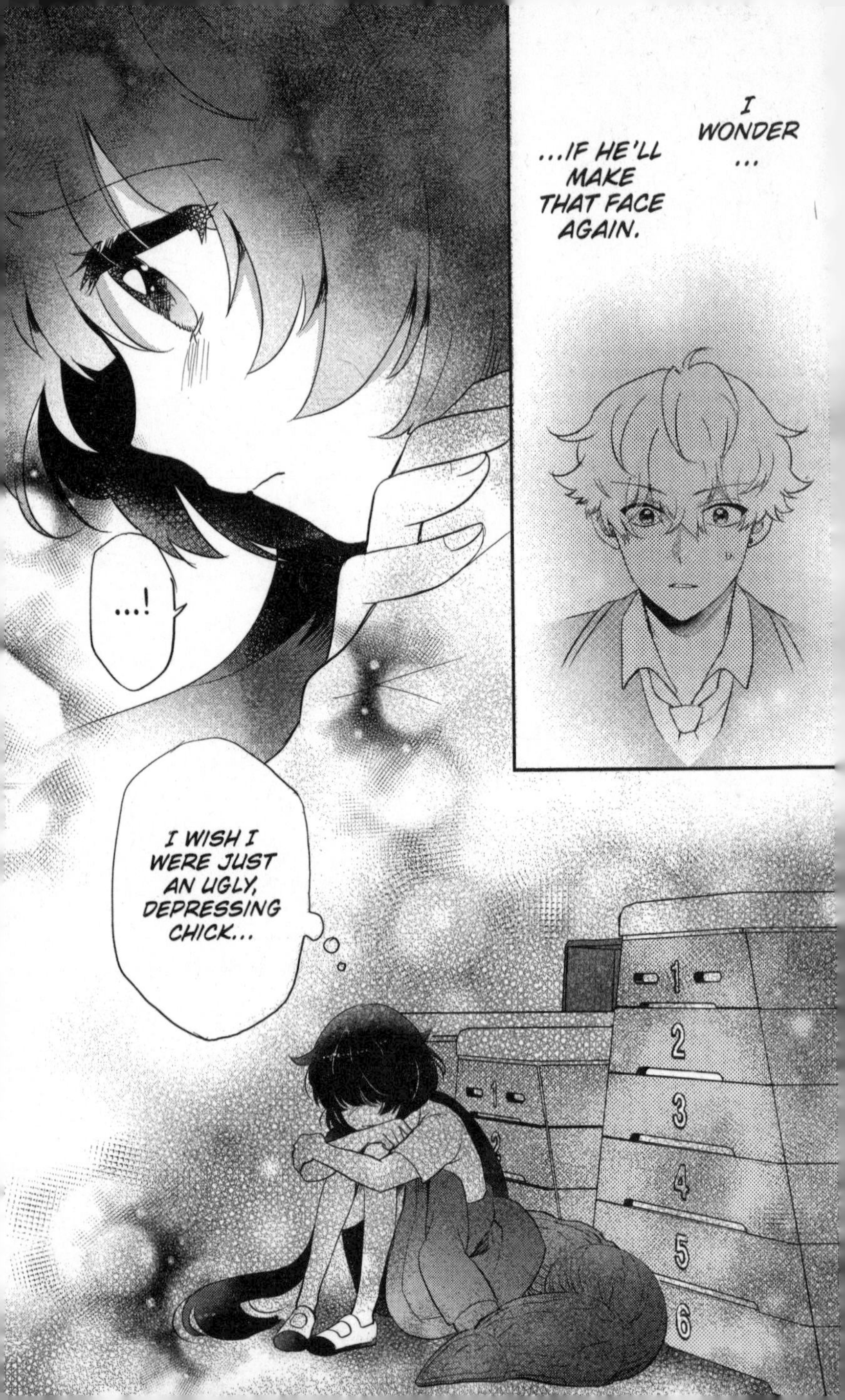
I WONDER...
...IF HE'LL MAKE THAT FACE AGAIN.
...!
I WISH I WERE JUST AN UGLY, DEPRESSING CHICK...

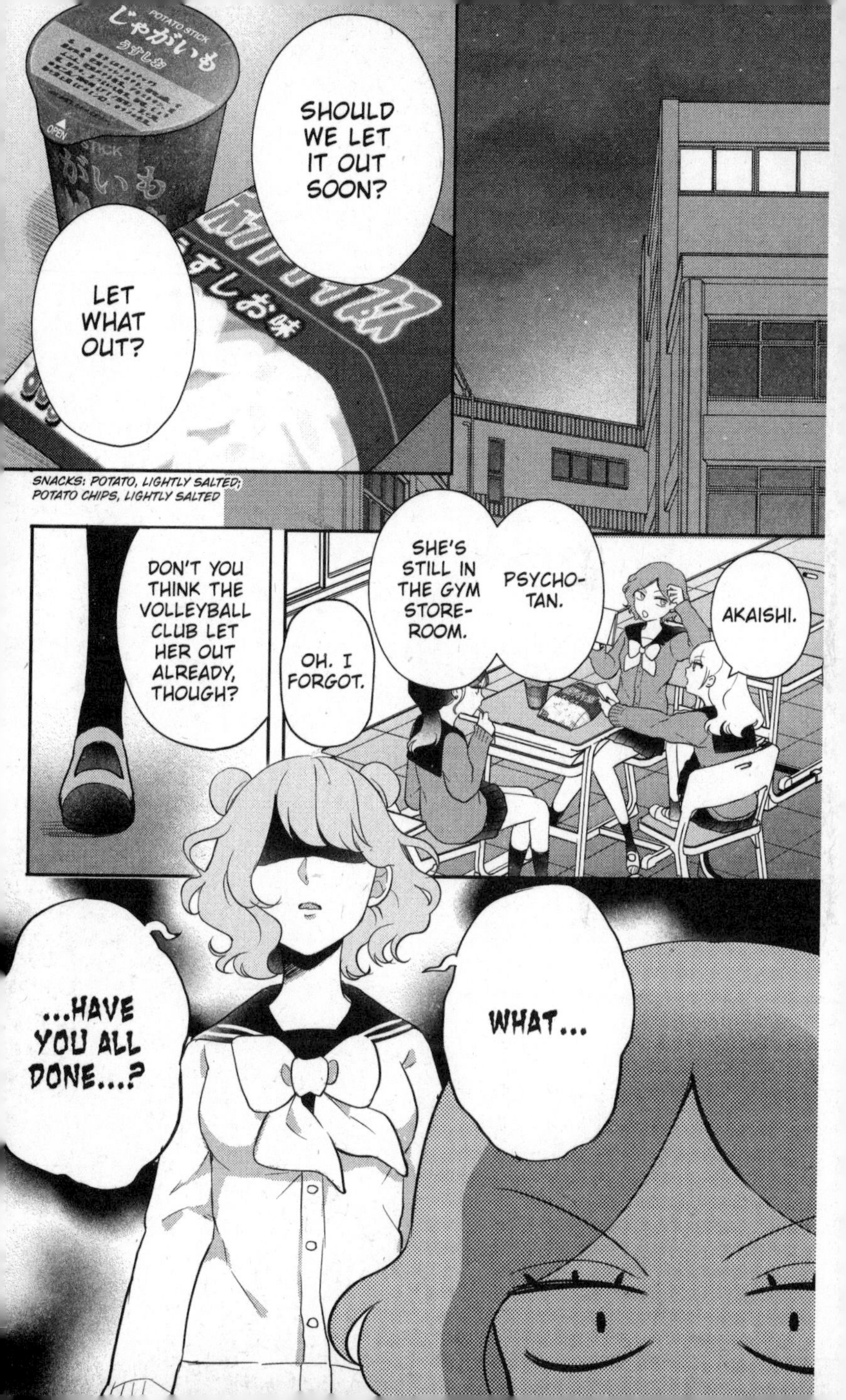
POTATO STICK
じゃがいも
OPEN
SHOULD WE LET IT OUT SOON?
LET WHAT OUT?
SNACKS: POTATO, LIGHTLY SALTED; POTATO CHIPS, LIGHTLY SALTED
AKAISHI.
PSYCHO-TAN.
SHE'S STILL IN THE GYM STORE-ROOM.
OH. I FORGOT.
DON'T YOU THINK THE VOLLEYBALL CLUB LET HER OUT ALREADY, THOUGH?
WHAT...
...HAVE YOU ALL DONE...?

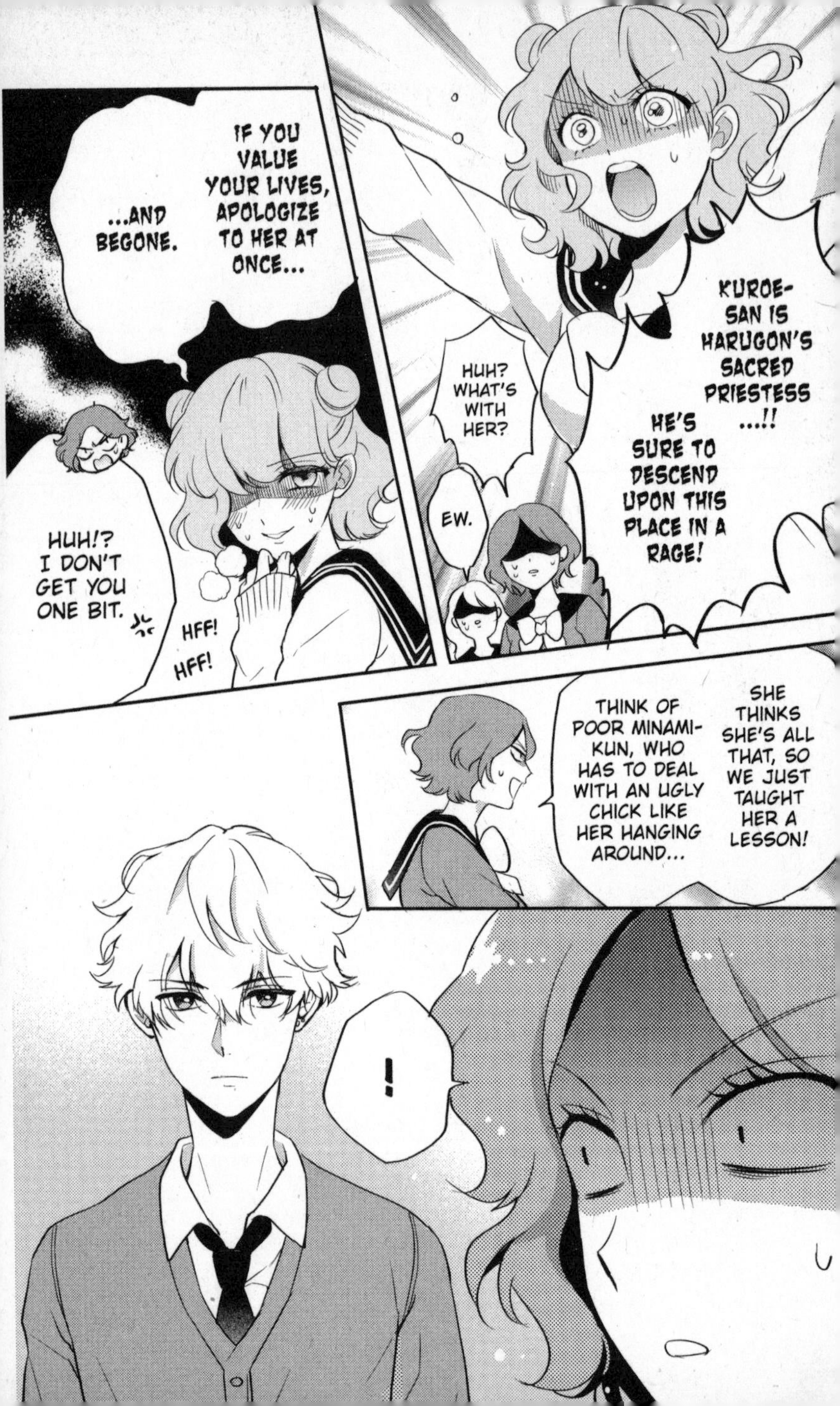
KUROE-SAN IS HARUGON'S SACRED PRIESTESS ...!!
HE'S SURE TO DESCEND UPON THIS PLACE IN A RAGE!
HUH? WHAT'S WITH HER?
EW.
IF YOU VALUE YOUR LIVES, APOLOGIZE TO HER AT ONCE...
...AND BEGONE.
HUH!? I DON'T GET YOU ONE BIT.
HFF!
HFF!
SHE THINKS SHE'S ALL THAT, SO WE JUST TAUGHT HER A LESSON!
THINK OF POOR MINAMI-KUN, WHO HAS TO DEAL WITH AN UGLY CHICK LIKE HER HANGING AROUND...
!

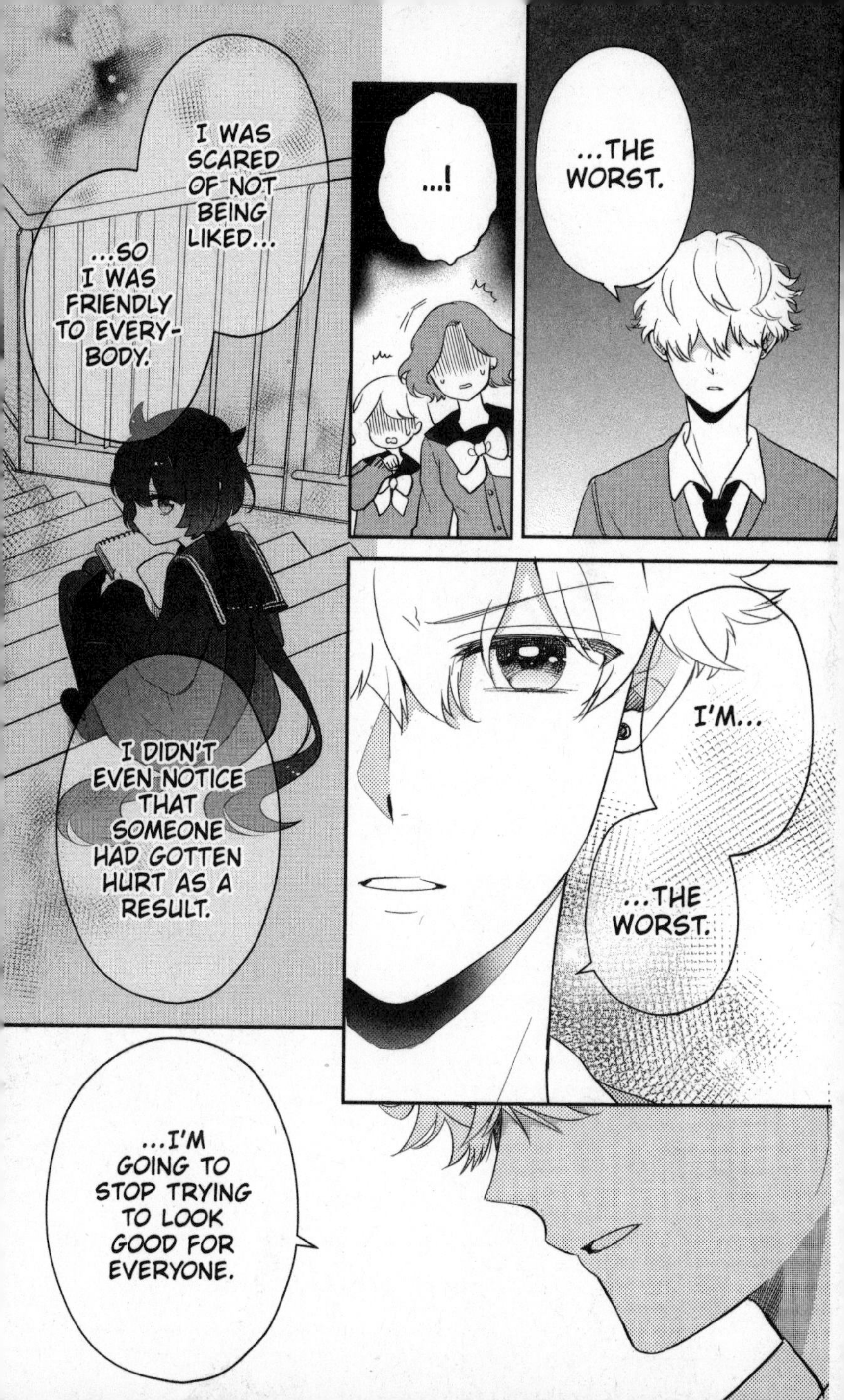
...THE WORST.
...!
I'M...
...THE WORST.
I WAS SCARED OF NOT BEING LIKED...
...SO I WAS FRIENDLY TO EVERY-BODY.
I DIDN'T EVEN NOTICE THAT SOMEONE HAD GOTTEN HURT AS A RESULT.
...I'M GOING TO STOP TRYING TO LOOK GOOD FOR EVERYONE.

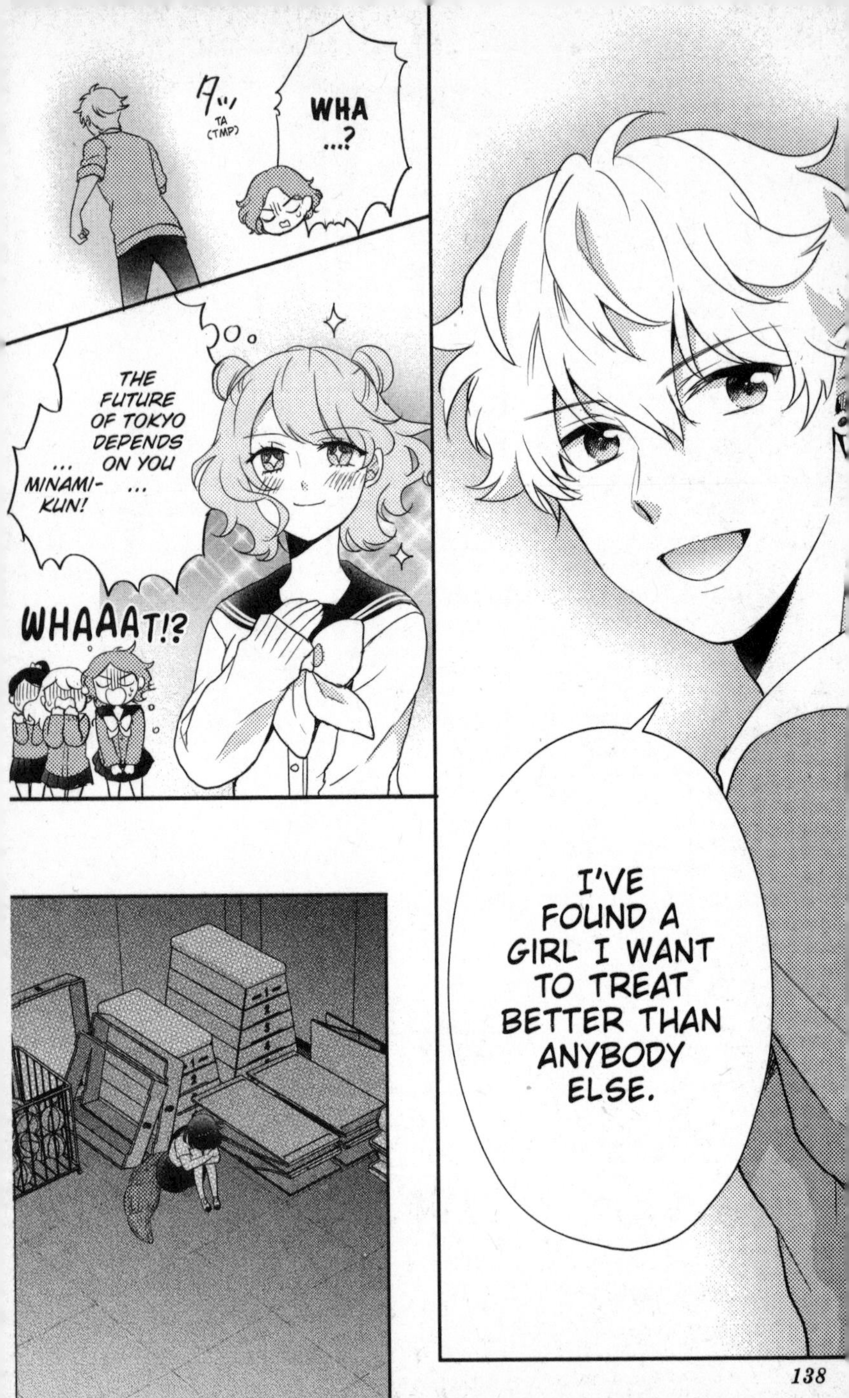
I'VE FOUND A GIRL I WANT TO TREAT BETTER THAN ANYBODY ELSE.
WHA ...?
タッ
TA (TMP)
THE FUTURE OF TOKYO DEPENDS ON YOU ... MINAMI-KUN! ...
WHAAAT!?

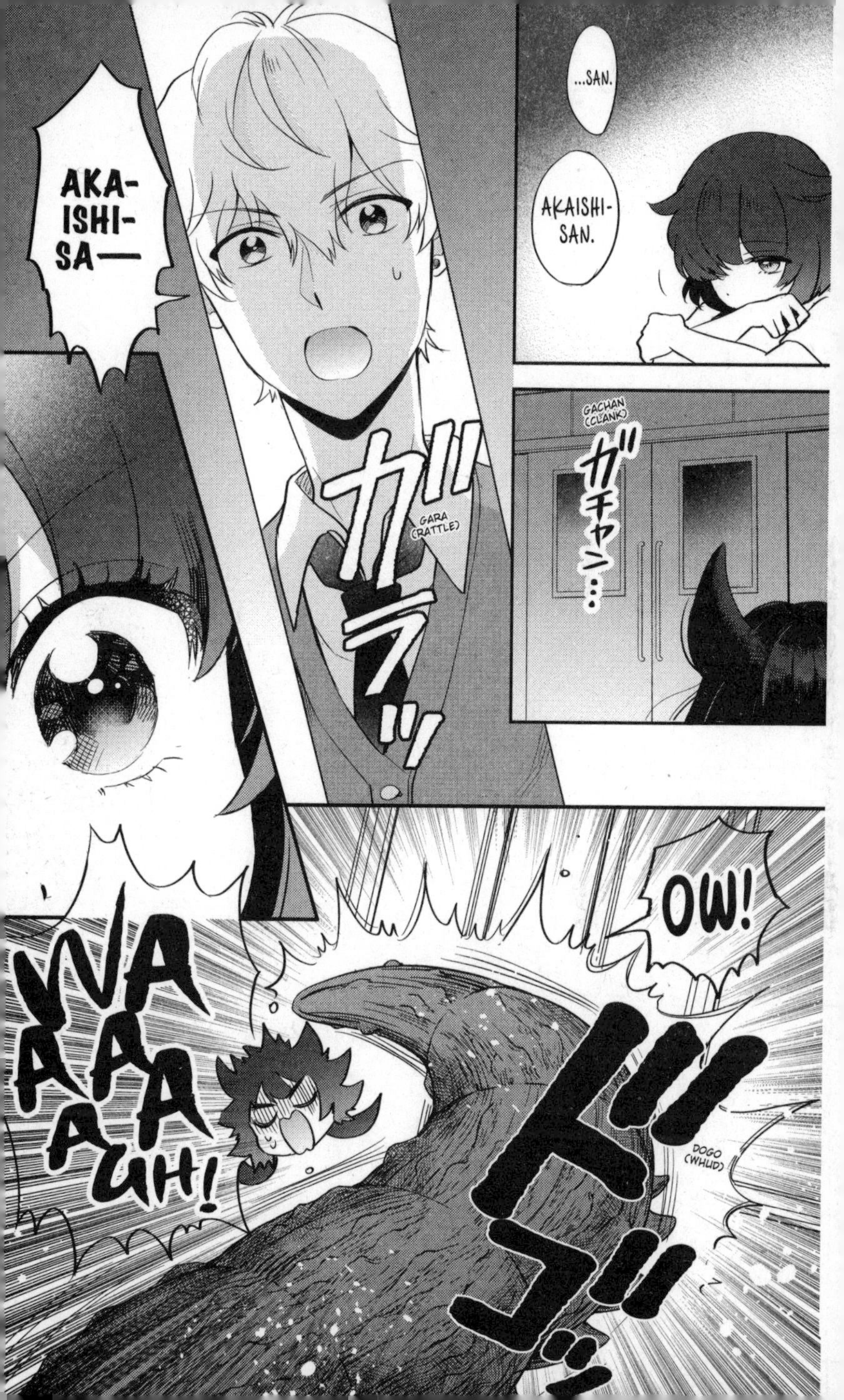
...SAN.
AKAISHI-SAN.
GACHAN (CLANK)
ガチャン…
AKA-ISHI-SA—
GARA (RATTLE)
ガラッ
OW!
DOGO (WHUD)
ドゴッ
WAAAAAAAUH!

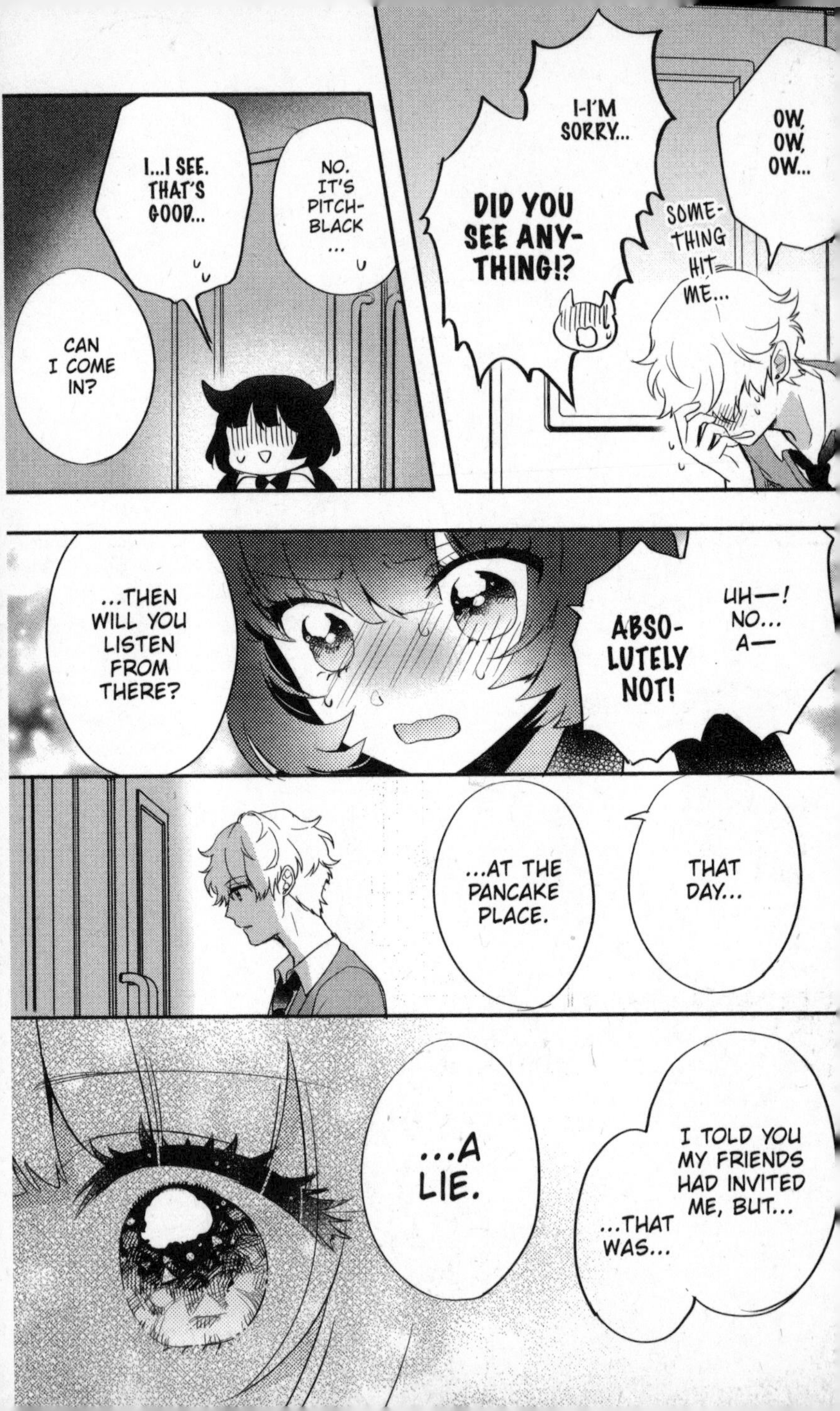
OW, OW, OW...
SOMETHING HIT ME...
I-I'M SORRY...
DID YOU SEE ANYTHING!?
NO. IT'S PITCH-BLACK...
I...I SEE. THAT'S GOOD...
CAN I COME IN?
UH—! NO... A—
ABSOLUTELY NOT!
...THEN WILL YOU LISTEN FROM THERE?
THAT DAY...
...AT THE PANCAKE PLACE.
I TOLD YOU MY FRIENDS HAD INVITED ME, BUT...
...THAT WAS...
...A LIE.

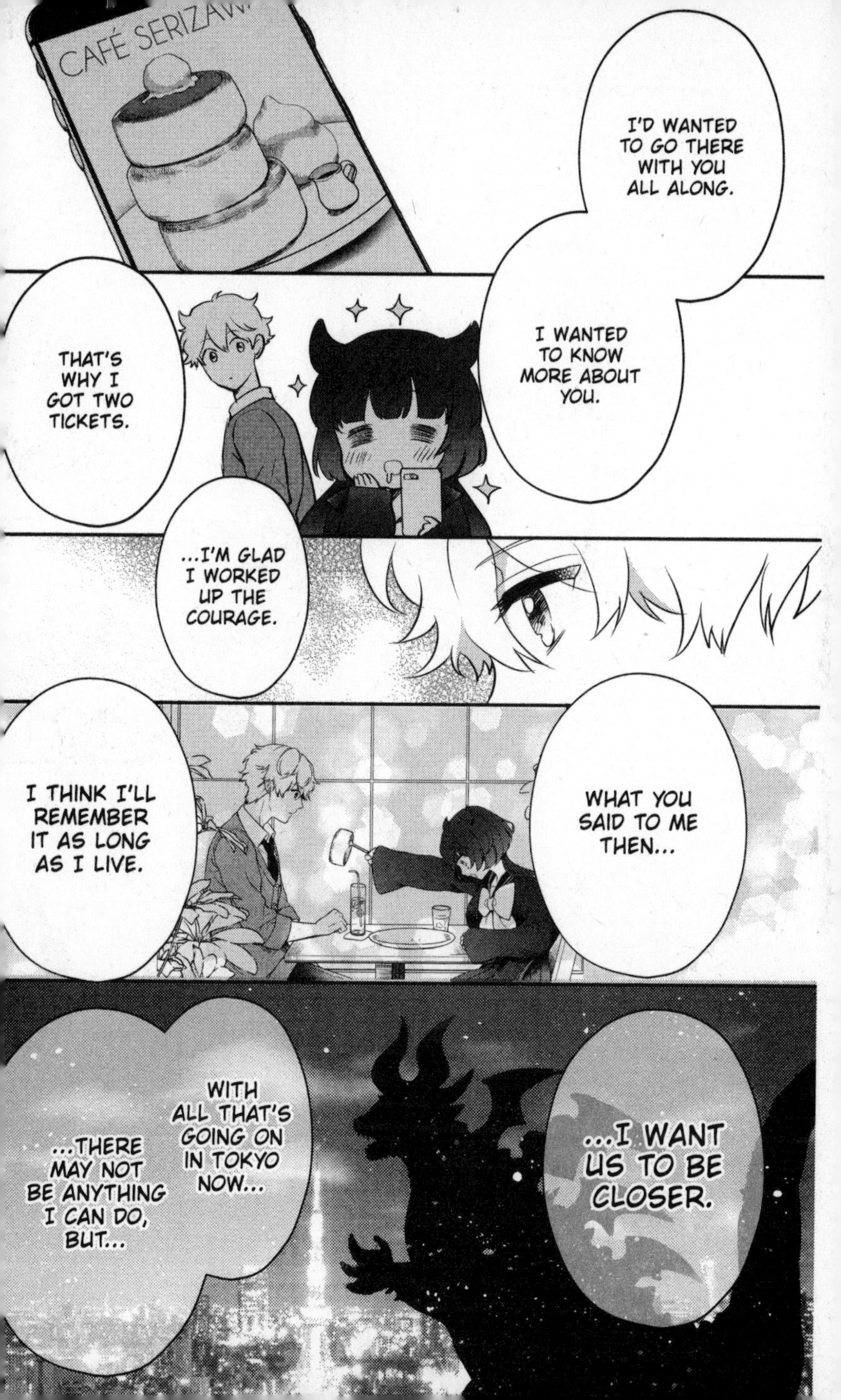
I'D WANTED TO GO THERE WITH YOU ALL ALONG.
CAFÉ SERIZAW
I WANTED TO KNOW MORE ABOUT YOU.
THAT'S WHY I GOT TWO TICKETS.
...I'M GLAD I WORKED UP THE COURAGE.
WHAT YOU SAID TO ME THEN...
I THINK I'LL REMEMBER IT AS LONG AS I LIVE.
...I WANT US TO BE CLOSER.
WITH ALL THAT'S GOING ON IN TOKYO NOW...
...THERE MAY NOT BE ANYTHING I CAN DO, BUT...

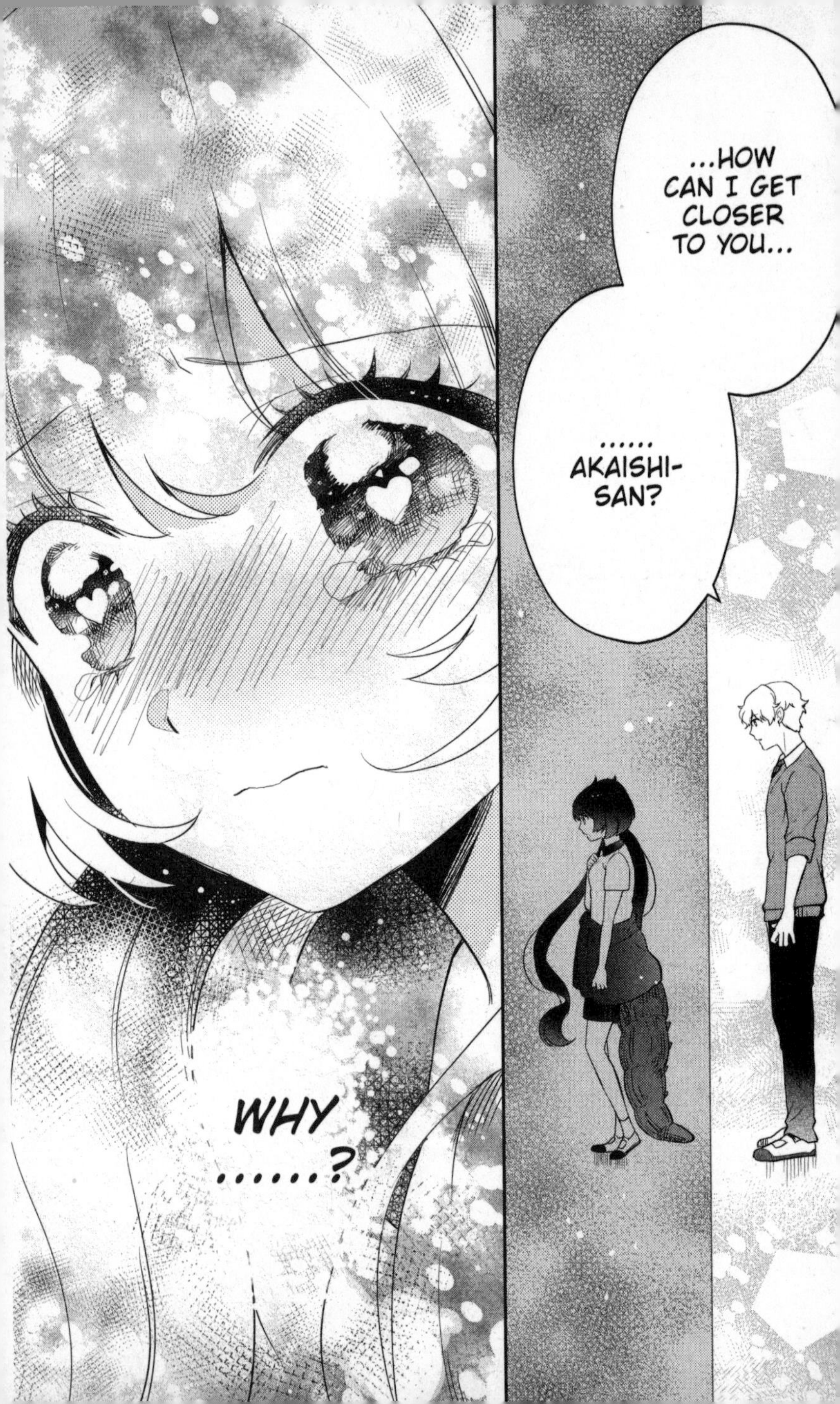
...HOW CAN I GET CLOSER TO YOU...
...... AKAISHI-SAN?
WHY ......?

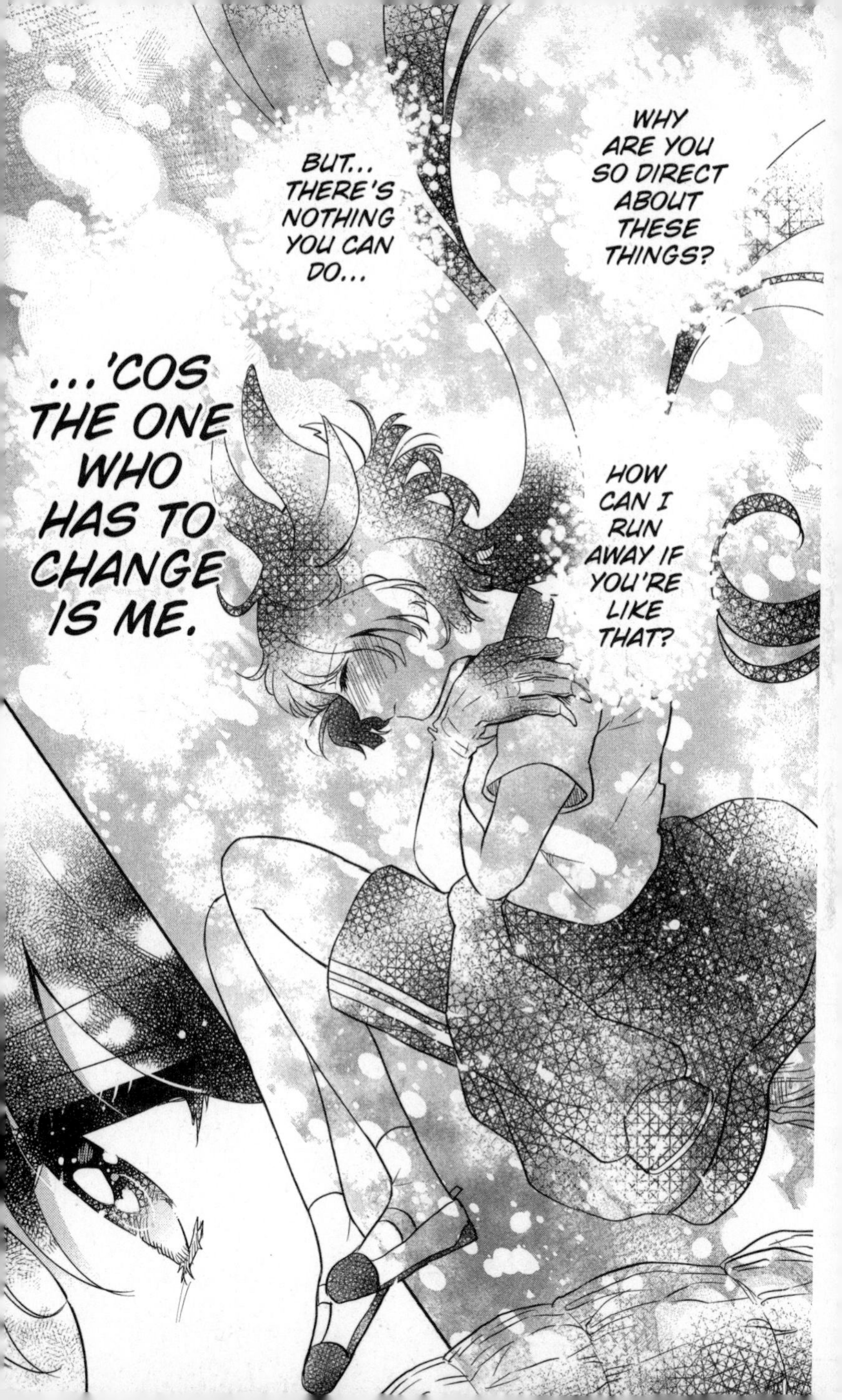
WHY ARE YOU SO DIRECT ABOUT THESE THINGS?
BUT... THERE'S NOTHING YOU CAN DO...
HOW CAN I RUN AWAY IF YOU'RE LIKE THAT?
...'COS THE ONE WHO HAS TO CHANGE IS ME.

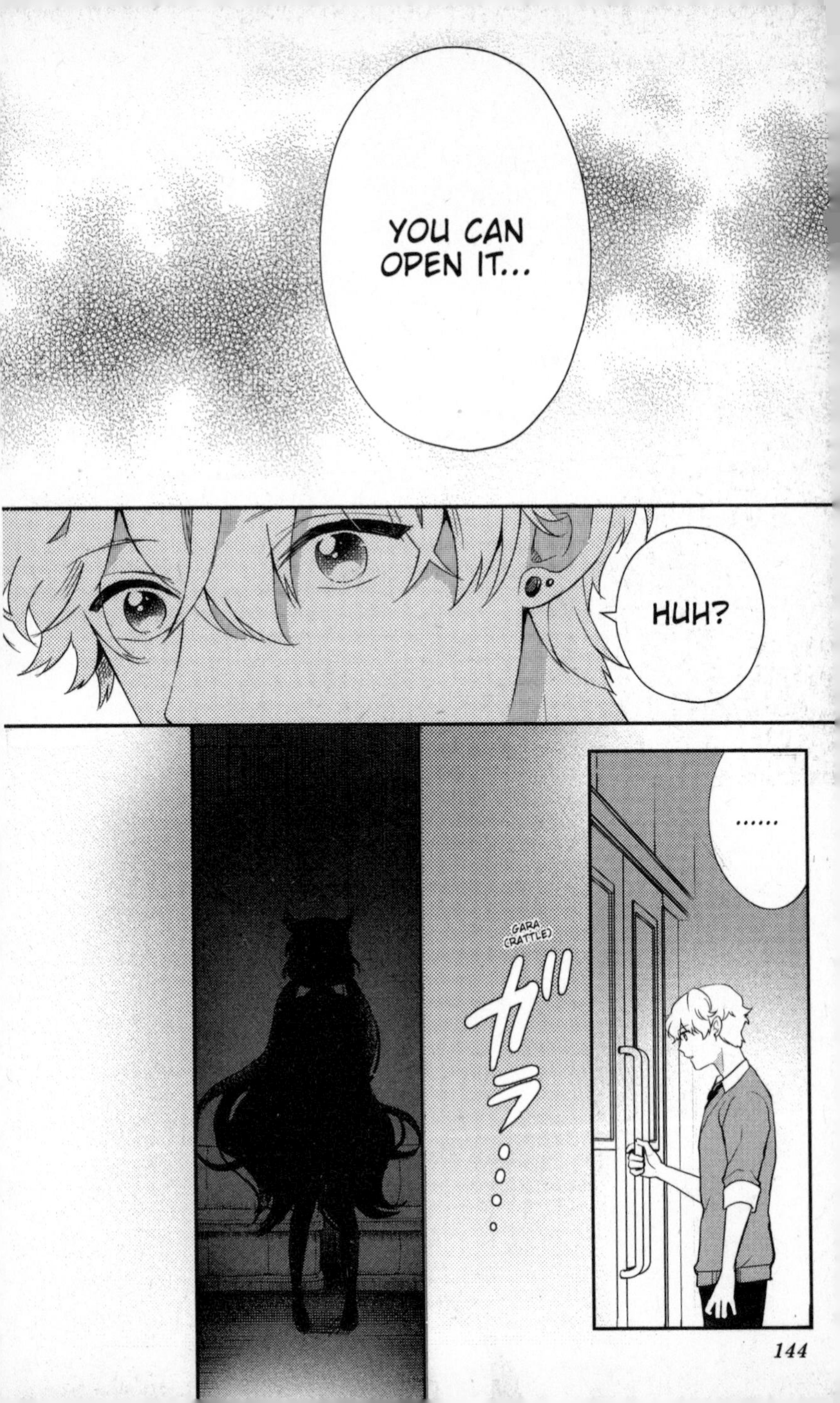
YOU CAN OPEN IT...
HUH?
......
GARA (RATTLE)
ガラ・・・・

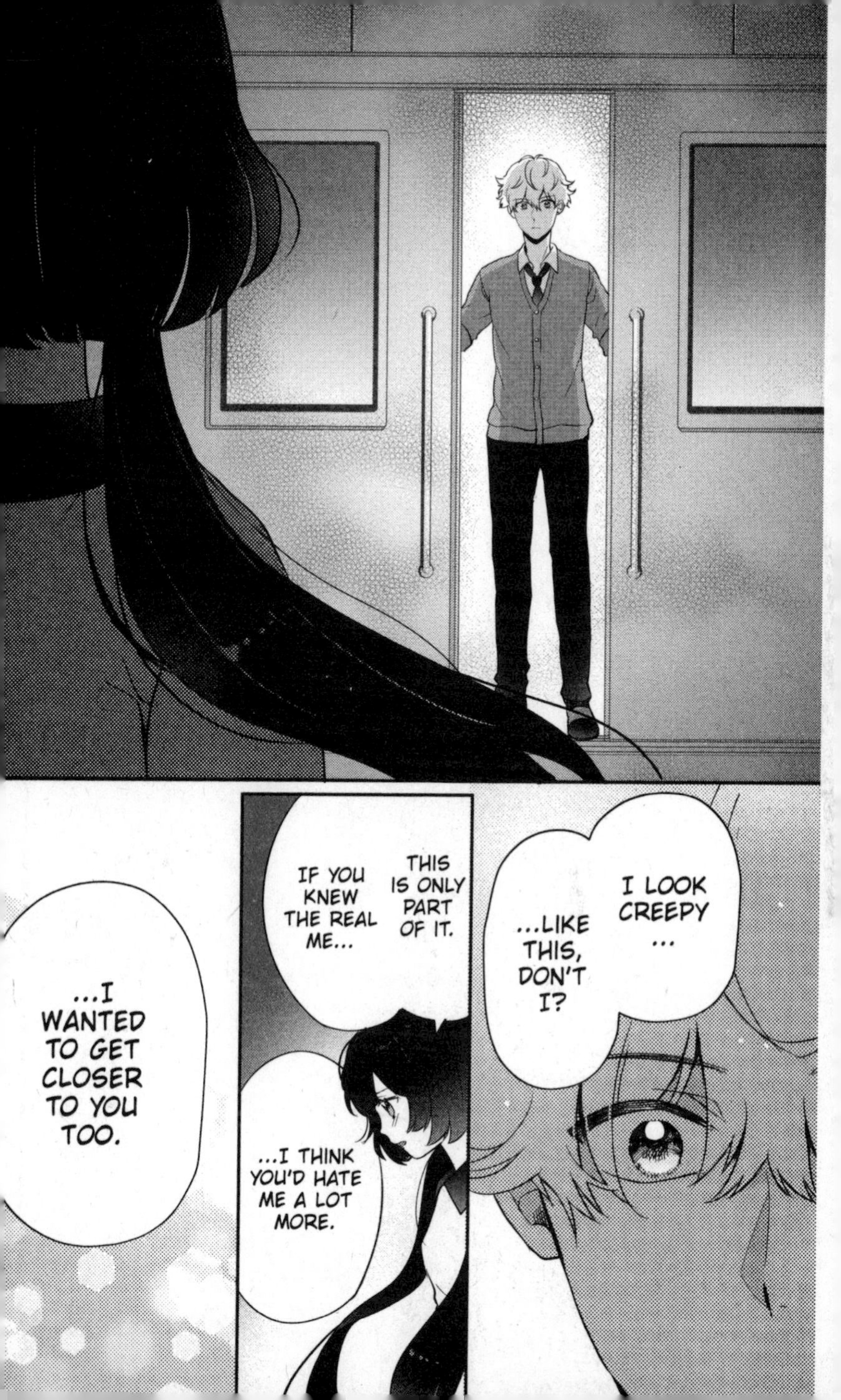
I LOOK CREEPY...
...LIKE THIS, DON'T I?
THIS IS ONLY PART OF IT.
IF YOU KNEW THE REAL ME...
...I THINK YOU'D HATE ME A LOT MORE.
...I WANTED TO GET CLOSER TO YOU TOO.

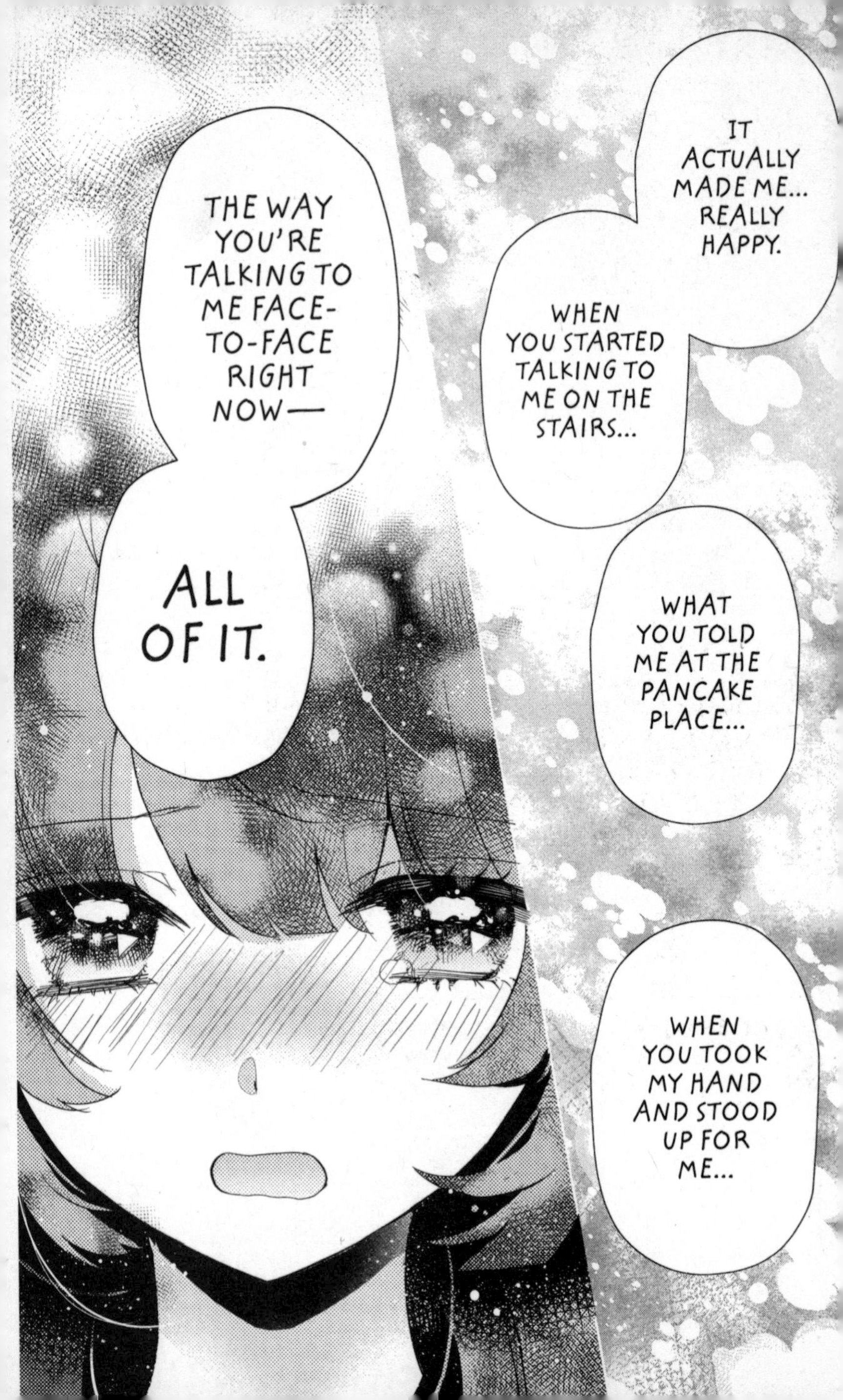
IT ACTUALLY MADE ME... REALLY HAPPY.
WHEN YOU STARTED TALKING TO ME ON THE STAIRS...
WHAT YOU TOLD ME AT THE PANCAKE PLACE...
WHEN YOU TOOK MY HAND AND STOOD UP FOR ME...
THE WAY YOU'RE TALKING TO ME FACE-TO-FACE RIGHT NOW—
ALL OF IT.

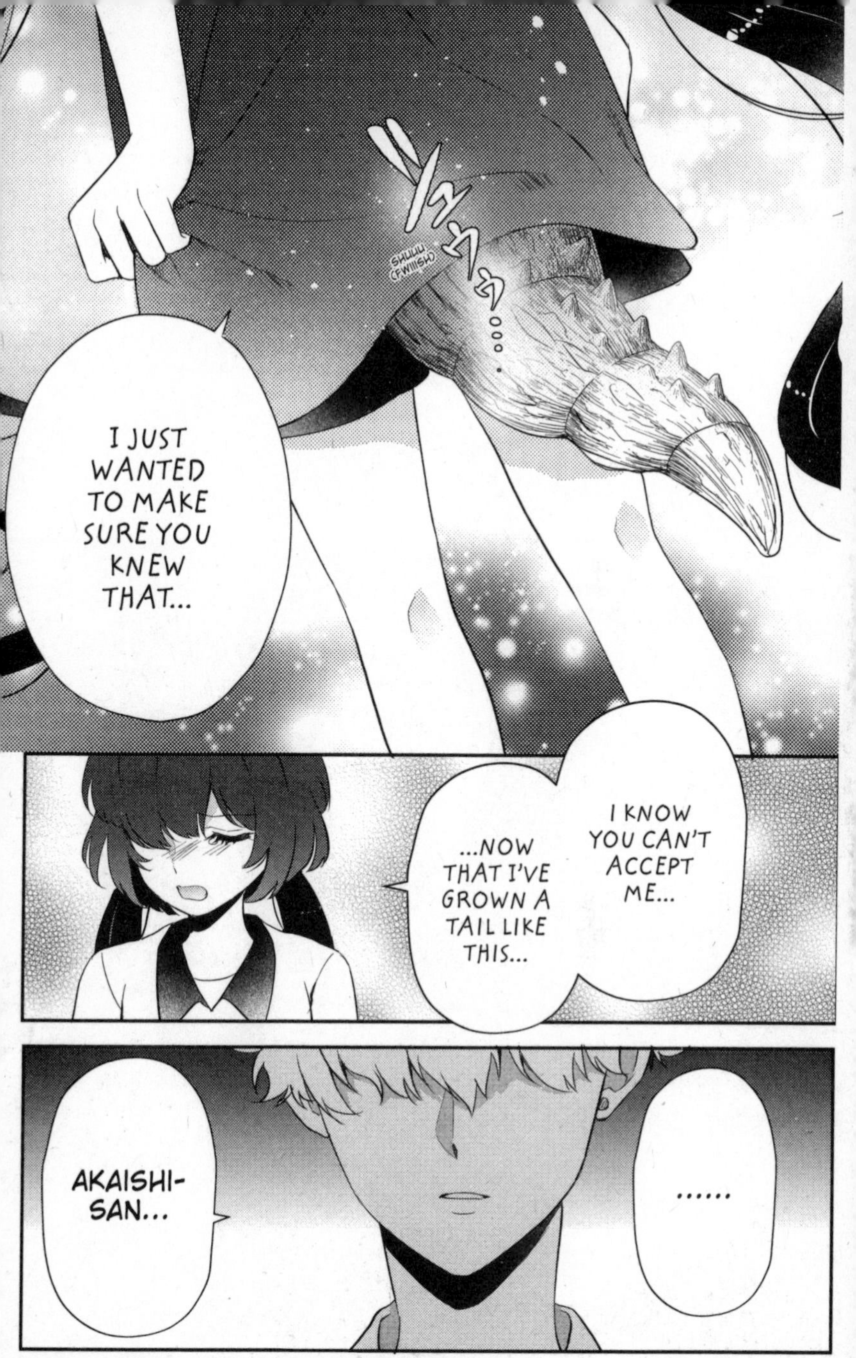
SHUUU (FWIIISH)
I JUST WANTED TO MAKE SURE YOU KNEW THAT...
I KNOW YOU CAN'T ACCEPT ME...
...NOW THAT I'VE GROWN A TAIL LIKE THIS...
......
AKAISHI-SAN...

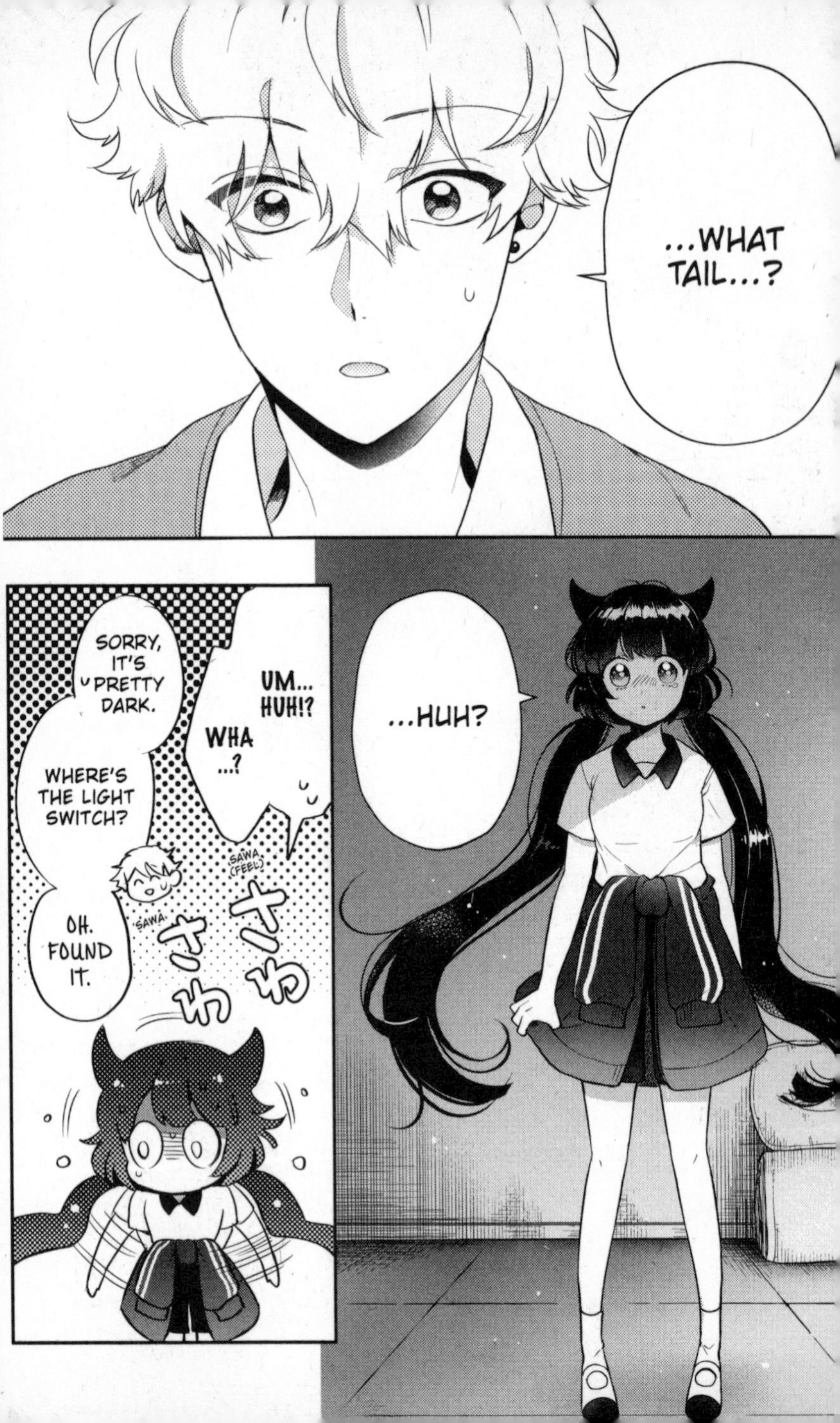
...WHAT TAIL...?
...HUH?
UM... HUH!?
WHA ...?
SORRY, IT'S PRETTY DARK.
WHERE'S THE LIGHT SWITCH?
OH. FOUND IT.
さわ
SAWA (FEEL)
さわ
SAWA

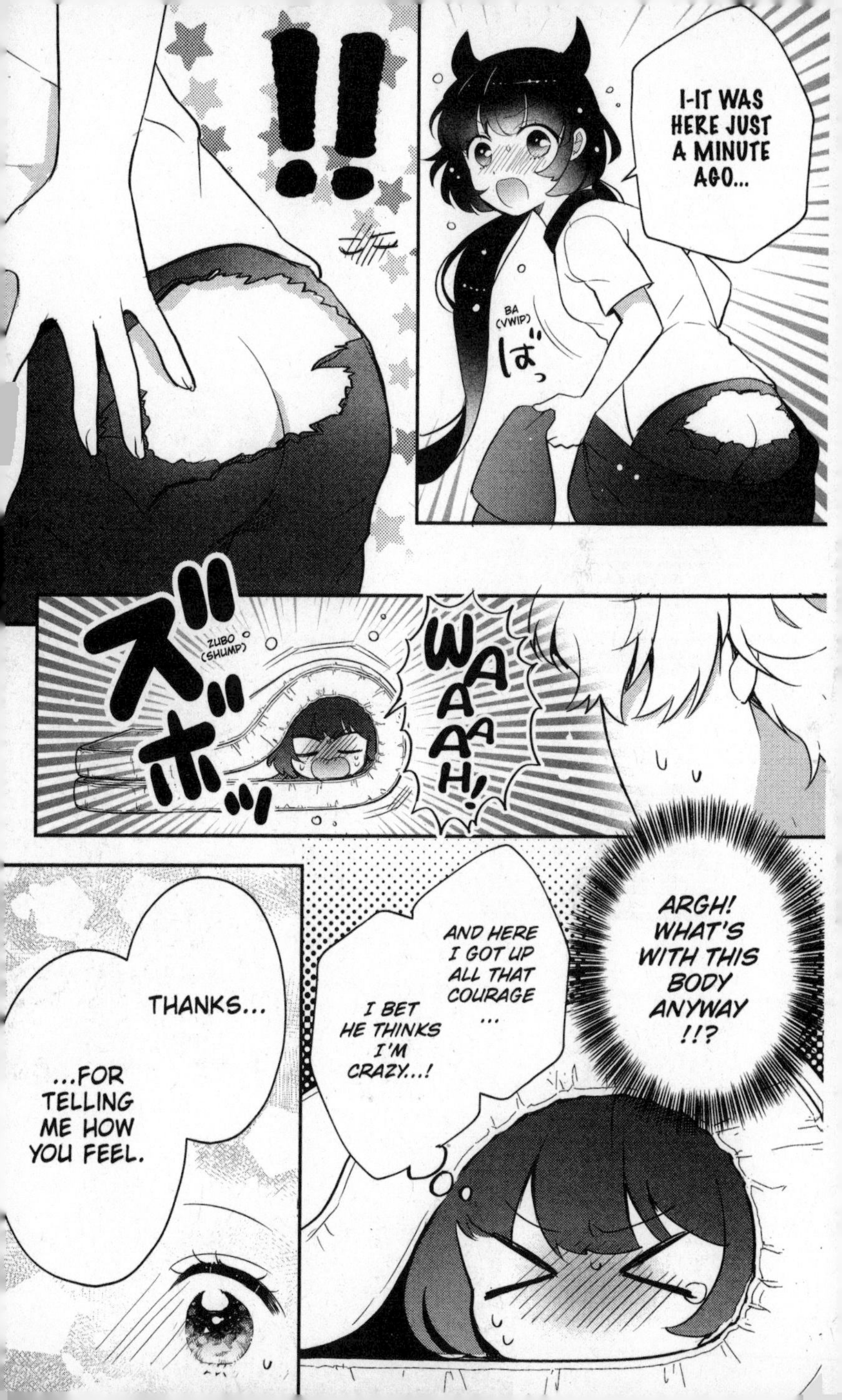
I-IT WAS HERE JUST A MINUTE AGO...
BA (VWIP)
ばっ
!!
WAAAAAH!
ZUBO (SHUMP)
ズボッ
ARGH! WHAT'S WITH THIS BODY ANYWAY!!?
AND HERE I GOT UP ALL THAT COURAGE...
I BET HE THINKS I'M CRAZY...!
THANKS...
...FOR TELLING ME HOW YOU FEEL.

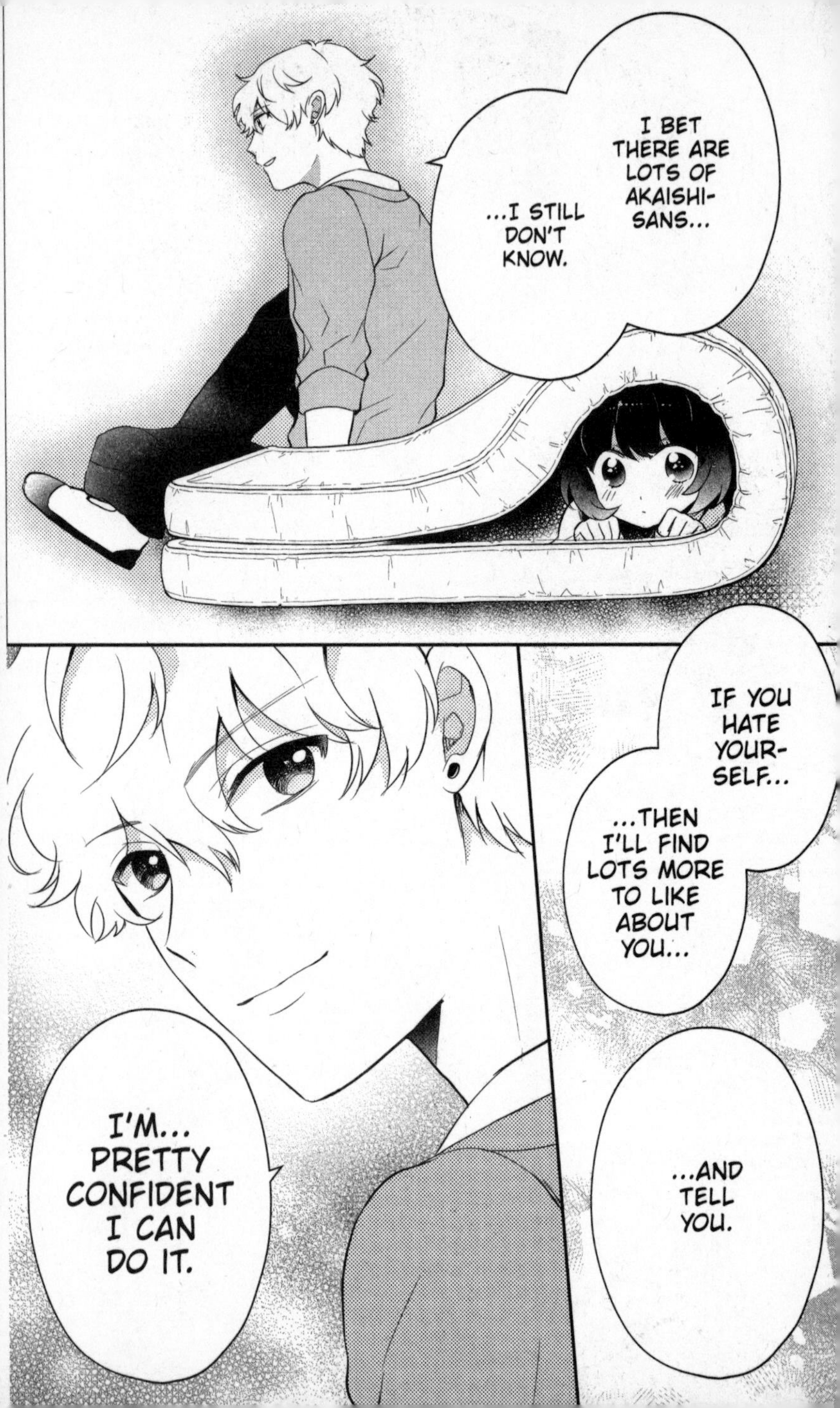
I BET THERE ARE LOTS OF AKAISHI-SANS...
...I STILL DON'T KNOW.
IF YOU HATE YOURSELF...
...THEN I'LL FIND LOTS MORE TO LIKE ABOUT YOU...
...AND TELL YOU.
I'M... PRETTY CONFIDENT I CAN DO IT.

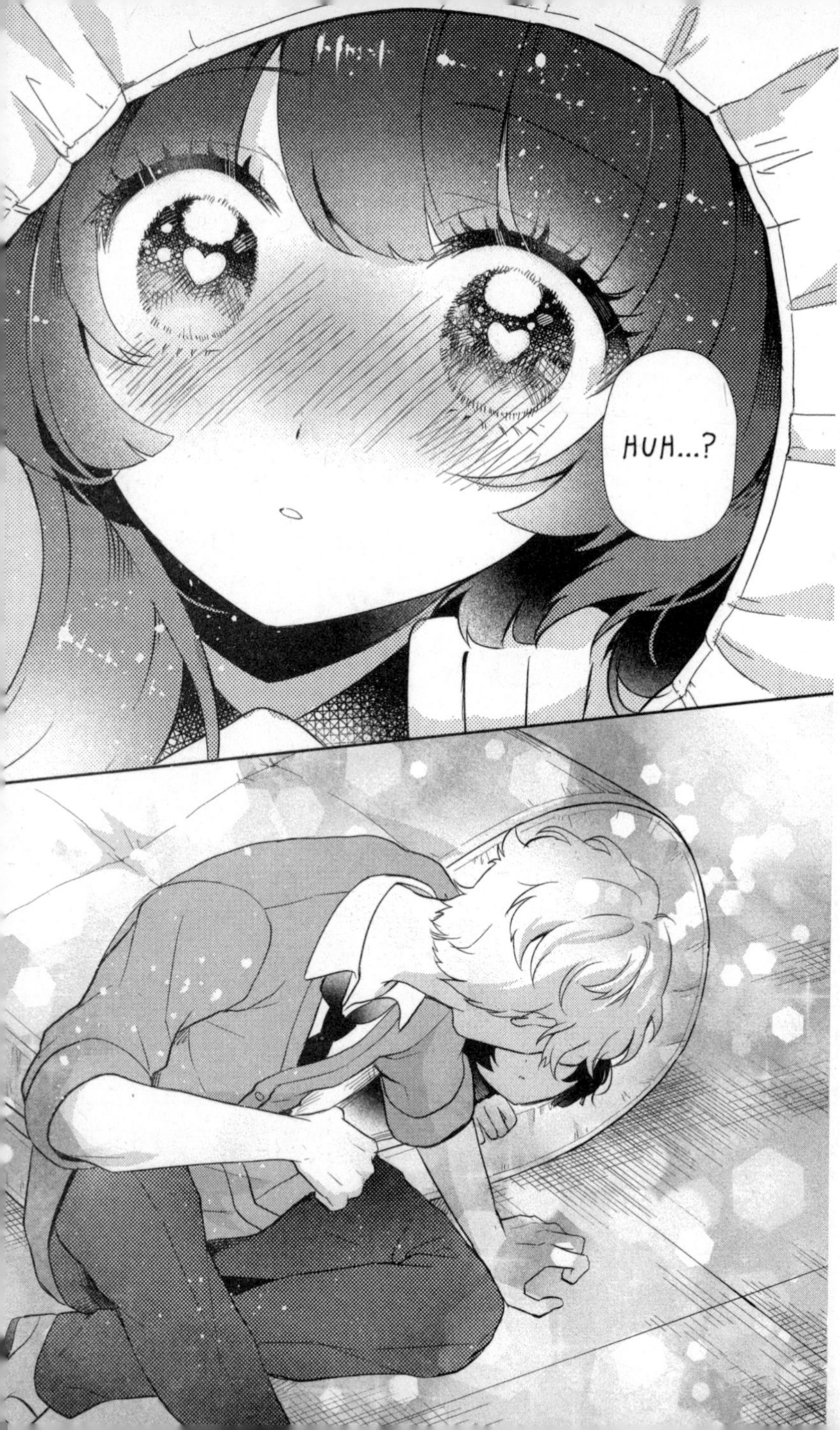
HUH...?

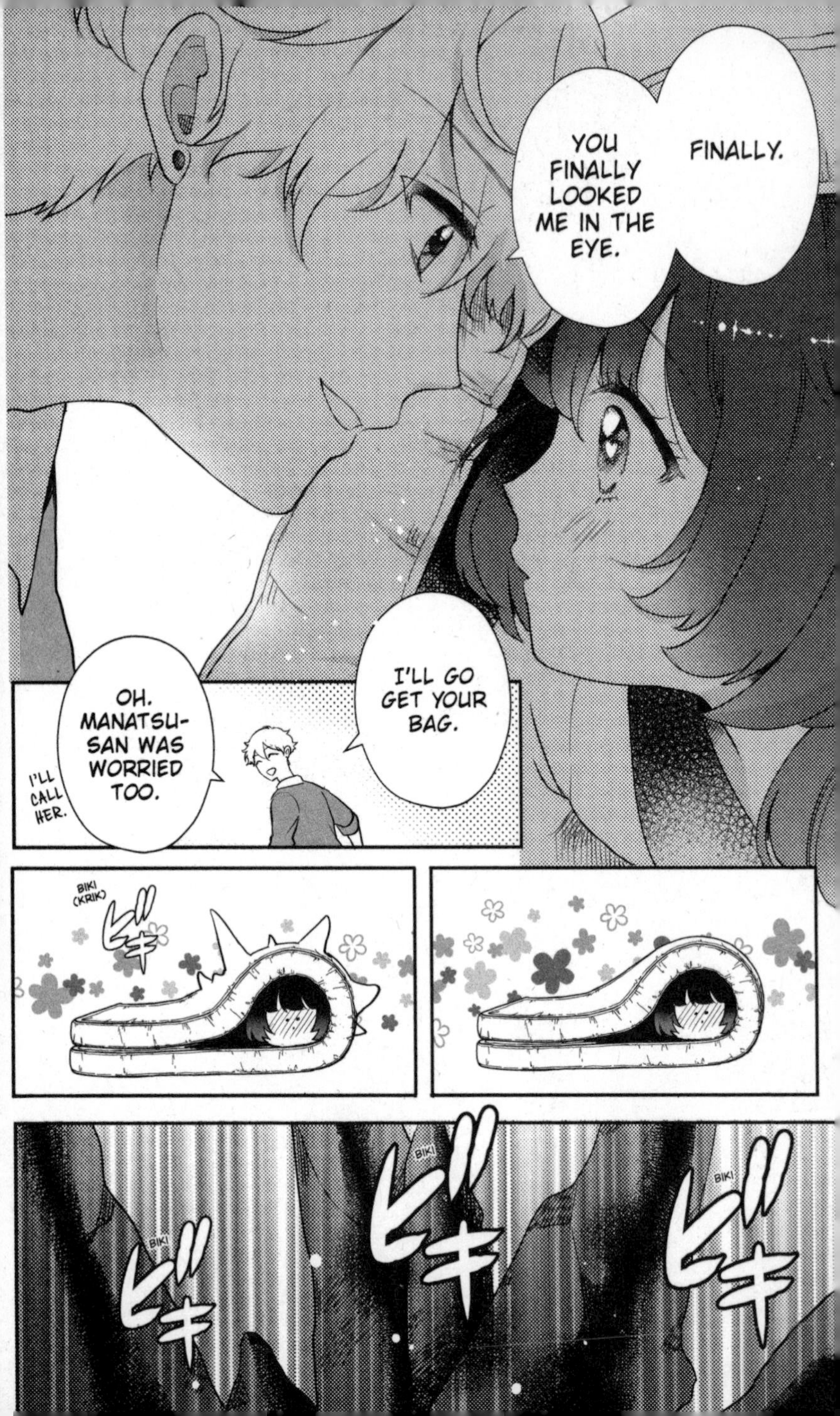
FINALLY.
YOU FINALLY LOOKED ME IN THE EYE.
I'LL GO GET YOUR BAG.
OH. MANATSU-SAN WAS WORRIED TOO.
I'LL CALL HER.
BIKI (KRIK)
ビキ
BIKI
ビキ
BIKI
ビキ
BIKI
ビキ

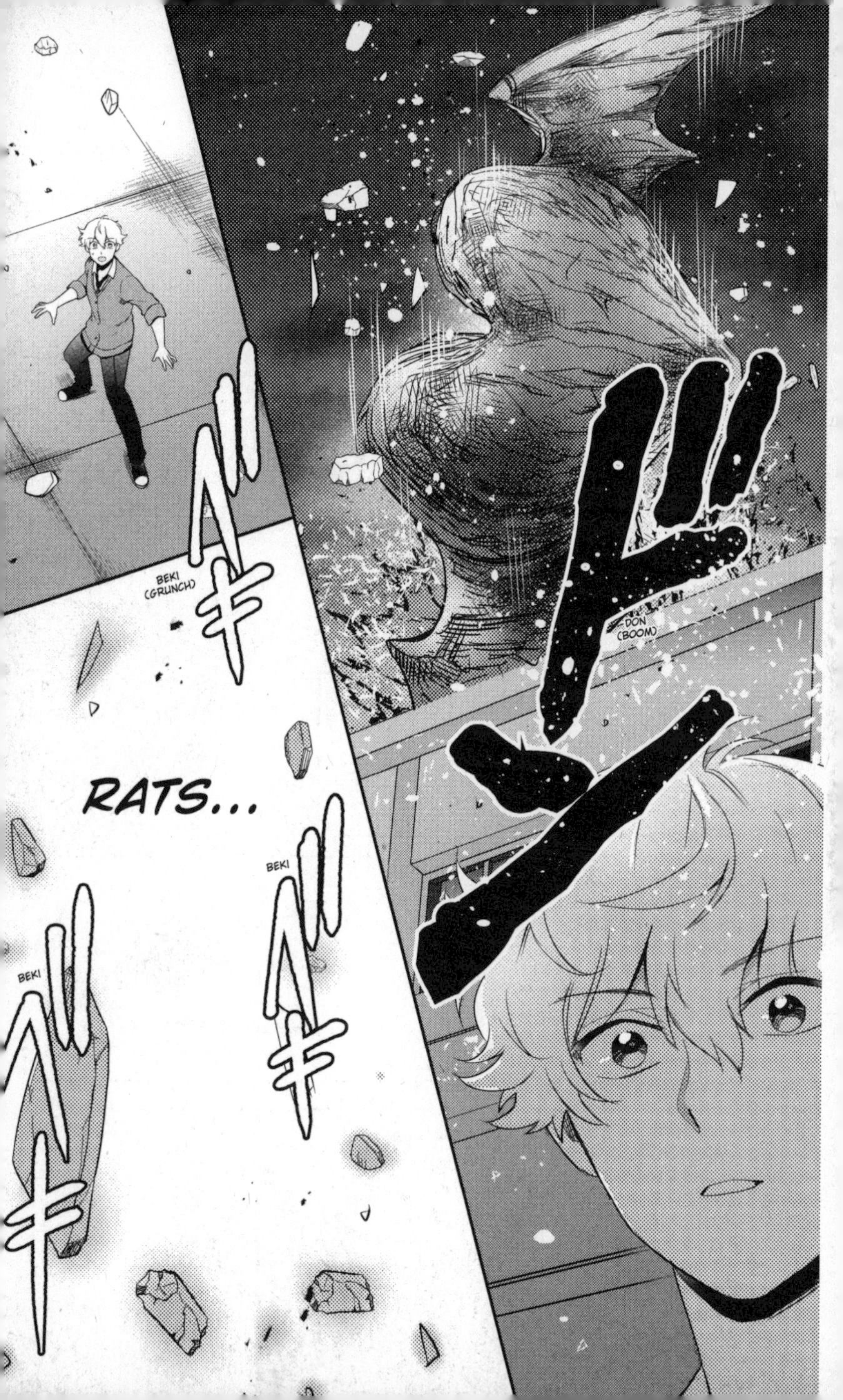
DON (BOOM)
BEKI (GRUNCH)
RATS...
BEKI
BEKI

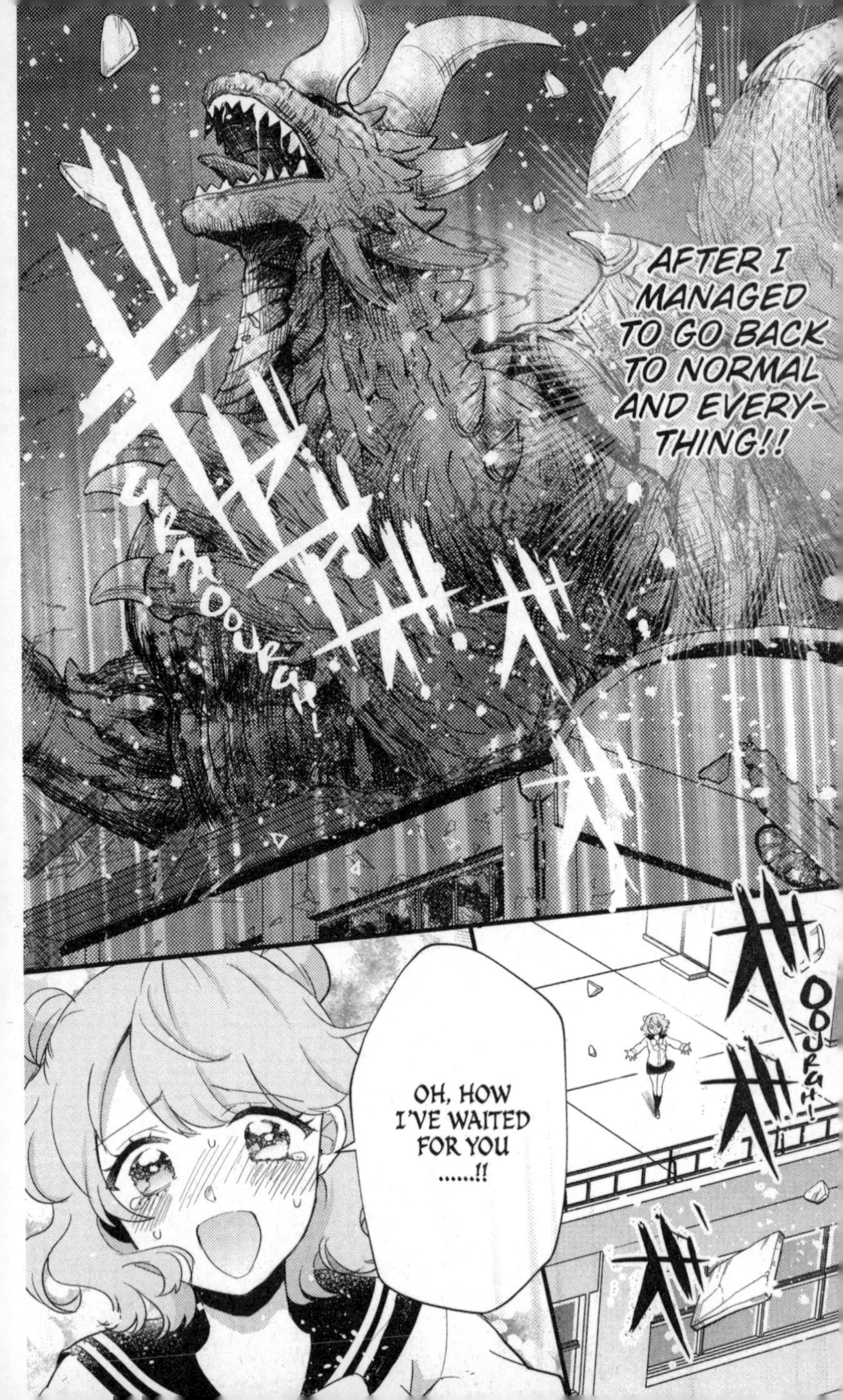
AFTER I MANAGED TO GO BACK TO NORMAL AND EVERY-THING!!
URAAOOURAH!
OH, HOW I'VE WAITED FOR YOU ......!!
OOURAH!

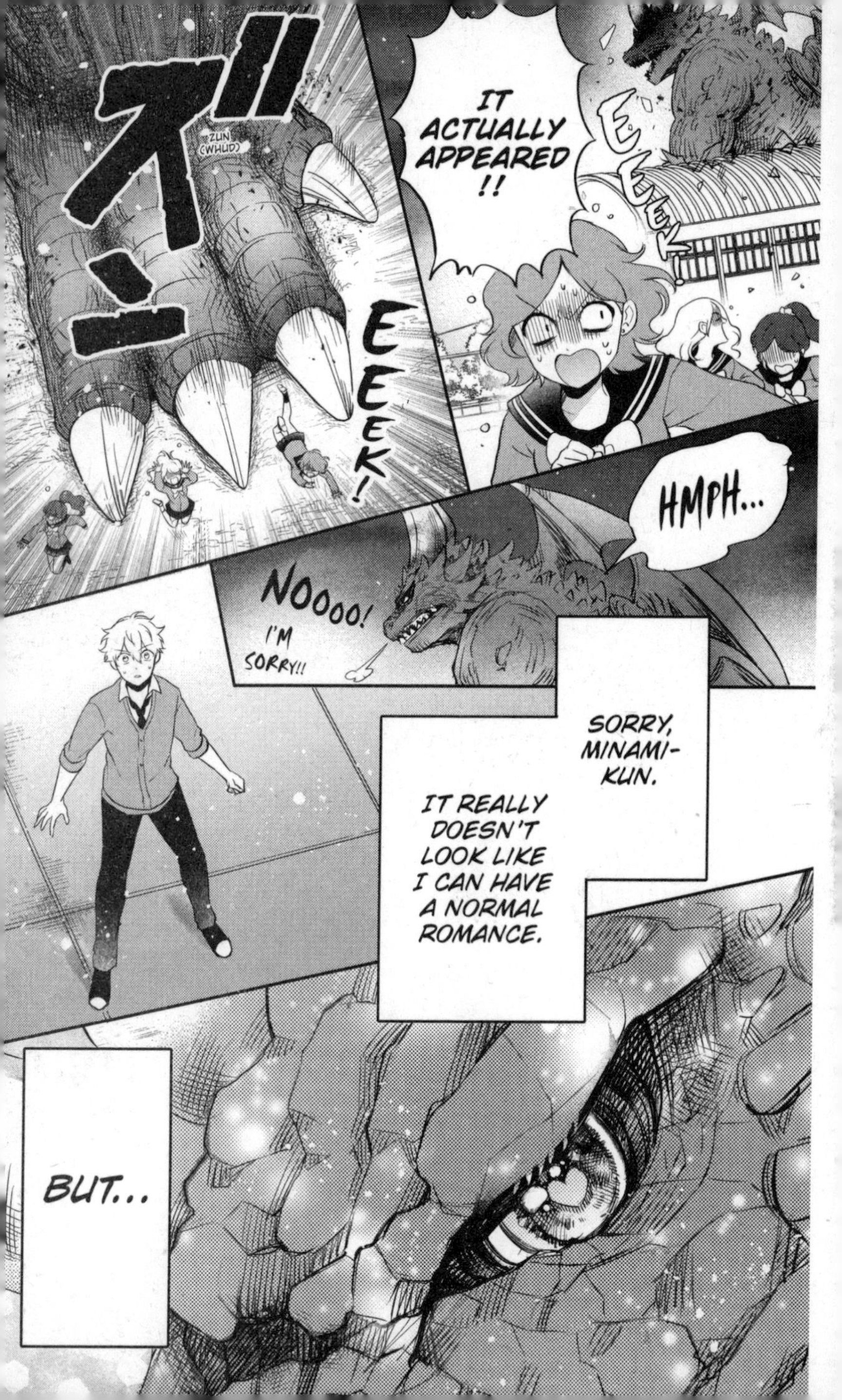
IT ACTUALLY APPEARED!!
EEEEK!
ズン
ZUN (WHUD)
EEEEK!
HMPH...
NOOOO! I'M SORRY!!
SORRY, MINAMI-KUN.
IT REALLY DOESN'T LOOK LIKE I CAN HAVE A NORMAL ROMANCE.
BUT...

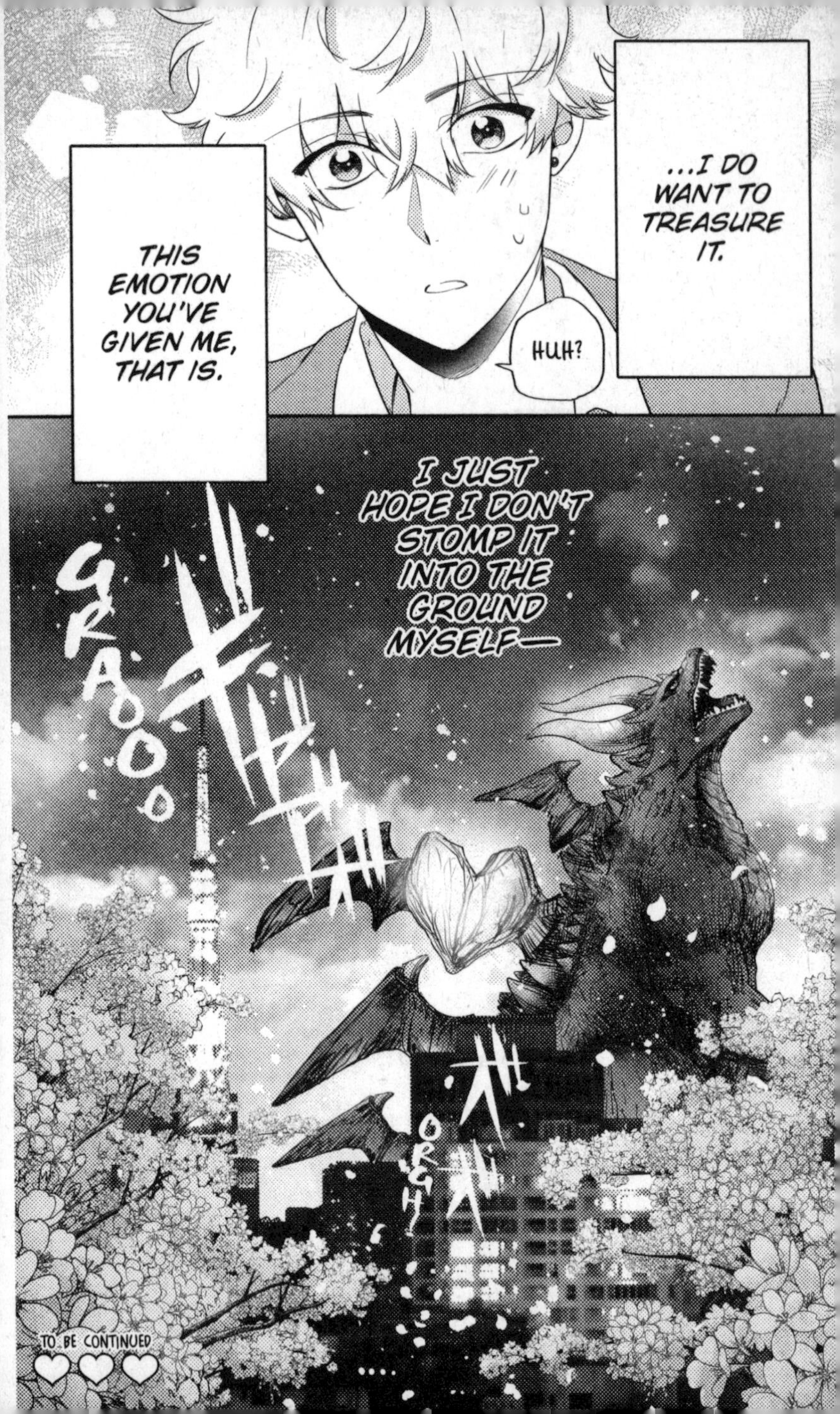

...I DO WANT TO TREASURE IT.
HUH?
THIS EMOTION YOU'VE GIVEN ME, THAT IS.
I JUST HOPE I DON'T STOMP IT INTO THE GROUND MYSELF—
GRAOOO
ORGH!
TO BE CONTINUED

TRANSLATION NOTES

COMMON HONORIFICS

no honorific: Indicates familiarity or closeness; if used without permission or reason, addressing someone in this manner would constitute an insult.

-*san*: The Japanese equivalent of Mr./Mrs./Miss. If a situation calls for politeness, this is the fail-safe honorific.

-*sama*: Conveys great respect; may also indicate that the social status of the speaker is lower than that of the addressee.

-*kun*: Used most often when referring to boys, this indicates affection or familiarity. Occasionally used by older men among their peers, but it may also be used by anyone referring to a person of lower standing.

-*onee-san*: A respectful way of referring to one's older sister or an older woman.

-*chan*: An affectionate honorific indicating familiarity used mostly in reference to girls; also used in reference to cute persons or animals of either gender.

-*tan*: A casual honorific that expresses closeness and affection; it is similar to *chan* in that it is used in reference to cute persons.

PAGE 7

In the Japanese book, Kuroe is called *Menhera-tan*. *Menhera* is short for "mental health" or "mental health-er" (-er added to refer to a person). This Internet slang is often used to describe a person who displays unconventional, creepy, or crazy behaviors that are often destructive to themselves and the people around them. Here, it is used as an insult.

PAGE 14

Eyelid glue, or *aipuchi*, is used in Japan to form a double eyelid, or a crease above one's eyelid.

PAGE 40

Line is a popular smartphone chat application used in Japan.

PAGE 56

The most common example being Godzilla, a *kaiju*, which literally means "monster," is a giant, dinosaur-like monster (based on creatures across the world) that destroys large cities. The term also refers to a Japanese film genre featuring these monsters.

PAGE 60

JSDF stands for the Japan Self-Defense Forces, which is a military force created in Japan after World War II for national defense purposes. Due to its active role in the war, Japan has been forbidden from forming an army, navy, or air force used in offensives.

PAGE 72

The nickname Harugon is a combination of "haru" from the Harumi River, where Kuroe suddenly transformed into a *kaiju*, and "gon" from "dragon."

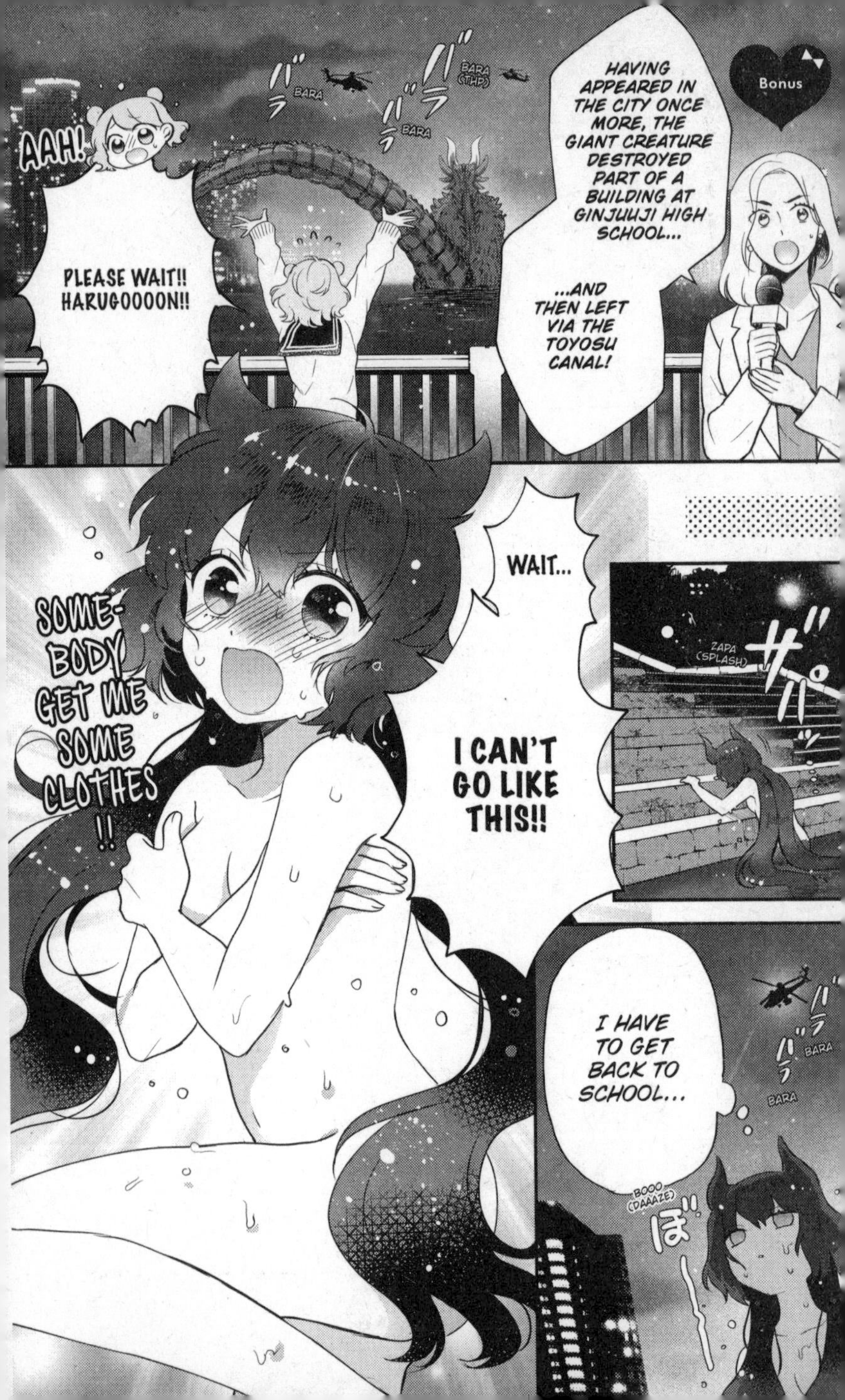
Bonus
HAVING APPEARED IN THE CITY ONCE MORE, THE GIANT CREATURE DESTROYED PART OF A BUILDING AT GINJUUJI HIGH SCHOOL...
...AND THEN LEFT VIA THE TOYOSU CANAL!
BARA (THP)
BARA
BARA
AAH!
PLEASE WAIT!! HARUGOOOON!!
ZAPA (SPLASH)
BARA
BARA
I HAVE TO GET BACK TO SCHOOL...
BOOO (DAAAZE)
WAIT...
I CAN'T GO LIKE THIS!!
SOME-BODY GET ME SOME CLOTHES!!

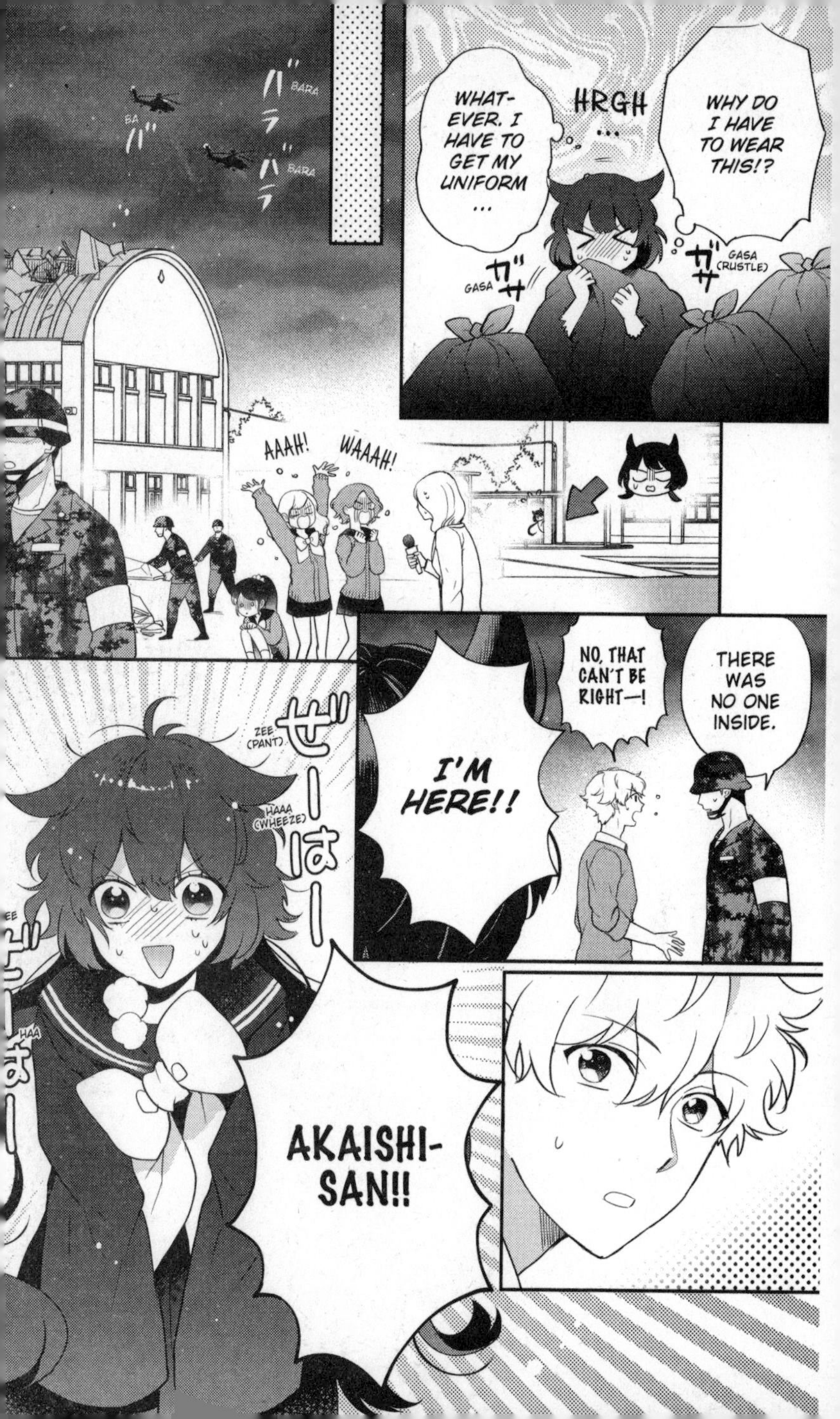
WHY DO I HAVE TO WEAR THIS!?
HRGH ...
WHAT-EVER. I HAVE TO GET MY UNIFORM ...
GASA (RUSTLE)
GASA
BARA
BA
BARA
WAAAH!
AAAH!
THERE WAS NO ONE INSIDE.
NO, THAT CAN'T BE RIGHT—!
I'M HERE!!
ZEE (PANT)
HAAA (WHEEZE)
HAA
AKAISHI-SAN!!

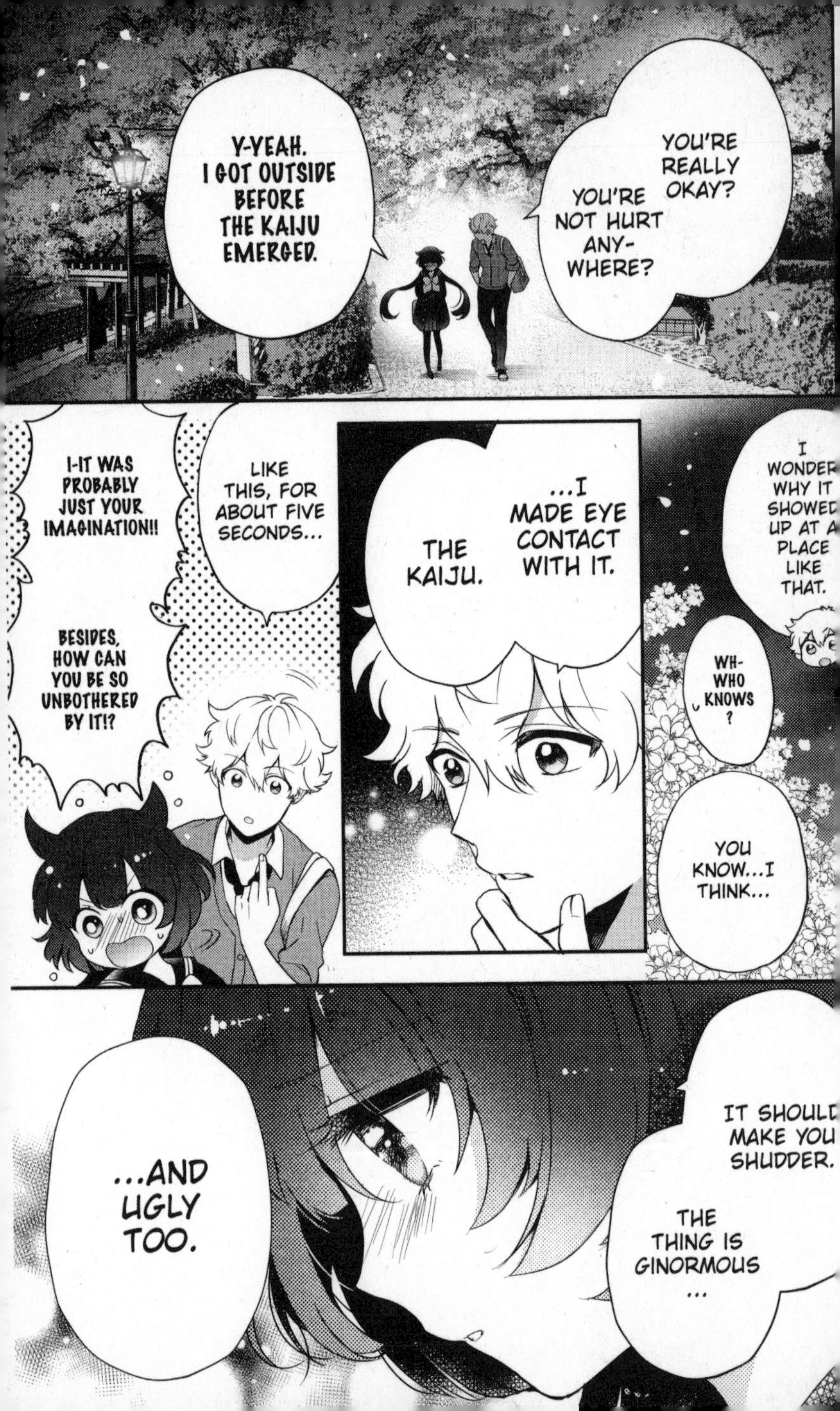
YOU'RE REALLY OKAY?
YOU'RE NOT HURT ANY-WHERE?
Y-YEAH. I GOT OUTSIDE BEFORE THE KAIJU EMERGED.
I WONDER WHY IT SHOWED UP AT A PLACE LIKE THAT.
WH-WHO KNOWS?
YOU KNOW...I THINK...
...I MADE EYE CONTACT WITH IT.
THE KAIJU.
LIKE THIS, FOR ABOUT FIVE SECONDS...
I-IT WAS PROBABLY JUST YOUR IMAGINATION!!
BESIDES, HOW CAN YOU BE SO UNBOTHERED BY IT!?
IT SHOULD MAKE YOU SHUDDER.
THE THING IS GINORMOUS ...
...AND UGLY TOO.

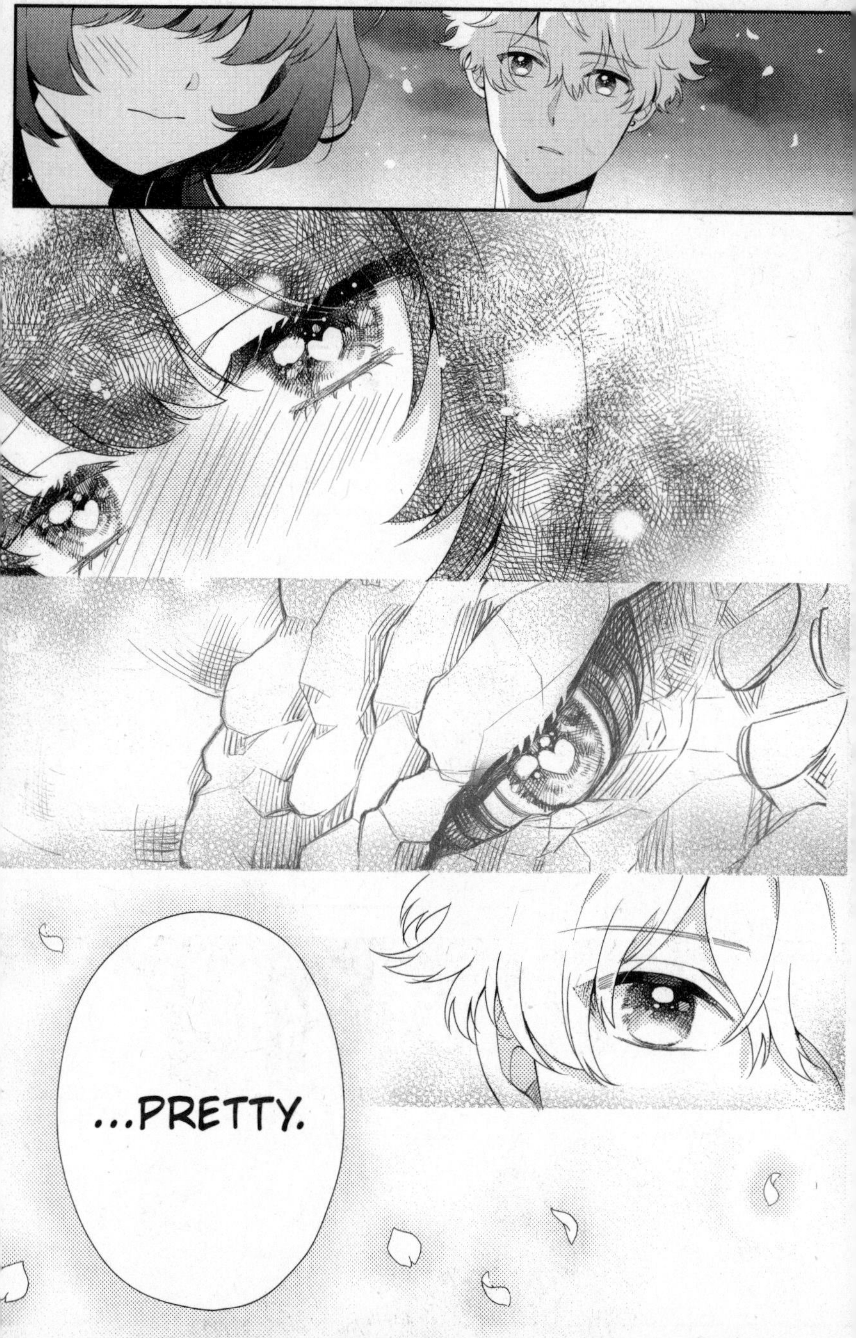
...PRETTY.

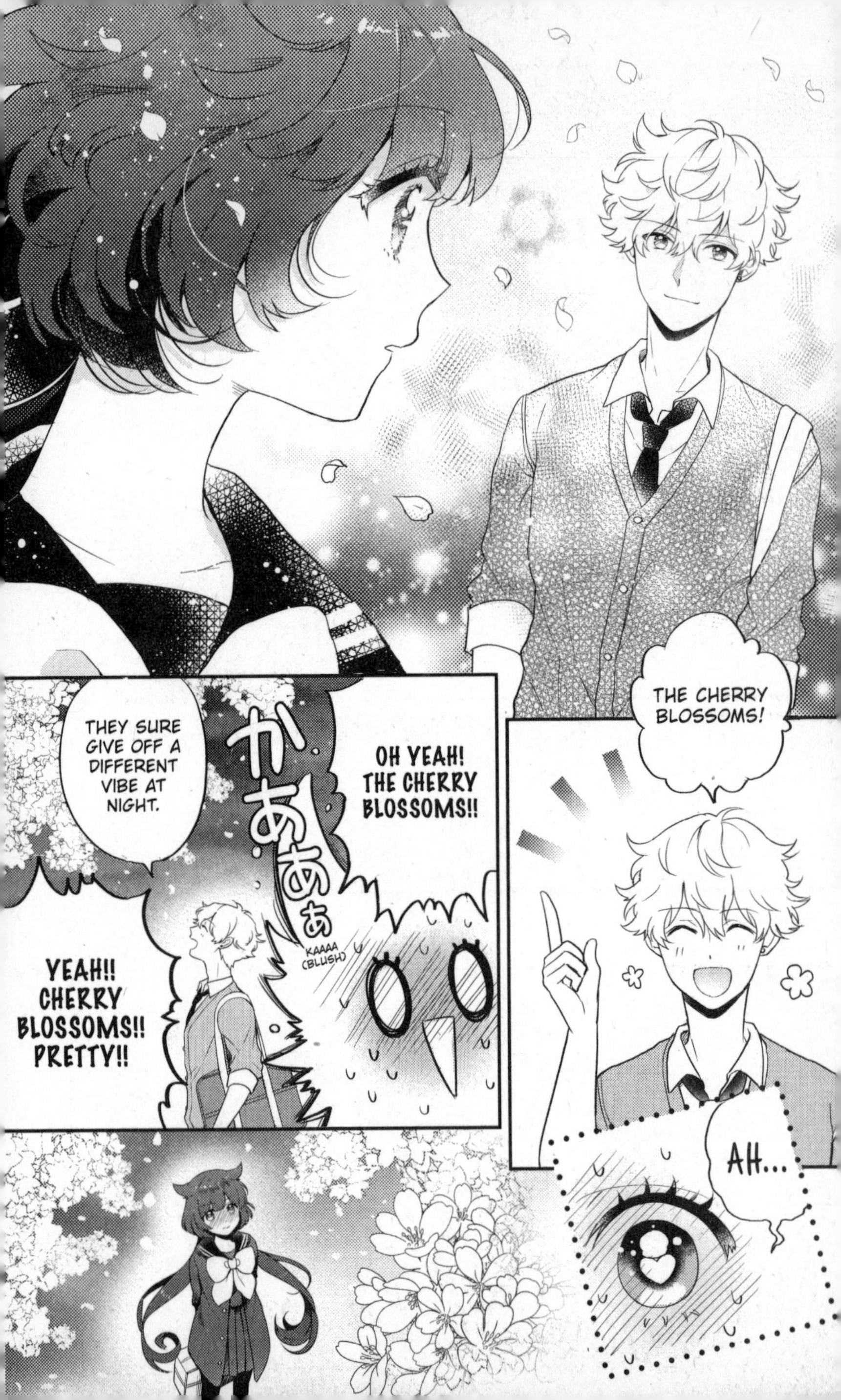
THE CHERRY BLOSSOMS!
OH YEAH! THE CHERRY BLOSSOMS!!
かあぁぁ
KAAAA (BLUSH)
THEY SURE GIVE OFF A DIFFERENT VIBE AT NIGHT.
YEAH!! CHERRY BLOSSOMS!! PRETTY!!
AH...

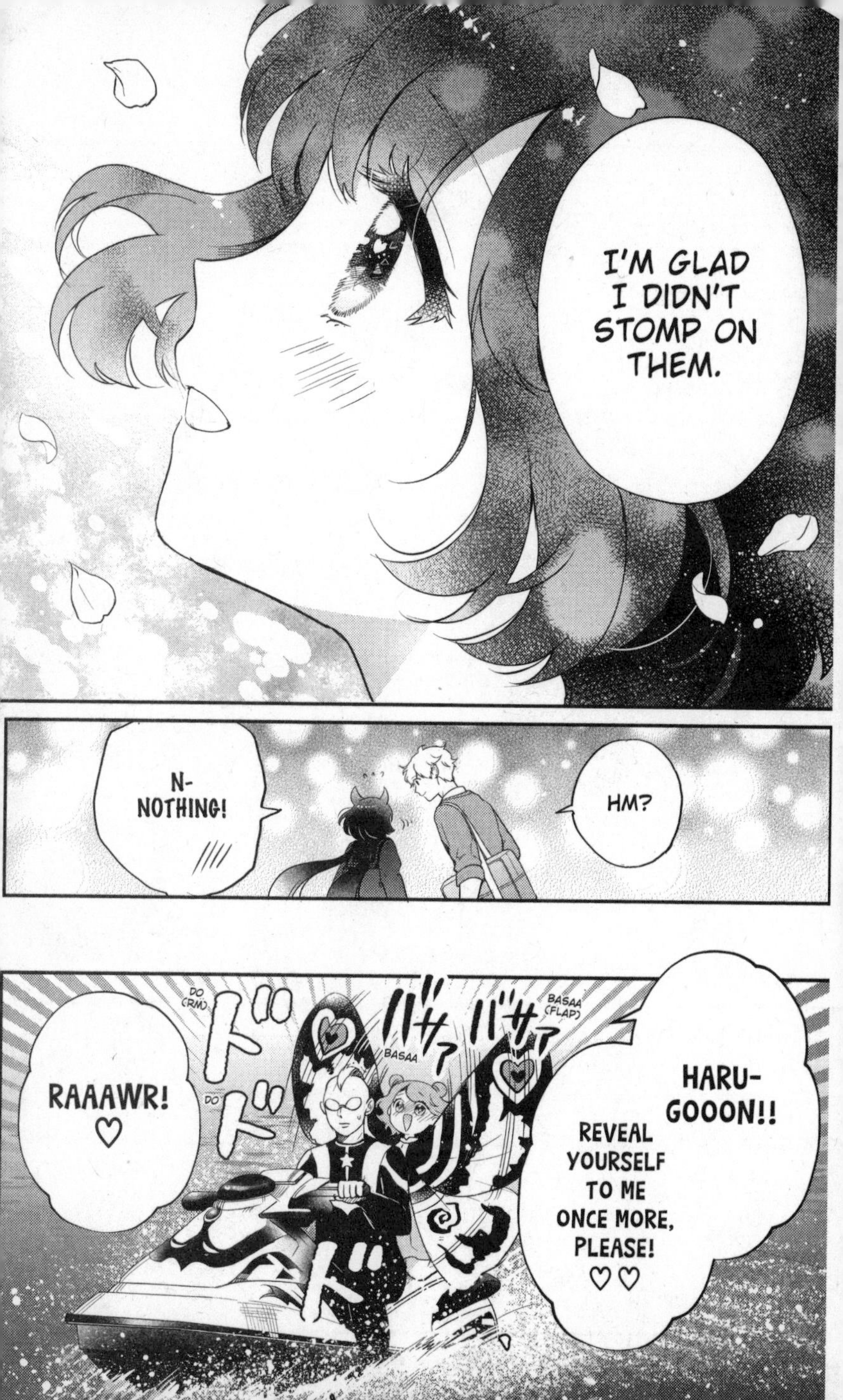
I'M GLAD I DIDN'T STOMP ON THEM.
HM?
N-NOTHING!
HARU-GOOON!!
REVEAL YOURSELF TO ME ONCE MORE, PLEASE! ♡♡
BASAA (FLAP)
BASAA
DO (RM)
DO
RAAAWR! ♡

AFTERWORD

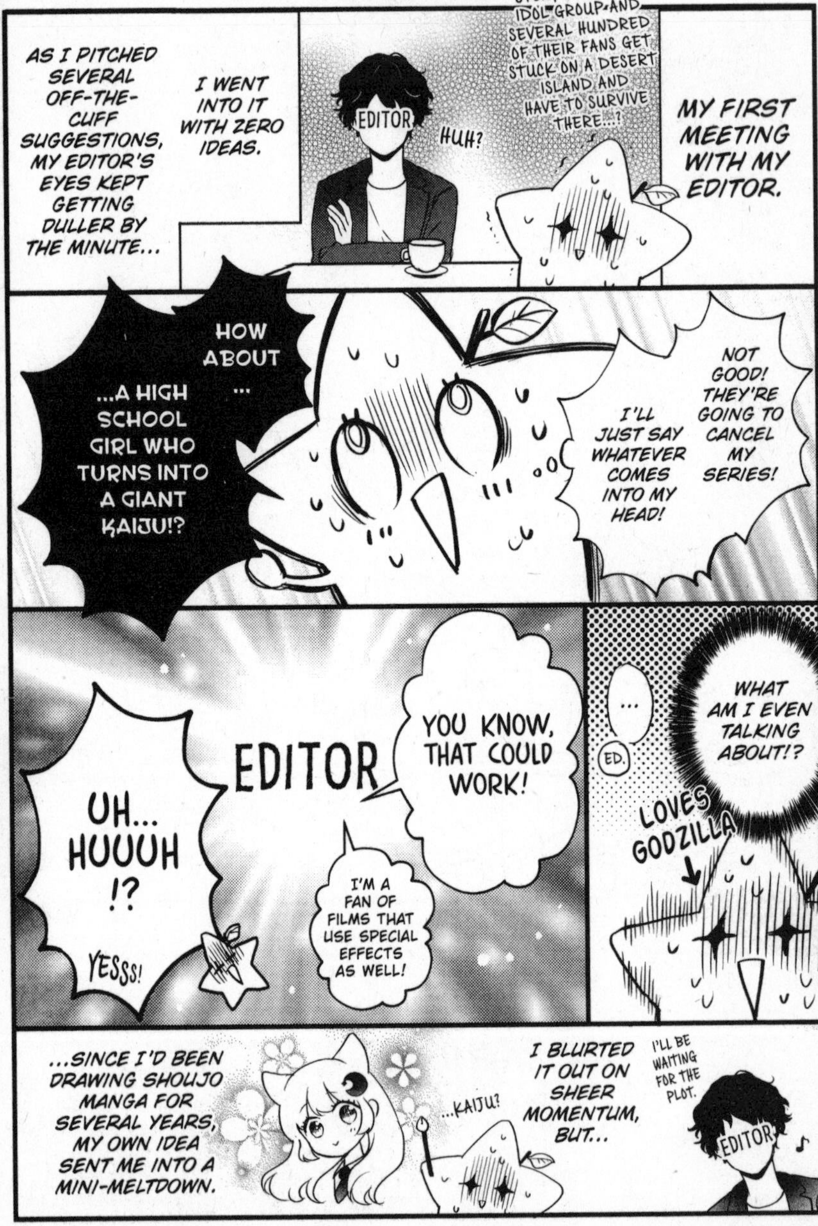
MY FIRST MEETING WITH MY EDITOR.
WHAT ABOUT...A STORY WHERE AN IDOL GROUP AND SEVERAL HUNDRED OF THEIR FANS GET STUCK ON A DESERT ISLAND AND HAVE TO SURVIVE THERE...?
HUH?
EDITOR
I WENT INTO IT WITH ZERO IDEAS.
AS I PITCHED SEVERAL OFF-THE-CUFF SUGGESTIONS, MY EDITOR'S EYES KEPT GETTING DULLER BY THE MINUTE...
NOT GOOD! THEY'RE GOING TO CANCEL MY SERIES!
I'LL JUST SAY WHATEVER COMES INTO MY HEAD!
HOW ABOUT ...
...A HIGH SCHOOL GIRL WHO TURNS INTO A GIANT KAIJU!?
WHAT AM I EVEN TALKING ABOUT!?
...
ED.
LOVES GODZILLA
YOU KNOW, THAT COULD WORK!
EDITOR
I'M A FAN OF FILMS THAT USE SPECIAL EFFECTS AS WELL!
UH... HUUUH !?
YESSS!
I'LL BE WAITING FOR THE PLOT.
EDITOR
I BLURTED IT OUT ON SHEER MOMENTUM, BUT...
...KAIJU?
...SINCE I'D BEEN DRAWING SHOUJO MANGA FOR SEVERAL YEARS, MY OWN IDEA SENT ME INTO A MINI-MELTDOWN.

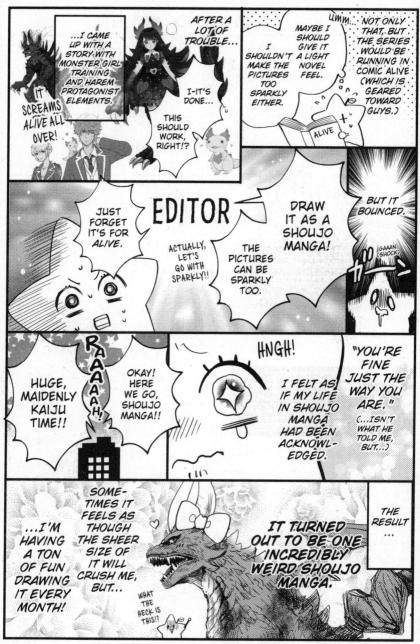

UMM...
NOT ONLY THAT, BUT THE SERIES WOULD BE RUNNING IN COMIC ALIVE (WHICH IS GEARED TOWARD GUYS.)
MAYBE I SHOULD GIVE IT A LIGHT NOVEL FEEL.
I SHOULDN'T MAKE THE PICTURES TOO SPARKLY EITHER.
ALIVE
AFTER A LOT OF TROUBLE...
...I CAME UP WITH A STORY WITH MONSTER GIRL TRAINING AND HAREM PROTAGONIST ELEMENTS.
I-IT'S DONE...
THIS SHOULD WORK, RIGHT!?
IT SCREAMS ALIVE ALL OVER!
BUT IT BOUNCED.
GAAAN (SHOCK)
EDITOR
DRAW IT AS A SHOUJO MANGA!
THE PICTURES CAN BE SPARKLY TOO.
ACTUALLY, LET'S GO WITH SPARKLY!!
JUST FORGET IT'S FOR ALIVE.
HNGH!
"YOU'RE FINE JUST THE WAY YOU ARE."
(...ISN'T WHAT HE TOLD ME, BUT...)
I FELT AS IF MY LIFE IN SHOUJO MANGA HAD BEEN ACKNOWL-EDGED.
OKAY! HERE WE GO, SHOUJO MANGA!!
RAAAAAH!
HUGE, MAIDENLY KAIJU TIME!!
THE RESULT...
IT TURNED OUT TO BE ONE INCREDIBLY WEIRD SHOUJO MANGA.
SOME-TIMES IT FEELS AS THOUGH THE SHEER SIZE OF IT WILL CRUSH ME, BUT...
...I'M HAVING A TON OF FUN DRAWING IT EVERY MONTH!
WHAT THE HECK IS THIS!?

KAIJU♥GIRL CARAMELISE 1

Spica Aoki

TRANSLATION: **Taylor Engel** ♥ LETTERING: **Lys Blakeslee**

OTOMEKAIJU CARAMELISE Vol. 1
©Spica Aoki 2018
First published in Japan in 2018 by KADOKAWA CORPORATION, Tokyo.
English translation rights arranged with KADOKAWA CORPORATION, Tokyo through TUTTLE-MORI AGENCY, INC., Tokyo.

English translation © 2019 by Yen Press, LLC

Yen Press
1290 Avenue of the Americas
New York, NY 10104

Visit us at yenpress.com ♡ facebook.com/yenpress ♡ twitter.com/yenpress ♡ yenpress.tumblr.com ♡ instagram.com/yenpress

First Yen Press Edition: June 2019

Yen Press is an imprint of Yen Press, LLC.
The Yen Press name and logo are trademarks of Yen Press, LLC.

The publisher is not responsible for websites (or their content) that are not owned by the publisher.

Library of Congress Control Number: 2019935205

ISBNs: 978-1-9753-5705-4 (paperback)
        978-1-9753-5706-1 (ebook)

10 9 8 7 6 5 4 3 2 1

WOR

Printed in the United States of America